Ecstasy
to Agony

Ecstasy to Agony

The 1994 Montreal Expos

*How the best team in baseball
ended up in Washington ten years later*

Danny Gallagher and Bill Young

Foreword by Bob Elliott

Scoop Press

Toronto, 2013

Ecstasy to Agony
The 1994 Montreal Expos – How the best team in baseball ended up in Washington ten years later

Copyright © Danny Gallagher, Bill Young, 2013
Printed and bound in Canada

Published by Scoop Press
694 Midland Avenue
Toronto, Ontario, Canada
M1K 4C6

Unless otherwise noted, all photos used in the text are courtesy of the Canadian Baseball Hall of Fame, St. Marys, Ontario.

Chapter organization by Bill Young. Cover design and book formatting/page layout by Carl Lemyre. Technical expertise provided by Greg Gallagher.

Front-cover: photos of Felipe Alou and Larry Walker taken by Denis Brodeur; photos of Pedro Martinez and Marquis Grissom obtained from the archives collection at the Canadian Baseball Hall of Fame, St. Marys, Ontario. Back-cover team photo obtained from the Canadian Baseball Hall of Fame, St. Marys, Ontario archives collection.

Library and Archives Canada Cataloguing in Publication

Gallagher, Danny, 1950-
Ecstasy to Agony: The 1994 Montreal Expos/ Danny Gallagher, Bill Young, 1940-

ISBN: 978-0-9681859-5-7

Montreal Expos (baseball team) – History. I. Young, Bill, (1940)
II. Title.
GV======

There are probably people who didn't grow up in that generation who don't realize how great an Expos team that was in 1994. They had great players, great coaching, a great manager. They were as good as any team that season. They were going to the playoffs. They were that good. They were loaded, no question.

– Tony Gwynn

Contents

Foreword

The Atlanta Braves and the Montreal Expos faced each other nine times in 1994.

Although working for the Toronto Sun as a baseball columnist that year, I saw the final six meetings: a three-game series at Olympic Stadium, a three-game series at Atlanta Fulton County Stadium ... and four Montreal wins.

My boss sensed a three-peat for Canadian teams winning the World Series.

Covering the Braves in postseason play, from 1991-93 and 1995–2005, it seemed some nights as if their starting pitcher would work a 1-2-3 first and opposing teams would ask in the dugout, "so, what time do we take batting practice tomorrow? This one's over."

The Expos were never like that.

Maybe it was because of manager Felipe Alou.

Maybe it was the line drives off the bats of Moises Alou, Larry Walker, Wil Cordero, Sean Berry, and Marquis Grissom.

Or maybe it was the simple fact that the two teams shared facilities at Municipal Stadium in West Palm Beach, Florida.

Whatever the reason, one thing was certain:

The Expos were never ever intimidated by the likes of the Cy Young Award–winning staff of Greg Maddux, Tom Glavine and John Smoltz. Or Steve Avery and Kent Mercker, the other two members of the rotation.

Maddux, the two-time defending NL Cy Young Award winner on his way to capturing a third straight (he won again in 1995) was 1-2 with a 2.28 ERA in three starts against the Expos that year, allowing 10 runs – six earned – on 19 hits and five walks.

Glavine, the 1991 and 1998 Cy Young Award winner, was 1-0, 2.25 in two starts, allowing four runs on 13 hits and four walks in 16 innings.

Smoltz, who won in 1996, was 1-1, 1.64 in three starts allowing five runs – four earned – on 13 hits and seven walks in 22 innings.

Avery did not face the Expos, while Mercker was 1-0 with a 1.29 ERA in his one start as he gave up one run on five hits and three walks.

Danny Gallagher, who wore Renfrew Red Sox when he played infield, and Bill Young, a founding member of the Montreal chapter of the Society for American Baseball Research, tell readers all about the Braves–Expos match-ups and all the insights into the 1994 season, one without a post-season.

Gallagher began covering the Expos in 1988 for the Montreal Daily News and as evidenced by his latest book has never stopped, while Young is a baseball enthusiast with a baseball-shaped heart – with an Expos logo on it.

Bob Elliott
Recipient 2012 J. G. Taylor Spink Award
for meritorious baseball writing, Cooperstown NY

Dedication

Charles Bronfman and Jim Fanning

Of all those who have had a hand in the direction and management of the Montreal Expos over the years, perhaps the two most faithful stewards were Charles Bronfman (left in photo below) and Jim Fanning. It is with humility that we dedicate this book to them in everlasting appreciation of their unstinting efforts to ensure baseball thrived in Montreal.

Mr. Bronfman stepped forward in 1968 to save the franchise when it seemed doomed to die before even seeing the light of day. He remained the owner and favourite of players and fans for 20 years, until the game's emerging complexities began to strip it of its joy.

Mr. Fanning joined the Expos as general manager about the same time. For the next 25 years he served the club in any number of different capacities – ranging from colour man on team broadcasts to field manager, taking the club to its only postseason appearance in 1981.

Photo: Bill Young

Charles Bronfman and Jim Fanning at the Canadian Baseball Hall of Fame in St. Marys, Ontario, 2010

Both men are symbols of a time when the summer game ruled in Montreal. For as long as the Expos dwell in our hearts, their deep loyalty and perseverance will continue to be cherished.

Mr. Bronfman and Mr. Fanning – thank you for making so many memories possible.

Preface

Bob Prince, the great and late Pittsburgh Pirates play-by-play announcer, had it all, especially when his baritone voice pounded out, "The G-r-e-a-t Roberto." He liked to call Roberto Clemente '*Bobby*' Clemente – not always, but much of the time.

It was the 1960s, and there I was with my good right ear anchored tight against the old relic, square-boxed, priceless RCA radio we had in our home in rural Douglas, Ontario, located about 70 miles west of Canada's capital city of Ottawa.

While the rest of the family was sleeping, including my parents Ed and Catherine, I stayed up – I grew up - listening to Prince. Somehow, incredible as it might sound now, once darkness set in and Canadian stations faded into static from reduced power, the signal from KDKA in Pittsburgh could be heard clearly all the way to Douglas. That voice, calling out "The G-r-e-a-t Roberto" resonates with me still to this day.

Even though I never became a Pirates fan, the simple joy I got from hearing Prince's voice, led me to baseball. With the support of my parents, I started playing the game around 1962 when I was about 11. Then somehow the Royal Canadian Legion peewee team in nearby Renfrew heard of my play in Douglas and invited me to join their squad in a tournament. Of course, I said yes.

What I remember most about that experience was a crucial play at the plate where I was waved home late in the championship game and was called out. Had I been safe, we would have won the tournament and, consequently, earned a free meal, courtesy of the Legion. I was so emotional, I cried.

Putting that disappointment behind me, I went on to play bantam-midget in Douglas and then adult, senior-sandlot baseball in various centres across Canada. I played under the likes of respected coaches Larry Moriarity in Douglas, Clair Seeley in Renfrew, Berk Keaney in Sudbury, Ontario, Lionel Ruhr in Regina, Saskatchewan, and a number of others.

I took that passion of playing the sport and parlayed it into writing for a number of newspapers, including the Montreal Daily News, the Ottawa Sun, The Associated Press and later the Globe and Mail as a freelancer – covering the Expos.

This is the third Expos book I have authored, the second in conjunction with co-author Bill Young. We produced the popular "Remembering the Montreal Expos," which was released just before Christmas in 2005.

We hope you enjoy this new book of ours.

DANNY GALLAGHER

One of the truly sad things about being a die-hard baseball fan is not having a team to cheer for. Since 2004, when the Expos were unceremoniously whipped out of town by the brain trust that ruled the game – remember the team was owned by Major League Baseball – and plunked down in Washington, D.C., not having a team to cheer for has been the lot of most Expos faithful. Washington doesn't work – too much residual bitterness; New York and Philadelphia were the enemy for too long to be viable – and the rest of the National League is just too remote to be taken seriously. Toronto is a logical choice – but the Blue Jays are an American League team where they play ten-man baseball, anathema to National League followers.

All to say that Danny and I have written this book to fill a void; to help bring back both the great and the melancholy memories – and perhaps fill the gap between the departure of the Expos from Montreal and the arrival of a new team, which, if the proponents of the Montreal Baseball Project and ExposNation are to be believed, is becoming closer to the real thing all the time.

Happy reading!

BILL YOUNG

The season was lost and I was at Municipal Stadium in West Palm Beach to get my stuff and I ran into Tom Glavine of the Braves. Glavine told me, "I feel bad for you guys. It was impossible to catch you guys. You guys were dominating the league."

– Felipe Alou

Prologue

It's a great day for Montreal and a great day for the National League ... Montreal is now a fully fledged member of the National League.

– Warren Giles, NL President, August 14, 1968[1]

In 1994 the Montreal Expos stood front and centre as the best team in baseball: by the end of July they topped both the National and American Leagues in winning percentage and seemed poised to tackle the postseason head on. Indeed, according to many observers, this edition of the club ranked as the best ever in team history. And as the season unfolded, folks in Montreal grew evermore convinced that the ball club they called *Nos Amours* was on the fast track to the game's ultimate prize, the World Series. It had been a long time coming.

Across the years, beginning with 1969 and their birth as an expansion franchise (their crib-mates in the National League nursery were the San Diego Padres, also hatched in 1969), the Expos had only managed one postseason appearance. It occurred in 1981 and ended with a heart-wrenching loss to the soon-to-become World Series champion Los Angeles Dodgers – on a Rick Monday home run in the final inning of the Championship Series final game. Ask any self-respecting Expos fan to explain what the expression "Blue Monday" means, and the response will be immediate – Monday, October 19, 1981.[2] The Expos never made it that close again.

But that was then. So when a special group of special players showed up on Opening Day in 1994, following an outstanding 1993 season, the fans, the media, the folks out on the street, began, albeit slowly at first, to concede that this might be the year when fortune would shift in our favour. For too long, we stolid stragglers from the north had reluctantly borne our Joe Btfsplk-like propensity for jinxes and bad luck with cold-weather stoicism[3]. But now, perhaps, we were about to discover that hope sometimes does trump despair, that sometimes good things do happen to good people.

Sadly, however, not very often, as we would soon learn. For in mid-August, even as the Expos sat nicely positioned out in front of everybody else, their world came to a shuddering standstill. On the twelfth of the month, the Major League Baseball Players Association (MLBPA) and the Major League Baseball team owners arrived at such an impasse in their collective bargaining negotiations that the players simply put down bat and glove and went on strike.

Their action was not entirely unanticipated. For over twenty years both sides had been mired in such a morass of nasty exchanges and debilitating deep suspicion they had lost sight of the business at hand – entertaining the patrons and filling the grandstand. By the time the bitter and protracted work stoppage was dramatically halted in the spring of 1995 via a temporary injunction issued in Manhattan by United States District Court Judge Sonia Sotomayor,[4] the credibility of players and owners, indeed the reputation of the game itself, lay pretty much in tatters. "It wounded the sport so deeply," wrote the *New York Times'* Richard Sandomir in 2009, "that baseball needed the record endurance of Cal Ripken Jr. and the home runs of Mark McGwire and Sammy Sosa, whose slugging is so retroactively tainted, to recover its equilibrium and popularity."[5]

Within the Expos camp, the devastation was almost apocalyptic, so shredded by disappointment and financial distress was the organization. As for the fans, that faithful collective which had dared to cast aside doubts and start believing this time it was for real, the heartbreak could hardly have been more shattering. Indeed, the havoc wreaked by the events of August 1994 reached so deeply that neither the fans nor the club itself ever truly recovered. Ten years later, following the 2004 season, when all of baseball had turned its back on Montreal, or so it seemed, the franchise was callously cut out from the herd and shipped to Washington, D.C. There, people call it the Nationals. *Requiescant in pace, Expos.*

Gone these Expos may now be, but they are far from forgotten. Ten years after their exile to the District of Columbia and twenty years after their championship dream was dashed, they still refuse to disappear. With each passing season more and more words are written about the club that was; with each passing season louder voices come forth suggesting that big league baseball belongs back in Montreal, and predicting its return.

There is little doubt that interest in the Expos is ever on the rise. In 2010 Major League Baseball produced a one-hour documentary film about the Expos entitled *Triumph and Tragedy* for broadcast on its own network. An excellent piece of reporting, it offered an intimate and unfiltered glimpse into the events of 1994 and the club's ultimate demise. That same year, filmmaker Ken Burns explored similar turf in the *Twelfth Inning*, an outstanding two-part supplement to his seminal series, *BASEBALL*, devoting considerable attention to the sad fate of the 1994 Expos. Might these modest glints of light on the fringes of our baseball horizon be the harbinger of promise and a new dawn of hope? Only time will tell.

In this book the authors have attempted to convey both the euphoria that surrounded the 1994 team, and the subsequent decade-long downward spiral that marked the Expos' slow descent into oblivion. As some wag once complained, "How many last-ever home openers am I expected to suffer through? Enough already!"

Beginning with events leading up to that summer of wonder, we have set out to trace the team's final decade, revisiting both the passionate joy that reigned until mid-August 1994, and the subsequent slow deterioration that ultimately resulted in the club's departure. Our goal is to tell the story as it really happened, sidestepping the myriad misconceptions, misinterpretations, false conclusions, and faulty hypotheses that circulated widely at the time and still occasionally bubble to the surface today. Our aim is to provide a balanced, dispassionate, yet frank assessment of the period, nuanced by the luxury that time and distance now allow. We intend that this effort offer clarity and a deeper understanding of a narrative that was and remains a source of intense interest, if not preoccupation, among baseball aficionados everywhere.

We feel we are well positioned to tell this story. We have both written extensively about the Expos and baseball generally, and in 2005 we co-authored the book, *Remembering the Montreal Expos*, which spent seven weeks on the best-seller lists and still remains the only comprehensive treatment of the Expos from conception to departure available in English.

Once again, for *Ecstasy to Agony* we turned to a variety of sources, from contemporary game reports to a range of relevant publications to personal interviews. We contacted many of the individuals who had donned Expos uniforms during this period – players, coaches, managers – as well as club executives and others close to the team. Journalists, broadcasters, ownership partners, opposing players and officials, and fans who had been close to the team throughout that last decade were also part of the discussion, as were MLBPA representatives, members of the owners group and officials from the Office of the Commissioner.

It was always our intention to complete the book and have it in stores by the start of 2014, the twentieth anniversary of the Expos' dream season – and of the wake-up call that brought it all crashing down.

We hope our story offers insight – and brings you pleasure.

Danny Gallagher
Bill Young

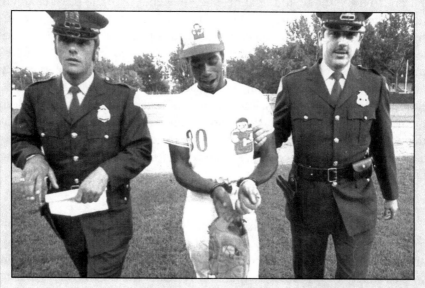

Back when hearts were light

Expos speedster Larry Lintz in 1974 being arrested by police in Daytona Beach, Florida, for theft – of second base.

Beginnings

1989

It was the end of the beginning;
It was the beginning of the end

Charles Bronfman (left) and Gene Mauch chatting at spring training in the early days when the Expos franchise was still new and fresh.

Chapter One

Changing of the Guard

Keep in mind that at that time baseball had bad economics, a bad labour situation, and very bad PR. Nobody in Montreal had the financial wherewithal, nor the operational ability to make a run at buying the franchise.

– Claude Brochu

To fully appreciate the rise and fall of the 1994 Montreal Expos one really should return to the tail end of 1989, to that darkening period when days grow short and autumn gives way to winter. For it was then that Charles Bronfman, owner of the Expos since before time began, met with team president Claude Brochu at Nashville's Opryland hotel, where baseball's annual winter meetings were drawing to a close, and declared his intention to step away from baseball and sell the club.

"Claude, I want to sell the ball club," he said, just like that. And even as Brochu desperately tried to mask his shock at the unexpectedness of the moment, Mr. Bronfman continued, "I don't have the strength to fight anymore. I'm not having any fun. I'm tired..."

Brochu protested vehemently, of course, but he knew in his heart that the decision was already final: there would be no reversal. As he conceded in his autobiography *My Turn at Bat*: "For Bronfman, the Expos weren't just a business; they were a true passion...The decision to get involved in this adventure [in 1968] was, above all, an emotional one. So was the decision to get out of it."[1]

The news was shocking, devastating, and deeply foreboding – for even as Mr. Bronfman's departure from the game signalled the end of an era, stamping *finis* on a princely twenty-year run of glory days, some chequered, some spangled - of far greater significance was the degree to which his unwavering stand would recast the club's future path and fortunes. What one might call the Charles Bronfman era had come to an end. Whatever lay ahead would belong to a new regime, one devoid of the

Bronfman touch. In the eyes of most observers across the baseball world, this was not seen to be a good thing.

Nor was it – as barely fifteen years later the club would play out its final string in Montreal and move to Washington, D.C., a town celebrated in baseball history for its interminable parade of struggling teams.

But before saying their final farewells, these new era Expos managed to scale great heights in 1994, putting together the best record in baseball. Unfortunately, that year, the season ended in mid-August, pulverized by a strike forced on the players by mendacious owners making impossible demands. Never before in the history of the major leagues had a schedule been prematurely aborted or a World Series cancelled. The work stoppage rocked the universe of the game to its core. Baseball eventually did recover, but barely. Except in Montreal. There it just managed to hang on for another ten years. Then it died.

There is no easy way to say this – but let's face it: the 1989 edition of the Montreal Expos was a monumental embarrassment – to the fans, to themselves, and most importantly, to their owner. The club had begun the season bursting with hope and promise, and for several months led their division. However, once August rolled around and every game began to count, the team collapsed, ultimately tumbling into an 81-81, fourth place finish.

This once proud ensemble, which had been within shouting distance of a berth in the 1981 World Series, apparently had, by 1989, run out of gas. No matter that they were blessed with a fine array of good players, a reasonable share of great players and two future Hall of Famers in their lineup (with a third one waiting in the wings), they seemed destined to forever fall short. Their 1989 collapse was the final straw. At least for Mr. Bronfman.

A scion of the family responsible for the immeasurable success of the multinational Seagram Corporation Distillers Limited, Charles Bronfman was one who believed in giving back. When in 1968 the newly birthed Expos franchise was on life-support and about to die in the cradle, Charles Bronfman was the man the city turned to for succour. He accepted the challenge and after quickly acquiring a 45 percent share of ownership, he was formally installed as the Montreal Expos' principal owner and Chairman of the Board. Mr. Bronfman hired John McHale, formerly general manager with the Detroit Tigers and Braves teams in both Milwaukee and Atlanta. From then on there was no looking back.[2]

At the time, Mr. Bronfman had acted mainly out of civic pride - but it did not take long for him to discover the extent to which baseball's many charms and wonders would find favour in his heart. Even before the launch of the club's initial 1969 season, he had grown so demonstrably enamoured of his Expos that he would occasionally appear at the team's spring training camp proudly sporting an Expos uniform emblazoned with number 83. That particular choice occasioned some chuckles at first: why would the owner of a baseball club who wanted his own uniform and number be so ill-informed as to give himself an unreasonably high number, one more suited to a football jersey? The answer lay with Seagram's 83 Canadian whisky. If not for the popularity of this product, there would have been no team! The

John McHale

laughter stopped. And some years later the number was officially retired by the club.

Over time, Mr. Bronfman's affection for the game and the people who played it deepened, and his commitment to the club's good fortunes rose to become his passion. Sportswriter Jerome Holtzman of the *Chicago Tribune* wrote: "He made sure the team had the financial means available to compete, and along the way became well regarded around ownership circles for his business acumen and commitment to the game. To many he was among the last of the "gentleman sportsmen" remaining in the game."[3] Jerry Reinsdorf, owner of the Chicago White Sox, considered Charles "just about the only guy in the room who votes and speaks for what's best for baseball, not what's best for his club."[4]

But by 1989, twenty summers had passed since the Expos first opened at Jarry Park. Mr. Bronfman was now acknowledged as the elder statesman among the owners of the National League, having outlasted all those who had been his compatriots over the years. Holtzman remembered Mr. Bronfman fondly, pointing out that this co-chairman of Seagram was among the wealthiest men in North America, possessing "more than enough money to buy the entire National League." He then added: "Bronfman doesn't flaunt it. Just the opposite. He puffs on his pipe, has a soft word for everyone and walks with a light foot. I have known him for many years and never once saw him do or say anything to draw attention to himself."[5]

And yet as Holtzman further noted: "Although he has been a gentle and concerned caretaker for 21 years, his players never rewarded him with a pennant or even a division championship." Actually that statement was untrue. In fact, the club did make one foray into the postseason. Who can forget 1981 when the Expos defeated the Phillies in the NL division finals and then lost their epic battle against the Los Angeles Dodgers who went on to win the World Series.

Of course, one could always factor in the memories. There were plenty of these.

Nevertheless, the fact remains that by the end of 1989 Mr. Bronfman was worn out. Worn out from coming close without much to show for it; worn out by the steady drop in attendance and the bitter spectre of rising costs; worn out by the relentless push for what he considered unreasonable salaries paid to star players which made the long-term financial viability of Major League Baseball problematic. He never really got over the contract demanded by Gary Carter in late 1982, eight-years and $16-million, (they settled for a seven year $13.1 million deal)[6]. It led directly to Carter's being traded to the Mets two years later. "I was Charles' scapegoat," Carter always maintained.[7]

Charles Bronfman was horrified by the reckless approach of his fellow owners to free agent signings at the end of 1989. "I mean you can have bidding for players," he declared, "but you don't have to be a damn fool about it. And right now, some people are."[8] And he was worn out by the haggling that had permeated the game at all levels. It was time, he knew, to call it a day.

As club president Claude Brochu explained at the time, "Charles was disappointed with the results of last season. And he doesn't like the labor strife, the direction baseball is taking. Charles has always said that what everybody should remember is that the game of baseball doesn't exist for the owners or the players; it exists because of and for the fans."[9]

Brochu had taken over as Expos president in early September 1986, upon the retirement of John McHale – the only president the Expos had known up to that time. Previously Brochu had served as executive vice president of marketing for Joseph E. Seagram and Sons, and it was in that capacity that he had become a close associate of the Expos owner. During the press conference at which Brochu was introduced to the media, Mr. Bronfman offered these comments: "One of the things that Claude Brochu will bring to us is expertise in general management and, more particularly, in marketing, in which he has a successful track record. That experience will stand him in good stead in bringing a freshness of ideas to the baseball club." Brochu was not, however, a baseball man, a fact that did not pass unnoticed.

Although Mr. Bronfman surprised everyone with the shocking year-end announcement that his Expos were for sale, he had actually tipped his weary hand somewhat earlier in the season. Indeed, as play began in the spring he instructed Expos general manager Dave Dombrowski "that no expense should be spared in bringing a flag to Montreal." That was all the impetus Dombrowski needed to leap head first into a rash of what Holtzman later described as "mid-season and late-season trades, none of which worked out. The biggest flop, of course, was the Mark Langston deal.

Brian Holman

Langston, who has since flown the coop, was acquired at the expense of three outstanding pitching prospects." These, of course, were Brian Holman, Gene Harris and a still very green Randy Johnson.

Langston, an impressive southpaw with the Seattle Mariners had been acquired by Montreal at the end of May, ostensibly to bolster the Expos' pitching rotation and spearhead a drive to the pennant. At the time, and during the early months ahead, he seemed to be the answer. Unfortunately, when the going got serious in August, Langston wilted, and a team of promise, which led the pennant race for much of the year, plum-meted into fourth place. As if that were not insult enough, at the end of the year, Langston rebuffed the Expos' attempts to re-sign him, opting instead to become a free agent and accept a five-year pact with the Los Angeles Angels. It was worth $16 million, the largest guaranteed contract in the history of the game to that point. Many observers believe that this turn of events was the final straw contributing to Mr. Bronfman's decision to divest himself of his beloved Expos.

Many now refer to 1989 as the year that free agency began its rampant run. On the Expos alone, as if to add bitter icing to an already bitter Langston-flavoured cake, Hubie Brooks, Damaso Garcia, Pascual Perez and Bryn Smith also launched themselves as free agents, out looking for a better deal.

Although Mr. Bronfman moved decisively in declaring that his club was for sale, he was anything but precipitous in his dealings with prospective purchasers. No "For Sale" signs hung on his clubhouse door. Rather, he chose to simply spread a quiet word that he was ready to talk to potential buyers, making it clear that certain conditions would have to be met. The new owner would pledge not to move the franchise from Montreal, and would retain the management team now in place. "That's typical of Charles," club president Claude Brochu said at the time. "He feels a great allegiance to his city and to his associates."[10]

In commenting on Mr. Bronfman's action, Chicago's Holtzman expressed the desire that he not be successful in finding a purchaser. He feared that "if [Bronfman] departs not only the ownership wing but all of baseball would be diminished."

As it turned out, Holtzman's fantastical musings were almost realized. Mr. Bronfman had charged Brochu with the task of securing new ownership, but the challenge soon grew far more daunting than anticipated. The local business community shied away, in part because of poor economic conditions generally, in part because of baseball's sullied reputation at the time, both in Montreal with the Expos' diminishing prospects, and across the board, "in the wake of the collusion fiasco."[11] There was some interest expressed by certain parties in the United States, but this always came with the underlying expectation of eventually relocating the franchise to an American city.

By 1991, with progress stymied, Mr. Bronfman loaned sufficient capital to Claude Brochu so that he, working in concert with Jacques Menard, an important Montreal businessman of the day, were able to pull together a syndicate of local investors prepared to purchase the club, one of whom was Stephen Bronfman, Charles' son. It had taken almost two years from the day Mr. Bronfman first declared his team for sale until he could officially step down, rid finally of the terrible burden the Expos had become.

Just how weighty a burden it was is perhaps revealed in Mr. Bronfman's dogged determination to free himself of the club, even in the face of a stalled economy. "As there was no real financial motivation for Bronfman to sell, and since his son Stephen was interested in maintaining a connection with the team," it has been said, "one must ask whether the sale really was unavoidable or simply reflected Charles Bronfman's frustration with the fractious state of Major League Baseball at the time."[12]

The evidence would suggest the latter held sway. Not long after the sale had been finalized, Mr. Bronfman spoke out one more time against the acrimony that now defined relationships between players and owners. "I have regretted it always, not only that we get into bitter disputes but that both sides are so silly. We get into an adversarial posture over something neither side owns. The owners don't own the game; the players don't own the game; the North American public owns it."[13]

Charles Bronfman continues to be regarded fondly by Montreal's baseball faithful. He was there to save the franchise at the very beginning and give it life, sustaining it for over twenty years. Responsibility for what happened after his departure, both the good and the bad, now lay at the feet of others.

And that, as we will see later, was a mixed blessing indeed.

Tributes to Charles Bronfman

When Charles Bronfman reigned as chairman and principal owner of the Expos from August 14, 1968 through the 1990 season, he held the longest consecutive ownership tenure of any National League club.

Ironically, he had stepped in only after the first major investor, Montreal's Jean-Louis Lévesque, backed out. Had Mr. Bronfman not been so willing to lend his considerable weight to Montreal's baseball project and provide the guarantees required, the whole effort would have been wasted and the franchise shifted elsewhere. Mr. Bronfman went on to purchase the majority of the shares – and thus the story unfolded.

Upon leaving, he received tributes from across the baseball world.

Bud Selig, at the time president of the Milwaukee Brewers, wrote: "He was the epitome of what baseball ownership should be. He constantly put the best interests of the game over his own and those of the Expos. Baseball is suffering an egregious loss with his leaving. Charles Bronfman has left an indelible imprint in the most positive ways on this institution."

Fred Wilpon, president and chief executive officer of the New York Mets, wrote: "Charles Bronfman's contributions to baseball in general and baseball in Canada in particular, are immense and will leave all of us in his debt for years to come."

Commissioner Fay Vincent wrote: "For better than 22 years, Charles Bronfman was baseball in Montreal. He is a true gentleman of the game, a good friend and baseball will sorely miss him."

Chapter Two

Remember Charles Johnson?

He could have been the second-best catcher in Expos history behind Gary Carter and should have been a member of Montreal's talented 1994 squad. But he wasn't, because he and his agent got tough at the bargaining table in the summer of 1989. He opted not to sign with the Expos even after they selected him as the tenth overall pick in the first round of that year's draft of amateur players.

"I blame myself for that," said Gary Hughes, the Expos scouting director at the time. "Believe me. I know very much how Charles would have meant to the Expos. He would have been their catcher in 1994. I messed up in '89."[14] A draft choice out of Westwood High School in Fort Pierce, Florida, Johnson was some kind of player. When you look back to those days of free-agent money for high-school and college players and compare it with what they now earn in the twenty-first century, the coin Johnson was seeking was miniscule.

At the time, Hughes didn't like the way Johnson's father, Charles Johnson Sr. and other advisors were dealing with him. "I didn't agree with the tactics. They were lying in the weeds and then they would come out," Hughes said in 2012. "Philosophically, I didn't agree with what they were doing. I was upset.

"Charles Bronfman, the best owner in the history of the game, came up to me and said, 'What about Charles Johnson? Are we not going to sign him? Really?' Charles put his hands up and said, 'OK.'

"I said, 'I don't think it's right for the game. At the time, I thought that it was the right thing to do. By that, I mean not caving into the tactics being tried on us by the player and his advisors."

The story, as Hughes relates it, goes back a year earlier when the Expos signed pitcher Reid Cornelius for $225,000 in 1988. Expos vice-president of baseball operations Bill Stoneman asked Hughes who he took as the team's first pick and Hughes told him.

"Oh, my God," Stoneman told Hughes. He had heard the rumours.

"Yes, Cornelius is thinking of going to Mississippi State, Bill, but let's take a chance," Hughes told Stoneman, meaning, take a chance that

Cornelius might sign with the Expos. Hughes and several members of the scouting department including Ed Creech travelled to Cornelius's home in Alabama to negotiate a contract.

Cornelius's mother did most of the negotiating, the father staying in the background. Out of the blue, Hughes offered $225,000. The player smiled and thought it sounded good. The mother was in agreement. The Cornelius folks couldn't believe what they knew was a generous offer. That same year, pitcher Andy Benes received $330,000 from the Cardinals, and pitcher Steve Avery accepted $211,000 from the Braves.

So the next year, the Johnson family, knowing that Cornelius received $225,000 from the Expos, wanted the same money. "We offered $200,000 and we were $25,000 apart," Hughes said. "We didn't budge. It was a stalemate."

If Hughes had to do it all over again, he would have offered $225,000 in 1989. "Definitely," he said 23 years later. "In retrospect I cost the Expos a major-league catcher, who turned into an all-star. The one thing I know is I can't be certain that $225,000 would have done it anyway, even if we ever got to that figure. Three years later, Charles was a draft pick of the Marlins but he held us up until the last minute."

What did Johnson get from the Marlins? Are you ready for this? $550,000. Just when the Expos were starting to roll in 1994, Johnson made his big-league debut with the Marlins, on May 6 of that year.

Over the course of his career, Johnson was not a star offensive player for the most part, finishing with a .245 average with 167 homers and 570 RBIs. His forte was his strong defensive play and throwing out runners trying to steal. He was a four-time all-star and helped the Marlins to the 1997 World Series title along with Moises Alou and a cast of other all-stars. But that's a whole other story.

Chapter Three

They Also Served - Silverman, Kozak, Giroux

Since 1977, John Silverman has been hanging around major-league clubhouses as equipment manager. It all started during the Toronto Blue Jays' first year of business in 1977 when he took over the post he would hold for four years. Then he joined the Montreal Expos in time for the 1981 season as assistant equipment manager under Harvey Stone. As a Christmas present on December 22, 1981, he was appointed the club's head equipment manager, beginning a run that would last until the end of the 2002 season.

Silverman's one of those Expos employees who can say he was around both for the wonderful playoff team of 1981 and the ill-fated, talented squad from 1994. Since 2003, he has served as chief equipment man for the Florida Marlins. When the 2013 season opened, Silver, as he is called, began working his 37th major-league season. Still youthful-looking and trim, he keeps in shape by jogging and has completed a few marathons in his time.

Silverman apprenticed for all of his clubhouse jobs from 1969-73, when he was an Expos clubhouse attendant under Harvey Stone. Back then, he was also completing his studies at Baron Byng High School on St. Urbain Street in Montreal, and later Dawson College. At the time, Baron Byng served a largely Jewish population – a number of whom went on to become leaders among Canada's cultural elite. These included actor William Shatner, writer Mordecai Richler, poet Irving Layton, and, of course, baseball's own, John Silverman.

Another unsung hero who enjoyed a lengthy run in Major League Baseball clubhouses is Mike Kozak, an assistant trainer whose career has stretched over 33 seasons. He too began with the Expos, on December 10, 1980, remaining with them through the 2002 season, when he followed Silverman to the Marlins.

Kozak calls himself "the only Canadian-born trainer on a big-league roster."[15] He holds a diploma in athletic training and management from Sheridan College in Oakville, Ontario, and a B.Sc from the University of Waterloo. He belongs to the National Athletic Trainers' Association, the Canadian Therapists Association and the Professional Baseball Athletic Trainers' Society. And, like all others in positions similar to his, Kozak is a full-fledged member of the Major League Baseball Players' Association. Yes, training staff belong to the MLBPA.

A colleague of Silverman and Kozak was Ron McClain. Called Ronnie Mac, he joined the Expos training staff in 1980 and remained until the 2004 season ended. Rather than move to Washington, he retired.

Then there is Monique Giroux, little known to the public but a favourite among Expos management and office staff. She was a business administration graduate from Montreal's St. Anne Academy and held a Sir George Williams/Concordia University degree in geography. In November 1968 Monique became an original member of the Expos communications /public relations department as an administrative assistant. In 1985 she was made Director of Media Services.

A friend to all media people, Monique wrote press releases and game notes in French, produced the regular-season and postseason media guides in two languages, coordinated press-box activities, issued credentials and oversaw photography at Olympic Stadium.[16] Her friends and colleagues considered her a mighty fine lady. High praise indeed.

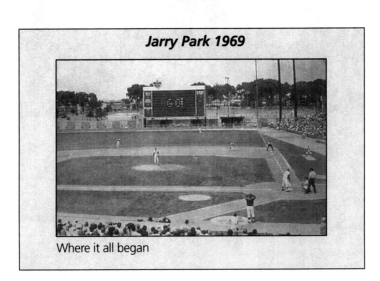

Jarry Park 1969

Where it all began

Ken Singleton was one of three players who came to Montreal in exchange for Rusty Staub. All three contributed to the club, although it took a long time for fans to accept that favourite Le Grand Orange had been traded to the Mets in early April, 1972.

Deep Despair

1990-1991

Life begins on the other side of despair
— Jean-Paul Sartre

Montreal Expos Hall of Famers

Andre Dawson

Gary Carter

Dave Van Horne

Chapter Four

First Came the Darkness

Yet I will love the darkness for it shows me the stars.

– Og Mandino

There was no official five-year plan, Expos scouting director Gary Hughes would say years later. But unofficially, there might as well have been, especially after the disaster that was 1989, when a talented Expos squad folded in the second half of the season.

Things were in a state of flux at the start of the 1990 season. With majority owner Charles Bronfman having grown so discouraged with his Expos that he decided to put the team up for sale, there was an absence of leadership at the top. For once Mr. Bronfman stepped back, the reins were now placed in the hands of Brochu, team president and chief operating officer since September 1986, although his powers to act were limited.

The ownership situation remained unstable well into 1991. It was not until mid-June of that year, when Claude Brochu was working with Jacques Menard of Nesbitt Burns to cobble together a consortium of 14 owners, that the transfer of ownership was complete. Brochu was named the club's managing general partner.[1] Unfortunately, even after this matter was resolved, the efficacy of the organization remained forever tenuous, principally because it was underfunded, a reality that would haunt its every move right up to the very end.

Claude Brochu

The Expos' record in 1990 was an improvement over their 1989 performance, but still not good enough. To compensate for players lost to free agency the Expos made several moves. Those with the most lasting

33

impact included the acquisition of Oil Can Boyd, Moises Alou (from Pittsburgh) and Ugueth Urbina. The club finished in third place, above .500 with an 85-77 record, but still 10 games behind the East Division–leading Pirates. Attendance dropped by 400,000 from the previous year to less than 1.5 million, ahead of only Atlanta and Houston in the National League. Tim Wallach led the Montreal hitters with a .296 batting average, 21 home runs and 96 RBIs. Larry Walker and Marquis Grissom took regular turns, but had not yet come into their own. Dennis Martinez and Boyd were the only starters to win 10 games, although reliever Bill Sampen collected 12 victories over the season. It was a tired team. As if to underscore that point, on December 23, the Expos traded their stellar outfielder Tim Raines, a strong candidate for baseball's Hall of Fame, to the Chicago White Sox for Barry Jones and Ivan Calderon.

Montreal did have some success with the draft that year, with nine of the team's selections eventually making it to the major leagues, including Rondell White and Shane Andrews.

Then came 1991, and unfortunately, things only got worse. This was the year the Expos reached the very depths of despair, a season when everything that could go wrong did, the ultimate in what Latin scholars might call the *annus horribilis*. Looked at from the vantage point of today, perhaps it is best just to treat the campaign as simply a false start and move on to better things. For soon enough, things did get better, infinitely better in fact.

Before the 1991 season began, in an attempt to put a new face on the club, management made several moves. They traded Otis Nixon to Atlanta and Tim Burke to the Mets, released Kevin Gross and Mike Aldrete, among others, and acquired Scott Service, Ron Hassey, Heath Haynes, Todd Haney, and Mike Lansing.

The home opener was a great success, with over 54,000 in the stands to watch Dennis Martinez, with late-inning help from Barry Jones and Scott Ruskin, lead the Expos to a 7–0 triumph over Pittsburgh. Larry Walker, Ivan Calderon and Dave Martinez knocked out three hits each. Calderon and the veteran Ron Hassey produced two RBIs apiece, and the year's first home runs came off the bats of Delino DeShields and Calderon. Hassey was wrapping up his career, and as a free agent had selected Montreal because he believed in the team's potential. "When the season began we thought we had a good team," he said in 2011. Speaking informally before a Florida State League game in Bradenton, where his Jupiter Hammerheads were in action, he admitted, "but it was a bad year for injuries. Walker was hurt, and so was Moises Alou."[2] Indeed, Alou was out for the entire season with a serious injury; Walker managed to get into 137 games, but his numbers (.290-16-64) were yet to rise to the levels he would attain over the next few years.

Hassey is an interesting story. Thirty-eight years old and entering his final year when he joined the Expos, he had consistently managed to overcome his modest numbers and earn his place, not only in Expos history but indeed in baseball history. Hassey was behind the plate on July 28, 1991, the day Dennis Martinez pitched a 2-0 perfect game over the Dodgers in Los Angeles, one of the few bright spots in a desperately miserable season.

Ron Hassey in 2011 at the ballpark in Bradenton, Florida

Martinez's accomplishment is still fondly remembered today, but he would be the first to acknowledge the stellar job Hassey did in guiding him through those nine flawless innings. According to Martinez, "Hassey was unbelievable that day...He made sure to put up a big target if he wanted me to throw inside or outside. He knew what he was doing."[3]

Yes he did. For one thing, Martinez's achievement was not Hassey's

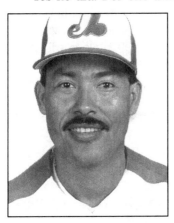

Dennis Martinez

first perfect game behind the plate. He had "been there" before, ten years earlier, on May 15, 1981, when he caught Cleveland pitcher Len Barker's nine-inning unblemished masterpiece against the Toronto Blue Jays. Hassey remains the only catcher in Major League Baseball history to have two perfect games under his belt. It is all the more remarkable that he split the accomplishment between the two leagues.

To the Dodgers' legendary broadcaster Vin Scully, the perfect game by Martinez was "a masterpiece." Expos iconic play-by-play giant Dave Van Horne followed Marquis Grissom's catch of Chris Gwynn's game-ending drive before exploding with the catchphrase "El Presidente...El Perfecto". These words still echo today as one of the most entrenched of all Expos slogans and expressions.

Photo: Van Horne handout

Dave Van Horne, voice of the Expos, in his perch at Olympic Stadium. In 2011 he was awarded the Ford C. Frick Award for Broadcasting, at Cooperstown.

It should be noted that the gem by Martinez was not the only stellar pitching exhibition in the game that day. Up until the sixth inning neither team had managed a hit. Ironically, when Dodgers hurler Mike Morgan's flirtation with fame was finally dashed, the perpetrator was none other than Hassey himself. It seemed almost as though the aging backstop was bound to ensure that no one was going to steal the lustre from his hurler's march into the history books. Even with that, the Expos managed only four hits off Morgan, who also pitched a complete game. Both Expos runs were unearned.

There must have been something in the air, for, strangely, in the same park only two days earlier, Montreal's Mark Gardner had taken a no-hitter into the 10th inning. He lost both his no-hit bid and the game on a couple of hits and a run in that final frame.

Nevertheless, the Martinez masterpiece, as marvelous as it might have been, appeared like a rose bush in a field of thistles. Before this game the Expos had lost eight of their previous 10 matches, and of the 10 games following they would win only one.

The team continued to bounce around the second division until early August when they comfortably descended into the National League east cellar, never to emerge again. They wrapped up the 1991 season with a 71-90 record, 26.5 games behind the division-leading Pittsburgh Pirates. The last time an Expos squad descended into the depths of such futility was 1972, only the club's fourth year in the league.

How bad was the 1991 team? It is telling that three years later, when the 1994 edition of the Expos took the field, only five members of the 1991 club still remained in the mix. On the positive side, all of them – Moises Alou (he had missed the full season due to injury), Jeff Fassero, Marquis Grissom, Mel Rojas and Larry Walker – were front-liners, fundamental to Montreal's success.

However, if the team on the playing field in 1991 had been done in by misfortune and bad play, those troubles paled in comparison to the hardships that hounded the organization off the diamond.

To begin with, even though the ownership dilemma had been resolved in mid-June, there was little about the solution to breed confidence in the hearts of Expos fans. Just the very nature of the Brochu-Menard consortium, a fractious group of strange bedfellows drawn from competing sectors – public and private, management and labour – and rife with overwhelming egos was enough to send warning signals clattering. A significant number of the partners let it be known that at best they were reluctant players in the game. Their contribution was intended as a public relations gesture and did not represent a financial commitment to the team's long-range future. They would never be prepared to put more money in the pot. So don't ask.

Thus when the crunch came, a decade or so later, the ill-equipped consortium lost its way. Many of the partners found themselves so politically and ideologically at odds with one another that consensus became impossible, and to make matters worse, few were willing to invest new capital into protecting their original investment. Complicating the problem further was the public's lack of confidence in the restructured new regime – not even conceding it the customary 100 days of grace traditionally accorded new administrations everywhere.

And with some reason perhaps. Even as the untested bosses were still signing for new keys and privileged parking at Olympic Stadium, another storm was brewing. On June 2, 49 games into the season, Expos general manager Dave Dombrowski fired Expos field boss Buck Rodgers, after over six years in the position. The Expos had only won 20 games to this point and Dombrowski felt that the team would have a better chance at success if third base coach Tom Runnells were at the helm. Brochu hints that he too might have found Rodgers a bit prickly. As president and managing general partner he seldom became involved in the baseball side of the operation, but there was one instance when he let displeasure get the better of him. Unhappy with Rodgers' persistent platooning of Otis Nixon and Marquis Grissom, he arranged to trade Nixon. And that was the end of that.

Rodgers greeted the news of his dismissal stoically. "I knew and the players knew that Tommy Runnells was [GM] Dave Dombrowski's man," said Buck. "I wasn't."[4] Rodgers was a popular pilot with both players and fans, and reaction to his sudden departure swept across Expos nation with tsunami-like intensity. The faithful were not pleased.

Unfortunately, or not, depending on how long range one's perspective might have been, Dombrowski's choice of Runnells, a first-time manager, was either foolish or prophetic. Runnells completed the season with a 51-61 record, good enough to warrant his re-hiring for 1992, even though it had quickly become apparent that on this team of veterans, he was operating far beyond his depth.

As it turned out, not only did Dombrowski rid himself of the trouble-some (to Dombrowski) Rodgers barely eight weeks into the 1991 season, a couple of months later he decided to remove himself from the scene as well. Hindsight would suggest that even as he was passing the buck on Buck (!), Dombrowski was already setting his own sights on fresh hori-zons. Before the season wound down, the new boy wonder of baseball's front offices had already moved to Florida to become the first general manager of Florida's fledgling expansion franchise, the Marlins. One of two expansion teams created in June 1991 (along with the Colorado Rockies, although they would not start playing until 1993), Florida's own-ers were in immediate need of an experienced architect to guide them through the November 1992 expansion draft. Dombrowski was their obvi-ous choice – and they were his.

Dave Dombrowski joined the Expos in 1987, perhaps the last good year for the 1980s team of glory, as director of player development. Previously, he had served as assistant general manager to Roland Hemond of the Chicago White Sox, one of the great men of baseball. Born in Rhode Island, Hemond was a product of the robust Franco-American community that long ago established itself in that state – and still today he is comfort-able speaking French. Given his deep Quebec–based roots, Hemond keeps a special place in his heart for the baseball fortunes of the province. And that affection is returned by the many members of the Quebec base-ball community who have come to know him. This recognition and respect was such that for a number of years there was hope he might one day become associated with the Expos in a senior executive role. It was felt that as a member of the Expos staff he would have brought an innate understanding of the Quebecois environment to the front office, some-thing sorely lacking through too many years of the team's existence. Regrettably, even though his years of service ran in parallel with the lifes-pan of the Expos, never, in all that time, did anyone in Montreal ever see fit to offer him a job. That was a pity.

Hemond's own baseball journey started in the early 1950s with the Boston, later Milwaukee, Braves. He eventually rose to become the orga-nization's assistant scouting director. From there, he moved on to hold a variety of executive positions with the Angels, White Sox, Orioles and Arizona Diamondbacks, all for extended periods of time. Now in his eight-ies, he remains active as a special assistant to the Diamondbacks presi-dent. In 2011 the Baseball Hall of Fame awarded Hemond the Buck O'Neil Award in recognition of "the profound impact he has had on the game, for his baseball intelligence as a keen talent evaluator and in building winning teams, to the universal respect he has earned for mentoring generations of baseball executives, past and present."[5]

In other words, Dombrowski had learned at the knee of a master. So too had another successful general manager, Chatham, Ontario's Doug Melvin, currently GM of the Milwaukee Brewers. He readily attributes much of his success to the lessons learned when he was teamed with Hemond in Baltimore, then serving as the Orioles' general manager. Inducted into the Canadian Baseball Hall of Fame in 2012, Melvin made a point to single out Hemond as his mentor. "Roland taught me the lessons of life," said Melvin. "He prepared me to someday take on the role of a general manager myself."[6]

Roland Hemond in the mid-2000s. The ring he is wearing is the Arizona D'backs' World Series Championship ring of 2001.

Dombrowski became general manager of the Expos in 1988 when he replaced Bill Stoneman. During his tenure, the Expos managed to hold their own, always finishing above .500, but seldom in contention by season's end. While Dombrowski is generally given credit for having put new muscle into the farm system, by 1991, perhaps the most disappointing year in Expos history, the team had tumbled into last place. With the club possessing the second-worst record in the National League, and with his decision to replace popular manager Buck Rodgers with Tom Runnells still rankling players and fans, his own fire seemed to be burning low.

That was confirmed in September when, as the team was in freefall and its fortunes about to hit their nadir, he abandoned ship for the embryonic Florida Marlins.

Fortunately, Dombrowski was replaced as general manager by his assistant, Dan Duquette, in what turned out to be a stroke of genius. The transition was smooth, as the two men had worked well together, and Duquette was equipped to handle the job. In fact, in the early 1990s, it was not unusual to see the duo jogging together on the warning track at Olympic Stadium before game time, staying in shape and talking baseball. Nevertheless, Dombrowski's departure became just one more blow in the

Dave Dombrowski

streak of unaccountable bad luck to strike the club in 1991.

For there was still more, especially with the aging dowager-like Olympic Stadium already suffering her own fall from grace, one of the too many misfortunes which marred her rocky reign. In September, on Friday 13, completely without warning, support beams snapped, causing a huge 55-ton concrete slab to crash down onto an outside walkway near a cluster of ticket booths. Because it happened in the afternoon, at a time when the Expos were on the road and the concourse empty, there were no injuries. But the accident sounded a harsh wake-up call, for had circumstances been different, the results could have been catastrophic.

It was not the first time the weary old edifice had misbehaved. In fact, ever since this gargantuan concrete structure began rumbling skyward in 1976, it had been rife with problems. Many of these were associated with the new-fangled, so-called retractable roof Parisian architect Roger Taillibert had designed to ensure that patrons would be able to enjoy the sporting life *al fresco* in balmy weather, while still being protected from the elements when the sun didn't shine. His plans called for a flexible

Dan Duquette

Kevlar roof cover that could be mechanically extended out or folded up like an umbrella as needed, simply with the push of a button. It took until 1987 before the roof was finally completed, and another year to be made operational.

The mechanical roof was a monumental flop, cumbersome to deploy, impossible to manipulate in even moderate winds, and susceptible to tearing. In the short interval this wonky structure was in place, it could never keep up with sudden wind or rainstorms. Consequently, the club was repeatedly embarrassed by the necessity of calling rain-delays or even postponements in a so-called covered stadium.[7]

The Stadium had been built for the 1976 Montreal Olympics, with the idea that it would serve into perpetuity the sporting needs of the citizens of Montreal. That these same citizens would also end up paying into perpetuity for the privilege was less evident at the time. In the final analysis, it is fair to say that the Big O – or Big OWE, take your pick – was quite wonderful in its day, far more so than expected, and for a number of years it did achieve its mandate. It became the centre for everything BIG that was Montreal – sporting events, raves, church assemblies, rock shows, monster truck shows, agricultural exhibits, and anything else that would bring out a crowd.

Sadly, by 1991 Olympic Stadium had become so plagued by a variety of calamities that paying customers began staying away, simply because they feared for their safety. Especially during the early post-Olympic years a variety of mishaps had occurred, many related to work on the leaning support tower for the roof. Fires, often caused by flying sparks, were always a concern, as were bits of steel that fell into the stands or on the playing surface.

Earlier in 1991, during an Expos game, strong winds had ripped a hole in the Kevlar roof, causing heavy rains to pour down on fans – final proof that Taillibert's retractable roof was impractical and impossible to make work. It was kept closed for all of the 1992 season, and thereafter.

Although the cause of 1991's breakaway concrete slab was not related to any structural deficiency, the experience was confidence-shaking enough to force Olympic Stadium authorities to shut down operations for the balance of the baseball season. This meant that the Expos had no choice but to play their final thirteen home games on the road, in the parks of their opponents. It was the first, but not the last time, that the club was forced to adopt the guise of a semi-pro travelling team, barnstorming its way across the land, with no place to call its own. It occurred again in 2003 and 2004, although this time the cause was not gravity but

Olympic Stadium in the late 1970s: Note the open roof, the tower designed to house the moveable covering and the Velodrome in the lower right.

rather the baseball elite trying to be cute. In those years, the Expos, by this time the property of MLB, were summarily dispatched to Puerto Rico to play a number of so-called "home" games there. The experiment was a disaster – and even today the very thought of this ignominy still makes Expos loyalists shudder.

Prior to the concrete slab's collapse, the club had been slated to open a two-game series at the Big O against the Mets on Monday, September 16. That series was moved to New York and played on the Tuesday as a doubleheader, which the clubs split. The "home-stand" then continued on to Philadelphia, where Montreal lost the two games scheduled. Chicago was next – although the anticipated three-game weekend series was reduced to a doubleheader played on Sunday. It was swept by the Expos.

At that point Montreal "really" took to the road, scheduled for a four-game series in St. Louis against the Cards (each team winning two), before "returning home" to meet the Pirates in Pittsburgh (losing two), and then the Cards again in St. Louis (losing three). They wrapped up the season as the true visiting team in Pittsburgh, taking only one of three.

All told, the season was an embarrassment, a season to forget, a season of 71 wins and 90 losses. (The lost game in September with Chicago was never made up.) Nor were admission revenues for the thirteen lost games at Olympic Stadium. Attendance for the year dropped to 940,000, last in the National League, and the first time since the final two years of the Jarry Park experience in 1975 and 1976 that the number of patrons in the stands fell below the seven-figure level.

At year's end, management actively began making moves to strengthen the team. They lost Junior Naboa on waivers and both Ron Hassey and Mike Fitzgerald to free agency. They picked up Gary Carter from the Dodgers and sent Andres Galarraga to the Cards for Ken Hill. Nelson Santovenia was released and Darrin Fletcher was acquired from the Phillies for Barry Jones. And, in a significant trade with Cincinnati, Montreal obtained Bill Risley and John Wetteland for Dave Martinez, Scott Ruskin and Willie Greene. Draft picks in 1991 included Cliff Floyd, Mark Grudzielanek, Derrick White, Brian Looney, Kirk Rueter, and Bob Henley.

Thus, although it was too soon to tell, the core of the 1994 club was beginning to coalesce. It still lacked the single binding force that would bring it all together, the catalyst to unify the different components and make them as one – a team capable of winning.

And that was how the year ended, with the Expos folding under the weight of a runaway GM in search of greener outfields, a fractious ownership group, a dysfunctional manager and no place to play. Could it get any worse? Actually yes – but then it would become so much better.

Andres Galarraga joined the Expos as a rookie in 1985 and remained with the club through 1991. A fan favorite and Gold Glove first baseman, his batting prowess so deteriorated from his Silver Slugger turn in 1988 to a sickly .219 average in '91, that he was traded. Galarraga discovered new life in Colorado, earning Comeback of the Year Awards in 1996 and 2000. He made a comeback of sorts with the Expos in 2002.

Chapter Five

Scout's Honour – Gary Hughes

G ary Hughes remembers spring training of 1991 when he, general manager Dave Dombrowski, manager Buck Rodgers and other members of the Expos brain-trust were in a boardroom in the West Palm Beach area discussing whether to trade veteran Otis Nixon or send either Marquis Grissom or Larry Walker to the minors.

"Buck loved Nixon. When it came to me for a vote, I said that we should keep both Grissom and Walker at the major league level," Hughes recalled. "I thought trading Otis was the thing to do. I felt it important to get those young guys playing. We now had reason to look into the future, at a better chance down the road."[8]

Thus, on April Fool's Day, Nixon was dispatched to the Atlanta Braves and Walker and Grissom remained in the majors. Good thing, too, for they were part of the core group that elevated the Expos to supreme status in 1994: Walker a Canadian free agent signed by the Expos in 1984, Grissom a draft pick signed in 1988.

"In the six years we were in Montreal, we drafted 65 guys that went to the majors, almost unheard of," Hughes said. "I remember two guys that stand out. We got Grissom in the third round. It was phenomenal, a great day for the scouts, Eddie Creech, Frank Wren, Bob Oldis. And the second guy was Kirk Rueter, who we got in the 19th round and scouted by Stan Belinski, a guy I had great respect for.

"It's not me, it's us. It was the scouts who found these guys. To get a player, it starts with a part-time scout, who tells the

Marquis Grissom

area scout, then he tells a cross-checker, and then the national cross-checker comes in. Finally, it gets to the scouting director and the assistant scouting director."

Hughes's two favourite Expos of all time? Grissom and Delino DeShields. Even though he was traded to the Dodgers for Pedro Martinez, DeShields has always stood tall in Hughes's book.

"The Expos got Pedro for somebody," Hughes said, meaning that DeShields was a heckuva player. "Going into the draft in 1987, we had seven votes in the room. Should we take a chance on DeShields, who was a star basketball player at Villanova? The vote was 6-1 in favour. I was the one dissenting vote. I remembered when the Expos decided to draft Pete Incaviglia. He wouldn't sign and we had to trade him.

Delino DeShields

"So we signed Delino for $75,000, well under the going rate. Three days into playing for us in the minors, Jerry Manuel said DeShields wants to play baseball only. That was him telling us, not us telling him. When I saw Delino in Bradenton, Florida, he told me he was going to play baseball and concentrate on one thing. I ended up giving him $125,000, instead of $75,000. I felt that was the right thing to do."

Before long, DeShields would be spending time at the Hughes' house. He remained there for three years, forging a life-long friendship with the scout and his family, especially Sam, Gary's son. In one of his last assignments as a scout with the Chicago Cubs, Hughes brought Grissom and DeShields along to help out at a workout camp before the free-agent draft.

"Marquis and Delino were throwing batting practice. It brought a tear to my eye," Hughes said. "At the hotel that night, Delino came to me and said, 'I just want to thank you for all you did for me. You are a special person in my life.'"

Hughes had a deep fondness and respect for Charles Bronfman. "I had a visit with him right after he announced that he was selling the team in the late 1980s. I asked him to give it two more years and we'd win it. He said he'd been hearing two more years for 20 years. I replied maybe so but not from me. He smiled and said that with all due respect he was getting out.

"It wouldn't have taken until '94 had Charles hung on."

All-Star Game Trivia

In 1994, the Expos sent five of their front-line players to the All-Star Game in Pittsburgh. They were: Moises Alou, left field; Wil Cordero, shortstop; Darrin Fletcher, catcher; Marquis Grissom, centre field; Ken Hill, pitcher.

Only once before had the club managed to place five players on the National League All-Star team – in 1982, when the game was played at Olympic Stadium. Can you name the players?

Answer: Gary Carter, catcher; Andre Dawson, centre field; Al Oliver, first base; Tim Raines, left field; Steve Rogers, pitcher.

Felipe Returns

1992

Everything about him was old except his eyes and they were the same color as the sea and were cheerful and undefeated.
– Ernest Hemingway, *The Old Man and the Sea*

Photo by Bill Young

Felipe Alou was the most charismatic and knowledgeable Expos' manager of them all. In 1992 he took over a team that had lost its way: two years later it stood out as the best club in baseball. Here he speaks with a fan in Montreal at an Expos' breakfast reunion, Montreal, 2011

Chapter Six

Turn, Turn, Turn

To everything there is a season, a time for every purpose under the sun[1].

– Ecclesiastes 3.1

Seldom has a baseball year begun so miserably only to end so well. But this year, what started out as an extension of the gloom that had defined the Montreal Expos in 1991 truly did wrap up under a canopy of winning, and happy fans. Signs that life was about to change first began appearing in the spring, and by the mid-point of 1992 it became increasingly evident that this year things were going to be different. It had taken almost three years after Charles Bronfman stepped aside as Montreal's owner and number one fan for the Expos' pitiful descent to run its course, but when it did, the change in club fortunes was almost miraculous.

Of course, none of this was apparent when Expos players showed up for spring training at West Palm Beach toward the end of February. Nothing seemed different from the year previous as the bad luck and sour karma that had embraced 1991 just refused to disappear. Manager Tom Runnells, in an attempt to show he intended to take charge from day one, announced at the opening of camp that he expected more discipline in the season ahead. It was a bold gesture, but an empty one – for as players and media alike and even fans quickly sensed, he lacked the wherewithal to back it up.

Then, when in a misguided, self-deprecating gesture meant to relieve tension and lighten the atmosphere, Runnells rolled into camp wearing army fatigues, his credibility fell to zero. To veterans like Tim Wallach and Dennis Martinez, it was the final straw. This was major league baseball, they seemed to be saying, how can you respect a manager who

Tom Runnells

shows up in army dress in some cockamamie attempt to make it clear he's the boss.

But Runnells didn't stop there. Somehow he got the idea he could strengthen the club by moving slick-fielding third baseman Wallach to first base and installing the untested Bret Barberie in his place. Ever the pro, Wallach acquiesced, albeit reluctantly, but the questionable logic behind the manager's decision quickly became another focus of dissent. Rumblings from the clubhouse confirmed the players' sense that Runnells was not up to the task of managing major league ballplayers. His style might have worked in the minors, but it was gratuitous and insulting in the bigs.

And as if the veterans on the squad were not snake-bit enough, at the end of April, while on a ten-game, West Coast road trip where the Expos had already lost five of seven, the club became entangled in the infamous Rodney King riots that set Los Angeles ablaze. The riots, which began towards evening on Wednesday April 29, were prompted by the acquittal of four members of the Los Angeles police force who had been caught on videotape beating Rodney King, a defenseless black man. The rampage quickly spread across the Los Angeles metropolitan area and by the time the California Army National Guard, supported by the U.S. Marines, was able to restore calm, 53 people were dead and over one billion dollars in damages incurred.[2]

The Expos heard of the uprising on Thursday as they were wrapping up a series in San Diego and preparing to fly into Los Angeles for three games beginning Friday, May 1. Concern gripped the team as the players learned about the expanding maelstrom of violence and destruction spreading across the city. *Los Angeles Times* scribe Scott Miller: "Minutes after their 9-3 victory Thursday over the Padres... the Montreal Expos dressed with one eye on their socks and the other on pictures from Los Angeles." He then added: "Subdued, withdrawn and nervous, they are due in Los Angeles today for a weekend series with the Dodgers, and they do not want to go."[3]

Vin Scully was broadcasting the Dodgers-Phillies game from Chavez Ravine that Wednesday night even as the city had begun boiling over with rage. As live shots from the streets played across the television sets in his booth, Scully knew he had to remain calm. He later wrote that he "was extremely aware of the obligation I had not only to broadcast the game, but my obligation to maintain the safety of…people at the ballpark. So I said nothing. It was very painful."[4]

When it became obvious that no baseball could be played for the next few days, there was talk of shifting the Expos-Dodgers series to Anaheim, or even moving it to Montreal. However, neither option proved practical. "A lot of us feel like the games won't take place," Tom Foley, the Expos' player representative said. "By looking at the TV shots they're sending out all over the world, how can you say, 'Everything is fine now, you go play the game?'"

In the end the Dodgers solved the dilemma for everyone: they postponed games for four days straight, including the Expos' weekend series. Larry Walker spoke for his teammates when he said that given the choice, "I'd rather go back to my own beautiful country."[5]

Relieved, the Expos headed back to Montreal and Olympic Stadium for a return engagement against these same three National League west coast teams. This time *Nos Amours* took five of the eight games played.

The impact of the riots on the Dodgers, both as a team and individually, was visceral and personal. Manager Tommy Lasorda pointed this out when his team finally made it back onto the field in Philadelphia, after almost a week of inactivity: "Everybody knows that what happened was bigger than our game. It put a tremendous scar on our entire city."[6]

It was simpler for the Expos. Life went on and the team's fortunes improved. The three games that were postponed in early May were integrated into the July schedule when Montreal returned to Los Angeles for a regular three-game series. The teams ended up meeting six times in three days – three double-headers in a row. The Expos lost both ends of the first twin bill, swept the Dodgers in the second, and split the finale. At this point the Expos' record stood at 42-42. They would not drop below .500 for the remainder of the season. Of course, by this time a new manager was at the helm.

Even before the Expos left Florida for Montreal to open the regular season, Runnells had become such a major distraction that his departure seemed inevitable, and imminent. Novice general manager Dan Duquette stuck with his rookie pilot as long as he dared, but by mid-May, as his team sat mired in fourth place with a disappointing 17-20 record and a league-leading 36 errors – and all this on the heels of the disastrous '91 season – he had no choice but to make a move.

Firing Runnells was the easy part: the struggling manager had simply failed to meet expectations. The tougher challenge was finding a suitable replacement, someone who could mould this collection of veterans and up-and-comers into a contender.

Duquette's solution was brilliant. In a move that overnight changed the club's fortunes for the better, he turned to the almost mythic Felipe Alou to take over the team. The date was May 22, 1992. From that day forward, right through until mid-August 1994, Alou took his charges on a one-way magical run. Montreal's won/loss record improved to 70-55 for the balance of the '92 season, setting the stage for an even more triumphant 1993.

Duquette received plaudits for not only sensing that the veteran Alou's experience and baseball knowledge would bring new life to the clubhouse, but also for possessing the insight and courage to offer the challenging job to a managerial neophyte. Alou, who played briefly for Montreal in 1973, at the close of his outstanding career, had been part of the Expos organization since 1976, serving as minor league batting instructor and manager. He had come to know intimately most of Montreal's budding stars – those currently on the roster and in the minors – and was well respected by them all. And he was already in the city, having joined the Expos as bench coach earlier in the year.

Alou was out fishing with the Expos' French-language broadcaster Jacques Doucet and friends the day he got Duquette's call. "At the time I thought it was premature to fire (Runnells)," Alou said later, "but Duquette said, 'If you don't accept the offer, we're going to pick someone else.' So I took the job before he could change his mind."[7]

The difference in the club, its approach to the game and its won-loss record, was immediate. "When Felipe took over things were different," said Marquis Grissom. "He knew he had a lot of young players, he was caring."[8]

Alou's promotion made him the first Dominican to manage in the major leagues. The only other minority managers then active were Cito Gaston of the Toronto Blue Jays and Hal McRae in Kansas City. Alou's appointment generated great joy and celebration in the Dominican Republic where, according to Manny Mota, himself briefly an Expo in 1969, Felipe "was looked on as a role model."[9]

Duquette never doubted he had made the right choice. He only wished he had made it earlier. "The biggest mistake I've made in my career," he said, "was not recognizing his ability before then to be a terrific major league manager. He is one of the best in the game."[10]

Duquette told Ross Newhan of the *Los Angeles Times* that "Felipe knows our personnel inside and out. He has the respect of the players and staff. His nationality wasn't a factor. We looked at his experience and his loyalty to the organization, and the way his clubs pitched and executed when he managed in our farm system. I believe we have some hungry players who will respond to the change. I don't think there's a dominant team in the division." To these accolades Alou responded, "I was proud to be one of the first Dominicans to play in the big leagues, and I am proud to become the first manager."[11]

While the resulting turnaround in Expos fortunes – a precursor to the accomplishments that lay ahead in 1994 – was shaped by Felipe Alou, one cannot ignore Dan Duquette's success in rebuilding the team. With little delay after replacing Dave Dombrowski in late 1991, Duquette made it clear that his mission was to achieve success – and then he set out to make it happen.

Duquette joined the Expos in 1987 as director of player development, working closely with Dombrowski. It was under their watch that Montreal drafted and/or signed many of the players who would become vital to the 1994 wonder team. That this remarkable collection of talent was never allowed to complete its mission that year was crushing: that it was never able to achieve its destiny, ruinous.

During Claude Brochu's tenure as general partner, he hired four general managers – Dombrowski, Duquette, Kevin Malone and Jim Beattie. "When I set out to hire I looked for young, smart, bold, strong candidates," he said. "And I was very lucky. I had four very good GMs working for me." While Brochu was highly satisfied with all of them, Duquette was the only one he would rate as a "full 10, on a scale of one to 10," principally because in putting together the 1994 team, he accomplished the most. According to Brochu, Duquette, and his staff – including Kevin Kennedy – had the "ability to see beyond the obvious and this helped them engineer a number of trades beneficial to Montreal. To do that, you've got to know your stuff and be able to take the chance that these new guys will produce." Brochu is convinced that Duquette was the magician who put together the 2004 Red Sox World Series winner, although Theo Epstein has been given the lion's share of the credit.

Dave Dombrowski was also outstanding (earning a rating of 9.5 from Brochu) although his decision to quit the club in September 1991, before the season ended and when Expos fortunes were at their lowest ebb, did leave a sour taste. Brochu respected his reasons for going: Dombrowski had been offered the GM position with the Florida Marlins, still in their infancy, and "I couldn't say no, not when he was given such an opportunity," said Brochu. In a 2011 interview, Brochu stated he would have preferred his GM to remain until the schedule had been played out. He also expressed dismay that Dombrowski had picked off over 20 key personnel from the scouting side of the Expos' operation on his way out the door. "It got so bad," said Brochu, "the commissioner had to step in and stop it."

Brochu regrets he never offered the GM job to Bill Stoneman, at the time in charge of financial operations, but in the early years a formidable pitcher for the Expos, with two no-hitters to his credit. "This is one of my big regrets in baseball,'" Brochu claims. "Stoneman knew and understood the game." Asked if Stoneman would have accepted the position, given that he always seemed to maintain a low profile and lived in the area year-round, Brochu replied, "absolutely." Stoneman eventually became general

Bill Stoneman

manager of the Anaheim Angels and soon built a World Series winner.[12]

However, in 1992, even as the Expos successfully put the brakes to another losing campaign, not every-thing was positive. As followers of the team know only too well, a recurrent theme running through its history is the profound way that bad timing and bad luck can shape a club's fortunes. And so it was in June 1992 when, far beyond the diamond, Montreal made a choice, not so much a bad choice nec-essarily, but the wrong choice – at least when considered in hindsight some twenty years after the fact. The Expos had a crack at drafting the player some consider to be the greatest of his gen-eration, perhaps of all time, and they passed him by. (See Chapter Seven)

Baseball's amateur draft that year took place via conference call on June 1. Because of the team's dismal finish in 1991, Montreal drafted third, with scouting director Kevin Malone representing the Expos.. He was looking for a left-handed pitcher. Faced with a full panoply of talent, Malone selected B.J. Wallace, a fire-balling southpaw from Mississippi State University. Sadly, Wallace flamed out in the minors, brought down by arm trouble, without ever getting a taste of the big leagues. Although Malone could not have known it at the time, by choosing Wallace he had let magic slip through his fingers.

The 1992 draft was not a total loss, as Montreal's prize selection that year was second baseman Jose Vidro. He broke in with the big team in

1997 and remained at his starting position through 2004. He played two more years in Washington before ending his career in Seattle in 2008. All of the others from the '92 draft who graduated to the Expos were pitchers. None lasted very long, although Rodney Henderson saw action briefly with Montreal in 1994.

As the 1992 season progressed, the Expos grew steadily stronger and more confident. With manager Alou guiding them from the dugout and Duquette cherry-picking the talent pool, those individual pieces that would form the *équipe du tonnerre* of 1994 were beginning to fall into place.

Ken Hill (16-9) and Jeff Fassero (8-7) set the tone among the starting pitchers, while in the bullpen John Wetteland (37 saves) and Mel Rojas (10 saves) served notice of their considerable skills. The all-star outfield of Larry Walker, Marquis Grissom and Moises Alou was already in place while future starting infielders Wil Cordero and Sean Berry (acquired from Kansas City in August) had begun to establish themselves. Catcher Darrin Fletcher was making strides as the back-up to Gary Carter.

Carter had come back to Montreal for one last hurrah – one last walk through the National League before retiring. The fans loved him once again, cheering on his every move. And he returned the love, responding with generous waves and smiles whenever they chanted his name. Fittingly, his last hit in baseball was made as an Expo, at home in Montreal, with only one week left in the season. Batting against the Cubs in the seventh inning and in the hole on an 0-2 count, Carter drilled a double deep into right-centre field just barely over the outstretched glove of his former teammate Andre Dawson. On the play Larry Walker scored with the only run of the game. The 41,000 fans in the stands went ballistic – cheering wildly and stomping their feet as the Kid made one curtain call after another. It still rates as one of the greatest moments in Expos history.

As for the Expos themselves, everything else was anticlimactic. They wrapped up the season with a six-game road trip, losing three in St. Louis (including one to their former teammate Bryn Smith) and two of three in Chicago, mostly because their bats had finally run out of hits. Nevertheless, the season was a success by any measure. With the difficulties of the brief Runnells stint long forgotten, the club finished second in the National League East with a very respectable 87-75 record. Their winning percentage of .537 was third best in the league, dominated that year by Pittsburgh and Atlanta. Marquis Grissom, followed by Delino DeShields, led the National League in stolen bases. John Wetteland was third in saves and second in games finished, presaging the good stuff that lay ahead. Larry Walker truly came into his own by being named to the NL All-Star Team and earning both the Rawlings Golden Glove and Silver Slugger Awards. Grissom was voted Expos player of the year:[13] Dan Duquette was named the *Sporting News* Executive of the Year. The biggest disappointment among the regulars was Tim Wallach, whose batting average dropped to .223, lowest in the league among everyday players.

Spike Owen was acquired by the Expos in 1988 in a trade with the Boston Red Sox. After five seasons as Montreal's starting shortstop, he was granted free agency following the 1992 season. He later signed with the Yankees.

Duquette remained busy during the off-season, releasing Spike Owen and taking on Frank Bollick, Lou Frazier, Curtis Pride, Tim Spehr and Jeff Shaw. His most shocking transaction was the trading of Tim Wallach to the Dodgers for shortstop Tim Barker, on December 24, 1992.

An original Expo, Wallach had played his first game with Montreal in 1980, and over the next twelve years had shone at his position. A five-time all-star with Montreal, Wallach was also twice named to the *Sporting News* NL All-Star team, while managing to garner three Rawlings Gold Glove and two Silver Slugger Awards over his career. He still reigns as the "Montreal/Washington all-time franchise leader with 1,694 hits, 360 doubles, 905 RBIs and 1,767 games."[14] Felipe Alou's immediate decision to return Wallach to his familiar spot at third base had failed to achieve its desired effect. Wallach's falling batting average continued to bottom out and by season's end it seemed that the fairest thing was to accord him a fresh start in Los Angeles.

It worked. Although Wallach needed the whole of 1993 to get his groove back, he returned to form in 1994, earning the *Sporting News* NL Comeback Player of the Year Award. Wallach wrapped up his playing career in 1996, but stayed in the game as a hitting coach for the Dodgers. In 2009 he was appointed manager of their Triple-A Albuquerque Isotopes, returning to Los Angeles the following year as third base coach.

Tim Barker never made it to the big leagues. He remained in the Expos' system through 1993, playing at both Harrisburg and Ottawa, before being shipped off to the Milwaukee Brewers' organization.

And that was the year that was 1992. No one could have imagined that a season begun in such a dysfunctional fashion would end so well, that the transition from Tom Runnells to Felipe Alou could have been so positive. Clearly the fanship was delighted. Over 1.5 million people attended games in 1992, a most welcome change from the previous campaign when the sky was falling and attendance dropped below one million.

Nevertheless, the time to enjoy this feeling of success was brief – for then it was on to next year and the surprises it would bring.

Three Tim-Bits

Although there was nothing tiny about either Tim Wallach or the Dodgers' Tim Barker, they could be forgiven for thinking they had tumbled into a baseball version of the Charles Dickens seasonal classic *A Christmas Carol*. They were traded even up on Christmas Eve, 1992. After all, who but a Scrooge-like character could have stage-managed that sort of heartless deed at the most family-oriented time of the year? So much for sitting around the Christmas tree waiting for Santa!

Oddly enough, this wasn't the first time the Expos played Scrooge, and with another Tim at that. Two years earlier, again on December 24, this particular Tim was dispatched to the Chicago White Sox, along with a couple of minor leaguers, for Ivan Calderon and Barry Jones. His name? Tim Raines, of course.

So how do you spell Grinch? If you ask these three Tims, they will probably say: E-X-P-O-S.

Chapter Seven

Missed Opportunity – Derek Jeter

If the Expos had taken Jeter instead of Mississippi State lefty B.J. Wallace, who never made the majors, would there still be a major league franchise in Montreal?
— Joe Sheehan, *Sports Illustrated*, September 23, 2013.

As noted earlier, when Expos players showed up for spring training at West Palm Beach, Florida, in 1992, they were not optimistic. Nothing seemed different. Not only did the bad luck and sour karma from the accursed year of '91 refuse to disappear, it stretched all the way to the 1992 amateur player draft and Montreal's choices.

Although, as noted earlier, the draft did have some positive results for the Expos (Jose Vidro is a case in point), it is mostly remembered for a spectacularly blown opportunity. Still today, one shudders at the realization that had events unfolded in a slightly different way, a sure first-ballot Hall of Famer might have ended up donning an Expos uniform, perhaps even in time to play for the talented 1994 squad. It was that close.

This is a player who, from his shortstop position in the 2001 postseason against Oakland, scrambled ten feet into foul territory beyond the first-base line to retrieve a wild throw that had missed the cutoff man, and then flipped the ball to a startled catcher, preventing a run and saving the season. The dash across the infield and that amazing play demonstrated this extraordinary athlete's uncanny heads-up, almost extrasensory ability to judge and react quickly to a critical situation. On the full run, he grabbed the errant ball in his bare hand and, tumbling, he side-armed it to catcher Jorge Posada, who tagged a startled Jeremy Giambi attempting to cross home plate standing up. The younger Giambi was so mesmerized by the scene unfolding before him that he failed to slide.

This bit of infield wizardry occurred during the third game of the American League Championship Series between the New York Yankees and the A's, and pretty much sowed up the playoff for the boys from the Bronx. It is regarded as one of the most extraordinary plays in the history of the game – and it cemented the young man's reputation as a clutch player forever. His name, of course, is Derek Jeter.

For the next 10 years and more, Jeter remained one giant step ahead of the pack – both a superstar and a corporate sponsor's dream. He has never been tainted by rumours of steroid use. He is the leader and face of the Yankees, he owns the patent on the inside-out swing, and he always seems to end up in the right place at the right time when it counts the most.

In his Kalamazoo, Michigan, Central High School yearbook Jeter defined his goal as: Professional baseball player, New York Yankees.

But he could have been an Expo.

Sketch by Jack Wong

Artist sketch of Derek Jeter and how he might have looked wearing an Expos cap.

When the Expos, selecting third overall in the 1992 amateur draft, made their first round choice, Jeter was still available. Scouting director Kevin Malone passed on him because he believed Montreal already had a solid shortstop in Wilfredo Cordero. "There's no question Jeter was available to us that year, but we had Cordero at shortstop and thought the world of him. We felt we were great at that position so we decided on B.J. Wallace, a left-handed pitcher with a wicked fastball instead," Malone recalled in a telephone interview.[15]

It's not as though Jeter was an unknown commodity. "I went to see him play in Michigan," said Malone, "and he had a badly sprained ankle. It was a rainy day. It was hard to get a good read on him. Even so, you could tell he would be a special player; you could see it in his make-up, the attitude, work ethic, upbringing, the athleticism. But let's be honest, he has surpassed everyone's expectations. He's been an all-star, a great player, even better than everyone thought. He stays out of trouble, he's special."

Chuckling ruefully, Malone continued. "He's great on and off the field. He's a quality human being, friendly, warm, appreciative. That's just how he is as a person. You never hear anyone say anything bad about the guy. He's turned out to be one of the best players to play the game."[16]

Nevertheless, in 1992, Malone and the Expos were happy enough with Cordero to forego the undeniable promise of the untested Derek Jeter. "At the time, we thought Wil Cordero was one of the best young shortstops in baseball. He did go on to become a major-league All-Star after all – it's not that he wasn't any good." Malone adds that while everyone knew about and liked Jeter as a prospect, there was never any discussion as to which of the two would turn out better. And indeed Cordero did enjoy some splendid moments, although he never quite lived up to his advance billing. Jeter, on the other hand, far exceeded his.

As far as *Kalamazoo Gazette* sports writer Paul Morgan is concerned, Jeter would have signed with the Expos or any other team drafting him, even though he would have been heartbroken not to go to his beloved Yankees.

"He would have signed, I think so," Morgan said in a recent interview. "He was excited to be drafted. His dream was always to play in the majors. Wherever he was chosen, he would have gone. He wouldn't have held out. The fallback would have been university (Michigan) because his family always prepared for everything, just in case he didn't get drafted high."[17]

Said Malone, "I don't remember who the Expos' territorial scout promoting Jeter was at that time but everyone loved the young man and thought highly of him. Everyone was promoting him. Claude Brochu (then managing general partner) allowed the scouting department to make decisions. He was very good that way, as was general manager Dan Duquette."

The team's priority in 1992 was left-handed pitching. "We already had an all-star at shortstop: now we were hoping to draft an all-star pitcher," Malone said. He does acknowledge that for the cash-strapped Expos coming off a crushingly disappointing season, money might have been a factor in the team's decision to pass on Jeter. But he insists this was not the main reason the club chose Wallace. Jeter, in fact, was never in the plans. Had a Plan B existed, it probably would have called for the drafting of Chad Mottola, whom Malone called a "big strong outfielder from Florida, although he wasn't really one of our top 10 choices."

Mottola certainly stimulated interest in other quarters: he was drafted fifth by Cincinnati, one spot ahead of Jeter. He too, like Wallace, never made the grade: he spent a spotty five years in the major leagues, seeing action in only 59 games for four different teams. In 2012 he was named hitting coach for the Toronto Blue Jays.

Malone understands as well as most just what a crap-shoot the scouting and signing of players can become. "Everyone knew Jeter was going to be a quality player, but no one ever can say if one guy will become one of the very best players ever in the game. An all-star, yes – but one of the best players of all time? Just not possible."

These many years later, Malone was asked if he would go so far as to say he regretted not taking Jeter. He replied: "I don't really know what the word regret means; it means different things to different people." He added: "To me, regret always carries with it a negative connotation. I would phrase the question differently... and I would say if I had it to do over again I would definitely select Jeter (and his 3,000-plus hits) instead of B.J. Wallace."

Jeter made his first appearance in a Yankee uniform on May 29, 1995 against Seattle at the Kingdome. He went 0-5 at the plate. But by the time he reached age 25 he had been named Rookie of the Year, possessed three World Series rings, won two All-Star selections, and owned a career .318 average, .289 OBP, .465 slugging and .855 OPS.

The only other current player who can claim a comparable record of achievements is Giants catcher Buster Posey. He has been named Rookie of the Year (2010) and MVP (2012), possesses two World Series rings, a batting championship (2012), one All-Star selection and a .314 career average with .380 OBP, .503 slugging, and an OPS of .855.

There is some consolation to be found in remembering that the Expos were not the only team to pass on Jeter. The Houston Astros had the first pick and they chose Phil Nevin, prompting scout Hal Newhouser, who had spent the summer monitoring the young Jeter's every move, to immediately resign in despair. When the Yankees' sixth-place turn came up, to their everlasting credit – and glory – they made no mistake, signing Jeter to a bargain-basement $800,000 bonus.

"That was," Malone says today, "the best $800,000 any team ever spent." The story goes that when the Yankees initially broached the notion of recruiting Jeter, someone mentioned he was considering a university scholarship offer. Yankees scout Dick Groch, who was one of the first to be convinced of Jeter's potential, responded quickly and decisively. "He's not going to Michigan," he said. "He's going to Cooperstown."

Indeed, he will be. Five years from the day he steps off the diamond for the last time.

Would Jeter have signed for certain as an Expo? Interviewed recently in Toronto, he readily admitted he was prepared to join the Expos organization had they selected him in 1992. "You have no choice. You have to go where you are picked," Jeter said. However, as the conversation evolved, Jeter revealed that the Expos had never entered into talks with his parents, Charles and Dorothy. "Never heard about the Expos," Jeter said. "Montreal was never discussed. I was pretty sheltered from the talks going on with the teams."

In the end, Jeter's dream of playing for the Yankees was achieved when they drafted him sixth overall. ""I was a Yankees fan growing up in New Jersey," he said.[18]

Sometime around 2020, you will see him headed for Cooperstown.

Chapter Eight

A Last Look at the Kid

By 1992, Gary Carter was on his last legs as a major league ballplayer. Celebrated wherever he went, he was lionized in New York, where his enthusiasm and determination had carried him and the Mets to the 1986 World Series championship. And he was revered in Montreal, the city where he had first made his mark. It is not an exaggeration to state that "for ten years (1974-1984), on the team that was to constitute Expos royalty, he was king."[19]

Carter started his career as an Expo, having been selected in the third round of the 1972 amateur draft right out of Sunny Hills High School in Fullerton, California. After three years in the minors (West Palm Beach, Quebec City and Memphis), he outgrew the graduated-A levels and made his major league debut with Montreal at the end of 1974.

Carter sampled his initial taste of professional baseball in Jamestown, New York, where long-time Expos general manager and gifted factotum Jim Fanning witnessed him in action for the first time. There was something special about the budding catcher, something intangible.

"My first impression of him came that first day I saw him in Jamestown where we brought in a lot of our young drafted players," Fanning said in an interview in 2012. "I saw hustle, enthusiasm, zest. He was all over the place, running here and there. I saw great ability, all of the good stuff in a player you have signed. He was really exciting, plus he had the size and strength. He was something special."[20]

Thus began a Hall-of-Fame career that saw Carter star on those talented Expos teams from 1978-83, particularly the 1981 squad that lost to the Los Angeles Dodgers in the NL Championship Series. Carter played 10 full seasons with the Expos before being traded to the New York Mets after the 1984 season.

Carter was a work of art and showmanship. In the batter's box, he would tug at his shirt-sleeves before each and every pitch, trying to get set. "Doing that was just something to get comfortable at the plate,"

Jim Fanning in the days before the 1982 All-Star game in Montreal. Gary Carter was selected as starting catcher. He was joined by fellow starters Expos Andre Dawson, Tim Raines and Steve Rogers along with reservist Al Oliver.

Carter told Danny Gallagher during the early '90s. "It got you into a comfort zone and got you mentally prepared. I didn't realize all those things in the batter's box until I bought a video-play machine for $1,200 in California in 1980. That's when those machines started coming out. I would see myself on the machine tugging on my sleeves."[21]

Some of his fellow Expos thought he was hot-dogging with his sleeve pulling, ever-present smile and his eagerness to go out of his way to talk to the media. One teammate once said, "You couldn't put enough mustard on that hotdog." He would earn the nickname Kodak Kid and some called him Camera.

"Gary was the most personable player the Expos ever had," Fanning said, laughing about the nickname. "He had more personality than anyone on the team ever had. He was a great interview. He would do so many interviews before a game that we had to cut him down a lot because he had to get ready to play the game.

"Carter satisfied more fans than everyone else on the team put together. On the road, when we were leaving the ballpark to go to the hotel, he was the last guy on the bus because he was signing autographs. He had to tell the bus driver to wait a few minutes."[22]

Carter exuded bravado, but he also delivered in the clutch, and over the years put together a stellar career, offensively and defensively. He played one of the toughest positions in baseball, one where you had to get down and dirty, an almost thankless task. He played hurt, participated in more than 2,000 games, hit 324 homers, drove in 1,225 runs and was an all-star 12 times. He was also a key figure in the New York Mets' drive to a World Series title in 1986.

As much as Carter wanted to be inducted into the Hall of Fame in Cooperstown wearing a Mets cap, hall officials advised him that he would have to wear the Expos tri-coloured hat. Carter took this decision in stride. "People will remember me as an Expo," Carter said years ago. "My identity is with the Expos, not anyone else. I've had the luxury and the pleasure of coming back to the organization where I started. Not many players can say that. The happiest day for me was signing with the Expos in 1972 and then coming back for the 1992 season. The saddest day was when I was traded to the Mets in 1984."[23]

Carter spent five years with the Mets followed by single seasons with the Los Angeles Dodgers and San Francisco Giants, before returning to the Expos for that last hurrah. By then, he was a shadow of his former self, batting .228 with five homers and 29 RBIs. However, being Gary Carter, he made his final plate appearance count, leaving a lasting impression and in many ways signaling just what a big-moment player he was. The black hole of oblivion that awaited so many others on the eve of retirement from the game was not for him.

As noted above, on Sunday September 27, with two out in the seventh inning of a scoreless contest against the Chicago Cubs, playing before more than 41,000 fans at Olympic Stadium and down 0-2 in the count, Carter drilled a fly ball just barely over the head of former teammate Andre Dawson for a double to drive Larry Walker home with the game's only run. Play was delayed for ten minutes as Carter received curtain call after curtain call. The YouTube video of that moment reveals a beaming Carter awash in a river of joy as youthful enthusiasm swept once again across his face. No wonder they called him the Kid.

Carter would not play again. By ending his career with a game-winning hit, he had achieved everything he ever wanted from baseball. His ultimate reward was his induction into the Hall of Fame in 2003.

Carter died of brain cancer on February 16, 2012.

Chapter Nine

John Wetteland – What a Relief

John Wetteland was eccentric. He could be funny and he could be ultra-serious.

"I was a rookie in 1993," remembers pitcher Kirk Rueter. "I had new clothes, good clothes, and Wetteland would squeeze grapes to put stains on them. I'd have new shoes and he'd spit tobacco juice on them just to aggravate me. I was so mad."[24]

Call it rookie initiation.

It was late in 1991, as Christmas neared, when Expos GM Dan Duquette pulled the trigger on a trade that brought Wetteland from the Los Angeles Dodgers to Montreal by way of the Cincinnati Reds.

Shockingly, on November 27 the Dodgers had sent Wetteland and fellow power pitcher Tim Belcher to the Reds for pitcher Kip Gross and outfielder Eric Davis. What were the Dodgers thinking – getting rid of two power pitchers just like that?

Two weeks later, Duquette, playing Santa Claus for the Expos, slipped Wetteland and pitcher Bill Risley clean out of the Reds' hands, in exchange for outfielder Dave Martinez along with journeyman pitcher Scott Ruskin and infielder Willie Greene. Once again, Duquette was in the right place at the right time. "Wetteland never threw one inning for Cincinnati," manager Felipe Alou remembered in 2012, trying to hide the grin on his face.[25]

"I'd been trying to get Wetteland from the Dodgers," Duquette said recently. "Then when the Reds got Wetteland, I talked to Reds GM Bob Quinn on (American) Thanksgiving weekend."[26] It was shortly after that the deal went through.

Someone who knew Wetteland was Expos catcher Darrin Fletcher, who grew up with the young pitcher in the Dodgers' minor-league system. They were as different as chalk and cheese – Fletcher, a regular guy from small-town Illinois in the mid-west, Wetteland from San Mateo, California, a muscular, blond surfer-type with Hollywood-handsome looks.

"John was a fun guy and when he came to the Expos he gave us a nice lift," Fletcher says. "He was a huge prospect with Los Angeles, a top prospect like Ramon Martinez. Getting him was a big pickup for us. When he fell in love with that closer role we knew he was going to be a star. He always wanted to be a stopper."[27]

Looking back on the deal today, one would almost think that the slick Wetteland trade was a preview of the slight-of-hand Duquette would pull in November, 1993, when, with the same Dodgers, he made what is now considered one

John Wetteland

of the five most one-sided trades of all time, obtaining hurler Pedro Martinez for second baseman Delino DeShields. Here, too, L.A. management gave up on a tremendous prospect too soon and lived to rue the day.

Wetteland's shift from starter to the closer role first occurred early in the 1991 season in Albuquerque, New Mexico, with the Dodgers' Triple-A club. As journalist Rich Griffin pointed out in his notes on Wetteland prepared for the 1992 Expos media guide, "John made a career decision, approaching the Dodgers, requesting a chance to be the stopper at Albuquerque. Given the opportunity, he excelled."[28] Duquette was in full agreement. "Wetteland was better as a reliever than as a starter. At Triple A, he was good for short periods of time but had trouble with a whole game."[29]

Indeed, he did excel as a closer. He would go 20-for-20 in saves that Triple-A season, something Duquette and his scouting staff certainly noted. And then following the 1991 season, Wetteland joined up with the Caracas club of the Venezuelan League. There he mustered a perfect saves record of 13-for-13 before the Expos acquired him and called him home.

Used strictly as a reliever in 1992, Wetteland blossomed in Montreal. In 67 innings of work, he saved 37 games with a 4-4 record and a neat 2.92 ERA. In 1993, he was merely spectacular with 43 saves, a 9-3 record and a nifty 1.37 ERA. Had he not gotten angry at himself in spring training in 1993 when he kicked a fence on a back field in West Palm Beach, he might have saved 50 games. Instead, he broke the big toe on his right foot and was out of commission from March 6 through April 22. Some of that time he spent in a Montreal hospital, no doubt embarrassed by what he had done to his foot and his teammates.

Wetteland struggled in the early days of the 1994 season, until fellow pitchers and his specialist catcher Tim Spehr suggested he start throwing more curveballs. All he had wanted to do was throw heat and that wasn't working so well anymore. "Wetteland wasn't too sharp and he got hurt once in a while," said setup man Mel Rojas, who, until Wetteland turned his game around, was also assigned the closer's role on occasion.[30]

"John was going with the fastball and sliders and (opposing players) were able to judge the speed when he threw hard up in the zone," Spehr said. "We finally got him to throw the curveball. When we got him to change, it finally sunk in with him. He had one of the best curveballs in the game."[31]

Largely because of Spehr's intervention, Wetteland got himself straightened away. He would finish that truncated season with 25 saves, somewhat ahead of bullpen mate Rojas who added another 16 saves to his record.

"I came into the game when Wetteland came in," Spehr said "That's how much he counted on me. I was not selfish, I was happy in the role I had. Darrin Fletcher would catch most of the game but I would come in on a double switch. I was not John's personal catcher. I was a defensive catcher late in the game. It was fun. I was just trying to make the team. As I look back on it, I'd take that job in a heartbeat when the game is on the line. Wetteland came into the game and I'd come into the game."[32]

Said reliever Gil Heredia, "John Wetteland was a special breed. Wett and Rojas were our sergeants-at-arms and what they said we usually did and didn't ask any questions. Wetteland and Rojas kept a tight rein while still having fun."[33]

Although he only played three seasons in Montreal, Wetteland and his wife Michele loved the city, even spending time in the nearby tourist community of Saint-Sauveur. He was traded to the Yankees in 1995 as part of Montreal's infamous fire sale, spending two years in the Bronx before joining the Texas Rangers as a free agent for four more seasons. He was a member of the 1996 World Series–champion Yankees, saving every one of the team's four victories over Atlanta and earning MVP honors.

But in June of that big season with the Yankees, Wetteland had already told author Gallagher he would not be back with the team the following season. True to his word, he was gone at season's end.[34] Wetteland signed with the Texas Rangers for only marginally more than he earned as a Yankee. Surprisingly, in 2000, at age 33, he took his leave from the game. Had he continued pitching for another five years, he might have accumulated the necessary numbers for induction into Cooperstown. He finished with a total of 330 saves, placing him 11th on the all-time list. In a longer career, he might well have amassed close to 500.

In a brief conversation with Gallagher at the Cummings Centre Expos 1994 reunion breakfast in Montreal in March 2011, Wetteland explained why he had been compelled to shut it down. "I broke my back throwing a pitch," he said, "even though I finished the inning."[35] That incident occurred in Minneapolis on September 20, 2000. The game had gone into extra innings and when the Rangers went ahead of the Twins in the eleventh, Wetteland was called upon to close out the win. Unfortunately for him, shortstop Christian Guzman tripled and later scored on a sacrifice fly. The save now blown, Wetteland completed the inning without allowing any more runs – but somehow he broke his back on one of those pitches. Then in the twelfth inning the Rangers took the lead again, and this time were able to hang on for a 6–4 victory. Wetteland was credited with the win, his sixth that season and 48th of his career. "I had eight surgeries on my back," Wetteland told Gallagher that day in Montreal. "The eighth one was the charm."

"Wetteland was a Christian, wild as a kid, born-again, a quirky guy," said Montreal broadcaster Mitch Melnick. "I talked to him a lot. He loved to talk about politics. He would get jacked up for games on caffeine and was always wired after games. After a game, because I knew John was not going to be good company when he came out of the clubhouse, I would accompany his wife Michele. She was a communications major from New Orleans."[36]

In 2009, Wetteland experienced a nervous breakdown at his Texas home, and after what appeared to be a suicide attempt, he sought and received help. When the authors met him in 2011, he appeared to be fully recovered.

They talk about ballplayers who will go to any length to help their teams win. "I would break my back for this club," they say, metaphorically. John Wetteland actually did.

Rusty Staub

Rusty Staub was the Expos' first superstar. He earned
his spot on the honour roll long ago.

Fly Me to the Moon

1993

Fly me to the moon
Let me play among the stars
Let me see what spring is like
On Jupiter and Mars

– Bart Howard (1954)

Bill Lee – the Original Spaceman

Left-handed pitcher Bill Lee was a favourite among local fans. Unceremoniously dumped by the Expos in 1982, he remained both unrepentant and fond of his former club. He makes Montreal one of his bases, is heard frequently on local radio and, even today, now well into his sixties, continues to pitch in organized games.

Chapter Ten

Spring Comes to Montreal

The bird is on the wing, the steaks are on the barbecue, the boots are in the closet, March has come in baaaaaing and who cares if it's Monday?

– Leonard Cohen[1]

Nineteen ninety-three: and what a year it was. As the new Alou era established its own identity, all the disappointments of the early 1990s simply faded into the distance, a forgotten prelude to an exciting present. Riding on the strong finish in 1992, Montreal sailed through the season, wrapping up the year with a 94-68 record and a winning percentage of .580, the second best in team history. In their 36 years of existence, only the 95-65 and .595 numbers put together by the 1979 club were superior. Of course, the very best edition of the Montreal Expos was still to come – the squad of 1994 whose march to glory was halted by an ill-considered strike.

The drama of 1994, which began with the skyrocketing success of the Expos, only to conclude in shocking disarray with the termination of the season in mid-August, so dominates the narrative of this period that we forget just how good this 1993 club was. In its greatness, it just narrowly missed finishing in first place, losing out to its nemesis, the Philadelphia Phillies, by three games. The Phillies' 97-65 record, a winning percentage of .599, was sufficient to buy them entry to the World Series.

There they were overwhelmed by the defending World Champion Toronto Blue Jays, 4 games to 2, done in by Joe Carter's ninth inning walk-off home run struck against closer Mitch Williams, with Rickey Henderson and Paul Molitor on base. Carter still dines out on that exploit and rightly so. It stands as perhaps the greatest single moment in Canadian baseball history.

Somewhat forgotten in the Blue Jays story is just how good the Expos were in 1993. And they were getting better. Their younger players were maturing and new additions were filling in the missing pieces; they were on their way to the top.

Far and away the most outstanding player on the 1993 Expos was outfielder Marquis Grissom. Drafted by the Expos in 1988, he made his first appearance with the big club one year later, after brief pit stops in Jamestown and Indianapolis. Voted National League Rookie of the Year in 1990, Montreal's starting centre fielder was emerging as a legitimate star. Indeed, in 1993, he was named to the All-Star team, won a Golden Glove, and led the club in stolen bases and RBIs. Joining him on the green grass beyond the diamond were Moises Alou and Larry Walker, who also picked up a Gold Glove. Collectively, they were considered the best outfield in the game. Not only could they cover a lot of ground, but they were equally menacing at the plate. They made their mark in 1993; glory awaited in 1994.

On the mound, the veteran Dennis Martinez led the club once again, posting a 15-9 record with a 3.85 ERA. Also outstanding were Ken Hill and closer John Wetteland. Hill had come to Montreal from St. Louis following the 1991 season, in exchange for a fan favourite, the power-hitting first baseman, Andres Galarraga. Hill made an immediate impression, winning 16 games in 1992. A quality pitcher, he had arrived.

John Wetteland, once a member of the Los Angeles Dodgers, appeared in Montreal in late 1991. In his first year with the Expos, he notched 37 saves. Manager Felipe Alou had seen something in Wetteland's mettle that suggested the cagey hurler was perfectly suited to the closer's role and he was right. In 1993, Wetteland's 43 saves and 9-3, 1.37 ERA record were major factors in propelling the club's rise to the top.

The Expos opened the season in Cincinnati before a capacity crowd, and made history in the process. When Montreal's Dominican-born manager Felipe Alou ambled toward home plate to meet with the umpiring crew, he was greeted by his Cincinnati counterpart – former Expos all-star Tony Perez, whose birthplace was Cuba. Their coming together marked the first time that opposing managers in a regularly scheduled major-league game had been born outside the United States. When made aware of this milestone after the game, both declared they felt privileged to have served as trailblazers in this way. As Perez told *The Sporting News*, "I am very excited now because I know Felipe and I have made history in the major leagues."[2]

Although the Expos lost the opener, 2–1, they did serve notice they were for real. Dennis Martinez took the loss, working seven innings before turning the game over to Jeff Fassero. Montreal's only run came on a Larry Walker home run in the ninth. The Opening Day lineup – Delino DeShields 2B; Alou LF; Grissom CF; Walker RF; Frank Bolick 3B; John Vander Wal 1B; Wil Cordero SS; Tim Laker C – suggests that Felipe had yet to settle his infield and catcher positions. By the end of the year, Greg Colbrunn was most often on first base and Sean Berry had settled in on third. The catcher was Darrin Fletcher. Others who saw action at various points in the year were Cliff Floyd, Lou Frazier, Mike Lansing, Rondell White, pitchers Kirk Rueter and Mel Rojas – and in one great moment of glory, utility outfielder Curtis Pride.

Curtis Pride was like many other young ballplayers of his generation, a strong African-American outfielder with power who batted from the left side. His only difference – and it was dramatic enough to set him completely apart from his peers – was that he was profoundly deaf, a condition brought on by German measles when he was born. Nevertheless, through the power of his bat and his strength of character, by 1993 Pride had made his way up the Expos' minor-league system to their Triple-A affiliate in Ottawa. There he enjoyed such a good year that in September he was called up to the big club. He had his debut on September 14, but it was not until three nights later on Friday, September 17, that he truly made an impression.

The Expos were playing before a raucous crowd of 45,000 and more, and with Montreal still in the pennant hunt, five games behind Philadelphia, and the Phillies were in town for a three-game weekend series, an Expos sweep would do wonders.

Things looked bleak for the home team as the Friday game moved into the bottom of the seventh inning. Montreal had blown a three-run lead in the sixth when starter Dennis Martinez and two relievers surrendered seven runs before the bleeding stopped. After rallying for one run in the bottom of the sixth, the Expos struck again in the seventh inning, placing runners on first and third with one out. With pitcher Chris Nabholz due to bat, manager Alou rolled the dice and sent Pride to the plate in his stead. This was to be his major league baptism by fire.

The crowd was standing and clapping – although the hearing-challenged batter could hear none of it. Totally unaware of the commotion surrounding him, Pride drove the ball into the gap in centre field, sending runners Randy Ready and Sean Berry home while he slid into second with a double. One out later he scored on a single by Mike Lansing to tie the score. The Expos went on to win 8–7 when Grissom doubled, stole third and scored on a DeShields sacrifice fly.

The Expos split the next two games, moving up half a game in the standings. But the story of the weekend was Curtis Pride and his clutch hit on Friday night. When he began dusting off his uniform after sliding into second, he had no idea that throughout the Big O, fans were stomping their feet and chanting out his name. None of it registered. Not until third-base coach Jerry Manuel drew his attention to the hullabaloo he had gen-

Curtis Pride

erated did Pride sense the euphoria pouring down on him. Remarkably, the cheering just kept rolling on.

And then "…something incredible happened." As the crescendo rose to the very top of Olympic Stadium it bore a vibrating roar in its wake, a roar that "grew more intense until, for the first time in his life, Curtis Pride actually 'heard' people cheering for him. The silent curtain that had separated him from his dream had parted."[3] Author Jonah Keri, whose comprehensive history of the Expos is to be released in 2014, has called this particular moment number one in his "favorite in-person Expos memories."[4]

That fall, Pride was nominated for the Arete Award, given annually to recognize courage in sports. He lost out to boxer Evander Holyfield. Pride was better served two years later, in 1996, when he received the Tony Conigliaro Award, "given annually to an MLB player who best overcomes adversity through the attributes of spirit, determination and courage."[5]

Although Pride never managed to find a permanent home in the major leagues, he was considered valuable enough that in times of need, a number of teams turned to him for bench strength. He returned to the Expos in 1995 and again in 2001 – and in other years suited up for Detroit, Boston, Atlanta, and the Yankees. His big-league career finally ended in 2006 following a stint with the Los Angeles Angels, thirteen years after it had all begun at the Big O in Montreal. Pride then poked around the minor leagues for another couple of years before calling it a career well lived. But he never really left the game and recently he was named head baseball coach for Gallaudet University in Washington, D.C., the world's first school for the advanced education of the deaf and hard-of-hearing.

The Expos started modestly in 1993, winding up the month of April a meagre three games over .500. In some ways this sluggish start seemed to confirm what certain observers, players included, were thinking, that not enough had been done to improve the squad. In January, Delino DeShields had been openly critical of general manager Dan Duquette's efforts in this regard. "We made some changes but we are not a better team than we were before," he said. "Even if myself, Marquis Grissom, Larry Walker, Ken Hill and Dennis Martinez all have great years, we are still going to need the other guys to play. I think management expects us five to carry the load. Anything's possible, but realistically we're not that much better."[6] Running counter to this bleak mid-winter assessment was the announcement earlier that the Montreal and Toronto chapters of the Baseball Writers Association of America had named Walker as Canada's baseball man of the year.[7]

Ironically, in an indirect way, that award might have influenced Walker's upcoming negotiations, for he also signed a new contract a few months later. It brought him to the $3-million mark, a full $500,000 ahead of Dennis Martinez as the Expos' highest-paid player.

That news could not have pleased Martinez, who was entering the final year of his three-year contract and was already disappointed with the club's unwillingness to open discussions on a new deal. By mid-winter he had made his feelings clear. "Either they talk to me before the year starts or we'll forget about it," he said. "I'll take my chances as a free agent, and this time they won't get first choice." Rumours that Martinez might retaliate by reporting late to spring training were quickly nipped in the bud by General Manager Dan Duquette. "(Martinez) always comes into camp in shape ready to do his best," he said. "I see no reason to expect that to change."[8]

Nevertheless, both Martinez and Walker figured in trade rumours as the season unfolded, and for the former, these were more than just unsubstantiated phantasms floating on ill winds.

After their somewhat mediocre first month the Expos picked up in May, expanding their margin above .500 to six games. They were in second place, though still a full seven games behind the streaking Phillies in the National League East and two ahead of both St. Louis and the Cubs. However, they were unable to hold their own in June. The club dropped into third place, 11 games out of first and 5.5 games behind the Cardinals. But that glitch proved to be an anomaly, and as things picked up in July they began climbing back up the standings – still 9.5 games back of the Phillies though, and 3.5 behind the Cards.

It became increasingly evident by mid-summer of 1993 that the Expos were ready to trade Dennis Martinez should the right offer come along. When Montreal rolled into San Francisco to play the Giants in a three-game series in late July, General Manager Duquette unexpectedly joined the club, confirming what many had suspected, that the Giants had set their sights on Martinez.[9]

However, nothing transpired: Martinez remained an Expo. When questioned about this later, Duquette said simply that at this stage "he's more valuable pitching for us." Or as beat writer Jeff Blair signalled, this meant that unless the club could get something better than the Padres received for Fred McGriff, Duquette was ready to pass.[10] McGriff had been traded to the Braves a few days earlier for three marginal players, an unfortunate bit of business if you were a San Diego fan.

With Martinez apparently staying put at least for the moment, a new batch of trade winds began swirling. These rumours, which had been circling as a slight breeze since Opening Day, indicated Montreal was preparing to trade Larry Walker. Soon enough, this chatter became sufficiently widespread that it prompted a reaction from the man himself. "I used to think that there was no way they would trade me," Walker said, "because I was a Canadian. Now I'm not so sure."[11]

It was about this time word leaked out that Duquette was preparing to join the Boston Red Sox in 1994. Expos President Claude Brochu was quick to deny the speculation, stating that Duquette was under contract to Montreal through the 1994 season.[12]

Back on the diamond, by the end of August the Expos had crept back into second – just ahead of the Cardinals – but still nine back of Philadelphia.

Life suddenly became more interesting, as Felipe Alou's men mounted a sustained run for the lead. Contributing to this late charge was a new face on the bubble-gum card, Rondell White. Called up from Ottawa in early September, he made enough of an impression that manager Alou declared him "one of the most fearless players that we have in the organization, majors or minors."[13]

It wasn't quite enough. On the last day of September Montreal still stood four back and while they gained one game before the season ended, that was where the charge stopped. While it had been too little, too late to reach the top, the good news was that the Expos wound up the 1993 season with the second-best won/lost record in club history. When the push was on and the chips were down, when clichés were dancing off the sports pages like bears at a Russian circus, when winning counted most, in September, the Expos put it all together and made a race of it.

September 1993 should also be remembered for two glorious moments – the time Curtis Pride set Olympic Stadium cheering to the rafters with hoots and hollers of delight, and the game in which Quebec-born hurler Denis Boucher took the mound for the first time as an Expo before a packed house at the Big O. Boucher was joined on the field that day by two other Canadian-born Expos players, Larry Walker and catcher Joe Siddall, a record regarding Canadian ballplayers at the time. All three were up to the task and the home squad won (see Chapter Fifteen for the full story).

But there was another momentous happening in September, a most unhappy one. On September 16, in St. Louis, Moises Alou fractured his left fibula and dislocated his left ankle in what one report described as a "grotesque base-running accident." Alou later recalled: "The first thing that went through my mind was, 'That's it.' The first thing I thought was, 'my career's over.'"[14]

He had surgery almost immediately, with two fixation screws inserted into the ankle and his foot and leg placed in a cast. The operation was considered a success and according to his father Felipe, it looked "like he could be back for spring training."[15]

The season ended on a winning note in Montreal on October 3, on a Sunday afternoon before 26, 277 fans. Stimulated by Denis Boucher's fine performance on the mound, the Expos closed out the year with a 3–1 triumph over Pittsburgh. Then, even before the blue Expos tarpaulin had been stretched across the Olympic Stadium turf following the final out, fans were already echoing the cry so familiar to old Brooklyn Dodgers fans: "Wait 'til next year!"

Such high expectations were not without pitfalls. The challenge now facing the front office was to generate that fine margin which would make the difference and bring a pennant to Montreal in 1994. They first looked toward their emerging stars to lead the way. And so did the players. When Marquis Grissom was honoured as the Expos' Player of the Year at season's end, he was clear and passionate as to what the team expected from management. "Keep us all together," he admonished, "and have the same attitude that we had when we were out in the field. When we need something, go and get it. When we need someone, go and get that player."[16]

Grissom's pleas notwithstanding, as the off-season marched on, rumours were rampant that Walker was being offered up as trade bait. When questioned about this, Walker answered, "It's all just talk. Most of me believes I'll be back in Montreal in 1994," he said.[17] He was right. He stayed put.

On the other hand, the outspoken DeShields, who had questioned management's commitment to winning at the beginning of the year but who had performed as one of Montreal's true shining lights in the field, as it turned out, was not so fortunate.[18]

Complicating matters for the Expos was the growing uncertainty surrounding Dan Duquette and his own future. Throughout the month of October the questioning never let up. While speculation had him going to Boston or Cincinnati, Duquette, who still had one year remaining on his Expos contract, insisted he was staying in Montreal. He had told his players as much on the final day of the season. "I told them that as far as I was concerned," he said, "we had unfinished business for next year. I meant that."[19]

Team president Claude Brochu was equally adamant. Although in similar circumstances he had allowed Duquette's predecessor, Dave Dombrowski, to sever his contract and join the Florida Marlins, Brochu insisted: "This situation is completely different from David's. I have not received any calls from anybody requesting to talk to Dan. And I wouldn't give permission. He doesn't want to go anywhere."[20]

Nevertheless, there was also some good news in the postseason mix. Cliff Floyd, who had spent much of the 1993 season with the Harrisburg Senators of the Eastern League and later the Ottawa Lynx in Triple-A ball, and who was a September call-up, took top honours as *The Sporting News* Minor League Player of the Year. He was already being pencilled in as the Expos' starting first basement for 1994. The other bit of good news was that Harrisburg manager Jim Tracy was named Minor League Manager of the Year by *The Sporting News*. Tracy, of course, then managed in Ottawa before the Expos promoted him up to the big club as the bench coach for manager Alou in 1995. Tracy went on to enjoy an extensive major-league coaching and managing career, moving to the Dodgers as bench coach in 1999 and becoming their manager two years later.

Tracy remained as Dodgers manager until 2005 when he moved over to the Pittsburgh Pirates in the same capacity. Two years after that, he became manager of the Colorado Rockies, where he remained until the end of 2012 when, dismayed at the poor season the Rockies had endured, the least successful in team history, he resigned.

The decision to make Cliff Floyd the Expos' starting first baseman did carry with it a certain measure of collateral damage. Greg Colbrunn, a natural first baseman who had served the Expos well in a limited role in 1993, was put on waivers. The Expos anticipated he would sail through the process with no takers and be able to join the Ottawa Lynx, as added insurance against the unexpected. Regrettably for Montreal, he was claimed by the Marlins. Colbrunn could not have been too dismayed, however. He performed well in Florida, establishing himself as a solid major leaguer. He reprised that effort later with the Arizona Diamondbacks as a member of the 2001 post-9/11 edition. It wrestled the World Series championship trophy away from the Yankees in one of the most dramatic, emotionally tinged Fall Classics of all time.

When November rolled around, Duquette found himself faced with a new set of pressing challenges. Nine members of the Expos – the heart of the team in fact – were eligible for salary arbitration. That number should have been ten, except that pitcher Jeff Fassero was five days short of meeting the eligibility criteria. This, of course, was good news for the cash-strapped Expos, for as baseball operations vice president Bill Stoneman noted at the time, "Jeff probably would have made at least in the upper six-figure area had he qualified," as opposed to the $187,500 he earned in 1993.[21] That still left the starting outfield of Alou, Grissom and Walker, second baseman DeShields and catcher Fletcher, and the heart of the pitching staff, Ken Hill, Chris Nabholz, John Wetteland and Mel Rojas, to be signed. Duquette had to find a way of making everyone happy within the strictures of a less-than $20-million budget. To create some needed wiggle room, the club chose to cut six scouting positions at the minor-league level.[22]

Then, in mid-November, came a shocking transaction, a move so dramatic, so unexpected, so bold, that it was widely interpreted as a foolhardy attempt by the team simply to realign its player salary budget. The Expos traded star second baseman Delino DeShields straight up to the L.A. Dodgers for a twenty-two-year-old, untested pitcher named Pedro Martinez (see Chapters Seventeen and Eighteen).

The move was immediately and loudly panned by the media and fans: they charged it was a case of trading away the corner piece of a promising team for an unwanted hurler simply to improve the balance sheet.

In one sense the accusation was accurate – after a fashion. To begin with, the Expos were on the look-out for a young arm to replace the aging Dennis Martinez, who had opted for free agency. They felt that given the choice they would have better luck filling an infield void than successfully replacing the older namesake. The Dodgers, meanwhile, were in the hunt for a quality second baseman after their incumbent Jody Reed chose free agency. For both organizations, DeShields seemed to fit the bill.

Los Angeles was prepared to surrender Pedro as they concluded he was not strong enough for the rigours of major league baseball. As for the Expos, the trade permitted the club to cut $3 million from the budget, money saved by avoiding arbitration with DeShields. According to Dan Duquette, this 'found' sum now placed the Expos in a better position to sign the other arbitration-eligible players, in some cases, to multi-year deals.

"We're going to try to keep our foundation together as best we can, and we'll see how it goes," Duquette said. "We'd like to talk about some multi-year deals; that's our intent."[23]

Although not evident at the time, it did seem there was method to Duquette's apparent madness. Montreal scouts had a good feeling about Martinez; they were confident that he could handle the demands of a regular spot in the rotation. And nobody was taking their opinions lightly. As scribe Peter Pascarelli had noted: "The Expos have shown the ability to recognize and acquire a young talent on the rise."[24]

In Montreal, however, the media and baseball fans were having none of this. To them, the transaction reeked of more mendacious stupidity. Calls to radio talk shows damning the move and similar screeds burning up the print media were relentless. Attempts by the Expos to explain and defend the trade were dismissed.

The normally sober-sided Michael Farber, these days with *Sports Illustrated* but then with the *Montreal Gazette*, called it "rotten to the core...Expos one big deal to balance books will sicken fans." Pat Hickey, with the same newspaper, joined the chorus. "There's no puzzle why the Expos made the deal," he declared. "Too many decisions are made to balance books." Pierre Ladouceur of *La Presse* snorted that in spite of team claims that the trade was made primarily for baseball reasons, "the Expos' executives are thinking only about reducing their payroll."[25] Critics even blasted the club for announcing the deal one day after season-ticket renewals were sent out, and they excoriated team president Claude Brochu for escaping to Florida the day the trade was confirmed.

The uproar grew so overwhelming that by the end of November Brochu decided to return from the sunny south and address his critics head on. "This was a baseball trade," he said, "not an economic move, and it will stand on its own like that." He concluded by saying: "If Pedro Martinez wins 15 or 16 games. I think we'll come out all right."[26]

Fifteen years later, Brochu recalled ruefully just how harsh the public criticism had been. "We were blasted....(they said) we were only doing it for the money...we would be able to use Dennis Martinez's uniform and not have to buy a new one...and yet when Dan made this trade he said to me, 'you know what? We're going to win in '94'"[27]

As much as the trade rattled fans and the media, it was even more disquieting for Delino DeShields. Speaking in December, the young player readily admitted the move had

Delino DeShields

unsettled him a great deal. "I'm probably not going to get over it until I put on my Dodgers uniform," he said. Sounding more like a traveler whistling past a graveyard, he added: "The more I think about it the more I know I'm going to be in a better situation. I'm going to miss the guys in Montreal; we all came up together. But as far as being a professional athlete and being seen, there's no doubt in my mind that playing in Los Angeles is a better situation."[28]

He did allow his displeasure to show, however, aiming a parting shot at Duquette, the man who had engineered the trade and whose own personal plans were now cloudy at best. Said DeShields, "I just hope that Dan stays in Montreal after doing this and doesn't jump ship the way that David Dombrowski did after he dumped everybody else."[29]

That was pretty well the way the season ended, with the second winningest team in Expos history on the ropes. Dennis Martinez, the ace of the pitching staff through the troubled times of the past few years, had taken the hint and in October left the club via free agency. He had signed originally with Montreal in 1986 and become another of their successful reclamation projects. Once the burnt-out former Orioles hurler found his comfort zone within the Expos family, he was an outstanding performer. Now this key member of the starting four was gone, with nothing coming back in return. And no one was convinced that his spot in the rotation would be adequately filled by the new kid, the Martinez called Pedro. And, did anybody know who was going to replace Delino DeShields? The suggestion that novice Mike Lansing might get the job done was almost laughable. Or so the experts said.

And what about Dan Duquette? The man who had put this promising Expos team together was still fending off rumours that he was headed to Boston. True or not, as the year wound down to its final moments, the disquiet was becoming more that a bit unsettling.

Auld Lang Syne indeed!

Chapter Eleven

The Miracle That Was
Mike Lansing

It was a miracle of sorts that Mike Lansing found his way to the Expos in a trade on September 18, 1991. Give most of the credit to the perceptive Felipe Alou, who had seen Lansing playing with the Single-A independent Miami Miracle.

Alou was managing the Expos' minor league team in the Florida State League and the more he saw of Lansing, the more he was impressed. The young man's statistics in 1991 were solid: a .286 batting average, six homers and 55 RBIs in 384 at-bats. This was a marked improvement on his 1990 numbers: a .242 average, two homers and 11 RBIs in 207 at-bats.

So what did Alou do? He approached Miracle manager Fredi Gonzalez (most recently manager of the Atlanta Braves) for a little chat on the field one day before a game. "Hey, Fredi, what kind of a guy is this Lansing?" Alou asked.

"He's tough and a winner," Gonzalez replied.

"What kind of money do you think it would take to acquire him?"

"Oh, about $40,000," said Gonzalez.

Alou called the Expos' front office to speak with Dan Duquette, and told him about his conversation with Gonzalez. "There's this guy here that I really like," Alou told Duquette. "His name is Lansing."[30]

"You say Gonzalez says he's worth $40,000. What do you think he's worth?" Duquette asked.

Alou quickly replied, "$100,000." It was not long afterward that the general manager acquired Lansing – but for a lot less than $100,000.

"The truth of the matter is that we signed him for $42,000," said Dave Jauss, who scouted Lansing along with Alou. "Guys like Lansing only come around once in a while. He was like a point guard, busy in so many ways."[31] Asked about this deal more than 20 years later, Duquette replied, "I thought it was around $35,000 that we paid for him."[32]

Drawing on a never-before-used rule, the Miracle, an independent minor-league team owned partly by comedian Bill Murray, had drafted

Lansing out of Wichita State University late in the sixth round of the 1990 MLB draft. Lansing put in two seasons with the Miracle before joining the Expos' organization.

He spent the entire 1992 season at Double-A Harrisburg, producing similar numbers to those of 1991: a .280 average, six homers and 54 RBIs in 483 at-bats. He made his major-league debut on April 7, 1993 when Delino DeShields came down with the chicken pox, contracted in spring training. At the age of 25, slightly older than the age when most players break into the major leagues, Lansing was finally in The Show.

His performance that first season was a surprise even to his biggest supporters. Four days after his first game, he collected five hits in seven at-bats in a 19-8 blowout of the Colorado Rockies. Overall, he hit .287 in 1993, with 29 doubles, three homers and 45 RBIs, playing mostly at short-stop once DeShields reclaimed his spot at second base after warding off the chicken pox.

When DeShields was traded for Pedro Martinez at the end of that season, Lansing became the legitimate replacement at second. In 1994, he was again solid with five homers, 35 RBIs and a .266 average. And he wasn't afraid to get his uniform dirty.

Marquis Grissom, who was best friends with DeShields prior to the trade, had the greatest of admiration for Lansing and what he did in 1994. "Lansing was tough as nails, had a great attitude, played his ass off every game," Grissom recalled. "He contributed big hits and great defence."[33]

Another admirer was catcher Darrin Fletcher. "We saw in spring training in 1994 that Lansing was good. I thought, 'This guy is going to fill in very well for DeShields,'" Fletcher said.[34]

"We bought out his contract and look at the kind of player he became," said Alou. "He was a tough guy, a fighter. He had his own ways but he got some big hits for us and played good defence."

Indeed, Lansing left a lasting impression on many people, including 1994 Chicago Cubs

Mike Lansing

skipper Tom Trebelhorn. "Lansing was kind of the epitome of that team, a tough son of a gun," Trebelhorn said. "He never gave up. He was a tough competitor. He exemplified the type of club they had, a solid, hard-nosed player."[35]

Because of this hard-nosed style, Lansing, who has lived all his off-season life in his native Wyoming, was reputed to be not the easiest person to get along with.

But out there on the diamond - he was miraculous.

Mr. Alou's Best Friends

Felipe Alou's best friend is not a baseball figure. He is Alfredo Cordero, a painter living in the Dominican Republic who is in his 70s and doesn't speak English. He and Alou have known each other since they were kids.

"Whenever Felipe goes to the Dominican, Cordero picks him up at the airport and then when Felipe goes back to Florida, Cordero brings him to the airport," said Luis Pujols, also a close friend of Alou's. "When I meet up with them, I just listen. They talk about history."

And now, even though there is a 20-year age difference between the senior Alou and Pujols, the two have also become very close friends.

"Felipe was my first manager in winter ball in 1973 with Escogido (Dominican Republic)," Pujols said. "For some reason or another, we have been friends for 40 years. We don't live too far from each other in Boynton Beach, Florida, about five miles apart. He treats me like a father. I have a lot of respect for Felipe," Pujols adds reverently. "We're pretty close because we've been together through the good and the bad. Some days, he'll drive by my house and see if I am there."

Thanks to Felipe, Pujols was Alou's first-base coach both with the Expos from 1993-2001 and then again with San Francisco from 2003-06. And in the intervening years, perhaps not so surprisingly, when Pujols finished out the 2002 season as interim manager with the Detroit Tigers, Alou was one of his coaches.

"We do a lot of fishing together in the West Palm Beach area," Pujols said. "So much so that when people want to find out where Felipe is they call me."

Chapter Twelve

Kirk Rueter – the Expos' Record-Setting Southpaw

It was about as good a beginning as one could have in a big-league uniform. His name was Kirk Rueter, and he started out with a bang with the Expos in 1993, going 8-0.

"Chris Nabholz and Brian Barnes had gotten hurt," Rueter noted in a telephone conversation. "I had success right away. It was beyond my wildest dreams. My first game was in San Francisco. I had made it to the major leagues. It was a huge accomplishment, a lifelong dream to go out and pitch well. Something I'll never forget, definitely the highlight of my whole career. It was my cake and ice cream. I burst on the scene."[36]

That year, 1993, was a whirlwind time for Rueter, a most unexpected success, for he had not even been invited to spring training with the major-league club. He spent February and March exclusively at the Expos' minor league facility. When the season began, he joined Double-A Harrisburg, where he quickly went 5-0. Then he moved up to Triple-A in Ottawa where he was 4-2. His performance in these two locations merited a call-up to the major-league squad in early summer.

Taking in the game before his first Expos start scheduled for July 7, the kid with the broad ears saw what he was up against – a powerful Giants club that would post a record of 103-59 that season. As the awestruck Rueter looked on, the Giants trounced the Expos 13–5, even worse than the 10–4 rout they had inflicted the day before. Some 20 years later, Rueter recalled, "It was a big step for me. I asked myself, 'how am I going to get these guys out?' The Giants had scored 13 runs the day before I started!"

So how did Rueter do in that first start? He was brilliant, stopping the Giants in their tracks, 3–0, with 8.1 innings of two-hit ball. During one stretch, he retired 18 batters in a row. This game was the beginning of an outstanding year for the young pitcher: he was equally impressive over the rest of the season, never losing a game.

"Rueter was a fan and media favourite, averaging two hours, 31 minutes for each of his eight wins," noted PR guru Rich Griffin in the 1994 Expos media guide.[37] According to fellow pitcher Butch Henry, he was "a guy that flew under the radar all year. He was phenomenal."[38]

When spring training rolled around in 1994, Rueter recalls looking around the clubhouse and thinking: "You could tell we would be good, there were all-stars everywhere. We had so much talent."

But 1994 was a melancholy year off the field for Rueter. Back home in small-town Illinois, his mother Marjorie was battling lung and brain ill-

Kirk Rueter

nesses that had developed the previous year and was "really sick." On a trip to Florida early in the regular season, Rueter received a call from his brother saying his mother wasn't doing well, that she was "just hanging in."

"Next day, we were coming back to Montreal and while we were in flight, I was told she had passed away. So as soon as we landed I turned around and went home. That helped put things in perspective. There were more important things than sports. I was only 23."

Upon his return to the team, Rueter won his first two games in 1994 to increase his consecutive wins streak to 10, tying Dodger great Fernando Valenzuela for the most wins before a loss to start a career. He would finish the 1994 season at 7-3.

"We almost caught the Phillies in 1993," Rueter said. "In 1994, we were almost the same team, even though we traded Delino (DeShields) for Pedro (Martinez). We were not really old. We were unbelievable, on a mission. We definitely had what it takes to go far into the playoffs. We were on some incredible run. It was a foregone conclusion that we were going to the playoffs. It was such a loaded team."

Then came August 12, 1994.

"It was tough," Rueter said. "We kept hearing from agents that the regular season wouldn't continue but that maybe there would be playoffs or that the teams with the best records would go to the World Series. No way anyone cancels the World Series. It was like a punch in the gut, especially for us."

Today Rueter believes: "If we had gotten to the postseason, this team could have been together a lot longer. You'd generate more revenue and be able to keep all of those guys, Larry Walker, John Wetteland, Marquis Grissom, Ken Hill. We could have been a mini-dynasty."

Rueter, himself, was soon gone, as well. He was mediocre in 1995 at 5-3 and was traded to the Giants in 1996, another year that became tough off the field when his father died. "I think his passing propelled my baseball career," Rueter would say in 2012. "It helped me refocus on the relative importance of things."

"I was disappointed when the Expos sent me down to Ottawa in 1996," Rueter said. "I asked to be traded. I had worn out my welcome. I looked at San Francisco as a new beginning. Still, I am forever indebted to the Expos."

Rueter thrived in the fabled city by the Bay. He would spend the remainder of his career there, becoming the career-winningest southpaw on the very team he had beaten in his first major-league start.

"I was happy with the Giants. I was there almost 10 years," he said. "I played on a lot of good teams with incredible bullpens behind me. I stayed healthy a lot and I was blessed to start 30-some games a year."

On top of his no-nonsense approach where he would take little time between pitches, Rueter gained a reputation as an excellent fielding pitcher, although he never won a Gold Glove.

"Rueter was the Mozart of fielding pitchers," wrote co-author Bill Young in a column about the pitcher on the Seamheads.com blog in 2010. Picking up on research done by John A. Knox on major league baseball's best-fielding pitchers and published in the Summer 2009 edition of the *Baseball Research Journal,* Young felt that Rueter's place in that pantheon deserved to be more widely known.[39]

Calling his research as much a pilot study as a definitive work, Knox limited his survey to 287 pitchers, all reputed to sound in fielding at their position, and who had accumulated a minimum of 1,500 innings pitched. By drawing on available statistics, he devised a ranking scheme to determine the top 100 fielders off the mound since 1900. Factors he considered were career fielding percentage, range, ratio of errors to double plays, and number of double plays turned.

The surprise in Knox's results lies in the degree to which its unanticipated findings differed from conventional wisdom. For example, by reputation and accepted criteria, two of the best-fielding pitchers have always been Jim Kaat (16 Gold Gloves) and Bob Gibson (9 Gold Gloves). However, Knox's ranking placed Kaat far down the list, at number 272, and Gibson even lower, at number 277. Rather than confirm their lofty status as fielders, Knox's statistical analysis in fact makes a strong case *against* Kaat and Gibson. Jim Abbott, who laboured with only one hand, shows at number 73; Tom Glavine comes in at number 30; Roy Halladay is up there at number 17.

According to Knox, the three best-fielding pitchers of all time were little Bobby Shantz (8 Gold Gloves), No. 3; Greg Maddux, No. 2, "a surprise given that he is the pitcher most often cited as having been the greatest (18 Gold Gloves);" and Kirk Rueter, No. 1 (0 Gold Gloves). Yes, Kirk Rueter.

As surprising as this first-place rating was, it was accurate, claimed Knox, for Kirk Rueter excelled at every phase of fielding. In fact, his numerical lead over second-ranked Maddux was as large as the gap between numbers 2 and 9. "When it comes to a wide range of reasonable interpretations of all-around fielding prowess," maintains Knox, "Kirk Rueter is king."

For a full explanation of the how's and why's of Knox's ratings, readers are encouraged to read the complete Knox article in the *Baseball Research Journal*, Summer 2009, published by the Society for American Baseball Research (SABR).

The modest, unassuming Rueter takes all of this 'king' stuff in stride. "My game of pitching was to put the ball in low, and get groundballs," Rueter would say in 2012.

Inevitably, some of those balls would be hit back to him.

"I took a lot of pride in fielding bunts, throwing to second or third or first on groundballs to me. It helped that I didn't throw hard to the plate. I was not a hard thrower. When I finished my release, I was in a position where I could field the ball."

There you have it: nothing complicated, a simple explanation from a country boy who calls Nashville, Illinois, home and doesn't even mind answering his own phone.

Rueter Rooter

It was several hours before game time in St. Louis one mid-September day in 1993 when Curtis Rueter walked down the steps at old Busch Stadium, leaned over the railing near the visiting team's dugout and called out, "Hey, Kirk, how are things going?"

Kirk Rueter kept walking, completely ignoring his first cousin, on hand to watch the young southpaw's start against the Cards. When Expos outfielder Moises Alou called out, "Do you know him?" Curtis replied, "I'm Kirk's first cousin."

"Well, don't feel bad," Alou told him. "Pitchers on the days they are pitching enter their own little world."

"Kirk always adored the Cardinals since he was a kid," Curtis mentioned in a telephone interview, "so to make a start in the majors in St. Louis was really something. What I remember about that game is that it was a nasty, rainy day. and Kirk still got the win."

Chapter Thirteen

Cliff Floyd –
A Man of Promise

It was spring training in Vero Beach, Florida, March 1993, and Montreal's latest up-and-comer Cliff Floyd was talking to a freelance reporter for Toronto's *Globe and Mail* newspaper about what he was going to do once he made it to the major leagues.

When the reporter's story was published in the *Globe* the headline read: *Expos' Prize Prospect Swings a Powerful Bat.* The story began: "Cliff Floyd, he of the Bunyanesque, Samson-like power, expects he will be hitting a few 500-foot dingers down the road in the majors." The reporter continued: "It isn't so much braggadocio as merely confidence borne out of the power the Montreal Expos prospect displays in his massive upper body and forearms. And he hasn't stopped growing. He's 6-foot-4 and even appears lean at 230 pounds."[40]

That's when Floyd himself entered the equation. "When I fill out, I won't be surprised if I weigh 250, but I'll still look good. It's a natural body. I take after my mom. She's a big woman," Floyd told the reporter. "When I get to the majors, I expect to be a real good hitter, hit 20 homers or so and drive in more than 100 runs each season consistently. I expect to hit a few long homers. I want people to know I hit that ball. People have been telling me I remind

Cliff Floyd

them of Willie McCovey. If I can live up to what Willie McCovey did, that would be great."[41]

At the time, Floyd, from the south side of Chicago and the tough side of the tracks, was considered a blue-chipper, Montreal's top phenom in the majors. In 1992, his first season of pro ball, Floyd was sensational at Class-A Albany, banging out numbers not expected of someone just starting out.

Get this: Floyd hit 16 homers that year but also legged out 16 triples to show there was speed inside that massive body. To boot, his RBI total was 97. Yet, when he arrived at spring training in 1993, the Expos weren't expecting him to stick with the club. He hung around long enough to become one of the last cuts as a non-roster invitee before being sent to Double-A Harrisburg, even though the major-league team had employed eight different first basemen in 1992.

"This is a dream come true," Floyd said of his invitation to big-league camp – before heading to Harrisburg. "I want to get stronger and work on my throwing arm."[42] In the meantime, he was considered the first baseman of the Expos' future, a player with a chance to dominate the game and show a thing or two to the Chicago high school coach who cut him when he was 15.

"He's a tremendous talent. He's close to Darryl Strawberry talent. Close," Franklin Stubbs, who auditioned unsuccessfully for the Expos in 1993, told the *Globe and Mail* that day.

With Harrisburg, Floyd continued his onslaught, batting .329 with 26 homers and 101 RBIs, before Ottawa's Triple-A Lynx came calling. Expos executives, media and fans awaited his arrival in the majors with great anticipation. It happened in September, against Philadelphia.

As Expos PR director Rich Griffin would write in Floyd's bio in the 1994 team guide, "Floyd's arrival in the majors on September 18 was the culmination of a five-month vigil by Expos fans that began at spring training when the young prospect participated in major-league camp for the first time."[43]

Floyd made his debut with the Expos in the sixth inning, playing first base. Stepping up to the plate in the bottom of the inning to face Phillies pitcher Tommy Greene, Floyd received a standing ovation from the Montreal fans. Feeling the pressure in that highly anticipated at-bat, Floyd struck out. There was some consolation in the fact that Greene was having a good season and was remembered for throwing a no-hitter against the Expos two years before. Floyd then fanned in his next four at-bats, too.

On September 26, Floyd, batting against Dave Telgheder of the Mets, hit his first home run. At 20 years, nine months and 21 days, he was the second youngest in Expos history to hit a home run. According to Griffin's notes, Gary Carter beat him by about four months when, at 20 years, five months and 10 days, he went deep for the first time in 1974.

"Floyd was a guy coming into his own," said 1994 Expos reliever Tim Scott. "Despite his size, he was probably the fastest guy on our team. He could run with Marquis Grissom and Larry Walker."[44]

Floyd stuck with the Expos for the entire 1994 season but it took a great deal of arm-twisting on the part of manager Felipe Alou to keep him in Montreal. "The front office wanted to send him down to the minors to start the season," Alou recalled. "He had a really good spring. We liked his speed, his energy and he was a big boy, so the last week of spring training, hitting coach Tommy Harper and I went to bat for Cliff. We told the front office people that we really needed to have this player for the first week. We asked to let us keep him one week and if he didn't do well, OK, send him down. Luckily, we started the season in Houston and he had a great series and went on to have a pretty decent season."

Scott, however, characterized Floyd as "all hype, a king-in-waiting who never pans out." While there might be some truth in that observation and while Floyd never panned out like Hall of Famer McCovey, in 1994 the freshman ballplayer did do his bit to make that club exciting

Floyd hit .281 and drove in 41 runs in 334 at-bats. He fell woefully short in home run production, however, hitting only four roundtrippers. One of those is a YouTube sensation and part of Annakin Slayd's video tribute to the 1994 Expos.[45]

According to manager Alou, when Floyd first arrived in Montreal from the minor leagues, he was using a high-leg kick at the plate. Alou and Harper found this action excessive and sought to tame Floyd's approach. They told him to forget about the high-leg-kick and just relax in the batter's box.

Floyd had felt comfortable with his familiar approach to a pitcher's throw and was none too thrilled with having to change his style. He knew it would cut down on his home run totals. "It was a tough pill to swallow," he said over breakfast in Miami one day in 2012. "There was a lot of frustration. I had really high expectations. Things were changed on the fly. It affected my whole batting stance. They didn't want a lot of movement."[46] Floyd's career with the Expos was shortlived and disappointing. He had some stellar seasons elsewhere but not on a consistent basis. Injuries played their role in slowing him down, but none was more gruesome than the shattered right wrist he suffered very early in the 1995 season when he collided with Todd Hundley of the Mets near first base.

The injury was similar to what a motorcycle rider or downhill skier might encounter after crashing at high speed, reported Expos orthopedic surgeon Dr. Larry Coughlin, when he spoke to a reporter shortly after the accident. The surgery called for eight screws to be inserted in the wrist to hold the shattered bone together.

After leaving the Expos, Floyd played five years with the Florida Marlins, winning a World Series championship in 1997. He was not an impact player that year, playing only part-time and having only three hitless at-bats in the Fall Classic. His next four years were more productive. He played four seasons with the Mets, and spent single seasons with Tampa Bay, the Red Sox, the Cubs, and the Padres. Over his career, Floyd experienced four seasons when he amassed at least 90 RBIs and four in which he batted .300 or better.

Thinking he might still have some gas in the tank, the Expos reacquired him in 2002 but he was gone again by the next winter. He finished his career in 2009, after 17 years in the majors. His career stats showed a respectable .278 average, 233 home runs and 865 RBIs. Certainly not McCovey-like numbers, but solid nonetheless.

The Cliff Floyd homer of 1994 that became a YouTube sensation and an integral part of Annakin Slayd's video tribute to that fabled Expos squad, shows the slugger going down to his ankles to reach for a Greg Maddux pitch, swinging like a golfer on a long par-5 and whacking it out of the yard. The cagey Maddux, famous for pinpoint accuracy, throwing to spots and nibbling at the strike zone, thought he could get it past the slugger with no problem.

Even though the pitch was near the ground and clearly not a strike, the powerful Floyd still managed to get his big bat down quickly and drive the ball up into the air and out. He had done something incredible with a pitch that was considered safe, even excellent, from a pitcher's perspective. "He golfed it out," Tim Scott recalled. "It was unthinkable, considering that Maddux was pitching. Maddux was shocked, absolutely shocked."

Floyd's incredible homer came in the bottom of the seventh inning at Olympic Stadium on the night of June 27. The score was tied 1–1 when Marquis Grissom, leading off the inning, singled to left and stole second. After Lou Frazier walked, Grissom stole third. In no time Frazier followed suit, stealing second. Moises Alou popped up to second baseman Mark Lemke, which led to an intentional walk to Darrin Fletcher to load the bases.

Wil Cordero broke the tie by lining a sacrifice fly to Ryan Klesko, scoring Grissom. Frazier quickly stole third, leaving runners on the corners. Then came the magic from Floyd: he went deep for a three-run homer to give the Expos a 5–1 cushion. They would go on to win the game.

"That was the highlight of that season for me," Floyd would say in conversation over breakfast as he dug into the fruit-plate.[47] "Dealing with the Atlanta Braves, they were our nemesis; they were the team of the 1990s. So when I did that, I felt that helped get us over the hump. In that moment, there was a packed house (45,291), it was something. He threw me a ball down low where I like to hit. I have looked at my stats against Maddux. I think I batted .240 lifetime in my career in 70 at-bats. I would pop up, ground out. He would throw a lot of balls down low where I like to hit and I missed that pitch many times. Maddux always had control, he knew actually what he wanted to do, what he had to do with what he had. He threw what and where he wanted to."

Even though Maddux threw the ball out of the strike zone, Marquis Grissom doesn't think it was such a great idea to offer that pitch to Floyd. "That's a no-no," he said. "You don't throw the ball down and in to a left-handed hitter. He hit the ball 450 feet."

Floyd's homer sent Maddux to the showers (he was replaced by Steve Bedrosian) and dropped his won/loss record to 10-4. Ken Hill emerged as the winning pitcher, bringing his record to 11-3. Ironically, both pitchers would end the season with 16 wins, best in the league. The Cy Young Award went to the Braves hurler, however, and deservedly so: he had an ERA of 1.56 compared to Hill's 3.32 and almost twice as many strikeouts (156 to 85).

"Cliff Floyd hit a lot of those types of home runs," said Braves president John Schuerholz, who was the team's GM for years. "He was remarkable and uncanny, a modern-day version of Yogi Berra. Both could go anywhere where the bat could reach. Floyd really had some kind of swing. As I have said before, he was a good comparison to Willie McCovey."

Yes, that Willie McCovey!

Card-Playing Foursome

So confident were the Expos in 1994 that a core group of players, Larry Walker, Moises Alou, Marquis Grissom and Mike Lansing would regularly play cards in the clubhouse after pre-game workouts.

They would get back around 6:15 p.m. throw their workout garb in the nearby laundry hampers, and head to a picnic table to play Casino or something similar. They would play until almost game time, before jumping into their uniforms and running back out for a 7:07 start.

It was a ritual that rookie Cliff Floyd found hard to fathom.

"You gotta be kidding me," Floyd would say in an interview later. "Are you serious? How could they be loose for a game? Sometimes Felipe would have to circle around from his office to get them ready on time."

Grissom started laughing when told of Floyd's comments, downplaying it all. "It was a form of relaxation," Grissom said. "We'd always get to the field and get our stuff done. Butch Henry and Ken Hill also liked to play cards. The young guys, we didn't allow them to play cards."

Chapter Fourteen

Au Monticule, Now Pitching – Denis Boucher

Top of the 12th inning. Houston Astrodome. April 4, 1994. Opening Day, a matinee encounter with 43,440 in the stands. Score tied 3-3 between the Expos and Astros, the first game of the season for both clubs.

To start the inning, Houston brought in reliever Mitch Williams, the Wild Man himself, who had been acquired late in spring training from the Phillies. After retiring the first two batters he faced, Williams gave up singles to Wil Cordero and Jeff Gardner, saw his catcher surrender a passed ball, and walked Sean Berry to load the bases. Now totally flummoxed, Williams issued two more walks, to Randy Milligan and Marquis Grissom, bringing home Cordero and Gardner – before he was mercifully replaced by Tom Edens, who summarily fanned Rondell White to end the inning. Expos 5, Astros 3

However, the Astros still had one more turn at bat – and they hadn't run out of gas just yet. Expos reliever Tim Scott, who entered the game in the 11th inning, was in trouble from his first pitch in the 12th. Scott walked lead-off batter James Mouton and then surrendered a single to Steve Finley, enough damage for Expos manager Felipe Alou to pull him and bring in Jeff Shaw.

Shaw struck out Craig Biggio before allowing a single to Jeff Bagwell. Mouton scored and Finley stopped at second. With the score now 5–4 Expos, Alou turned to Lachine, Quebec, native Denis Boucher, a southpaw, to face left-handed batter Luis Gonzalez.

Coming on in relief was unfamiliar territory for Boucher. All the way through the minors and at his various, albeit short, major-league stops with the Indians, Blue Jays and Expos, he had always been a starter. The one exception, his only appearance out of the bullpen, had occurred with the Indians in 1992.

Was Boucher intimidated coming in against the Astros? Not really. In conversation 18 years later, he recalled how the late and great umpire

John McSherry rang up Gonzalez on a called third strike with that slot-machine pull of his right arm. "I struck Gonzalez out on three pitches," Boucher said.[48] Now there were two men out.

Next up was the switch-hitting Ken Caminiti, who batted right-handed against the lefty Boucher. To this point in the game, Caminiti had gone 0-for-5 and "was due" – as they say in baseball parlance.

"John Wetteland and Mel Rojas had already pitched and were out of the game," Boucher explained. "Gil Heredia and I were the only relievers left."

Boucher seemed to fool Caminiti on a critical changeup, but somehow the all-star third baseman still managed to get his bat on the ball. "Caminiti hit a ball off the end of the bat, but it went into the gap for a double to score both runners," Boucher recalled with a grimace.

That walk-off double gave the Astros a stunning 6–5 win. It was a heart-wrenching loss for Montreal. The winning pitcher was Tom Edens, the loser, Shaw. But the damaging blow had been given up by Boucher.

"After striking out Gonzalez, I thought I would be out of the game," Boucher said. "Mentally, I wasn't

Denis Boucher

ready to be a reliever. The bullpen, it was big adjustment, a different mentality. It was a bad start to the season. It could have been a save in my first opportunity.

"I made the team out of spring training," Boucher explained. "I got a couple of starts. They wanted to try more young guys from the minors. I pitched sporadically, a little bit, once in a while. It was a good team and they jelled together as the year went on. It was a good mixture of veterans and younger players."

By May 6, the Expos could see no future for Boucher and demoted him to Triple-A Ottawa, where he finished out the season. He wasn't happy with the move. "I was a little mad," Boucher said. "I thought I could still pitch but I wanted to get back in a starting role, a normal routine and show them in Montreal. I did pitch really well the rest of the season. I thought I had a good chance of going back up to the Expos but the team was doing so great and then the strike came up. My arm wasn't always feeling right. I should have gotten surgery done before then, but you know how it is, you stay up there in the majors, keep pitching and you overuse the arm. I tried to do too much when it wasn't 100 per cent."

Boucher would never pitch again in the majors, although he did manage to extend his professional career through 10 seasons. In all, he strutted his stuff with close to 20 teams before calling it quits in 1997.

No chapter on Boucher would be complete without mentioning his acquisition by the Expos and all of the excitement that surrounded his first game with the club on Labour Day, September 6, 1993, at Olympic Stadium.

Originally signed as a free agent by Toronto, Boucher made his major league debut with the Blue Jays on April 12, 1991. Two months later, however, he was traded to the Cleveland Indians. He remained with the Tribe through 1992, until Colorado selected him in the expansion draft and then traded him to the San Diego Padres a few months later. Boucher spent the early part of the 1993 season in Las Vegas toiling for the Padres' Triple-A team. His uncertain odyssey finally ended on July 10 when Expos GM Dan Duquette plucked him out in exchange for a minor leaguer player and cash.

"When (Las Vegas manager) Russ Nixon called me in and told me I was traded to Montreal, I had tears running down my cheeks. I was going home," Boucher told a media conference call on the day of the trade. In 2012, Boucher reiterated these comments. "I was very happy with the trade because I wasn't having a good season in Triple A with the Padres," he said. "I was real happy to be coming home."

Boucher didn't actually join the major-league club until September 1 and that after an excellent 6-0 stopover in Ottawa. When it was announced that he would make his first Montreal appearance on Labour Day, September 6, fans and the media were wildly enthusiastic. After all these years, a home-grown Quebec pitcher would finally be starting a game for the Expos.

Boucher, a modest ballplayer by nature, but one who possessed a profound sense of the possible, was deeply appreciative of the chance – call it a reprieve – granted to him. He made no special requests, not even for a favourite uniform number. Readily accepting his assigned number 38, he was stoic: "I've been with a lot of teams, had a lot of different numbers...some were lucky. Some weren't."[49]

At Olympic Stadium, on game day, over 40,000 fans poured into the stands for this emotionally charged moment and an incredible 192 accredited media types jostled for space in the press box.

Boucher made an excellent debut, allowing his opponents, the Colorado Rockies, only one earned run over six innings – a fourth inning home run by former Expos favourite Andres Galarraga. The Big Cat, as he was called, had been traded to St. Louis following the 1991 season for Ken Hill, the ace of Montreal's 1994 league-leading club.

Boucher left the game after six innings with the Expos leading 2-1, his job done. He did not get the win, however, as the Rockies scored two more runs before the Expos came back with two of their own in the eighth inning. Final score: Montreal 4, Rockies 3.

To add magic to the affair, Boucher's catcher that day was Joe Siddall of Windsor, Ontario, and the right fielder was Larry Walker of Maple Ridge, British Columbia. The presence of three Canadians in the starting lineup represented the first time in modern major-league history that three countrymen from Canada had been on the diamond at the same time and with the same team. In a similar vein, that day Boucher and Siddall also became the first modern-day all-Canadian starting battery.

This Labour Day caper was easily the highlight of Boucher's short tenure with the Expos, indeed of his career. Hollywood couldn't have asked for a better script.

"It was a big day. I always say it was good that it was a day game," Boucher recalled in 2012. "I didn't have much time to think about it. I had no time to get nervous. I had a good breakfast and was ready to go. The first inning was really good with five or six pitches."

After the game ended at 4:10 p.m., Boucher still had to face waves of reporters, wrapping up his last media session almost three hours later at about 7:00 p.m. Then he adjourned to a Lachine restaurant for a large family gathering. Life in an Expos uniform was starting out well for Boucher. He had the honour of becoming only the second Quebec-born player, after Claude Raymond, to suit up and play for the team.

"I pitched really great that month in September," said Boucher, who went 3-1 for the season. "It was a big month. We were in contention until the last weekend before the Phillies beat us out. We drew 100,000 for a three-game series on the final weekend."

In the pressure cooker as a French Canadian, Boucher never felt uncomfortable when it came to dealing with the francophone media. "With the French media, there wasn't more pressure, because you always need to perform to win games anyway. The pressure is always there. Yes, with the French media, there was more attention; yes, you're looked at more closely; you're under the microscope every day, talking to media every day."

Denis Boucher was born in the Lachine area of Montreal in 1968 and right from his earliest years he was drawn to baseball. The left-hander quickly rose through the ranks of Baseball-Quebec's development programs. He was so highly regarded that by age 19 he was named to the Team Canada squad that finished fourth in the 1987 Pan American Games held in Indianapolis. He had been scouted extensively by Blue Jays bird-dog Bill Slack, and scouting director Bob Prentice saw him in action at the Pan Am Games, Boucher was signed to a Toronto contract for $20,000.

This was an era when few Canadians made it to the majors, a far cry from the present day when one can expect to see close to 20 in the bigs at any one time. As Boucher explained it, "That was in the days when Canadians were still considered as free agents. Today, Canadians go into the draft. I probably could have gotten more money from other teams. The Yankees wanted to sign me and Dan Duquette was a scout with the Brewers and he said he was interested in me."

"If you are interested in talking more, give me a call," Duquette told him.

"It's funny. Dan traded for me in 1993 for the Expos," Boucher said. "But I thought I would sign with the Blue Jays because they had been following me for a while."

In recent years, Boucher has been a Canadian scout for the Yankees and is the pitching coach for the Team Canada senior team that participates in the World Baseball Classic and Pan Am Games.

"I've been coaching for Team Canada for 10 years. I'm also in charge of the baseball association in Lachine (Quebec)," Boucher said. The former Expo has also received a number of honours over the years. In 2012 he was inducted into the Quebec Baseball Hall of Fame; he had already been named to the Quebec Sports Hall of Fame a year earlier.

In retrospect, it seems odd that the Expos didn't show interest in Boucher in the late 1980s. "The Expos didn't have much interest in Canadians at the time," he remembers. "(Expos employee) Ron Piché invited me to the stadium once or twice and I threw on the sidelines a few times for the Expos."[50]

Chapter Fifteen

Dennis Martinez
Leaves the Expos

The Expos' 1993 season was a season to remember, but it was not without its surprises and intriguing elements. Perhaps the most intriguing of all was the saga of pitcher Dennis Martinez, El Presidente, the ace of the pitching staff.

It all began when Martinez put his foot down and said no to a trade. The San Francisco Giants had fashioned a deal to acquire Martinez but since it required that he first clear waivers, the Atlanta Braves managed to step in and block the move. Set to make another pennant run in August, the Braves, seeing that Martinez was available, decided they wanted the talented hurler for themselves. Martinez was a 10-and-5 player, meaning he had spent at least 10 seasons in the majors, the last five (or more) with the same team. As such, he was entitled to veto the deal.

"I stopped the trade because I was going to become a free agent and I knew the Braves weren't going to give me an extension at the time of the proposed trade," Martinez recalled. "They said they would not start talking contract at that point. So I said I was not going to Atlanta just for the hell of it. Also, they told me that I would be the sixth starter so I figured I might get one or two more starts.

"By staying in Montreal, I would get maybe four, five, six starts. I wanted to get my 100th win in the National League and I wasn't going to do it by going to the Braves. There was no reason to go anywhere else."[51] Martinez, who ended the year with a 15-9 record, also wanted to be part of the team's run at a '93 playoff spot.

Nevertheless, even before the 1993 season ended, it was almost a foregone conclusion that Martinez would not be re-signed as a free agent by the Expos. One reporter sensed this and arranged to have a plaque made and presented to Martinez during a pub crawl near the end of the season in the company of other journalists. In the eyes of Expos management, Martinez had become too expensive. He was completing the last year of a three-year contract worth $9.5 million. He was not expecting an offer from the Expos and when none came he accepted a two-year deal from the Cleveland Indians worth more than $9 million.

"Maybe the Expos were upset at me because I turned down the trade to Atlanta," Martinez would say close to 20 years later. "I was not unhappy at all that the Expos didn't make an offer and I wasn't going to go after them for an offer. I loved the city of Montreal and I loved playing for the Expos."

That warmth was reflected at the Rogers Centre in Toronto on July 26, 2013, when Martinez was there with the Houston Astros for whom he was working as bullpen coach. It was only two days away from the 22nd anniversary of his perfect game against the Dodgers, and he was asked if he remembered the moment as if it were yesterday. "No, not like yesterday," he replied. "I'll remember it like it was today…because this time [the anniversary] is going to be in Canada. I pitched for Canada. I pitched for a Canadian team…so who knows? Maybe something special will happen again."[52]

Ironically, when it became apparent to general manager Dan Duquette that the Expos were about to lose Dennis Martinez, the shrewd Duquette just happened to find a way to pull another gifted pitcher named Martinez from his sleeve. But that's a different story.

Chapter Sixteen

Anatomy of the Trade – Pedro Martinez to Montreal

Dennis Martinez said it best: "It was one Martinez for another Martinez."

That other Martinez was, of course, Pedro, a reliever with the Los Angeles Dodgers. Los Angeles GM Fred Claire and his Expos counterpart Dan Duquette would spend several weeks discussing the trade that finally saw second baseman Delino (Bop) DeShields sent to the Dodgers for Pedro on November 17, 1993.

Media and fans in Montreal couldn't believe Duquette would make such a trade. In Los Angeles there were similar feelings about Claire.

The misgivings in Montreal about the trade concerned the fact that in 1993, DeShields had been named a second-team All-Star in the National League. Earning $1.5 million, he seemed a bridge to the future. He hit a mere two homers and had only 29 RBIs in 481 at-bats but his average that year and the previous year were very close to .300 and he was a leading basestealer. He was considered to be entering the prime of his career.

"I never thought I'd be a Dodger," DeShields said in a conference call from his home in West Palm Beach, Florida, the day of the trade. "I'm excited. I'm a little bit surprised, but I'm excited. This is a good opportunity for me. I know a lot of the Dodger players. They have a real good group of guys. I'm looking forward to it. I really felt in the second half (of last season) they were one of the best teams in the league. They have some young players, (Mike) Piazza, (Eric) Karros, (Jose) Offerman. It's going to be a nice mix with the veterans they have there."[53]

In an interview with *The Montreal Gazette*, DeShields said he'd had to take a deep breath in his backyard to digest the news. He called his good friend and teammate Marquis Grissom to tell him about the trade but Grip simply would not believe it at first. "Marquis thought I was bull-jiving, just like I usually do, and said he wouldn't believe it until he saw it on ESPN," DeShields told the paper.[54]

That same day, in a conference call, Claire told reporters: "The point of all of this was simply an opportunity to add a young player who we feel is one of the top young players in baseball. I believe that in Delino, we have acquired one of the finest young second basemen in major league baseball. He gives our ballclub great speed, and will help us both offensively and defensively."

When manager Felipe Alou was queried about the trade, he replied, "I just hope that Mr. Martinez takes up the slack of that other Martinez. This is a kid with a great arm. I know him well. Delino is on his way to being a superstar. If Martinez pitches well, this could be a good trade for both teams. This could possibly be a 20-game winner. He was one of the best in the league last year, you know – out of the bullpen."

Pedro Martinez as a Dodger

In making the move, Claire's hand had been forced by the actions of incumbent second baseman Jody Reed, who mystified the baseball world by declining a Dodgers offer of $7.8 million over three years. For some reason, he and his agent thought he was worth much more over that time-frame, upwards of $11.5 million. Embarrassingly for Reed, there were no takers, and when the dust settled he was forced to accept a rock-bottom poverty-line salary of about $750,000 with the Milwaukee Brewers. One observer said stupidity doesn't begin to describe it. Even Claire's pro-posed signing-bonus offer was $800,000, $50,000 more than what the Brewers gave him for one whole season.

"I was going home after work one night and I had the radio on and Jody Reed was degrading the Dodgers for their offer," a smiling Duquette recalled in an interview in Sarasota, Florida, in March 2013. "I thought to myself, that was three years for pretty good money. I said, 'Keep talking, Jody, keep talking.'" Then he turned serious. "That's when I thought we had a chance." A chance to ship DeShields to the Dodgers for Martinez.

"We needed a trade to get better in our starting pitching," Duquette said. "At the end of the 1993 season, we knew we needed someone to replace Dennis Martinez because we couldn't afford him as a free agent. The Dodgers had been looking to trade Pedro Asticio but the club also suggested Pedro Martinez might be available as well, because they didn't think he would hold up under the workload of a starting pitcher. Fred Claire and (manager) Tommy Lasorda always liked DeShields since they saw him a lot during spring-training games when the Dodgers played out of Vero Beach. They saw him as a great defensive player."

Duquette added: "There was a lot of criticism in Montreal toward the trade because Delino was our most recognizable player, our leadoff hitter. He was the face of the Expos, and so the trade was not well received."[55]

Gazette columnist Michael Farber was unequivocal in expressing his disbelief and distaste for the trade. "Trading DeShields for a middle reliever, even one that projects for something grander, is a stab-in-the-dark deal by a franchise that keeps trading its assets for precocious chil-dren," Farber wrote. "This trade was rotten to the core."[56]

Duquette saw things differently, of course. "Delino always played hard. I just wondered what kind of power he would have."

Duquette noted that baseball men had a higher opinion of Pedro. "Tim Johnson, one of our coaches, was familiar with Pedro because of the time he spent with the Dodgers. Tim gave us a very strong evaluation, saying Pedro was the type of pitcher that was ready for combat. Scout Eddie Haas was very helpful, too. Felipe Alou told me that what he liked about Pedro when he saw him in the Dominican was his fearlessness, that he had attitude out there."

There was also the question of money: "We were getting Pedro at a smaller salary. He was not eligible for arbitration. He had less than two years of experience and gave us someone who met our payroll requirements. Anytime you can trade for Pedro is a good deal."[57]

Over at the Fred Claire camp, the GM was telling Reed's agent J.D. Dowell that his offer, made before the free-agent filing period following the World Series, was the Dodgers' best and only offer. Ignoring that warning, Reed decided to test the open waters, figuring there had to be some teams willing to spend more than what Claire put on the table. When Reed did in fact file for free agency, Claire took his offer off the table. He had pressed Dowell to accept the deal and when he was rebuffed, Claire told Dowell he was making a mistake. And was he ever.

Claire had acquired Reed in November 1992 in a trade at the expansion draft and while not a star, the infielder filled the team's needs more than adequately. In 1993 he batted .276 with two homers and 31 RBIs, and was solid defensively, committing only five errors. "Jody's hustling style won our fans over in one season," Claire wrote in his autobiography "My 30 Years in Dodger Blue."[58]

Now faced with a vacancy at second base, Claire first talked to free agents Robbie Thompson of San Francisco and Harold Reynolds of the Seattle Mariners and their representatives. When Thompson eventually re-signed with San Francisco for three years and $11.6 million, Dowell called Claire to say the Giants had set the market for second baseman. Claire responded by saying that this wasn't the Dodgers' market. It was then that Claire started talking to Duquette, who told him that the price for DeShields was Martinez.

Assessing the situation, Claire knew what DeShields had done for the Expos. He picked the brains of Lasorda and Ralph Avila, the man in charge of the organization's baseball operations in the Dominican Republic. Interestingly, Claire told Lasorda and Avila they had veto rights on the trade. "Both agreed it was a good deal for the Dodgers in that we would solve our problem at second with an outstanding young player," said Claire. "The deal was made. If Jody accepts our offer, we keep Pedro."

Another potentially limiting factor that Claire considered was Martinez's health. Claire says he acted on a report by Dr. Frank Jobe, who called into question the young pitcher's body build and endurance. Jobe had also operated on Martinez's non-throwing left shoulder in October 1992. "I know he felt bad about the trade," Claire said of Jobe in response to a reporter's question in the 1990s. "I told him, 'Frank, don't think about that. You've done incredible work and made a great contribution to baseball and the organization.' It was more a reflection of the philosophy I took. Get the information (from Jobe), use the information and take the responsibility. Particularly take the responsibility if it doesn't work out."

To set the record straight about the trade and Jobe's influence, long-time *Los Angeles Times* baseball writer Ross Newhan coaxed the normally reticent Jobe to talk in 1999.

"I don't think I said get rid of him (Martinez)," Jobe told Newhan, talking about the situation for the first time. "I'd never say that, but the circumstances kind of spoke for themselves. His shoulder had come out once, and once an injury of that type occurs, you can't say it won't reoccur. He had a kind of a delicate stature to start with and there were already questions about his stamina. It's a judgment call, but you had to kind of wonder, 'Golly, is this kid going to break down?'"

Mitch Melnick, host of TSN sports radio in Montreal, shared that view. "I was one of the guys who wrote to Dan Duquette because all I knew was how skinny Pedro Martinez was…Tommy Lasorda, his own manager, said he wasn't strong enough to be a starting pitcher."[59]

In "My 30 Years in Dodger Blue," Claire talked extensively about the Martinez/DeShields trade. "My buddy George Green, who used to run KABC Radio, believes you are entitled to a mulligan on the first tee," Claire wrote. "This was one baseball trade where I could have used George's mulligan, where I wish I could have had a second chance. One thing I want to make clear is that I think the world of Delino. I liked him as a player and I like him as a person. It's not a question of personality. The trade just didn't work out for the Dodgers. I really didn't want to trade Pedro, whom I respect a great deal. What I wanted to do, as we looked to the 1994 season, was to fill a need at second base, to provide our team with speed along with good defense."[60]

Was the Martinez/DeShields trade the worst Claire ever made? "I would think so, no question about that," Claire told the authors in 2011. "I always take responsibility for the trade. Pedro never got a chance to start for the Dodgers. The trade obviously didn't turn out well for the Dodgers. As time went on, I felt bad about it. We lost a great pitcher in Pedro. I did feel Delino was really a key player, however. He looked as though he was a team leader. I'm the only person charged with the responsibility with the trade. A lot of things went into it, a lot of weight, a lot of thought process went into it."[61]

As it turned out, DeShields' career had mixed results from then on, but Martinez became Hall of Fame material. At spring training in Vero

Beach with the Dodgers in 1994, DeShields was injured and didn't get to play much. Then he was stricken with chicken pox. The pattern persisted throughout the regular season when he repeatedly missed time because of injuries. As a result, his production fell far below his 1993 level.

Reflecting on the trade, journalist Newhan, an elite baseball mind, had this to offer: "There were several aspects of the trade that come to mind. One is that Jody Reed turned down the contract offer. He never got that offer on the open market and the Dodgers absolutely had a vacuum at second base. The second aspect, Newhan said, "is that Tommy Lasorda didn't know what to make of Pedro. He thought Pedro didn't have the size and stamina to pitch out of the bullpen and to start regularly. There was uncertainty around the best role for Pedro. The third aspect was the report they had from Dr. Jobe on (Martinez') left shoulder. The Dodgers felt they needed a second baseman but DeShields had a terrible year and Pedro had a spectacular year. Every chance he has, Pedro lays it on Lasorda."

Martinez made an exception in an interview in Montreal on March 27, 2011 following the Cummings Jewish Centre Sports Celebrity Breakfast, which feted the 1994 Expos. There, the pitcher avoided criticizing the legendary Lasorda. Rather, he would talk about "they" in reference to the Dodgers. "I was so small they thought I was going to break down," Martinez said. "When I joined the Expos, I weighed 164. Now I weigh 195."[62]

There was no stopping Newhan's criticism, however. Writing in 1999 he declared: "In a 1993 deal that keeps slapping Claire and the Dodgers in the face, Martinez was traded to the Montreal Expos for Delino DeShields only to have the young prince of a second baseman become a frog in Los Angeles while Martinez became king of the hill in Montreal."

Newhan was even blunter in a column that appeared in the *Los Angeles Times* on April 22, 2008. "The worst trade in the 50 years that the Dodgers have been in Los Angeles?" Newhan asked rhetorically. "From casual fans to dedicated seamheads, no prompting is needed: the 1993 trade that sent Pedro Martinez to Montreal for Delino DeShields continues to produce the loudest moans, with obvious justification."

DeShields spent three seasons with the Dodgers, with a lacklustre record overall. Despite his limited production in la-la land, he did stun the baseball world in 2000 when, playing with the Baltimore Orioles, he registered a career-high 86 RBIs. He also batted .296 with 43 doubles and 10 homers during that wonderful season but, incredibly, two years later he was out of the game at age 34.

Despite his up-and-down career, baseball fans need not feel too badly for Bop DeShields. He did become a multi-millionaire, grossing over $28 million during his career. He later started a clothing line of his own and then went on to become a minor-league manager in the Cincinnati Reds' system.

DeShields didn't feel comfortable talking in public and was anything but a media celebrity. He was more of a quiet, brooding personality – but still likeable in his own right.

As to who would replace DeShields at second base, the answer was already waiting in the wings: Mike Lansing. As a freshman in 1993, Lansing opened up eyes with a .287 average, three homers and 45 RBIs in a utility role. "This (trade) is a surprise and, now that I think about it, a little bit of a disappointment," Lansing said the day of the deal. "Delino did a lot for me last year. He'd tell me to keep my head up if it looked like I was having a rough time. He had something to do with the kind of year I had."

Gazette sports columnist Jack Todd joked that the Expos made the trade for another Martinez simply so they wouldn't have the expense of getting a new uniform made up. They could just reuse the one marked "Martinez" on the back.

How quickly the jibes and insults were forgotten though, as the magical 1994 season unfolded and Pedro emerged as a quality starter. He fashioned an 11-5 record and launched an amazing big-league career – quite the start for the pint-sized, fireballing string bean. Shame on those experts who were so wrong in their assessment of the trade and their predictions about Pedro. Sadly, it was typical of a negativism that had permeated the media at this time – and which in some ways was as responsible for the Expos' eventual downfall as were tight-fisted owners and carpetbaggers. The few who saw the wisdom of the trade were the smart ones.

Martinez for Martinez. What sounded at first like a bad joke became one of the most glorious moves the Expos ever made.

Chapter Seventeen

Avila's Take on Pedro

If there is one baseball mind that knows Pedro Martinez inside out, it would have to belong to Rafael (Ralph) Avila of Pembroke Pines, Florida – who also calls Cuba his homeland and the Dominican Republic his adopted country.

Avila, a scout since 1966, signed Pedro's older brother Ramon in 1985 for the Los Angeles Dodgers when the young lad was a mere 16 years of age. Often when Ramon would show up in the Dominican to strut his stuff for Avila and other scouts, a little skinny guy would tag along. They called him Pedro.

"Pedro was only 14 when I signed his brother Ramon," Avila recalled in a spring 2011 telephone interview. "Pedro was always fooling around. He was a very active kid, you know. I signed him when he was 16 too, for $5,500. It was pretty good money in those days. Most organizations were paying $1,500 to sign a player, even in the Dominican Republic."

"I loved Pedro's makeup and intelligence," recalls Avila. "You only had to tell him something once. He would literally do what he was told and more. He wasn't even 5-foot-10: Ramon was 6-foot-3." Avila chuckled, remembering the "many times Pedro would give me a hard time when he came to see his brother work. He was always moving around, a tough guy. The youngster had good stuff, pretty good stuff for someone only 16 years old. Even then, he was throwing 85-86 mph fastballs. He would tell jokes, but would watch a lot: he was very observant."

When asked if Pedro was the best pitcher, period, he ever signed, Avila quickly gave his answer: "No doubt in my mind; of all of the players I signed, I thought Pedro had the most potential and would have the most production because his makeup was better than anybody else I saw. My report on him as a pitcher said he possessed a lot of potential, not because of his stuff but due to his brains and intelligence. That report is now in the Hall of Fame at Cooperstown."

Fast forward to the fall of 1993 when Dodgers GM Fred Claire realized his team was in dire need of a second baseman after incumbent Jody Reed had turned down a generous three-year contract offer.

Claire called his Expos counterpart Dan Duquette to see if Delino DeShields was available for the taking. Names were tossed around as to who would go to the Expos if DeShields was sent west.

"We needed a second baseman," Avila said. "We offered Pedro Astacio, Ramon and all of the pitchers on the 25-man roster."

But, Avila pointed out, Expos manager Felipe Alou, and ultimately Duquette, held out for one guy: Pedro Martinez. And as indicated previously, Claire gave Avila and Dodgers manager Tommy Lasorda veto rights over whether Pedro should be traded or not. Their decision was ultimately based on the status of a left-shoulder (non-throwing arm) injury that Martinez had incurred earlier, caused by one false swing of the bat. That injury had forced the Dodgers' surgeon Dr. Frank Jobe to operate – and raised questions about Pedro's overall toughness and durability.

"My opinion and Tommy's opinion were different. We spent two weeks going back and forth," Avila said. "We couldn't stop the trade. Pedro had a lot of potential. Dr. Jobe was a very honest person. In an article in the *Los Angeles Times*, he accepted responsibility for how the trade turned out. He called Fred Claire and said, 'Hey, it was my fault. I recommended to the general manager that Pedro's left shoulder was a very

Pedro Martinez and Ralph Avila at a sweater presentation ceremony.

Photo - courtesy Ralph Avila family

weak shoulder. People were blaming Tommy Lasorda, blaming Fred Claire but it was my responsibility.'

"We had no choice but to trade him because his shoulder was very fragile for his size. That's part of the business. Better trade him now because later on it might get worse. I didn't want to see us trade Pedro but we needed a second baseman," Avila said. "Delino was one of the good second basemen in those years but he wasn't the same player he was in Montreal after he came to Los Angeles. It's one of the worst trades we ever made. I was against the trade but I felt Fred had no choice."

Does Cooperstown await Pedro's arrival some day, in fulfillment of that report of Avila's on him?

"Pretty good chance," Avila says. "Three Cy Young Awards and he has pitched great in both leagues. He's one of the greatest players produced in the Dominican. He's been a great human being off the field and on the field.

For a kid who grew up in a poor family in Manoguayabo, Dominican Republic, Pedro Jaime Martinez has been a godsend, not just for that country but for baseball in general.

While scout Ralph Avila knew Pedro Martinez very well, so did many others, including Expos catcher Darrin Fletcher, who saw firsthand in the late 1980s and 1990s just how good the youngster was.

After all, Fletcher was a Dodgers prospect as well. He got to know Pedro at spring training in Vero Beach, Florida. Looking back at the trade, Fletcher sort of sniffs at how the Dodgers didn't truly appreciate Pedro's talents and how they were too concerned he might be injury prone.

"People underestimated Pedro," Fletcher said. "He was given an opportunity in Montreal and adapted very well. I never saw him with a sore arm. He was very durable. He fit in great. He had an explosive fast-ball, big sharp curveball, and he had one of the best changeups in the game. He was a top-of-the-line-pitcher, just unstoppable.

"When I was in the Dodgers' organization, I saw Pedro was a good player. I kept it to myself but I saw his potential; that he was a good player, a good worker, a solid prospect. He was a bit more fiery than his brother, had more edge and flair. He had outward intensity and he was more extroverted."

Fletcher's assessment was bang on, perhaps more accurate that even he would have believed.

The Gathering Storm

Gentlemen, we have the only legal monopoly in the country and we're f—king it up.

– Ted Turner

Steve Rogers

Steve Rogers was one of Montreal's most successful pitchers and the only established Expos player who never toiled for another major league team. He was a member of the Major League Baseball Players Association's four-man negotiating committee during the period leading up to and including the strike of 1981. He currently works with the Major League Baseball Players Association.

Chapter Eighteen

Collective Bargaining (Dis)Agreement Strike One

And now the leather-covered sphere came hurtling through the air,
And Casey stood a-watching it in haughty grandeur there.
Close by the sturdy batsman the ball unheeded sped-
"That ain't my style," said Casey. "Strike one," the umpire said.

From "Casey at the Bat" by Ernest Lawrence Thayer

Some thirty years ago, a quirky new scientific concept called "chaos theory" exploded with such authority across the learned community that it found its way into the mainstream as well. In simple terms, the underlying premise of 'chaos theory' holds that within any moving system tiny fluctuations can have tremendous effects over the long range: in everyday parlance this phenomenon became known as the "butterfly effect" – as in the possibility of "a butterfly flapping its wings in Taipei affecting the weather over Montreal." Such illustrations were both odd and funny enough to catch the attention of the non-scientific majority, running the gamut from *The Simpsons* to *Jurassic Park*. It was great fun while it lasted, but once this curiosity outlived its 15 minutes of fame, it quietly returned to the bosom of physics and mathematics where today it continues to be taken seriously.[1]

Perhaps it's a stretch, but in a way "chaos theory" helps explain how one 'tiny fluctuation' in the norm, experienced in 1965, managed to alter the essence of owner/player relations in major league baseball from a patronizing form of benign neglect to a power struggle of such immense proportions that it ultimately ignited the devastating season-ending strike of 1994. That 'tiny fluctuation' was released the moment the floundering Major League Baseball Players Association (MLBPA) engaged the very un-baseball-like Marvin Miller to become its executive director. There is no question but that this single action, innocuous in itself, would alter the relationship between player and owner to the core. Bit by bit, as Miller established his presence, the ground shifted out from under the owners and toward the players, until almost thirty years later, it imploded with enough force to almost destroy the game.

When the dust settled in 1995 and efforts to pick up the pieces were set in motion, baseball had been brought to its knees, left in tatters and stripped of all honour and dignity. In Montreal, the aftermath spelled the beginning of the end.

Until Miller appeared on the scene, players had little or no say in determining their working conditions or pay scales. At the time, the average salary was $19,000, with the minimum barely reaching $6,000. The pension plan offered players but a pittance when they retired. Trapped by the notorious 'reserve clause,' players served owners as modern-day vassals, locked into their clubs until the owners discarded them. The reserve clause, a relic of a nasty past, enabled teams to repeatedly renew a player's contract for one or more years without ever allowing the player to terminate it. The prospect of free agency, an alternative that would grant players the right to negotiate and sign with other teams under certain conditions once their contracts expired, was still far beyond the horizon.[2]

Efforts by players to take a firmer stand, to show a bold face, were met by howls of disbelief from the owners. For the lords of baseball held all the cards – and they knew it: they called the shots.[3] But that was before Marvin Miller.

Often described as a "calm, patient, even-keeled professional who nonetheless got results," Miller had formerly been employed as leading economist and negotiator for the United Steelworkers. Upon entering the dysfunctional wonder-world of baseball contracts, he quickly recognized that his first order of business was to change the mind set of baseball players, to get them "to think like steelworkers – to persuade members of the professional class to learn from members of the working class."[4]

Miller remained in office until 1982: by the time he retired he had transformed the game. During his tenure, baseball adopted sport's first collective bargaining agreement, salary arbitration was introduced and, in 1975, the principle of free agency was solidly launched. The MLBPA had come to be regarded as one of the most powerful unions in the United States. But perhaps most significant of all, during the Miller era, the average salary of players increased from that paltry $19,000 in 1966 to $241,000 in 1982. Baseball had been transformed, as *Sports Illustrated* columnist Ben Reiter wrote, "from a fiefdom into a business in which profits are fairly shared."[5] No longer did it serve as the owners' private sandbox: the focus now was on the players. Not by accident did legendary broadcaster Red Barber declare in 1992: "Marvin Miller, along with Babe

Ruth and Jackie Robinson, is one of the two or three most important men in baseball history."[6]

Miller died November 27, 2012 at age 95. To the shame of everyone associated with the game and who benefitted from his dogged approach to negotiations, he is yet to be enshrined in the National Baseball Hall of Fame in Cooperstown, NY. The fault lies not so much in the stars, but in the community of baseball itself. Its inability to see through petty grievances, combined with a myopic vision of the game, have prevented it from taking full measure of the man.[7] In some ways, it is immaterial, for "what really matters," wrote Reiter in the same *Sports Illustrated* article, is "that his legacy – as the visionary behind a labor system that has resulted in unprecedented prosperity for all parties – was long ago cemented."[8] Everything else is window dressing.

By introducing a trade union approach to collective bargaining, the MLBPA changed the rules of the negotiations game. Perhaps the most direct consequence had to do with work stoppages. During the period 1972–1994, baseball suffered through seven such interruptions, three of which were initiated by the owners. Of these, up until 1994, only one had a major impact on the regular season. That occurred in 1981, when an impasse on appropriate free-agent compensation led to a players' strike and 712 regularly scheduled games were cancelled.[9]

Before Miller took the helm, the division of labour in the game had been starkly one-sided. The owners paid the bills and made the money; the players played the game and drew the glory – for which they received a salary and other benefits. However, compensation was pitiful when compared to today's standards and hardly commensurate with their contributions, both to the game and to the owners' bottom line. What few negotiations between player and owner did occur were mostly ugly and rarely satisfactory. Players were afraid to stand up for what they considered to be their fair due for fear they would be traded, or cut, or held up to ridicule as self-centered heels, ready to sacrifice the team for their own well-being.

Nevertheless, there were a bold few who tried. One of the most highly publicized attempts took place in 1966 when, on the eve of spring training, Los Angeles Dodgers pitchers Don Drysdale and Sandy Koufax declared they would not report to the Vero Beach training camp until they both received a substantial salary increase – they were demanding $100,000 each – and that neither would sign without the other. At the time, the Dodgers were reigning world champions and the two hurlers were perhaps the best in baseball. In 1965, Koufax (his salary was $85,000) had gone 26-8 with an ERA of 2.04 and 382 strikeouts. Drysdale (salary $80,000) was not far behind, with a 23-12 record, a 2.77 ERA and 210 Ks.

According to author John Helyar, author of *Lords of the Realm: The Real History of Baseball*, a thorough and captivating look into baseball's labour relations woes during this period, when the team balked, the two pitchers "hired a Hollywood agent, and shot the moon, demanding a three-year $1-million package deal for the two of them."[10] They eventually settled, Koufax for $125,000 and Drysdale for $110,000. Of greater importance perhaps, their example had "shown colleagues what was possible by exercising a little leverage."[11] Even Dodgers general manager Buzzie Bavasi agreed, telling *Sports Illustrated* in 1967: "I wasn't too successful in the famous Koufax-Drysdale double holdout…I mean, when the smoke had cleared they stood together on the battlefield with $235,000 between them, and I stood there with a blood-stained cashbox…they had a gimmick and it worked."[12]

However, the experience was anything but an epiphany for Bavasi, as he revealed in the following afterthought: "Be sure to stick around for the fun the next time somebody tries that gimmick. I don't care if the whole infield comes in as a package; the next year the whole infield will be wondering what it is doing playing for the Nankai Hawks."[13]

And thus the die was cast. For the next thirty years or so the major league owners' group and the players association would both scramble to increase their bargaining power. At times their constant bickering morphed into full-blown hostility, until invariably, the owners, moved to action by sinking bank accounts, would finally back off. But regardless of who was to blame, across the land this spectacle of owner vs. player slowly became embarrassing, to the point that the public started to lose respect for the game itself. And, as the debacle of 1994 revealed, once lost, that respect was almost impossible to recover.

The players association began flexing its muscles for real toward the end of the 1960s, targeting both the pension scheme and the Topps bubble gum company, manufacturer and sole purveyor of collectible baseball cards. At Miller's urging, players agreed in droves to not sign their bubble gum card contacts, scheduled for renewal, unless the folks at Topps upped the ante. Faced with this dilemma, Topps readily agreed to double the players' yearly stipend, to $250.

In 1968, Miller negotiated the first ever collective bargaining agreement (CBA) with the owners, convincing them to raise the minimum salary from $5,000 to $10,000. When that agreement came up for re-negotiation in 1972, Miller presented an expanded set of demands which he considered to be fair and reasonable. The owners turned them down flat. As Gussie Busch, the volatile proprietor of the St. Louis Cardinals put it: "We voted unanimously to take a stand. We're not going to give them another goddam cent. If they want to strike – let 'em".[14]

So they did, boldly declaring that "as of March 31, 1972, the Major League Baseball Players Association is on strike."[15] For the first time in modern baseball history, players were prepared to withdraw services during the season. Teams were still in spring training, and immediately the players announced they would no longer show up for pre-season games, nor would they be available on Opening Day. The players held firm – they would not return to the diamonds of the nation until an agreement had been reached.

Fortunately, cooler heads prevailed, and by the time the first week of the new season closed without baseball, the owners were looking for a way out of the dilemma. On April 11, they found enough room for agreement and on April 15 the 1972 season officially began. Although players had to forfeit salaries for games missed, the MLBPA managed to secure adoption of the principle of salary arbitration. And an additional $500,000 was added to the pension fund.[16]

But in some ways the victory was a pyrrhic one. Few fans attended the opening games, and those who did were angry at the players, including their current heroes. When the Expos opened in St. Louis, barely 7,000 people showed up, all of them prepared to heckle even the likes of Bob Gibson and Joe Torre, National League MVP in 1971. And, noted Helyar, "It was that way across America."[17]

The bitterness engendered by the 1972 strike carried over into spring training the following year, and with salary arbitration still the sticking point, the owners shut down operations from February 8 to February 25. This meant camps opened late, but the schedule of spring training games was not affected. Ultimately, the parties agreed to a new three-year collective bargaining agreement. Owners added more to the pension fund and increased minimum salaries.[18]

To Helyar, Opening Day 1972 was a turning point in the history of Major League Baseball. "Never again," he would write, would fans ever "view baseball in quite the same light. Neither would the players. For the second time in four years, the Lords (of the Realm) had refused to give them peanuts. Instead, they had ultimately handed their adversaries a great victory. Santa Claus was dead. But then the players didn't need him now; Marvin Miller's union had come of age."[19]

Over the next two decades the players association would see its influence on the game grow in leaps and bounds. Base salaries went up, as did licensing rights and pension funds. In 1974, the union parlayed a dispute between Oakland A's owner Charles Finley and his star pitcher, Jim 'Catfish' Hunter, into the legitimizing of free agency for all players. The infamous reserve clause was thrown into question and the notion of salary arbitration gained traction.[20]

But still, most owners kept looking at the future through the rearview mirror. To Expos president John McHale, this stubborn myopia was just an accident waiting to happen. "It was becoming obvious to some of us that some relaxation of the reserve clause was needed. But ownership refused to do that. They wanted the pleasant, paternal relations with players before Miller came along. They'd been brought up to think of baseball as a privileged business…Somebody was going to do a number on us."[21]

Ironically, little did McHale realize at the time that he was about to become a party to the 'us' factor. Or that when the challenge came it would indeed be centered on the reserve clause, an arcane piece of baseball policy which bound a player to his team forever – or until the team cut him. To the owners, this was the tool that kept the game viable. Without it, they feared players would be free to sign with the highest bidder: weaker teams would be powerless to keep their best players from jumping ship. On the other hand, the times were changing, as MLB attorney John Gaherin told his charges: "Fellas, this is the 20th century. You can't get anybody, drunk or sober, to agree that once a fella goes to work for A&P, he has to work for A&P the rest of his life."[22]

The challenge to the reserve clause came head-on in 1975, with pitcher Andy Messersmith furnishing the test case. That year, Messersmith completed the season without having ever signed a contract: according to the union's interpretation of the Uniform Players Contract, this made him a free agent, and they were ready to fight in support of that principle. To reinforce their case, they turned as well to pitcher Dave McNally of the Expos. He had come to Montreal from Baltimore at the end of 1974, along with outfielder Rich Coggins, in what was without question the worst trade in Expos history. For, in return, the Expos effectively gave up the farm, surrendering outfielder Ken Singleton and pitcher Mike Torrez, both of whom went on to stellar careers in the big leagues. On the other hand, Coggins, who soon developed a thyroid condition that put him out of baseball, was sold to the Yankees after appearing in only 13 games, and McNally quit, playing his last game on June 8, 1975. Not only had he developed a sore arm and was struggling with a 3-6 record, he was so unhappy with the trade and the Expos' offer that he never signed his contract. According to the union's view, this made McNally a free agent, and when Miller invited him to become part of the Messersmith challenge, he agreed.

The owners were, of course, furious. They believed the reserve clause bound a player for life, and feared the chaos that would follow if they lost that right. In late 1975, the matter was finally brought before baseball's arbitrator Peter Seitz. After lengthy, bitter debate, Seitz presented his ruling in a sixty-four page report on December 23. At its crux, it held: "The grievances of McNally and Messersmith are sustained. There is no common bond between these players and the Los Angeles and the Montreal clubs, respectively."[23] In other words, the principle of free agency had been recognized.

According to McHale, this was a disaster, especially for Montreal. "We've got so many negatives in drawing and keeping players here," he told Expos investors.[24]

The immediate consequence of the Seitz decision was for the owners to again shut down spring training activity in March 1976, and appeal the mediator's ruling. But once it was upheld, the owners knew they had run out of options. Commissioner Bowie Kuhn ordered the training facilities opened and instructed that negotiations toward the next collective bargaining agreement begin. In all, the work stoppage had been little more that an inconvenience, lasting from March 1 to March 17.[25]

Except for one thing, and that changed the course of baseball: the dreaded spectre of free agency has now become fact. Ironically, in spite of all their huffing and puffing about the havoc that would result should the reserve clause be eliminated, it took the owners no more than a nanosecond to accommodate this new reality and begin coveting players. Gussie Busch, ever a hardliner within the ownership group, was not impressed. "If anyone does not believe that we had our ass kicked in this labor matter, they are dead wrong," he said. "We have lost the war, and the only question is, can we live with the surrender terms."[26]

First, however, the 1976 season had to be completed. And completed it was, in memorable fashion, by Cincinnati's Big Red Machine. That finely tuned combine ate up the Yankees in four games to take their second consecutive world title in a workman-like victory that was the antithesis of the '75 barn-burner series when the Red Sox stretched the Reds to a seventh-game Cincinnati victory. It is still considered by many the most exciting World Series ever.

As soon as the gates of Yankee Stadium slammed shut for the last time following the Reds' 7–2 triumph, free agency's first feeding frenzy exploded on the scene, changing forever the very fabric of the game. As

Cincinnati general manager Bob Howsam ruefully acknowledged, even his 1976 squad, which he regarded as his greatest triumph in baseball and "the last of the great teams," could not survive intact: as soon as the free agent market opened for business he knew his empire would crumble.[27]

The first free agent 'mart' took place in New York's Plaza Hotel in November, with what folks called a 're-entry draft.' Picking in reverse order of their club's final position in the standings, owners were invited to 'draft' a maximum of twelve free agents apiece – of which they would be permitted to sign a maximum of two. Any thoughts that the owners might get together and refuse to make even a single bid were quickly diffused when the Expos' Charles Bronfman, picking first, announced, "The Montreal Expos are proud to draft Reggie Jackson." So, too, as it turned out, was an equally proud George Steinbrenner of the Yankees. The deluge had begun.[28]

In the end, Jackson signed with New York, despite Bronfman's best efforts to reel him in, including a lavish dinner in Montreal at the owner's Westmount mansion and an offer of nearly $5-million over five years. It was not enough, even though Steinbrenner's best offer fell about $2-million short – but came with a $63,000 Rolls-Royce thrown in. "He hustled me like a broad," said Jackson.[29]

Life in the country of baseball was about to enter a "we're not in Kansas anymore," moment, one dramatic enough to prompt Jackson to fantasize: "Do you think there will ever be a million-dollar player?"[30] Indeed!

By the end of the '70s, free agency had become fact, but that did not make the pill any less bitter for the owners to swallow. In public, they insisted that their primary concern was to ensure a competitive balance was maintained in both leagues. They contended this could best be achieved, given the new realities, through some sort of fair and equitable free-agent arrangement in which teams losing a player would be adequately compensated by the player's new owners. Otherwise, the top talent would inevitably migrate to the wealthiest clubs, while the lesser ones would have to settle for the cast-offs.

However, the owners' true concerns lay elsewhere. While they were alarmed by the rapid increase in player salaries – the average salary almost tripled between 1976 and 1980 – they were most distraught over their loss of control. Donald Fehr, later to head up the MLBPA, noted that the owners considered "it was an affront for a player to declare free agency."[31] The union was adamant, of course. As Marvin Miller told

Commissioner Bowie Kuhn, "[the owners] will get compensation over my dead body."[32] And thus were the battle lines drawn.

Negotiations on the next CBA were already well underway in 1980 by the time the owners introduced their free-agent compensation plan. But the players weren't buying. Bargaining broke down, and the MLBPA launched an abbreviated work stoppage at the very end of spring training. No baseball was played during the week of April 1–April 8. However, although these last games of the pre-season were washed out, the sides did manage to come to a common understanding on most issues, sufficient to reach a four-year agreement in time for Opening Day. Doing so, however, required a dangerous bit of legerdemain: the parties deferred the contentious free-agent compensation issue to the following year.[33] When it did then return to the bargaining table 12 months later, both sides were loaded for bear.

That hard-line attitude led to the 1981 mid-season strike, the first significant work stoppage in the history of baseball, the first to erase a major portion of the schedule. Clearly, the owners were out to wage war against Miller and the union. They advanced a free-agent compensation protocol so one-sided, so restrictive, that had it come into force it is doubtful any owner would have dared to sign any free agent. And then they belligerently hunkered down, prepared to defend their position to the very end.

Nevertheless, in the early months, all was smooth sailing. Spring training proceeded without disturbance and the regular season began as scheduled, even though the players had made clear they wanted no part of the owners' dodgy offer. Years later, the Pirates' Phil Garner, one of four members on the players negotiating committee, spoke about their position. "Free agency was a right," he said. "We had it. We'd fought to get it. We'd fight to keep it. They could not win that fight."[34]

As if to establish that point, the players declared that unless the issue was settled to their satisfaction by May 29, they would walk. True to their word, and allowing for a grace period, they waited until June 12 before shutting everything down.

Throughout most of the strike period the union's chief representative was lawyer Donald Fehr, backed up by the players' four-man negotiating committee, one of whom was Expos ace Steve Rogers. Rogers had been active in the union from the beginning, taking over as National League pension representative in 1976. His "calm, analytical voice in the committee's caucuses" made him a natural for the role.[35]

The strike lasted 50 days, from June 12 to July 31, and resulted in the cancellation of 712 games. It ended because the owners, tired of losing money, announced they were ready to settle. An agreement, one which returned very little to the owners, was hammered out between Miller, who assumed the leadership role at the end, and Lee MacPhail, representing the owners. Clubs lost the right to demand direct compensation for players who took their free agency to other organizations, although they did gain the authority to hold onto players for six years.

And so once more, ballparks prepared to open their gates and cries of 'Play Ball' were soon heard across the land. Because so many games had been lost to the work stoppage, MLB +decided that to rekindle fan interest, the schedule would be jiggered to create a split-season model. This meant that in each league the winners of the first half, i.e. those games completed before the strike, would play the winners of the second half, i.e. those games completed after the strike, to determine the division champion, much like today's Division Series. The division winners would then meet in the league Championship Series, with the victor heading to the World Series.[36] This arrangement was generally dismissed as bogus, making a mockery of the game; *Time* magazine called it "confusing and laughable."[37]

By the time the second-half season began, several things became obvious. For starters, the owners' hegemony over the players clearly lost most of its oomph as their attempts to regain control had failed. Instead of breaking the union, they had inadvertently strengthened it. Free agency was a reality. That battle had been won. And with it, the balance of power started shifting noticeably from owners to players.

Sadly, in the process, the two sides developed a genuine dislike for one another. Collectively, they had poisoned the well, giving rise to a bitterness that would carry over through every negotiation period, right up to the impasse that was 1994. According to Donald Fehr, "The (1981) strike left such a foul taste with me, it permanently colored the way I viewed people and their motives. It left significant scars that were there five years later."[38]

To some, especially in these parts, the 1981 strike represents the moment baseball lost its innocence. Romantic notions of the game as a bucolic pastoral endeavour, what the scholarly Jacques Barzun once characterized as the key to the American heart, took a pretty severe kick in the teeth. To A. Bartlett Giamatti, in a *New York Times* article published when he was president of Yale University and before he became commissioner of Major League Baseball, the strike was utter foolishness. He called it "an example of deny-side economics, which says you withhold from the consumer what he most desires so that you may substitute discipline for satisfaction." He urged both parties to "resume your dignity and remember that you are the temporary custodians of an enduring public trust."[39]

To Marvin Miller, this kind of talk was poppycock, and he was having none of it. He reminded the man from Yale that what he was calling a 'squalid little squabble' concerned an issue vital in the players' professional lives.[40] Miller never forgave Giamatti for this slight.

And yet, the second half of the 1981 season did get underway, first with the All-Star Game on August 9 in Cleveland, and then with regular league play, which resumed the next day. When the schedule wrapped up two months later, the Phillies and Dodgers emerged as the National League first-half winners and the Astros and the Expos as the second-half winners. All four teams were going to the postseason, the only time in their history the Expos ever made it that far.

The details of the 1981 playoffs are now legend in Montreal. Led by Steve Rogers' arm and bat, the Expos overcame the Phillies and their ace Steve Carlton, three games to two, and prepared to meet the Dodgers. After the teams split the first four matches, it all came down to the rubber match, the fifth game, in Montreal's Olympic Stadium. The World Series awaited the winner.

The facts are carved into the soul of Expos supporters everywhere. The score was tied 1-1 with two out in the ninth inning when Dodgers right-fielder Rick Monday homered to win it all for his team. The Dodgers then went on to defeat the Yankees and capture the World Series in six games.

Baseball in Montreal was never quite the same again. At least, not until the summer of 1994.

Chapter Nineteen

Collective Bargaining (Dis)Agreement Strike Two

With a smile of Christian charity great Casey's visage shone;
He stilled the rising tumult; he bade the game go on;
He signaled to the pitcher, and once more the spheroid flew;
But Casey still ignored it, and the umpire said, "Strike two

From *"Casey at the Bat"* by Ernest Lawrence Thayer

The legendary South African golfer Bobby Locke once famously claimed: "You drive for show but putt for dough." A similar parallel can be found within the twin towers of baseball negotiations – free agency and arbitration. While free agency commands the headlines, salary arbitration is the beast that drains the well.

Axiomatic or not, in the bitter battle of wills that effectively shredded the 1981 season, all the attention was focused on the perceived menace of free agency and the damage it would wreak – to the bottom-line, to the game, to the players – and to the very essence of what was still considered the National Pastime. However, the devil in those details, the bargaining equivalent of the six-inch putt, was, of course, salary arbitration. As John Helyar observed, the owners "had fought the wrong war. Obsessed with getting free-agent compensation, they didn't see the real enemy: salary arbitration."[41]

Baseball's system of salary arbitration, in place since 1974, is intended to soften the negotiations gap for players with fewer than six years of service and who are thus not eligible to file for free agency. The particular system employed – called 'final offer arbitration," sometimes referred to as "baseball arbitration" given its notoriety – is used in situations where younger players and their teams are unable to come to terms. A very straightforward process that kicks in around mid-January, arbitration requires each side to propose a salary figure, with accompanying rationale. In February, a single arbitrator, selected from a list of professionals agreed to by both the players union and the owners, hears each case. If, at the end of the hearing, the issue remains stalemated, the arbitrator is obliged to select either the player's proposed figure or the number specified by the club. It is one or the other – there is no room for negotiation, no room for appeal.[42]

No matter which option gets selected, however, the very process has led to a dramatic increase in players' salaries. "Indeed, the perception is that even when a player loses in arbitration, he wins, as in all cases the award has been higher than what the player received previously." Murray Clemens, a Canadian legal authority who writes on the subject, cites Whitey Herzog from his days as general manager of the California Angels: "Arbitration is the strongest vehicle the players have and the worst thing that happened to owners. When baseball owners gave players the right to arbitration, they sold out the house."[43] The A's Mike Morris put it succinctly: "I was either going to wake up rich…or richer."[44]

It is no wonder then that the owners devoted the next decade trying to get it back.

Left in the hands of the wrong people, i.e., unprepared owners or rapacious agents, final-offer arbitration can be a high-stakes venture that risks leaving a bitter and lasting effect. Helyar gives the example of Tony Bernazard, an original Expo who was traded to the White Sox after two years in Montreal. Bernazard suffered such damaging criticism during the arbitration ordeal in his days with Chicago that "he wouldn't speak to White Sox VP Jack Gould for years afterwards."[45]

While some clubs such as the Milwaukee Brewers tried to avoid arbitration at all costs, figuring that compromise was better than confrontation in the long run, others, notably the Expos, seemed ready to leap at every opportunity. In explaining the Brewers' cautious approach, general manager Harry Dalton said:

Tony Bernazard

"I think the club and the player are best suited to know what contribution or lack of contribution has been made, and they should work it out."[46] In contrast, the trigger-happy Expos turned to arbitration four times in 1985 alone, even though their only victory was to hold part-time catcher Bobby Ramos to $115,000, down from the $150,000 he was seeking. They then released him before the season began, signalling the end of his playing career.

Edward Bennett Williams, owner of the Baltimore Orioles (1980–1988), called the arbitration process crazy. "You spend all this time building up a kid," he said, and "then use this process to tear him down."[47] Tim Raines understood all too well what Williams was talking about when his 1985 negotiations with the Expos collapsed and ended up before an arbitrator. At issue was the biggest offer in arbitration history, and the organization and Raines were both represented by heavyweights. Bill

Stoneman, Expos vice president, spoke for the club. As reported in *Sports Illustrated*, this exchange, which lasted almost five hours and involved more than 100 pages of exhibits and well over 1,000 hours of research, illustrated the conundrum that final-offer arbitration presented.[48]

Management approached the issue by seeking to demonstrate that as good as Raines might be, his offensive numbers paled against the likes of Wade Boggs. Speaking for the club, Tal Smith, a baseball consultant who served as an agent of sorts for many of the owners, highlighted an undeclared but terrifying fear that haunted the owners. "The salary decided upon today," he said, "will serve as a base for Mr. Raines's subsequent salaries. One million

Tim Raines

dollars is more than ample recognition. Anything more would be frankly premature."[49] In the end, Raines got the $1.2 million he demanded, making him baseball's 36th million-dollar-a-year-man. But, more significantly, this decision planted the seeds for another dispute with the club in 1986. But by then, the issues had taken on a very different hue. And so it went.

Projected onto a larger screen, owners believed, and players and agents could not disagree, that even if a player shot high and lost, he was still ahead of the game. It was what one agent called a brilliant system. "You don't have to win them all, or even most of them. As long as there are a few settlements or decisions that are high, the players can peg off that. The whole structure goes up."[50]

And go up it did: between 1980 and 1984 the average salary more than doubled. "The [owners] had been crying poverty before the 1981 strike, but now, some teams were really experiencing it," Helyar wrote.[51] Increasingly, the owners lost confidence in Commissioner Bowie Kuhn, sensing that he had fallen out of touch with the new realities of the baseball business, and that it was probably time he stepped down. "The economics of the game were in bad shape and Bowie wouldn't do anything to help," Charles Bronfman said at the time. "As salaries started to escalate, you had to improve the revenue streams."[52]

Throughout the early 1980s, salaries continued to rise and owners became increasingly concerned – both with the economic impact on their businesses and the reckless spending proclivities of some of their partners. Commissioner Kuhn, anticipating the conflicts that lay ahead, chose this moment to step down, passing the baton to a man of a very different personality who would stir up the owners as never before. His name was Peter Ueberroth. He was fresh off a great triumph as the organizer of the 1984 Los Angeles Summer Olympics. The games had been a surprising success, financially and otherwise: in recognition of his Olympian achievement *Time* magazine named him its 1984 Man of the Year.[53]

No sooner had Ueberroth moved into his commissioner's digs than the next round of collective bargaining began. Once more the tone was fractious and the mood hostile. This time, though, the stickiest issue of them all concerned the pension fund. The players sought $60 million; the owners were offering $15 million. As negotiations spilled over into 1985 without resolution the players declared their readiness to strike, and set a deadline of August 6. When the day arrived with no settlement, the players walked. Ueberroth, not about to allow anything of this sort on his watch, demanded both sides settle, and fast. Remarkably, his posturing had an effect. An agreement was reached the next day. It called for: "three years for arbitration, no cap on arbitration increases, and $33 million for the pension."[54] The minimum salary went up from $40,000 to $60,000.[55] By August 8, everybody was back in business. And a new "bad" word was about to enter the baseball lexicon. It was called collusion.

Although the owners had signed the 1985 collective bargaining agreement, they were unhappy with its provisions and desperate to find new ways of reining in their budgets. Ueberroth laid the blame for rising costs right in their own backyards. He was uncompromising: "...if you are so dumb that you are paying all kinds of money to players that aren't playing and don't have money to pay players that are playing ... it's your fault," he told the owners. "Let's try to operate in a businesslike way before we, as a sport, are bankrupt." This time they were ready to listen. Ueberroth believed that the teams' salvation lay not so much in the nuts and bolts of agreements as within the clubs themselves. They just had to learn to work together.[56]

In Ueberroth's eyes the problem lay with free-agent signings and the maniacal impulses that were driving owners in their efforts to get a jump on the competition. Bringing that part of the game under control, he intimated, would go a long way toward resolving their problems. "Spend big if you want to" he said, "but don't go out there whining that someone made you do it."[57] He added: "You all agree we have a problem. Go solve it."[58] And so they did – by shutting down the marketplace. They tightened up their salary arbitration offers and turned their backs on free agents. Suddenly the rich opportunities of the recent past were drying up.

The owners called it "fiscal responsibility" and, mindful that the CBA prohibited them from "acting in concert," insisted they were acting on their own. The union called it collusion, a charge Ueberroth rejected. "I don't think the owners are capable of colluding," he said. "They couldn't agree on what to have for breakfast."[59]

Nevertheless, Donald Fehr, since 1983 the executive director of the players association, filed a grievance, charging collusion in the 1985-86 free-agent market. Baseball's arbitrator, Tom Roberts, launched hearings on the 1985 season but did not issue his ruling until September 1987. A second grievance pertaining to collusion charges for the 1986 season was heard separately. Meanwhile, collusion, by whatever name, continued unabated.[60]

When Fehr was asked how one could force clubs to engage free agents, he indicated that if what he called the "restraints" were removed, surely some clubs would want to improve themselves and sign players. If this were not to happen, he told the *New York Times*, "courts have the authority to enforce arbitration awards. But I hope that won't be necessary."[61]

Arbitrator Roberts's conclusions were unequivocal. As reported in the *New York Times*, he noted that not one club had pursued free agents unless their 1985 clubs had already relinquished interest in them. "This," he concluded in his 16-page report, "in itself, constitutes a strong indication of concerted action," and was, consequently, in violation of their agreement with the players. Roberts added that never in the history of free agency had one experienced "the sudden and abrupt termination of all efforts to secure the services of free agents from other clubs." Even though "they surely had a value at some price…yet no offers were advanced," underlining the word "no."[62]

Among free agents affected by the Roberts ruling were high-profile names such as Kirk Gibson, Donnie Moore, Carlton Fisk, Butch Wynegar, and both Phil and Joe Niekro. In fairness, however, it should be pointed out that both Gibson and Moore were, nonetheless, handsomely rewarded by their respective clubs (Detroit and California).

Colouring the atmosphere between the owners and the players association was the frightening spectre of recreational drug abuse, specifically cocaine, and the damage it was doing to the game. Montreal's premier sports-radio host, Mitch Melnick, reflecting on this period 30 years later, opined that the failure of the great Expos teams of the late 1970s and early 1980s to reach the pinnacle can be traced directly to this problem. The saga of Ellis Valentine and his drug-shortened career is well known, as is Tim Raines's successful battle to overcome a cocaine addiction, but not before he had damaged his reputation and hurt his team. "Just look at Raines's numbers and how they dropped after his great rookie year," Melnick pointed out on one radio broadcast years later. "It's all there."[63]

In this regard, the Expos were not alone. Indeed, the Pirates went so far as to sue Dave Parker "for failure to perform up to his ability because of drug use," while three Kansas City players actually went to jail on drug charges.[64] Ueberroth, commended for his anti-drugs stance at the Olympics, was quick to don his Sherriff's star and six-guns once again. "It is imperative that we rid baseball of drug use," he said. He followed up his words by introducing mandatory drug testing of players four times per year.[65] The union, claiming that drug policy was part of the collective bargaining agreement, launched a grievance, which they won. The owners, of course, were aghast –

Ellis Valentine

and the divide between the two parties grew that much greater.

The class of 1986 free agency–eligible players included the likes of headliners Jack Morris, Lance Parrish and Willie Randolph, along with two perennial all-stars from the Expos, Raines and Andre Dawson. All encountered the same ownership reluctance to act as demonstrated in 1985.[66]

The cases of both Raines and Dawson merit comment if for no other reason than at a local and visceral level they served as harbingers of what was to come. In 1986, Raines, fully recovered from his descent into drug abuse, led the National League in both batting average and on-base percentage. He was also eligible to become a free agent. When he met with

Expos brass to explore his options, Raines was advised by team president John McHale to move cautiously. Nevertheless, Raines chose to opt for free agency, and when he and the club could not come to terms by the January 1987 deadline, he began looking elsewhere.

At that time, the rules governing free agency were very specific. If the player and his current club were not able to reach agreement through arbitration or otherwise by January 8, the player was then prohibited from returning to that team until May 1. Free agency was a risky affair, especially given the climate of the times, and Raines was one of the few to take the chance. He felt justified: he just happened to be the reigning National League batting champion. Surely he could do better than the Expos' three-year $4.8 million offer – barely $100,000 per year more than his current salary. Raines was not pleased. "I was coming off the best year of my career," he later remarked, "and I just wasn't going to cave in."[67] By holding out, Raines joined a group of seven other players – folks called them the "January Eight" – prepared to venture "beyond the signing deadline and into the teeth of collusion."[68]

Raines, along with his agent Tom Reich, did meet with three clubs, all of which declined to make an offer. As his options ran dry, Raines began training with a high school team in preparation for his May return to Montreal. When in late April the club presented a slightly improved three-year deal, Raines signed. Finally, on Saturday May 2, he was back in the lineup and on the field, facing the Mets in a nationally televised day game from Shea Stadium. The Expos, suffering a three-game slump and desperate to salvage something from this trip to the Big Apple, were hoping Raines's presence might turn their fortunes around. The game was a 10-inning affair, and all Raines managed to do was go 4-for-5, including a triple and a stolen base that led to a run.

His fourth and last hit, however, was the most important one. With the score tied 6-6, the result of two Montreal runs in the ninth, the Expos loaded the bases in the 10th inning with none out, setting the table for Raines. It was one of those days when the storybook ending did occur – Raines hit a grand slam home run and gave Montreal the badly needed win. It was a blow that continued to resonate for years afterward, a salute to the mettle of the man, his "screw you" moment. And just to put a bit of mustard on the occasion, in the Sunday matinee that followed, he homered in his first plate appearance, accounting for the winning run in a 2-0 victory.[69]

Raines remained with the Expos through the 1990 season when he was traded to the Chicago White Sox. He spent another 12 years in the big leagues before retiring and these days is touted as a future Hall of Fame inductee at Cooperstown. In 2013 he was enshrined into the Canadian

Baseball Hall of Fame. As an aside, the Expos ended the 1987 season with 91 wins against 71 losses, one of the best records in team history. However, they finished third, four games behind first-place St. Louis. The Cardinals advanced to the World Series, losing to the Twins in seven games. One has to wonder, had Raines not been forced to sit out all of April, would his presence have been enough to carry Montreal into the postseason.

The other high-profile Expo who became a free agent following the 1986 season was Raines's close friend, Andre Dawson. An outstanding outfielder, Dawson was named to baseball's Hall of Fame in 2010, joining catcher Gary Carter as the only original Expos players currently installed at Cooperstown.

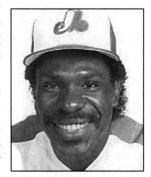

Andre Dawson

When Dawson filed for free agency, his Expos salary was $1.27 million. This time around, the club was offering an even $1 million for each of the two following years, an offer his agent Dick Moss called insulting. Highly combative by nature, Moss was never one to settle for less than top dollar. He had made that very clear in late 1981 when he wrestled a new deal for Gary Carter from Expos owner Charles Bronfman, securing an almost unheard-of $13.1 million spread across seven years.

This amount left the club "thirty to forty percent over where we wanted to be,"[70] according to Expos president John McHale, more than the team could afford. Four years later, Montreal traded Carter to the Mets, receiving Hubie Brooks, Mike Fitzgerald, Herm Winningham, and Floyd Youmans in return. Owner Bronfman later called the Carter signing the biggest mistake of his baseball life, and cited it as one of the principal reasons he decided to sell the team in 1989. According to Mitch Melnick of TSN 690 radio in Montreal, Bronfman "simply did not enjoy turning ballplayers into millionaires."[71]

Given this climate and mindset, the Andre Dawson negotiations went toxic very quickly. "Bronfman seemed to enjoy telling [Moss] the new ways of the world, and explaining how those ways would affect the size of his offer to Andre Dawson," wrote John Helyar. Unmoved, Moss insisted that the Expos owed the prize outfielder greater consideration. "He owns more of the Expos' records than anybody," Moss pointed out. "Given everything that's happened...*don't f*ck with Andre Dawson* (sic.)"[72]

Moss then set out to do precisely that to the owners. When Dawson elected to walk away from an Expos offer of $2.4 million for two years by letting the January 8 deadline pass, what Helyar called the "Dick Moss guerrilla method of free-agent marketing"[73] kicked into gear. Dawson set his sights on the Chicago Cubs and the friendly outfield grass of Wrigley Field. Cubs general manager Dallas Green was interested, even though he was under strict orders not to sign any high-priced players. So the wily Moss took a different approach. He left a blank contract with Dawson's name on it in Green's office and invited the GM to fill in any number he wanted. Aware that Moss was infamous for his gamesmanship and doubting that the agent's ploy was on the up-and-up, Green wrote in a low-ball figure of $500,000 plus another $200,000 in performance bonuses, half of what Dawson had earned with Montreal the previous year.[74]

To the surprise of everyone, Dawson (and Moss) said okay. All of a sudden, the quiet Andre was a Cubby, beginning what would become a beautiful friendship. He was outstanding that first year – leading the National League in both home runs and runs batted in. He was named league MVP, even though his club finished in last place, 18.5 games behind the first-place Cardinals. Dawson remained with the Cubs for six seasons before moving on to the Red Sox and a klatch of other clubs, retiring in 1996. It would be 14 years before he made his way to Cooperstown. Like Gary Carter, Dawson was exceptionally gracious toward Montreal in his induction address.

And then there was the strange case of Expos pitcher Bryn Smith. Montreal elected not to renew his contract, making him a free agent. With no serious offer coming his way, he had little choice but to resign with Montreal. His new contract was $250,000 less than he had earned in 1986.[75] Smith remained with the club through 1989, putting in the innings, winning 32 games against 30 losses, and keeping his ERA respectable. In those three years, never did his salary come close to the level he had reached in 1986.[76]

By the end of 1988, the spectre of collusion had pretty well faded from view. The MLBPA 1987 appeal against the owners had also declared the owners guilty of colluding with each other – and so that game was up. From start to finish it had been a monumental debacle, punctuated with comic relief worthy of The Three Stooges. Because the different arbitrators' collusion rulings freed up 21 players to return to the marketplace, owners began stumbling all over each other once again in their anxious desire to sign them – to free-agent contracts.

At another, darker level, however, the public relations hit suffered by the owners in their costly and embarrassing take-no-prisoners plunge into the shady world of collusion left scars that have still not healed. It also spelled the end for Commissioner Ueberroth himself. When his five-year term of office ended in 1989, he chose not to stand for renewal.

Peter Ueberroth's replacement was A. Bartlett Giamatti, a former president of Yale and at the time president of the National League. Although he was a literary scholar and master of the written word, Giamatti's first love – his passion – was baseball. In fact, when he had been appointed president of Yale he reportedly said, "All I ever wanted to be president of…was the American League."[77]

That dream of a presidency of major league baseball did come true, sort of, when, in 1986, he was asked to head the National League. Of course, he said yes. And with gusto. Never at a loss for words, Giamatti added, "I'm almost fifty years old and I've just fallen in love and run away with a beautiful redhead with flashing eyes whose name is baseball."[78]

Not all those connected with the game applauded his appointment, starting with Marvin Miller. Giamatti had earned Miller's everlasting enmity during the 1981 strike when, still holding down the top spot at Yale, he penned that scathing *New York Times* op-ed piece condemning the work stoppage. Writing with all the flourish and delight one might expect from an English professor, he castigated both sides in the dispute. His words resonated far beyond the diamond, and ring true even today, especially given the way professional sports have apparently abandoned the interests of their fans with their incessant billionaires vs. millionaires disputes. Giamatti wrote:

> *Call it a symptom of the plague of distrust and divisiveness that afflicts our land, call it the triumph of greed over the spirit of the garden. Call it what you will, the strike is utter foolishness… O, Sovereign Owners and Princely Players, masters of amortization, tax shelters, bonuses and deferred compensation, go back to work. You have been entrusted with the serious work of play, and your season of responsibility has come. Be at it. There is no general sympathy for either of your sides. Nor will there be.*[79]

An apoplectic Miller responded to Giamatti, in kind, letting it be known that he thought the Yale man's screed "was anti-union and that he didn't sound much different than an uninformed, bigoted fan."[80]

Giamatti was named Commissioner of Baseball on April 1, 1989. And then, tragically, on September 1, only 154 days into his mandate, he died, struck down by a massive heart attack at the age of 51. Giamatti's untimely death cut short his efforts, and those of others, to restore some vestiges of the pride and honour that had been so callously stripped from the game. One can only wonder at what might have been.

Giamatti's successor was his friend and colleague, Fay Vincent. Unfortunately, Vincent was no Giamatti, and all too quickly the already difficult relationships between players and owners, and between owners and the commissioner, deteriorated further, leading the newest round of contract negotiations in 1990 to break down yet again.

Chagrined by the way the collusion fright-show had played out, and alarmed by ever-climbing salaries, the owners – even though they were the ones electing to pay the money – grew ever more determined to dismember the union, even if this meant another lockout. They began insisting on a salary cap. Then they sought to limit the impact of salary arbitration through the introduction of a statistical formula that could measure performance.[81] The union, however, was having none of it.

At this same time, in the bi-polar world of baseball ownership, the bosses were also busily casting aside self-imposed restraints on free-agent hiring, setting off an orgy of new signings. Once again, salaries rose dramatically. Where the upper limits had remained around the $2 million figure throughout the collusion years, in late 1989 they soared above $3 million.

It became a circus, and it left Expos owner Charles Bronfman outraged. "People are being financially irresponsible," he said at the time. "The big clubs in the big markets can afford what they are doing. We can't afford to compete from a dollars standpoint."[82]

He was reacting, at least in part, to the negative impact that free-agent signings were having on his own club. For, included among those benefitting from this newfound largesse were pitchers Mark Langston and Pascual Perez, both of whom had abandoned ship for the balmy shores of some-other-place.

In 1989, Langston, a gifted southpaw, was in the final year of his contract with the Seattle Mariners and about to become a free agent. Seeking to salvage some return for him before the season ended, the club shopped him around, hoping that an organization with pennant-contending ambitions might take the chance on him. All they sought in return was three untested youngsters.

The Expos were the first to bite. Right from the earliest days of 1989 they believed they were in a position to go all the way. Adding a talent like Langston to the rotation might well be enough to take them to the top. They understood that keeping him beyond the season would be problematic, but perhaps it was worth the gamble. After all, in exchange, the Expos only had to send back "three young [inexpensive] pitchers."[83]

136

"Sure, it was a gamble," Expos vice president David Dombrowski admitted as the season ended, "but if you don't gamble when you've got a chance to finish first, when do you gamble? Obviously, we'll make every effort to sign Mark, but if he leaves Montreal, I can assure you it will have nothing to do with financial considerations."[84]

Mark Langston

As it turned out, the Langston deal was among the most unfortunate personnel moves ever made by the Expos. To begin with, although the pitcher started strong, in the end he was a disappointment, especially when Montreal still held a slim lead in the division and every game counted. Instead of rising to the occasion, first Langston and then the club folded, plummeting from first to fourth place and dropping to the .500 level.

Before arriving in Montreal on May 25, Langston's '89 Seattle pitching statistics were a modest 4-5, 3.50 ERA. Once he landed in the Expos' camp, however, he was strong in the early going. By August 11, his record stood at 10-3 and with the Expos sitting on a 64-51 record, the team remained very much in the chase. One month later, he had dropped to 10-6. He finished at 12-8.[85] Of his last seven decisions he won only two.

Following the season, Langston was the most coveted of all free agents still unsigned. Up until December 1 that is. Then, with barely a glance back at Montreal, he inked a five-year, $16-million contract with the California Angels. It was, at the time, the largest guaranteed sum ever offered in the history of the game. When asked to comment, a downcast Claude Brochu, in his new role as club president replacing Charles Bronfman, replied, "As a club, we're still in a state of shock. It's really quite incredible. And I guess a little scary," adding, "I don't know what the impact is going to be."[86]

Langston remained with the Angels for seven years, winning 86 games and losing 70. His only postseason appearances, with the San Diego Padres at the end of his career, were brief, and in relief.

For the Expos, the echoes would bounce back forever and not in a positive fashion. What a difference those "three young inexpensive pitchers," all of whom had been drafted by Montreal, could have made to the team's fortunes. Of the trio, the best known at the time was Brian Holman:

he had appeared in 28 games as an Expo in 1988-89 before the trade. He lasted another three years with the Mariners. Gene Harris had also appeared briefly with the Expos before heading west: he went on to put in seven years as a big leaguer, mostly with Seattle. The third pitcher was

something else again. A tall, gangly leftie with terrifying speed but little control when in Montreal, he soon became one of the most effective hurlers of his generation. Observers agree he will be a sure-fire first-ballot Hall of Famer as soon as he becomes eligible in 2015. Teammates called him "The Big Unit." In the record books, he appears as Randy Johnson.

Johnson's major league career lasted 22 years. He won almost twice as many games as he lost, 303-166. He appeared in the postseason on eight occasions and in one World Series, the 2001, post 9/11 classic that pitted the New York

Randy Johnson

Yankees against his Arizona Diamondbacks. He was the pitcher of record for three of his club's four victories, including both games six and seven. For the Expos, the overpowering Johnson was definitely the big one that got away.

If the Expos' reaction to Mark Langston's departure had been mixed – part shock-and-awe and part good riddance – they were more even-keeled about losing Pascual Perez. Perez was a flake, a troubled prisoner to drugs through much of his career, until he found redemption, and some glory, in Montreal. Folks called him "I-285" because when with the Atlanta Braves at the start of his career, and shortly after he obtained his driver's license, he got lost on Atlanta's Interstate 285, a beltway circling the city, and missed a scheduled start against, ironically, the Expos.[87] Nevertheless, the right-hander did enjoy success in Atlanta before blowing out his career in 1985 with a 1-13 record. He was released the following year and missed all of that season before Montreal signed him in early 1987 as another of their (mostly) successful reclamation projects.

With the Expos, he enjoyed reasonable success over his three years and became a fan favourite. He is remembered for the way he would hop around the mound "as if he has a pesky mosquito in his uniform pants," and pitching with flare, mixing 90 m.p.h. fastballs with his low velocity eephus pitch, a rainbow of a thing that arced so high and was so slow in coming to the plate batters almost had time to sign autographs before they swung, and missed. So it was with some regret that the club said good-bye when Perez signed as a free agent with the Yankees in November 1989 for almost $1.5 million, almost double what the Expos were paying him. That sum was increased by close to $1 million the following year. In return Perez put together a two-year won-lost record of 3-6. Apparently the attractions of the Big Apple's wild side were more than he could resist. In 1992, he failed a drug test and was suspended for a year. That was the end of his career.

Perez died in November 2012 at his home in the Dominican Republic, the apparent victim of a home invasion. It seems there were several assailants who ransacked the house in what seemed to be a search for money. His passing was widely noted.

Then there was the case of Bryn Smith, who became a free agent once again following the 1989 campaign. After re-signing in 1986, he had played three more years with the Expos. The team was hoping to keep him, but not at the price the St. Louis Cardinals were prepared to pay – $6 million over three years, the second highest salary in team history. Even Smith was surprised. "I'm still kind of stunned by the whole thing," he said at the time.

Bryn Smith

Expos president Claude Brochu explained candidly why the club chose not to pursue Smith. "Bryn's a good average pitcher," he said. "That's what he is – a .500 pitcher. If you triple his salary, it's not suddenly going to make him a 20-game winner."[88] For the record, Smith was reasonably successful in St. Louis, posting a record of 25-19 over the three years he was there.

Brochu was troubled by the recklessness of clubs keen to land a free agent. "What we have right now is a market that's out of control," he said. "Rather than make a mistake or do something that's not going to help us, we're going to wait and see what develops." Donald Fehr, however, disagreed. To him, the thaw in free-agent signings was "welcome news and one of the things we have been waiting for: returning to contracting patterns of past years." Player agent Arn Tellum, who represented Mark Langston, took it a step further: "Who knows, if there wasn't collusion, how high the salaries would be now." He added, "I still believe that there's an effect on this market, that players are being damaged by prior years' collusion."[89]

Two divergent points of view. And for those who might have thought that the worst was over, they were reminded that the existing collective agreement was scheduled to expire on December 31, 1989. There was trouble ahead.

Preliminary discussions in 1989 between owners and the MLBPA had done little to clear the air. The former were committed to the performance-centered amendment they intended to introduce into the current arbitration process. And they were equally insistent on the absolute need for a salary cap. Their version called for players receiving a percentage of gross revenues, what they called "revenue participation."

But they couldn't fool the old-time union faithful. As Marvin Miller repeated time and time again, "no mechanism that limited a player's earning power was acceptable."[90] When Donald Fehr asked pointedly, "in the aggregate, does this produce higher, lower or about the same pay?" ...and the owners answered, "We don't know," he knew they were looking to the players to fix their problem. They were saying, "We want you to agree to this and we will spend ourselves into oblivion if you don't."[91]

Still, even though neither party was keen to live through another period of protracted labour squabbles, both were hard-pressed to see any way of carving out an acceptable agreement before the start of the 1990 season. The more bellicose among the owners saw this probable impasse as the opening they were looking for. On February 15, in an attempt to display resoluteness of purpose, they shut down spring training and locked out the players yet again.

This time both sides had trouble keeping their membership in line; it seemed that unless they came to some agreement quickly, it would be lose-lose for both sides. But even faced with such reluctance, it still took a month to find a compromise. Commissioner Vincent made the announcement: "Finally we have reached what we all sought. Despite the travails, despite the difficulties, this is the proper way for baseball to resume."[92] The lockout extended from February 15 to March 18. Spring training was modified accordingly. The season started on schedule.

The agreement achieved little. Modifications to salary arbitration were adopted but the existing principles held. Pension-fund contributions were raised to $55 million while the minimum salary jumped to $100,000. And the salary cap matter once again ended up on the back burner. Nevertheless, its ominous echoes had already begun to swirl, foreshadowing the cacophony the issue would generate four years later, when once more it was brought back to the table.[93]

While the players were, of course, delighted with the result, most of the owners were furious. "Not only had the union decisively won," Helyar noted, paraphrasing the owners, "but the bastards had taken over the commissioner's office."[94]

There was no way, they were saying, they would ever let this happen again.

Camelot

1994

Ask ev'ry person if he's heard the story,
And tell it strong and clear if he has not,
That once there was a fleeting wisp of glory
Called Camelot[1]

Chapter Twenty

Happy Days

With the outfield speed they had in Alou, Grissom and Walker, not many balls were going to hit the ground. They had a lot of great arms on that team. Their bullpen was unbelievable.
– Former Expo Greg Colbrunn, with the Florida Marlins in 1994.

When manager Felipe Alou was invited to comment on his 1994 Montreal Expos for the Ken Burns documentary, *The Tenth Inning*, a coda to the film-maker's brilliant nine-part television series on the history of baseball entitled simply *Baseball*, he was unequivocal.

"That's the best team I ever managed at any level," he said. "We had a club that we developed through our minor-league system…we had tremendous pitching, we had defence. And it was young and eager and very hungry."[2]

Today, most observers would agree: the 1994 Expos were the finest Montreal team ever assembled – greater even than the 1981 edition, the only one ever to make it into the postseason. That club featured two Hall-of-Famers (Gary Carter and Andre Dawson), with another worthy candidate, Tim Raines, waiting in the wings.

Given the Expos' outstanding success in 1993, one might have thought that fans and the media would be chomping at the bit in anticipation of Opening Day, especially given the rich promise the club's maturing young players brought with them into the new campaign.

But no: instead, the club found itself buried in controversy and suspicion, its every move questioned, as an unholy alliance of fans and media alike sniped ceaselessly at its heels. Consider the following vessels of dissatisfaction:

Dennis, the wily Martinez, was gone, ensconced in Cleveland with the Indians. His spot in the rotation was to be assumed by Pedro, the lightweight Martinez, a move nobody thought was a good thing. Then there was (or wasn't) Delino DeShields, the anchor of the infield in 1993, now dispatched to Los Angeles in exchange for Pedro. DeShields' unheralded replacement was a still-wet-behind-the-ears Mike Lansing who, it appeared, had been simply handed the job. Larry Walker, only one year away from free agency, had elected to turn down his latest contract offer. Desperate to keep the all-star right-fielder in their fold, the club had laid out a three-year package (plus option year) valued at something close to $15 million. According to Walker's agent, Pat Rooney, this amount wasn't even within shouting distance of a deal. His client was seeking four years-plus, at $5 million-plus per year, numbers consistent with agreements that had been recently signed by Travis Fryman (Detroit Tigers) and Gary Sheffield (Florida Marlins). Said a frustrated Rooney: "We're so far apart, there is nothing to negotiate."[3] And hanging like a dark cloud over all of the above were persistent rumours that Dan Duquette, the Expos' rock-solid general manager, was headed for Boston and the Red Sox. Both organizations denied the chatter, of course, with Expos team president Claude Brochu publicly pointing out he had already refused the Sox permission to even talk to Duquette.[4] All this uncertainty so overshadowed the potential inherent in the team that as Opening Day approached the springtime promises of baseball's return were almost extinguished by the pessimism that engulfed the team. There was little joy: the Expos faithful preferred to just wait and see.

But even that was a delicate dance, for given the success of the 1993 club there emerged the very real possibility that this year's version, even including its "perceived flaws," could well make it to the postseason, and perhaps right to the World Series. If that were to happen, it would mark the third year running that a Canadian-based club participated in the Fall Classic. The Toronto Blue Jays set the standard by winning it all in 1992 and 1993. If *Nos Amours* were to follow in those same footsteps, their victory would leave the Commissioner's Trophy, awarded annually to the World Series champions, sitting beyond the borders of the United States for a third consecutive season. Horrors!

At first glance, Montreal's chances were given a boost by an MLB initiative to reconfigure league structures in time for the 1994 season. Both the National and American Leagues added a third division, called the Central Division, to complement the existing East and West Divisions, and relocated teams accordingly. The new East and Central Divisions in each league took on five teams per division, while only four teams were incorporated into each West Division. A newly modified playoff structure brought into play a second layer of postseason competition. Now, the three division champions in each league would be joined by the best of the non-leaders, designated the wild-card team. Following the regular season, these four teams would enter the first round of playoffs, called the

League Division Series, with the two winners coming together to determine the league champion. The two league champions would then face each other in the World Series.

If there was a downside to this arrangement for Montreal fans, it lay in news that the perennial champion Atlanta Braves were to cross over to join the Expos in the National League East, along with the Phillies, Mets and Florida Marlins. Unless Montreal could find a way to best the Braves in its quest for postseason action, the club would have to depend on the vagaries of the wild-card structure. [It is interesting to note that had the new structure been in effect in 1993, Atlanta (104-68, .642) would have won the East Division and Philadelphia (97-65, .599) would have captured the NL wild card spot. The Expos, even with their excellent numbers, would not have qualified.]

Old-school traditionalists, including John Schuerholz, the Braves' general manager at the time, were not in favour of such a dramatic change, at least not initially. "I wasn't a fan of the wild card at first," Schuerholz said. "The distinguishing feature of baseball was that the winner, the champion in each league, was determined over a grinding, 162-game season, and that this was the true measure of how you structured your team. If you prevail, you get to the postseason dance."

Over time, Schuerholz has mellowed. "I have come to a different position," he said recently. "The wild card adds a lot to the game for the fans."[5]

And as if that wasn't enough uncertainty to complicate the Expos' universe, the fractious MLB owners group had finally, and remarkably, come to an agreement amongst themselves on a revenue-sharing scheme that seemed to satisfy both the small- and large-market clubs. With that elephantine issue now out of the way, they were free to direct their attention to other matters, not good news for the players.

Nor was it smooth sailing even within the team. Marquis Grissom missed the first week of the Expos Caravan – a well-supported club initiative designed to keep fan interest at a high level during the long Quebec winter – even though he was listed as a featured guest at a celebrity dinner where he was slated to receive his Expos Player-of-the-Year Award. Although Duquette passed his absence off as "a mix-up in dates," there were whispers that Grissom stayed away because he was "miffed at the team's trade of close friend Delino DeShields."[6]

On the topic of DeShields, Larry Walker revealed he had long been convinced that if the club ever intended to trade anyone in order to expand its salary manoeuvrability, he, not DeShields, would have been the target. "I would not have been shocked if it had been me," Walker said. "Delino had matured and become a very good second baseman ...I don't think this team is as good without him."[7]

There is no doubt that rumours of Walker being on the trading block had bubbled up periodically in the past year, and even as team members assembled in West Palm Beach to prepare for the year ahead there was still talk that he might soon be on the move, most likely to Baltimore. However, Claude Brochu maintains that such speculation was purely that – speculation. Commenting in 2012 on the topic, in response to a query from the authors, he wrote: "If there was talk of trading Larry in early 1994, I really don't remember the substance of it. In principle, if Baltimore was willing to overwhelm us we would certainly have considered it, as we would have for any potential trade. It is quite possible there could have been exploratory and very preliminary talks, but it never went far. Don't forget, Dan (Duquette) was of the opinion that the '94 team, with the addition of Pedro, was a winner and our payroll was in the $18-million range. There was not much incentive for change."[8] Even when spring training rolled around, the winds of discord continued to bristle with the newly arrived Pedro Martinez expressing his disappointment that the Expos had arbitrarily renewed his contract for $200,000 rather than reward him for the success he had enjoyed with the Dodgers. "Just because it was with another team doesn't give them the right to do what they did," Pedro said. The club was unapologetic.[9]

While such skirmishing was hardly productive, it was, in the end, a passing thing. But the same could not be said for the soap opera-like drama swirling around Dan Duquette. Was he or wasn't he? Was Boston his destination or would he remain with the Expos for at least one more year? With each passing day the waters grew murkier as comments from the various principals sounded increasingly hollow. By the end of January the buzz had reached such a point that *The Sporting News* was reporting that, for all intents and purposes, the deal had been nailed down. All that remained were the details.

According to columnist Peter Pascarelli, there seemed little doubt that Duquette, a native of Massachusetts, would be in place and working as the Red Sox new general manager by March 1. Pascarelli, declaring that the Expos were now ready to eliminate the barriers blocking this move, said: "Expos President Claude Brochu…is expected to work out a compensation agreement with the Red Sox that will allow Duquette out of his Montreal contract." Pascarelli went on to suggest that Duquette's Montreal duties would be divided between vice president Bill Stoneman and Kevin Malone, the team's scouting director.[10] Not surprisingly, one week later Duquette was unpacking his bags in Boston, ready to lay the groundwork for a new era of baseball in Beantown. Malone was doing something similar in Montreal.

But of all the frustrations gnawing at the soul of Expos fandom, the most troubling pertained to money. Ever since Charles Bronfman had sold the franchise to Claude Brochu and a consortium of local businessmen, the club had been strapped for cash. Capital was in short supply, the Canadian dollar was valued well below its American counterpart, the economic climate had grown harsh and expense were up – not the least of which was the meteoric rise in player salaries, especially as these were paid out in costly American funds.

With so much focus on financial woes and the desperate measures called upon to survive, it is little wonder that the ever-doubtful fan moved cautiously. Consequently, 1994 season ticket sales were down, weakening the cash flow situation ever further and forcing the organization to reduce expenditures wherever it saw an opening. Scouting, travel and salaries were the most vulnerable. Plans for signing the current contingent of youthful players to long-term contracts were suddenly less attractive – and there were even rumblings that it was time the club be put up for sale and moved elsewhere. *The Sporting News* was already speculating that "with their foundation of great talent built by Duquette and Malone (and Dave Dombrowski and Gary Hughes before them), the Expos would be far more valuable an acquisition for a baseball-starved community such as St. Petersburg than would an expansion franchise."[11]

Although Claude Brochu was far from ready to suggest the club leave Montreal, he did acknowledge that the situation was dire, very much a day-to-day adventure. In a prescient *Globe and Mail* article by Danny Gallagher, which appeared as the Expos prepared to open the 1994 season in Houston, Brochu was asked if he thought the Expos would have to resort to a fire sale of their core of top players should the upcoming season prove disappointing. Deflecting the question as hypothetical, the club president did admit "our margin of error is so small that we can't afford to make one mistake…It's simply a miracle that we operate. It's a testimony to our system that we hang on." Don Wolfe, a player agent representing pitcher Tim Scott, was more forthcoming. "I certainly agree there could be a fire sale," he said. "I hope the Montreal fans embrace the team this year because they're going to be a good team."[12]

As if Brochu's problems were not already stacked sufficiently high against him, there was even more trouble in the wings. The Expos were at war with their landlord, the Olympics Installation Board, regarding their lease. Or, as President Brochu described it: "Relations between us and them are extremely poor."[13]

Then the Expos went out and lost their season opener to the Astros. Not an auspicious debut to a season that at this stage was layered more with problems than promises.

Now for the good news! As Dan Duquette and others insisted repeatedly, the Expos had put together a very good team, poised to enjoy an excellent year. And they had gone about building it in the right way: they had made the development of young talent a priority. (Some might say they didn't have a choice, they were too impoverished to do anything else, but that's beside the point). Duquette underscored the brilliance of this approach shortly after settling into his new digs at Fenway Park. "The best way to build a successful franchise," he said, "is with a foundation built around developing your own players. It has always been that way and even with all the changes in the game over the last several years, player development remains the best way to build a club.

When it came to player development, the Expos were always at the forefront in discovering and forming new and promising talent. Starting from Day One at Jarry Park in 1969, this approach remained a hallmark of the club right up until those final days in 2004 when the last candle glowing deep within the empty recesses of the Big O finally surrendered to the wind.

As Opening Day of 1994 rolled around, the pundits were generally predicting that while the Expos posed little threat to the Braves, they were in line for a wild-card spot. Pitching was the big concern, and it began with Pedro. Did he have the strength to sustain a spot in the starting rotation? Or were his "nasty stuff" and combative spirit better suited to the closer role he exercised in Los Angeles? Until this uncertainty could be sorted out, GM Malone was not about to tinker with his stellar bullpen. Any thoughts the club had of trading away highly prized relief pitcher Mel Rojas were put on hold, for good as it turned out.[14]

The season-opening loss in Houston was a close one, 6–5 in 12 innings. The starting lineup, pretty much a set piece for the entire year, included: Darrin Fletcher, catcher; Cliff Floyd, first base; Mike Lansing, second base; Wil Cordero, shortstop; Sean Berry, third base; Moises Alou, left field; Marquis Grissom, centre field; and Larry Walker, right field. Other position players appearing that first day were Rondell White, Lou Frazier, Tim Spehr, Freddie Benavides, Jeff Gardner, and Randy Milligan. Starter Jeff Fassero completed six innings and left with the score tied 3-3. He was followed by Mel Rojas and closer John Wetteland, both of whom pitched flawlessly. The game eventually slipped away in the bottom of the 12th inning when a trio of Tim Scott, Jeff Shaw and Denis Boucher surrendered three runs – and this after Montreal had scored twice in the top half of the inning to grab the lead. It was a bittersweet defeat. The team performed well as a whole, managing to manufacture five runs, including the two in the 12th inning, on only six hits. Moises Alou, still testing the repairs to his broken fibula suffered the previous September against the Cards, looked solid. Nevertheless, the club's inability to hold onto a two-run advantage in extra innings was unsettling.

This opening game was in some ways a harbinger of what lay ahead over the first month – middling results. When April ended, the Expos were playing slightly better than .500 ball (14-10) and holding down second place in the East Division, one game back of the Braves.[15] The Cincinnati Reds, with a winning percentage of .714, were the National League's hottest team.

In general, Montreal's pitchers were winning more games for the club than the hitters. Walker had socked three home runs by month's end, and Alou seven doubles, but generally power numbers were low. On the other hand, the pitching was first rate. Although Pedro did not win his first game until April 30, after losing his first two decisions, Ken Hill pushed his own record to 4-1, with Rojas collecting seven saves. And the imperturbable Kirk Rueter managed to extend his consecutive win streak to 10 games, although he was no longer pitching with the same authority he had shown in 1993. Eventually his problems would be reflected in his statistics; though his record at year-end was 7-3, it came with a troublesome ERA of 5.17.

Over in the American League the Red Sox had grabbed the early lead. Except for Detroit, however, all the other AL East teams were playing above .500 and snapping at Boston's heels. As for the rest of the junior circuit, the only team offering any hint of an early pennant run was the Cleveland Indians.

At the end of May the Expos (28-22) remained in second place but were now 3.5 games behind Atlanta. Still, they were four games up on the Mets, and folks sensed they had begun to make themselves known – that this was a club to be reckoned with. Pitching continued to be a strong suit; Hill's record climbed to 8-2 and Fassero was at 4-2; the relief pitching was stepping up, with Rojas, the early-year closer now used mainly as the set-up man, showing 10 saves while the recently appointed shutdown man, John Wetteland, had already accumulated seven. Among the position players the heavy hitters had begun to stretch their bats. By June 1, Walker had hammered out seven home runs and 25 doubles, Floyd added another 11 two-baggers and Grissom 10, along with 13 stolen bases.

It was not until the end of June that the real pennant race took shape. Both the Braves and Expos were winning more and losing less all the time. As the Canada Day July 1 holiday rolled around, these were the only clubs in the senior loop showing winning percentages above .600. And Montreal, at 47-30, had crawled to within 1.5 games of Atlanta.

The Expos were where they were because all the usual suspects were doing everything expected of them. Alou was up to 15 home runs to go along with his 22 doubles; Walker's round-trippers totaled 13 while his doubles flipped that number to 31. The pitchers remained solid, starting with Hill and his 11-3 record; Pedro had found his footing, climbing to 6-4; and Butch Henry was 4-1, with the relief pitching more than holding its own. Wetteland was showing 13 saves although his 2-5 record was somewhat disappointing. Rojas was 3-2 with 12 saves. It was all good but the best was yet to come.

One month later, the Expos were firing on all cylinders. They had reached the top, passing the Braves and sitting 3.5 games ahead of the pack. Their winning percentage of .635 was the best in baseball. Finally, Montreal's team of destiny had arrived.

July had begun in a fairly non-descript way with Montreal losing two of three games to the Giants in San Francisco. Then the club moved on to Los Angeles where *Nos Amours* took two of three from the Dodgers, before rolling into San Diego to sweep the Padres in four games. Remarkably, over those four games the pitching staff surrendered only three runs. Both Hill and Rueter gained shutout victories: Hill pitched a five-hit complete game, while Rueter, cruising along in a 14-0 laugher, gave way to reliever Jeff Shaw after wrapping up seven innings of three-hit ball.

On July 12, before the Expos returned to the Big O to open a home stand against a West Coast invasion, five Montreal players - Moises Alou, Wil Cordero, Darrin Fletcher and Marquis Grissom, along with pitcher Ken Hill - made a detour to Pittsburgh's Three Rivers Stadium to take part in the All-Star Game. Former Expos pitchers Randy Johnson and Lee Smith, now representing the American League squad, were also on the scene.

Although none of the Expos' five had been named to the starting lineup, they all shone once they got into the game. The key blow was a Moises Alou double in the 10th inning to drive Tony Gwynn home with the winning run, 8-7 for the NL squad, the first win by the National League since 1987. But even more important for Montreal fans, the game provided clear evidence that the Expos were now on everybody's radar.

Typical was the Baseball Almanac game summary: "While much of the media's pregame attentions were focused on the American League's Frank Thomas and Ken Griffey Jr., it was three Expos, Ken Hill, Marquis Grissom and Moises Alou, who stole the show. Hill pitched two scoreless innings; Grissom staked the National League to a 5-4 lead with a sixth-inning homer; and Alou delivered the game-winning double in the 10th."[16] Not to be outdone, Wil Cordero played errorless ball in the field, and

Darrin Fletcher was flawless behind the plate for the game's critical final two frames.

For the 1994 Expos, the All-Star Game came to symbolize the gateway that opened up to perhaps the most glorious starburst in team history. But not until they first had to contend with a bump or two in the road, all bearing the stamp "Giants of San Francisco." It was not pretty.

Immediately following the All-Star Game, the Expos opened a four-game series at home. Uncharacteristically, they delivered a stink-bomb of epic proportions, losing every game convincingly, before crowds ranging from 26,000 to 38,000. The pitchers who bore the brunt of the blame were no slouches: Pedro, who dropped to a 6-5 record; Henry, who lost for only the second time against his seven wins; Hill, the best hurler in the National League, who suffered his fourth defeat in 17 decisions; and Fassero, now 7-6.

As things turned out this was just the storm before the calm, easily weathered and just as quickly forgotten. For even as the Expos and Braves jockeyed for top spot in the NL East, in those late July days, Montreal began to establish its supremacy - and on July 22, pulled ahead for good. In fact, between July 18 and August 11, when the season was ruthlessly gutted, the Expos powered to a remarkable 20-3 record, emerging as the most dominant team in the game and perhaps the greatest squad in club history. And, oh yes, over in the American League the Yankees were similarly leaving their opposition in the dust.

Montreal's late-July surge came about because all the pieces started clicking at the same time. The synchronicity was a marvel to behold. A case in point would be its last game in

Wil Cordero

July, a 13-4 romp over the Marlins in Miami. Everybody contributed – and that was the way it would continue until the curtain dropped. In Miami, Pedro, who left the game after the sixth inning (not of his own volition), was credited with the win, his ninth of the year against five losses. Reliever Gabe White picked up the save. On the hitters' side, the Expos' bats were loaded. Lead-off man, centre fielder Marquis Grissom, hammered out four hits, scored three runs, and drove home another. Larry Walker, this day playing first base, also knocked out four hits, enough to produce five runs – three he drove home and two he scored himself. Of the starting eight position players, only shortstop Wil Cordero was held hitless. Cliff Floyd in right field, Darrin Fletcher behind the plate and infielders Juan Bell, second base, and Sean Berry at third, all had two hits apiece. Rondell White managed one hit. Floyd, Grissom and Berry connected with home runs; Walker and Fletcher hit two doubles apiece and Grissom added icing to his own cake with a triple in the sixth. But there was more, and it was here that some say the true mettle of the team was honed.

It was the third game of the Expos' three-game sweep, and after having been thumped 8-4 and 7-3, Marlins players were, frankly, upset and ashamed. Tempers flared throughout this final match, with retribution never more than one sideways glance away. Stare-downs, bean balls, plunks, even the occasional pitch behind the batter's back became the order of the day. Perhaps the most bizarre sequence of get-evens began in the sixth inning when shortstop Wil Cordero tried to foist the old-fashioned hidden-ball trick on an infuriated Chucky Carr. That led to a shoving match between the two, with Cordero being ejected by the second base umpire. By the time the inning was over, Martinez had surrendered a two-run double to Gary Sheffield, walked Greg Colbrunn and thrown wildly at Benito Santiago, before eventually striking him out to end the inning. Two frames later, Marlins manager Rene Lachemann brought reliever Yorkis Perez into the game for one purpose only – to throw at Expos catcher Lenny Webster, which he did. Perez's action was so blatant that as soon as his toss struck Webster, he turned and walked toward the dugout, not even waiting for home-plate umpire Tom Hallion to throw up his right arm and signal ejection. Then, just to underscore his displeasure, Hallion also tossed manager Lachemann.

"That's a helluva job Yorkis has, coming in to hit a guy," Felipe Alou said later, more than a little annoyed. "When you see him walk off the way he did, you knew he was in the game to hit someone."[17] (Alou would have had some understanding of what was going on in Perez's head, for Perez had been a fixture in the Expos' minor league system during the late 1980s and early 1990s. Although the pitcher never made an appearance with the big club, he and Alou would have come to know one another well. Being called upon to throw at one of Felipe's men must have been especially galling for Perez.)

But adversity of this sort only made the Expos stronger, reinforcing even more their closeness as a team. Now, after six games on the road they were heading back to Olympic Stadium and the comforts of home. It was like they were living the old Dave Dudley song, "Six days on the road, but we're gonna make it home tonight."[18] The feeling was uplifting, for in this brief moment of time the Expos were kings of the world. It was Camelot.

Chapter Twenty-One

Braves and Expos – Rivals

Anyone contemplating old-time baseball rivalries in the National League would be hard pressed to find any more fiery than the constant tug-of-war that pitted the Expos against their arch-enemies, the Atlanta Braves.

The strife wasn't just limited to the regular season either. Its origins lay in spring training, where from approximately February 20 until April 1 the feuding would evolve, all because the two teams shared facilities at the old Municipal Stadium, 715 Hank Aaron Drive in West Palm Beach, Florida.

"We trained together. We spent six weeks looking at each other every spring. As they say, familiarity breeds contempt in a way," recalled John Schuerholz, the Braves' current president, who was their GM from 1990-2007. "We had more success than they did but whenever you get to sharing a room with someone it can be aggravating – how they act, the way they talk, the way they walk – it was all part of the bragging rights for West Palm Beach."[19]

The Braves would traditionally take over the stadium's main field, the one used for Grapefruit League games, while the Expos' pre-game workouts would be relegated to the back fields. "The Braves had the big field. We were second to them," Marquis Grissom recalls. "It added fuel to the fire. You don't really appreciate that, always having to go on the back field. They had the front field but we wanted to play on the main diamond also."[20]

What it all came down to was seniority rights. The Braves had relocated to West Palm Beach in 1963 when they were still called the Milwaukee Braves. To accommodate them, local authorities renovated the old Connie Mack Field and renamed it Municipal Stadium. The Johnny-come-lately Expos didn't appear on the scene until 1969 when they opened their camp.

The Expos moved their spring-training operation to Daytona Beach following the 1972 season, but returned to West Palm Beach in 1981, remaining there through 1997.

That was the year both the Braves and Expos moved on to glitzier real estate – the Braves to Disneyworld, the Expos to a state-of-the-art facility in Jupiter, located about 20 minutes from West Palm Beach.

Thus in the latter part of 1994, when the Expos finally began to pull ahead of the Braves, each victory carried an extra-special measure of satisfaction. The Braves, on the other hand, were not cowed by what they saw as an anomaly. Many from that team will say today that they would have overcome the Expos' six-game lead had play not ended in August. "We felt our team was performing well," Schuerholz said. "We could see the elements finding their groove. We actually thought we were going to catch Montreal. The Expos had a talented team on both sides of the ball, they were athletic, they had team speed, aggressiveness, good pitching, all the pieces a team needs to win, but we felt we had that, too."

Larry Walker and the Bubble Gum

"Larry Walker was always the playful type,"' said Sean Berry. "If a player was getting a rubdown by trainer Ron McClain, Walker would take some spray can or other and spray it on the player's left leg or shoulder and it would be painful. McClain would set it up for him. Walker was a practical joker: he would do this sort of thing all the time."

Juan Bell has his own Walker story.

"A lot of times, some of the players would put bubble gum on top of other players' hats. Walker used to do that to me. One time in Pittsburgh, I did it back to him and he got mad. Everybody was laughing," Bell said.

"Why did you do that to me?" Walker shouted at Bell. "You can't do that to me."

Chuckling, Bell said: "He was angry, mad at me, but that's what made it fun."

Juan Bell

Chapter Twenty-Two

Larry Walker's Near Miss

It was in the month of April 1994, and Larry Walker and the Expos were not off to a great start; there was even talk of a trade, one that would have rattled the Expos' organization to the core.

Baltimore Orioles GM Roland Hemond was on the phone, chatting with Expos GM Kevin Malone about Walker's availability: could he be obtained in a trade? Malone indicated he was open to discussing it.

It seems the deal was pretty much done, recalls Montreal's premier radio sportscaster Mitch Melnick. "There was a potential trade that would have sent Walker to Baltimore for pitcher Armando Benitez and outfielder Alex Ochoa but Orioles owner Peter Angelos nixed the deal," the TSN Montreal radio host said. "A whisper campaign against Walker had begun, with a well-known broadcaster complaining about Walker smelling of alcohol and taking a nap on a trainer's table."[21] As it turned out, Benitez and Ochoa, both untested novices in 1994, remained in the major leagues for ten years or so, compiling decent records. Neither was the equal of Walker or close to it.

In any event, Hemond wanted Walker.

"I would have been happy to make that deal to bring Larry Walker to Baltimore," Hemond would say in September 2012, confirming the trade talks. "He would have been well suited for Camden Yards. He was a good, all-round top offensive player and defensive player." Then, serving up a dash of irony, he added, "If we had acquired him, I'm sure my tenure with the Orioles would have lasted longer."[22]

Of course, 18 years after a trade that didn't go down, Hemond was not about to bad-mouth Angelos, the team's long-time managing partner. "I don't like to go into details about it. I try to avoid that. That's best, you know. You have to respect your elders," he said, referring to his then-boss. At the time Angelos had only been in command of the Orioles for one season but from the start he had made his hands-on approach very evident to his general managers. A meddlesome, reclusive, high-stakes lawyer in Baltimore the 80-ish Angelos remains as the Orioles' controlling owner.

Larry Walker – swinging for the fences

Washington Nationals manager Davey Johnson once said of him, "I don't know that anybody has a good relationship with Angelos."[23]

But most certainly, had Walker landed in Baltimore, the Orioles would have threatened the Yankees for first place.

"The Yankees were 70-43 and we were 63-49 at the time of the strike," Hemond said. "We had a legitimate club but in the end, I paid the price." Hemond's seven-year run as Orioles GM ended following the 1994 season and he was replaced by Jays departing GM Pat Gillick.

On the flip side of the coin, Melnick was asked how he thought the Expos would have fared through the remainder of the season had Walker become an Oriole. After all, Walker went on to have a great year with Montreal, hitting 22 home runs and driving in 86 runs.

"Potentially, Walker could have had the most doubles in one season," Melnick pointed out. When the season shut down, Walker had already posted 44 two-baggers, within striking distance of the major league record of 67 set by Earl Webb of the Red Sox in 1931. At the time Warren Cromartie held the Expos' season record with 46 doubles established in 1979, a mark Walker would have broken easily. The franchise-high mark now belongs to Mark Grudzielanek who hit 54 in 1997.

"Walker was the best right fielder to play for the Expos and I include Vladimir Guerrero," Melnick said. "In a Game 7, if you needed one right fielder, I'd take Walker. His arm was not as strong as Guerrero's but it was a lot more accurate."

Chapter Twenty-Three

Fletcher, Moises and the 1994 All-Star Game

When asked for his own personal highlight of the 1994 season, perhaps of his career, Expos catcher Darrin Fletcher didn't hesitate: "The All-Star Game," he said. "That was the biggest memory for me. I was honoured to be there. We were the talk of the town in Montreal. It made me proud, for myself, and for the organization, to be lined up on the National League side as a member of the Expos."[24]

Although he never got to bat, the self-effacing backstop appeared in the game defensively for the all-important ninth and 10th innings, playing errorless ball and registering three putouts.

"Fletcher was outstanding that season," said French-language broadcaster Jacques Doucet. "He was no Gary Carter but he was more than a decent catcher."[25] Doucet's broadcast counterpart on the English side, play-by-play announcer Dave Van Horne, concurred. "Because Fletcher didn't produce like Larry Walker and Moises Alou he probably didn't get as much attention as he should," remarked the award-winning Van Horne recently. "He did a remarkable job, doing things very quietly behind the plate. He handled a great pitching staff. He was the unsung hero on that team."[26]

Darrin Fletcher

Manager Felipe Alou saw his rearguard in the same light. "Fletcher was a great man, a real good ballplayer," he noted not long ago. "He was a really good receiver. His arm was not so strong but he was accurate. He hit a lot of balls to left field, good RBI guy, good leader behind the plate, leader of the pitching staff. We all loved Darrin Fletcher."[27]

Almost forgotten today is that this All-Star Game, the basis of Fletcher's great baseball memory, might never have taken place had not cooler heads stepped in at the last minute. It seems the owners' group was prepared to delay a payment to the players' pension-benefit fund, a questionable gesture at best. Had that happened, the players unquestionably would have boycotted the game. "There was talk the All-Star Game could have been cancelled," said Fletcher, who was the Expos' assistant player representative, behind John Wetteland. "We could have voted to cancel the game."

But they didn't, and when Alou doubled off the wall in left-centre to score Tony Gwynn with the winning run in the 10th inning, putting the cap on the Expos players achievements, that day everyone was talking about the club. Assistant trainer Mike Kozak derived special satisfaction from Alou's achievement. "Moises being selected to the All-Star Game and hitting that game-winning double was a big moment for me. I consider it the highlight of that season, because of what happened with his broken leg the year before, a highlight because I helped him rehab the leg."[28]

On September 16, 1993 at Busch Stadium in St. Louis, Alou suffered a gruesome injury. Going all out as he always did, Alou rounded first base after a hit and tried to draw a throw from outfielder Bernard Gilkey. Expos media relations guru Rich Griffin described the scene: "As Alou went from full speed to a dead stop in the baseline, his spikes caught in the artificial turf and his leg collapsed underneath him like a folding chair."[29]

Moises Alou

Shortly after Alou got back to Montreal following several days in hospital, director of team travel Erik Ostling happened to be in the Expos clubhouse when the phone rang. He answered and there, on the other end of the line, was former CFL and NFL quarterback great, Joe Theismann. "Theismann wanted to talk to Moises to wish him good luck," Ostling said, "because he had suffered a similar, horrific leg injury back in 1985."[30]

Alou had dislocated his left ankle and broken his left fibula. He underwent surgery in Montreal on September 18 with Dr. Larry Coughlin doing the honours. The outfielder remained in the city, undergoing daily therapy with Kozak, until November 24. It was this experience that caused Kozak's delight with Alou's wonderful recovery and appearance in the All-Star game.

Just two days before the big game, Alou and the Expos had completed a four-game sweep of the Padres in San Diego. Immediately following that final match, he and his All-Star teammates flew directly to host city Pittsburgh, along with others selected for the game. Alou was assigned a seat next to Tony Gwynn, San Diego's lone representative at the mid-summer classic. "We took the same plane and Moises was really nervous about his first All-Star Game," Gwynn recalled, chuckling. "He was wondering how he would react to seeing all those stars in the clubhouse in Pittsburgh. I told him I had the same nervousness at my first All-Star Game."[31]

When asked to name his favourite player from the 1994 Expos, former Expo great and Hall of Famer Andre Dawson didn't have to think twice. "I liked Moises Alou a lot," said Dawson, who that season was lined up with the Red Sox. "Because of his passion and intensity, he came to play every day. He was a gamer. He worked really hard. Of course, he had the right genes!"[32]

Just to give this period of Expos history some context, Sean Berry had this interesting observation: "That outfield of Moises Alou, Larry Walker and Marquis Grissom – you could compare them to any of the best in baseball history."[33]

Hats off to Felipe Alou

"Even if we were down a bunch of runs, we had that killer instinct every day, something we got from Felipe. He gave us that attitude. Man, he rode my ass and I probably deserved it. Even when I went to San Francisco to play for him, he still pushed me to the max every single day."

– Marquis Grissom

Chapter Twenty-Four

Pedro Revisited

"**P**edro was outstanding, hard fastball, throwing inside consistently. That was his game: he came in on guys, to establish the inside part of the plate." This was the way Freddie Benavides saw his Expos teammate Pedro Martinez in 1994.[34]

Catcher Darrin Fletcher said: "Pedro knew how to play the game. He was just coming into his own in 1994. He had a slight build – 155 pounds soaking wet. He was pretty amazing. He could throw a no-hitter with the stuff he had. He just frustrated batters."

Pedro showed that no-hitter stuff on April 13, 1994 at Olympic Stadium when he was throwing heat against the Cincinnati Reds.

Freddie Benavides

Unfortunately, in the eighth inning, with the Reds hitless and the Expos holding a 2-0 lead, and with an 0-2 count on Reggie Sanders, Pedro accidentally nailed Sanders on the elbow with an errant pitch. Even though it was obvious the plunk was unintended, the hotheaded Sanders regarded it as a purpose pitch and charged the mound. "Pedro had struck him out several times before, so that's why he came out," recalled former teammate Tim Scott. "Sanders was becoming frustrated."[35]

Benavides, a backup Expos infielder, admits he "was kinda shocked. That's not like Reggie. He was a roommate of mine in Cincinnati. We came up through the Reds' system. It all happened so fast. What's going on? He charged the mound? It was the heat of the battle, the competition."

As Martinez and Sanders grappled near the mound, both benches cleared and a host of other players joined in. Quickly it became the kind of melee that causes managers and team officials to turn grey, knowing there is a risk of injury with every bear hug, every punch thrown.

"I got a black eye out of it," Benavides recalled, chuckling. "No idea how I got it. I was under the pile somewhere. I was trying to get people off the bottom."

Cliff Floyd's first reaction was to think, "Damn, he hit him. It breaks up the perfect game but he still has the no-hitter." That was just before the brawl gained momentum and he found himself paired off with Kevin Mitchell of the Reds. "I look up into Mitchell's face and he's got a gold tooth, a real tight shirt and a head full of curls," Floyd said, starting to chuckle.

"Where's Pedro?" Mitchell shouted at Floyd and others nearby. "I don't know," Floyd replied. Of course, Floyd was not about to tell Mitchell anything. He knew the rough-and-tumble Red was desperate to get his hands on Martinez. "Mitchell shoved me off and went looking for Pedro. He was mad as hell," Floyd said.

Discretion, they say, is the better part of valour, and Davey Johnson, the Reds manager that season, well appreciated Floyd's dilemma. "I wouldn't want Kevin Mitchell mad at me," said Johnson. "I had him two times as a player (Reds and Mets) and we had some disagreements. I don't know the history between Reggie and Pedro but I don't think he was trying to purposely hit him. I think he just wanted to brush him back."

Sanders was the only player tossed from the game, and the inning continued with Jerome Walton running for him at first base. As Floyd noted, Pedro still had a no-hitter going. Nevertheless, his confidence was somewhat shaken and after striking out Roberto Kelly he threw a wild pitch, allowing Walton to advance to second. But then he coaxed Willie Greene to fly out to Grissom in centre and end the inning, his no-hit masterpiece still intact.

According to an Associated Press report from that game, Martinez, in only his second start of the season and 0-4 in his four previous big-league starts, was aspiring to become the second pitcher in a week to throw a no-hitter in his first complete game. Kent Mercker of the Atlanta Braves had managed to do just that against Los Angeles a few days earlier.

Unfortunately, it was not to be. Journeyman Brian Dorsett, swinging on an 0-2 count, singled to break the spell in the top of the ninth. That was enough for manager Alou. He could see Pedro was bushed, and now that the promise of a no-hitter had vanished, he moved quickly to offer him rest. He called on closer John Wetteland to wrap it up and preserve the shutout. Regrettably for Pedro, it was not Wetteland's day. Another single and then a walk loaded the bases with none out. Two sacrifice flies later the score was tied.

Although there would be no decision for Pedro, the Expos managed to eke out a 3-2 win in the bottom of the ninth. They loaded the bases and then, with two out, Lou Frazier poked a single past the infield to send home the winning run. Wetteland, who had squandered the lead and Pedro's brilliant effort, was credited with the win.

For the record, Martinez was becoming identified as a headhunter, a reputation some felt was well deserved. In 1994 alone he hit 11 batters in 23 starts, an NL high, and all by himself touched off three bench-clearing incidents. Pedro was never one to back down from the criticism. "I'm not going to quit pitching inside. I don't care if I hit 1,000 batters," Martinez said repeatedly. "I'm going to keep pitching inside. That's the way I do the best." While catcher Darrin Fletcher acknowledged Pedro "had a reputation as a headhunter and perhaps appeared to be a bully out on the mound, it was a facade. In the clubhouse, he had a gentle way about him. He wasn't a bully by any means."

It wasn't long before Pedro's aggressive approach got him into trouble again. On April 30, in the fifth inning at Olympic Stadium, this time facing the San Diego Padres, Martinez first brushed back Derek Bell with a high fastball and then struck him out. Oddly, Bell waited until he had whiffed to take exception to the inside pitch and rushed the mound. In fact, he had already made his way back to the dugout, showing his frustration, and only reacted after s teammate Bip Roberts pressed him into action. As catcher Darrin Fletcher saw it: "Pedro threw a fastball around Derek's neck. Bell got mad, then he struck out and headed to the dugout, dragging his bat and hanging his head. That's when Bip Roberts told him to charge the mound. It was a funny moment."

Once again there was a skirmish on the infield grass – and once again the only player banished was the charging batter. As happened after the Sanders incident, Martinez had trouble settling down and Alou pulled him at the end of the inning. This time the Expos won the game, defeating the Padres 5-3. Pedro was credited with the victory, his first in an Expos uniform, and first as a starting pitcher. His winning ways had just begun.

Chapter Twenty-Five

The Bullpen

In discussions about the 1994 Expos, the focus is usually directed either toward starting pitchers or to the array of players enjoying career years at the plate and in the field. Seldom does the bullpen get much recognition, beyond John Wetteland and Mel Rojas. This is too bad because a major reason for the Expos success in '94 was the strength and versatility of the relief corps. Tim Scott, a mainstay of the group, put it best. "After the sixth inning if we were winning," he said, "it was pretty much game over. We were that dominant a bullpen."[36]

Scott was one of three middle-inning relievers the club could regularly count on, along with Gil Heredia and Jeff Shaw. He broke into the major leagues with the San Diego Padres in 1991. Two years later, on June 23 and quite out of the blue, he was traded to Montreal for infielder Archi Cianfrocco. Credit Dan Duquette for finding yet another gem of a player. During the first half of 1993, Scott had provided the Padres with solid pitching, putting up a 2-2 record and a 2.39 ERA over almost 40 innings of work.

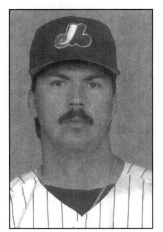

Tim Scott

Thus, as Scott recalled, "The trade was a big surprise to me. The Padres were conducting a fire-sale." Yet, Scott was hardly expensive, earning only $125,000 that season. "It worked out! I ended with a pretty good team in Montreal," Scott said. Indeed, with a fastball, curve and slider in his arsenal, Scott became an integral element of the bullpen as a middle-innings reliever. He was part of the system. Most often he would get the call in the sixth inning: Shaw would follow in the seventh; Rojas would take over as the setup man in the eighth; and Wetteland would bulldoze his way through the ninth.

Gil Heredia

In 1996 Shaw was traded along with Kirk Rueter to the San Francisco Giants in exchange for pitcher Mark Leiter. After brief stops in San Diego and Colorado he finally left big-league ball behind him a year later – although he continued to hold his own in the minor and independent leagues until 2002.

Gil Heredia was another castoff who blossomed with the Expos. He'd had brief stints with the San Francisco Giants in 1991-92 before Duquette took an inexpensive gamble on him, acquiring him August 18, 1992 for minor-league infielder Brett Jenkins. In the waning days of the season, Heredia impressed the folks in Montreal with 14 innings of work and an ERA of 1.84. He further improved in 1993 and was even better in 1994, going 6-3 with a 3.46 ERA in 39 games, 36 of which were out of the bullpen. "I was the long guy," said Heredia recently. "When any starter was having any problems early, I was the guy."[37]

Outfielder Marquis Grissom had his own ideas about the bullpen's effectiveness. "Some of the guys like Jeff (Shaw) and Gil had trouble making teams where they were – they had to work their way into the big leagues. It was the bulldog in them that kept them going."[38] Heredia remained with Montreal through 1995 when he was picked up by the Texas Rangers. Following a year in Triple A he returned to the big leagues with the Oakland A's where he was very successful. Over four years with that club he nailed down 38 wins against 30 losses – evidence, some might say, of the "money-ball" principle at work. During this period Heredia's salary with Oakland rose from $275,000 in 1998 to over $3 million four years later.

Jeff Shaw hailed from a town with the unlikely name of Washington Court House, Ohio. After three futile years in his home state where he managed only three wins in 10 decisions with the Cleveland Indians, he was let go as a free agent and ended up with the Kansas City Royals' organization. Before he could even suit up with them, Expos mastermind Dan Duquette, having recognized something in Shaw, acquired him and Tim Spehr in exchange for pitchers Mark Gardner and Jeff Piatt on December 9, 1992. With this transaction, which turned out to be another steal of a deal, Duquette was living up to the billing of those who suggested he had a divining rod as a scouting device, so finely tuned was his nose for buried talent.

Once in Montreal, Shaw, a forkball specialist, began to get better. Though his record in 1993 was only 2-7, with an ERA of 4.14 in eight starts and 95.1 innings of work, manager Felipe Alou liked what he was seeing and so did Duquette. Shaw was kept on for the 1994 season and he blossomed. His record was 5-2 with an ERA of 3.88 in 67.1 innings, due in large measure to the stark effectiveness of his forkball/screwball delivery. Nevertheless, his catcher Darrin Fletcher did concede that "Shaw was like a mop-up guy, a forgotten guy on the staff."[39]

Shaw remained in Montreal until late 1995 when he was traded to the White Sox for Jose DeLeon. Declared a free agent at season's end, he signed with Cincinnati in 1996 and there his career as a reliever truly took root. In 1997 he led the National League in saves and earned the Rolaids Relief Award. The following year he was named to the NL All-Star team, but shortly before the summer classic was held, he was traded to the Dodgers for Paul Konerko. He remained with Los Angeles through the 2001 season, when he was selected to the All-Star squad for a second time. By the end of the year, however, he was released as a free agent. He was 35 years old, and with 12 years of service under his belt, he decided to step away from the game.

Jeff Shaw

Unsung heroes, every one of them – but credit them with their share of the glory. Without their perseverance, the story of the 1994 Expos would have been much less interesting.

Vlad - Boy Wonder

As the Expos were making a splashy run in 1994, they had a young colt drawing rave reviews in the Gulf Coast League that same season.

He had been signed the year before out of Bani in the Dominican Republic. At age 18, he batted .314 in 37 games and was named the No. 4 prospect in that league by Baseball America behind a second baseman named Sergio Nunez, pitcher Scott Elarton and outfielder Andruw Jones.

He would go on to become the only player in major-league history to hit at least 30 homers, drive in 100 runs, collect 200 hits, steal at least 40 bases and hit for an average of .320 or better in a single season (2002). His name?

Chapter Twenty-Six

Joe Kerrigan –
Among the Very Best

Joe Kerrigan was way ahead of his time when he was pitching coach of the Expos, what with his books, notes, charts, stats, and whatever else he figured gave his club the edge.

In every pre-series meeting with his staff, Kerrigan would carefully speak about each opposing hitter, identifying their weaknesses and so on. "Pitchers hated Kerrigan," Cliff Floyd pointed out in 2012. "He went by the book but I tried to look at the other side of him. He was not an aggressive guy."

Sportscaster Mitch Melnick was less diplomatic. "Joe was anal, "he said, adding, "but he was so good. He did his job so well."

Joe Kerrigan

Former GM Dan Duquette concurred. "He got results," Duquette reminded those who might not have liked the way Kerrigan operated. "The pitchers got return on Joe's program; he helped them make a lot of money. His teams were usually near the top in ERA."

And then Duquette would frame this thought with a smile: "Remember, Joe pitched in Baltimore for Earl Weaver, one of the best managers in the game with a .583 winning percentage." In other words, he had the opportunity to see managerial genius at work. To this day, Duquette keeps in touch with Kerrigan, along with several others he respects greatly, including Felipe Alou and Pedro Martinez.

"Joe Kerrigan was incredible and Felipe Alou was incredible," pitcher Butch Henry said, looking back. "Those were two guys I still hold in the highest regard as consummate professionals. They taught me how to be a pitcher, the way to go about it. It was not about throwing the ball past people. I had no overpowering stuff. I had to work. I only threw about 85-86 mph."

Kerrigan's good work as a pitching coach in the majors took him to the Red Sox, Pirates and Phillies where he carried out the same role. He was even a short-term manager for the Red Sox under Duquette in 2001.[40]

Expos Friendships

A characteristic of the 1994 Expos that seems to come out in every conversation about the club is the closeness team members felt toward one another and their commitment to the mission they had undertaken – winning the World Series and establishing a dynasty in Montreal. That they were ultimately foiled only brought them closer and fostered even stronger friendships.

Take Cliff Floyd and Rondell White, for example. Today they are so tight they live on the same street in Davie, Florida, just west of West Palm Beach. Their friendship began in the early 1990s when Floyd and White patrolled the outfield as top Expos prospects. They first formed a bond playing together in Harrisburg and later in Ottawa in 1993. They were teammates in Montreal from 1994–1996, and ever since, they've been close as apple pie and ice cream.

"It's amazing, having a relationship you cherish," Floyd said. "We care so much about each other. We work out together. We just hit it off from the first time we met. The camaraderie between us is great." White concurs: "We're like brothers. We had a plan to become neighbours. A lot of guys say during their careers that they will get together and be just as close after their careers are over but they don't do it."

Floyd moved to Davie close to 10 years ago and White followed a few years later, buying a house near his friend in 2007.

"The wives agreed to it," White said. "We had to get the wives' approval."

Other 1994 Expos who have remained friends include Jeff Fassero, Sean Berry, Butch Henry, Gil Heredia, Pedro Martinez, Mel Rojas, Felipe Alou, and Luis Pujols.

Where Are They Now?   Compiled by Danny Gallagher

Who	Where he resides	What he's up to
Manager Felipe Alou	Boynton Beach, Fla.	Special assistant to Giants GM
3B coach Jerry Manuel	Sacramento, Calif.	Promoting blacks in base-ball
Pitching coach Joe Kerrigan	North Wales, Pa.	Semi-retired
Hitting coach Tommy Harper	Sharon, Mass.	Red Sox special consultant
Bench coach Tim Johnson	Las Cruces, N.M.	Manager of El Paso inde-pendent team
1B coach Luis Pujols	Boynton Beach, Fla.	Orioles' minor-league manager
Bullpen coordinator Pierre Arsenault	Montreal	Scout with Florida Marlins
Darrin Fletcher	Fithian, Ill.	Taking it easy
Lenny Webster	Atlanta, Ga.	Working with youth
Tim Spehr	Waco, Tx.	Investments advisor
Randy Milligan	Baltimore	Taking it easy
Larry Walker	West Palm Beach, Fla.	Baseball coach with Team Canada
Cliff Floyd	Davie, Fla.	Daily radio show on Sirius & pre-game with Marlins
Mike Lansing	Casper, Wy.	Taking it easy
Freddie Benavides	Laredo, Tx.	Minor-league employee, Cincinnati Reds
Juan Bell	Santo Domingo, D.R.	Teaching youth baseball teams
Wil Cordero	California	Involved with batting schools
Sean Berry	Paso Robles, Calif.	Hitting coordinator with San Diego Padres
Marquis Grissom	Atlanta, Ga.	Runs his own baseball association
Rondell White	Davie, Fla.	Owns tree-cutting com-pany in N.C.

Who	Where he resides	What he's up to
Moises Alou	Santo Domingo, D.R.	GM of Escogida team in Dominican league
Lou Frazier	Phoenix, Ariz.	Runs hitting school in the desert
Ken Hill	Fort Worth, Texas	Taking it easy
Pedro Martinez	Dominican Republic & Boston	Special assistant to Red Sox GM
Jeff Fassero	Paradise Valley, Ariz.	Triple-A coach, Chicago Cubs
Butch Henry	El Paso, Texas	Taking it easy
Kirk Rueter	Nashville, Ill.	Taking it easy
Gabe White	Sebring, Fla.	Loves racing monster trucks
Denis Boucher	Lachine, Que.	Pitching coach for Team Canada
John Wetteland	Argyle, Texas	Bible/baseball tutor at Liberty Christian School
Mel Rojas	Santo Domingo, D.R.	Taking it easy
Jeff Shaw	Washington Courthouse, Ohio	Taking it easy
Tim Scott	Hanford, Calif.	Working with kids' baseball teams
Gil Heredia	Phoenix, Ariz.	Minor-league coach for Arizona D'backs
Jeff Gardner	Newport Beach, Calif.	Taking it easy
Joey Eischen	Port Charlotte, Fla.	Colorado's A-Class pitching coach in Asheville, N.C.
Rodney Henderson	Baltimore	Minnesota scout
Heath Haynes	Phoenix, Ariz.	Investments advisor
Brian Looney	Cheshire, Conn.	Playing ball in Italy at last word

1994

The Good, the Bad
and the Ugly

I've never seen so many men wasted so badly.
– Clint Eastwood, 1966[1]

Photo: Denis Brodeur

Top row left to right: Tim Spehr, Ken Hill, John Wetteland, Moises Alou, Cliff Floyd, Rodney Henderson, Larry Walker, Kirk Rueter, Freddie Benavides and clubhouse attendant Sortirus (Moose) Athanasiou.

Third row: Equipment assistant Pat Ross, Gil Heredia, Jeff Shaw, Lou Frazier, Wil Cordero, Tim Scott, Butch Henry, Jeff Fassero, Randy Milligan, Pedro Martinez and unidentified clubhouse attendant.

Second row: Equipment manager John Silverman, Jeff Gardner, Mel Rojas, Sean Berry, Mike Lansing, Denis Boucher, Marquis Grissom, Darrin Fletcher, Lenny Webster and team-travel director Erik Ostling.

Front row: bat-boy Scott Abramovitch, assistant trainer Mike Kozak, hitting coach Tommy Harper, bullpen coordinator Pierre Arsenault, bench coach Tim Johnson, manager Felipe Alou, pitching coach Joe Kerrigan, first-base coach Luis Pujols, third-base coach Jerry Manuel, head trainer Ron McClain and bat-boy Jamie Abramovitch, Scott's brother.
Of course, mascot Youppi is in front.

Chapter Twenty-Seven

The Guns of August

Men could not sustain a war of such magnitude and pain without hope – the hope that its very enormity would ensure that it could never happen again...

– Barbara Tuchman[2]

These were the best of times: they were soon to become the worst of times. For, as even the average fan could hear, ominous rumblings had begun to cut through the hazy days of August. Strike talk was in the air, and unless some drastic change occurred in the interim, the players were set to walk out on August 12.

As the Expos entered what would become their doomsday month, they were cruising, sitting alone in first place, winning series after series, and playing hard-nosed baseball. People started comparing them to the Montreal Canadiens, whose dashing fire-wagon brand of fast and bruising hockey had produced record numbers of Stanley Cups for the trophy room.

It was 3 a.m. on August 1 when the Expos returned to Montreal from visits to Atlanta and Miami, ready to begin a brief four-game home stand against the Cards. As it happened, this would turn out to be their final home stand of the season. But nobody was thinking in those terms, not even the players themselves. All-star centre fielder Marquis Grissom said simply: "We're blocking out the strike and we're blocking out first place. We're just going to win as many games as we can and see what happens." After all, even White Sox majority owner Jerry Reinsdorf appeared to be having second thoughts, musing that perhaps he would prefer the salary cap be scrapped.

By now, local fans and the media alike were starting to believe that in all likelihood the Expos were on their way to the postseason. *Montreal Gazette* columnist Jack Todd was calling them the finest team in baseball. For the next two weeks the best place in the world to be was in the bosom of Expos fandom.

The evening of their early-morning arrival home, *Nos Amours* nipped the Redbirds 3-2, mainly because of the stellar performance offered up by Grissom himself, whose feats had fans talking long after the final out. It can still be found on a YouTube highlight reel someplace, one of the happiest highlight reels in franchise history.

The game was a pitcher's battle all the way, and going into the ninth inning the Expos led 2-1. On the mound, John Wetteland took over from Mel Rojas, who in turn had replaced starter Butch Henry in the seventh. Wetteland was intent on securing the victory: it was time for everyone to get some rest.

The Cards had other ideas, however. After Wetteland struck out the first batter and coaxed the next one to loft a lazy fly ball to right field and into Cliff Floyd's glove – Larry Walker was holding down first base that night – and with the crowd of 30,000–plus stomping their feet and cheering in anticipation of the final out – the closer had to stand and watch in disgust as Geronimo Pena circled the bases after hammering a drive over the fence to tie the game. Keeping his cool, Wetteland retired the next batter out. When the Expos failed to score in their half of the frame, sending this beyond-exhausted group of ballplayers back onto the field for extra innings, even the hardest hearts felt sympathy for them.

Wetteland, with the help of a double play, made quick work of the Cardinals in the tenth. Now it was the Expos' turn, and Marquis Grissom was first up. He swung at the first pitch he liked, belted the ball deep into centre field, and started to run. And run. He kept running right past third base and toward home, sliding across the plate in a cloud of dust. Safe. An inside-the-park home run. The Expos had won 3-2. The noise was deafening. The joy was palpable.

August Second

The following night the Expos won again, 5–4, as pitching ace Ken Hill notched his 15th win, the earliest an Expos pitcher had reached that total in a season, beating Charlie Lea's old mark by 14 days. "It was just one of those things where I happened to be on top in wins," Hill (15-5) said later. When someone compared him to Greg Maddux, Hill replied: "I think Greg Maddux is the best pitcher in the game. I'm just happy to be mentioned in the same breath."

There was some sad news that day as well. The team received word that manager Alou's father (and Moises' grandfather) had died in the Dominican Republic.

August Third

Upon hearing of his father's passing, Felipe Alou left Montreal to attend to his family's needs, delegating bench coach Tim Johnson to take over as skipper. Under his guidance the team never missed a beat, burying the Cardinals 8-3.

Making life a bit simpler for their interim manager – and for their starting pitcher, Gil Heredia – the club scored four runs in the first inning. Marquis Grissom led off with a single, and after Sean Berry flied out, Moises Alou's single put runners on first and third. Larry Walker doubled, driving the first run home, and before the frame ended both Alou and Walker had scored and catcher Lenny Webster had homered, a solo shot. That was all Heredia needed to keep the Cards off the score sheet. He was lifted in the seventh inning for Jeff Shaw, and while the reliever did surrender three runs, the damage had been done.

Following the victory, in Felipe Alou's office just off the clubhouse, Johnson made a point of not sitting in the manager's well-worn, comfortable recliner, choosing the corner of a nearby desk instead. "I have too much respect for the man to sit in his chair," Johnson said.

The Expos had improved their record to 68-38. They were 30 games over .500, experiencing a storybook season – on the field, that is.

Out on the labour front, things were far less promising. Strike talk was still clouding the air, and Expos managing general partner Claude Brochu was telling reporters and anyone else who would listen that, of all the teams in the major leagues, a strike would hurt the Expos most. "The timing for us couldn't be worse," he said.

A day earlier the owners, stirring the pot, had thrown a high hard one at the union, holding back on a $7.8-million payment owed to the players' pension fund. This action, clearly intended to provoke, so infuriated players association executive director Donald Fehr and his deputies that they held a conference call with all team representatives to ask if they might consider advancing their projected strike date of August 12 by a week. Discussion was loud and lively, but in the end, cooler heads prevailed. The reps made no secret of their displeasure with the owners and their seeming arrogance, but recognizing that it was in no one's interest to act rashly, agreed to a continuation of play.

August Fourth

The fourth and final game in the home stand against the Cardinals was played on Sunday, August 4. As it turned out, this was the last one the Expos would play in 1994. In many ways that match served as a harbinger of what was to come – none of it good. The 39,044 fans who lustily greeted *Nos Amours* as they took the field that afternoon constituted one of the last big crowds to see an Expos home game for the rest of time – except for each Opening Day. The season opener had long served as a celebratory event for revellers in search of spring. Throngs of people, from the committed to the casual fan along with their friends and loved ones, would pour into the Big O for that first game, bearing all the verve and joy they could muster. It was the one day in the baseball season when the concrete confines of the much-maligned stadium took on the noise, the enthusiasm, and even the eye-candy, of a Formula One Grand Prix–type event. Sadly, while this was an impressive and not-to-be-missed tradition, it was ephemeral and all too soon over. On the morrow, the stadium and the team would be pretty well forgotten as the festival drifted elsewhere down the street. In the club's final decade in Montreal, seldom, if ever, would a collection of 40,000 baseball–mad enthusiasts crowd into the stadium during the season just to watch a regular season game.

The Expos lost this final game, 7–3. Not only did they fail to sweep the Cardinals in this, one of their last important home stands ever, but by so doing seemed to set in motion a foretoken of doom they would bear for the rest of their days, and beyond.

Kirk Rueter, an Expos original who would be traded to the Giants halfway through the 1996 season, was the losing pitcher that day. Larry Walker, the all-Canadian lad from British Columbia, a true national star on the cusp of even greater things, went 2-3. Both his hits were home runs; his three runs batted in were the only runs the locals scored. He would never get the chance to do anything like that again in an Expos uniform.

Sometimes the sadness seeps in and takes hold even before you know it's there. This was one of those moments.

August Fifth

The Expos now moved out on the road to complete their truncated season and quickly returned to their winning ways, and with panache, right up to the end. Almost.

The team first stopped in Philadelphia for a three-game series, opening with Pedro Martinez on the mound. He ran his record to 10-5 by pitching a two-hitter and mystifying the 1993 World Series–finalist Phillies 5-0 as Alou's squad kept surging. The key to his performance, which included eight strikeouts and four walks, the sturdy Martinez said later, was to keep the dangerous, tobacco-chewing leadoff hitter Lenny Dykstra from doing any damage. "Lenny's the key. Keep him off the basepaths and you control the game." Phillies second baseman Mickey Morandini saw it another way: "He (Martinez) stuck it up our butts. Hey, everybody knows how good his changeup is. He's the best in the league now."

August Sixth

Montreal had a tougher time this day, finally pulling things together at the last moment to eke out a 4-3 win in 11 innings. All had been in order through the first eight innings. Batting against former Los Angeles Dodger Fernando Valenzuela, the artisan on the mound for Blue Monday in 1981, the Expos scored single runs in the third, fourth and sixth innings, thanks to some timely hitting by lesser-lights Mike Lansing, Lenny Webster and Sean Berry, while Montreal hurler Butch Henry limited the Phils to a single score.

When the teams entered the bottom of the ninth with Montreal ahead 3-1, closer Wetteland came in to wrap up the victory.

Unfortunately, things did not go as planned. With one runner on base, pinch-hitter John Kruk slammed the ball out of the park, one of only five circuit-blows he struck all year. The game was going into extra innings.

It remained even until the top of the eleventh, which Wil Cordero opened by reaching second on an error. A sacrifice bunt and a fielder's choice later, Montreal's all-star shortstop crossed the plate, giving his team the lead. Jeff Shaw took over from Wetteland in the home half and managed a quick three-up/three-down effort for the save. Wetteland was credited with the win.

August Seventh

Montreal took the final game of the series 6-4, sweeping the Phillies and putting an exclamation point to the disappointment that had blanketed the 1994 baseball season in the City of Brotherly Love. For Phillies faithful, the shortened season must have been a blessing, so far and so ignominiously had their team fallen since 1993 when only a misdirected Mitch Williams pitch to Toronto's Joe Carter prevented them from tying the World Series at three games apiece. "By the time play was halted on August 12, injuries, ineffectiveness, and overall ineptitude were [the] contributing factors to the team's 54-61 final record," noted one Phillies supporter.[3] The team ended the season holding down fifth place in the reconfigured NL, 20.5 games behind the league-leading Expos.

In this last outing of the three-game series the Phillies took an early 3-1 lead, only to have the Expos first tie the game and then move ahead for keeps in the sixth inning. Moises Alou was the offensive star, going 3-for-5 with a double, a triple, two RBIs, and two runs.

Ken Hill worked into the eighth inning to earn his league-best 16th win of the season against only five losses. That record was good enough to earn him an All-Star spot and place him second to Greg Maddux in voting for the Cy Young Award. Hill was having a career year, and most observers agree that, had it not been for the strike, he was on his way to 20 victories or more. This would have made him only the second Expos pitcher to reach that pinnacle: Ross Grimsley went 20-11 in 1978.

Now that the Phillies had been taken care of, the Expos were off to Pittsburgh and a four-game series with the struggling Pirates.

August Eighth – August Eleventh

The Pittsburgh Pirates, much like the cross-state Phillies, were out of the race and faring poorly. Since their hearts had been irreparably broken in 1992 when, for the third consecutive season, they had made it to the National League Championship Series only to be shut out of the World Series, the Pirates had become a pale shadow of their former selves. In fact, 1992 was the last winning season the Pirates experienced in a generation. From 1993 through 2012 the team never once enjoyed a season above .500. Thus, one can imagine the joy that embraced Steel City in the autumn of 2013 when finally the Pirates not only achieved a winning season, with conviction, but also made it through the wild card lottery to the NL Division Series.

But in 1994, with the Expos steamrolling into Three Rivers Stadium full of confidence, the Pirates had little to look forward to. And sure enough, Montreal took the first three games, all low-scoring affairs – before being shut out by the Pirates in the final match…the final match of the series, of the season, and of their good fortune.

The Expos won the opener 3-2, with all three runs coming on a Moises Alou home run in the sixth inning. Starting pitcher Gil Heredia held Pittsburgh to single tallies in the second and seventh innings to earn the win, his sixth of the season. He received help from Tim Scott, who made short work of the Bucs in the eighth inning, and John Wetteland, who earned the save pitching the ninth. The Expos won in similar fashion the next day, August 9, when they eked out another one-run victory, this time by a 4-3 score. Starting pitcher Kirk Rueter, who got the win, was responsible for all three runs, although the last of these came off a Dave Clark double surrendered by reliever Mel Rojas in the seventh inning. Then, in what seemed like just another day at the office, closer Wetteland took over to wrap up his 24th save.

Expos runs were scattered across four different innings. Grissom had four of the club's ten hits, scored one run and drove in two. The other runs came courtesy of Larry Walker's solo homer in the sixth, his nine-teenth, and his groundout, which brought Grissom home from third for the team's first run.

Montreal's third win of the series – and last of the season – was much more convincing, and epitomized just what a well-oiled machine these Expos had become. Staked to an early lead, Pedro Martinez pitched another gem, shutting out the Pirates 4-0. He struck out five and limited his opponents to five hits, only one of which was for extra bases. It came in the ninth inning on Pedro's final pitch of the game, a two-out double by Andy Van Slyke with Orlando Merced on base. Manager Alou, unwilling to risk further damage, did what he always did in these situations. He ambled out to the mound, took the ball from Pedro, patted him on the butt, said *gracias* and called for his closer. One batter later the game was over. John Wetteland had chalked up save number 25. Three of the Expos' four runs came in the third frame on a Grissom solo home run and RBI hits by Alou and Walker. The fourth run was the product of a Moises Alou double in the ninth.

The series finale seemed to foreshadow what lay ahead for the proud Expos. They lost. Pirates hurler Zane Smith, once an Expo himself, virtu-ally duplicated Pedro Martinez's performance of the day before by holding his former club to only five hits in throwing a 4-0 complete-game shutout. Expos starting pitcher Butch Henry allowed two runs in the six innings he worked. The Bucs managed to score two more runs in the ninth off Tim Scott and Gil Heredia.

And then came the strike call. It was all over. There would be no base-ball on the 12th: there was nothing left for the Expos to do but pack their bags and head for home. Surprisingly, most players were caught short by the melodramatic suddenness of the work stoppage, even though they knew it was coming.

"As a player, I, and most other players, let strike talk take a back seat during the season," said Larry Walker years later. "The issues were com-plicated, hard to understand and, what with the way we were playing, all our focus was on the field. Still, the way it ended caused a lot of anger, especially with the way we were playing. We had a real shot; we were very disappointed."[4]

"It was surreal," said Butch Henry. "We were going home but we all felt we had unfinished business. I got back to Montreal and my wife and I were packing our stuff in a U-haul truck and we were telling people we'd be back to work in a coupla weeks or so."

But that was not to be.

By the time the 1994 season ground to a halt, the Expos had played 114 games, winning 74 and losing 40. Going by the numbers and ignoring the inconsistencies inherent in a truncated season, this meant that the Expos were not only the best team in Major League Baseball, they were the best edition of the club, ever. Their .649 winning percentage topped the .594 achieved by the 1979 team and the .580 attained in 1993. They were six games ahead of the perennial front-runners, the Atlanta Braves, and, until the guillotine's blade cut the season short, they showed every sign of pulling further away.

So, what made this team special? Collectively, when it came to measuring their hitting, pitching and fielding outputs, the Expos generally fell somewhere in the middle of the pack. They just seemed better at rising to the occasion when it mattered most. Nevertheless, a number of individuals did enjoy very good years.

Pitcher Ken Hill's 16 wins tied him with eventual Cy Young Award winner Greg Maddux and earned him second place behind Maddux in the voting. Marquis Grissom won the Gold Glove Award and both Moises Alou and Wil Cordero received Silver Slugger Awards. Alou, Cordero, Grissom, Hill and Darrin Fletcher all were selected to the All-Star Team.

Others in the starting lineup – Sean Berry, Mike Lansing and Cliff Floyd – also enjoyed better-than-average seasons, as did super-subs like Rondell White, Lenny Webster, Juan Bell, and Lou Frazier.

Right fielder Larry Walker, the Canadian colossus, was especially effective in 1994, playing about one third of his games at first base. Walker led the league in doubles with 44 and batted a healthy .322, to go along with his 19 home runs and 86 RBIs.

Then there was the steady pitching staff. All five starters (Hill, Martinez, Fassero, Henry and Rueter) ended the season with winning records, while the outstanding relief core led by Wetteland and Rojas managed to win 24 games outright and save another 43.

Manager-of-the-year Felipe Alou, the guru whose mystically flavoured brand of leadership set the tone, has called this squad "the best team I ever managed, no question about it." Kevin Malone, Montreal's general manager in that magical year, goes even further: "I have been around a lot of teams," he said, "but not only on the field, these guys were a special group." Pedro Martinez, by this time a devoted Expo, declared proudly: "I was convinced that we could beat any team; 100 per cent. We were going to win it all! Felipe had confirmed it!" Rookie Rondell White exclaimed: "Best team I ever played on. It was electrifying. Everything that could go right went right. We couldn't wait to get to the game, to the park."

But it was John Wetteland who brought perspective to this shared sense of infallibility. Wetteland was one of several star players traded by the Expos in early 1995, victims of a fire sale driven by cash-flow problems. He landed in New York with the Yankees, and, as a Bronx Bomber, finally won the biggest prize of all in 1996. Wetteland was credited with the save in all four World Series victories, and was named the series MVP.

He later recalled: "When I was traded to the Yankees in 1995 and got to spring training, I was often asked 'Do you think your guys could have beaten the Yankees in '94?'" Smiling, he said: "My answer always began with the same words…'With all due respect…'"[5]

By way of comparison, on August 12, the Yankees had compiled a 70-43 record through 113 games. They were leading the AL East Division by 6.5 games and had scored 670 runs (5.93 per game) and allowed 534 runs (4.73 per game). The Expos, on the other hand, had compiled a 74-40 record through 114 games. They were leading the NL East by 6 games and had scored 585 runs (5.1 per game) and allowed 454 runs (4.0 per game).

As it unfolded, and even as it ended, 1994 was a season that meant everything to Montreal. Pity that the coterie of officials charged with preserving the well-being of the game didn't see things the same way.

Chapter Twenty-Eight

Collective Bargaining (Dis)Agreement Strike Three

The sneer is gone from Casey's lip, his teeth are clenched in hate;
He pounds with cruel violence his bat upon the plate.
And now the pitcher holds the ball, and now he lets it go,
And now the air is shattered by the force of Casey's blow.
— *"From Casey at the Bat"* by Ernest Lawrence Thayer

The 1994 season opened with the sword of Damocles hovering above the fragile neck of baseball. Owners and players were not close to coming to terms with an already past-due Collective Bargaining Agreement and time was running out. Whatever negotiations did take place seemed always to end with the inevitable stalemate. Both sides grew more frustrated with every passing day. It was only a matter of time before something would blow.

Not that any of this was especially surprising, except, according to Fred Claire, former general manager of the Los Angeles Dodgers, this time the owners were determined not to give in; this time they intended to change the system. Since the Marvin Miller era, maintained Claire, there had been "a dramatic increase in players' salaries, and a greater division between payrolls of large and small-market teams, but no more."[6] This time the owners balked, determined to draw their line in the sand and stand firm. They declared a readiness to confront the elements that they felt were killing the game – free agency and salary arbitration – and restated their commitment to drive home "the absolute necessity for a salary cap."[7]

The players were having none of it. To leave no doubt, the union, under the direction of Donald Fehr, responded to the owners' ultimatum-like pronouncement by immediately setting a strike date – August 12,

1994. If nothing changed by that date, they made clear, the players would walk. And with that, the game of chicken was on!

At the time, as Claire pointed out, the union's action was thought to be a negotiating tactic, a response to the owners' bellicose bluster. "No one," he wrote, "not owners, players or negotiators, would have dared predict [that games played on August 11] would be the last games of the [1994] season."[8] Or that the 1994 postseason would be cancelled – an unheard-of possibility that had never before transpired in the history of the major leagues. Or that major league baseball would not resume in earnest until April 24, 1995, 232 days later! For the first time since 1904, the year the Fall Classic was established, there would be no World Series.

When the strike was called on August 12 and players put down bat and ball and walked off the diamonds, the shock waves swept across the baseball world. To the amazement of all, the impossible had finally occurred: Chicken Little was vindicated, the sky really was falling. There was no other logical explanation.

By the same token, among those on the inside and closest to the heat, no one was surprised. George Will, the noted columnist, described the "terrible legacy …where it was expected that when the collective agreement expired the two sides would be at daggers drawn, and you would have a work stoppage. This bitterness and suspicion festered because a number of owners frankly were un-reconciled to the existence, not just of this or that behaviour of the union, but to the existence of the union."[9]

Ever since the 1990 round of negotiations had ended bitterly, and the phony March lockout had dissipated unnoticed, owners were seething: "never again would they let the bastards win," they were saying, "never again would they let them take over the commissioner's office."[10] And yet, salaries still jumped dramatically in 1990 and 1991 as a result of both generous arbitration decisions and unequalled free agent contracts. Jose Canseco (Oakland) and Darryl Strawberry (Dodgers) signed five-year deals averaging $4 million per year. Other players were in close pursuit of these numbers, including Expos ace Dennis Martinez, who signed a multi-year agreement with Cleveland at $3 million–plus per year. It was in the face of such insanity that Charles Bronfman made his decision to leave the game entirely. As author John Helyar pointed out, "It wasn't because he could no longer afford it…it was because he could no longer stand it."[11] Bronfman had attempted to encourage his colleagues to develop a formula that would allow for sharing "revenues with the players, and reward them handsomely on a basis that is economically fair to all – club, player, and the public. There is so much more than economics to be considered.

There is our society."[12] But his was a voice in the wilderness: the owners ignored his suggestion.

And the more they railed against the greed of the players and the unfairness of the system, the more money they foolishly kept pouring into salaries. Eventually, the smaller franchises, seeing they could no longer compete with the behemoths of the game, began to bow out, creating a tapestry of 'have' and 'have-not' organizations across both leagues. Helyar noted that by 1991 "the gap between the team with the biggest gross (Los Angeles) and the smallest (Seattle) had now grown to $80 million...The payrolls of three teams – the A's, the Red Sox and the Dodgers – now exceeded the Mariners' total revenues."[13]

By 1993, as both sides began strategizing for the next round of negotiations, the climate continued to sour. And to make matters worse, the owners had lost confidence in the Commissioner of Baseball, Fay Vincent. Too frequently, at least in their eyes, he seemed to lose sight of the fact he was their employee, and not, as some of his early predecessors had been, commissioner of all things baseball mandated to protect the best interests of the game. This difference of opinion led to strained relations and deepening tensions until finally the owners asked for his resignation. He stepped down as baseball's eighth commissioner on September 7, 1992, almost precisely three years from the day he was appointed.

Vincent was replaced by Allan H. (Bud) Selig, owner of the Milwaukee Brewers, who was named acting commissioner. He remained in that role until July 9, 1998, when the owners formally and unanimously removed the 'acting' designation and elected him Commissioner of Baseball. There were those who never took him seriously: to them he was simply "Bud Light."

Hardly an intellectual, Selig always seemed short on style. He lacked that hard-to-define quality some call presence. But he was hard-working, determined, and able to get the job done. And he was an owner, firmly positioned on the owners' side: he wasn't going anywhere.

Selig loved the game of baseball and mixed comfortably with his players – until it came to money, and then he left compassion outside the door. Helyar described Selig "as a hawk on labor matters and an apocalyptic voice on the baseball economy."[14]

Speaking years later, after he was named Commissioner, Selig allowed that: "Unfortunately, the acrimony between the parties was so intense that we just couldn't get anywhere. By '93 and '94 you knew that disparity had set in, the small and medium-market clubs were really feeling that they had no chance. The system needed significant economic change and we were getting nowhere, and you couldn't go on the way we were going."[16]

In late 1991, the owners hired Richard Ravitch as the fourth and most recent head of their Player Relations Committee (PRC) and gave him the task of getting the negotiating jump on Donald Fehr and the MLBPA. In his earlier life, Ravitch had been a high-profile businessman comfortable in both private and public sector activity.

For a host of reasons, Ravitch and Commissioner Fay Vincent soon found themselves at loggerheads, mainly regarding the chain of command and the commissioner's role in labour negotiations. Once Vincent departed the scene, Ravitch was free to prepare for the next round, unfettered. While the existing 1990 contract was to run until 1993, provision had been made for the possibility of reopening it as early as 1992, if either side so requested by December of that year. Ravitch encouraged the owners to do this.

The owners were far from unanimous, however. The small-market clubs supported the Ravitch plan, for they were dying under the current agreement. Mark Sauer, owner of the Pittsburgh Pirates whose club had lost $10 million in 1992, was unequivocal. Speaking with Jay Bell, the Bucs shortstop and player rep, he couldn't have been more direct. "Jay," he said, "the point is, you have won. But now you have to decide whether you're going to burn the bodies, bury them, or put us in intensive care. What are you guys going to do?"[17]

On the other hand, the big-market clubs were less than convinced that starting talks prematurely would be a smart move. They feared it would lead to one more protracted work stoppage and further loss of revenues. Baltimore, where "the Orioles loathed losing a single sellout at Camden Yards,"[18] was given as an obvious case in point.

Confusion reigned, owners were conflicted, the whole system seemed poised to run amok – and yet general managers were tossing money around like confetti. One of the first players to benefit was Barry Bonds – signed by the Giants in the winter of 1992 to a six-year contract worth $43 million.

It fell to Ravitch to finds ways of restoring some measure of order, and he placed his faith in a negotiating strategy built around the notion of a salary cap. Unfortunately for him, some owners could see nothing good in that approach.

The mounting disharmony among the owners was causing increasing uncertainty, and this worried Donald Fehr very much. "[The owners] are utterly disorganized and have no plan," he said, "but they've created the conditions where things could get out of control."[19] When someone suggested that the owners were cooking the books to make their situation seem even bleaker, Ravitch apparently fired back, "the owners aren't crooks; they're assholes!"[20]

Nevertheless, for many teams these were very trying times. Stan Kasten, current president of the Dodgers who once held the same post with the Braves, recalls: "It was a difficult economic time; some teams were losing a great deal of money." Speaking in an exclusive telephone interview with Danny Gallagher, he continued, "Collectively, as an industry, we were losing money. It was not a good situation. It was costing teams more money every day just to play the game. There was not any recognition or admission by the union that we faced economic problems. It was too easy for the union to say the owners are rich and making lots of money."[21]

The fundamental divide separating the two camps was perhaps best articulated in a minority report written by a member of baseball's Economic Study Committee, one Henry J. Aaron, an authority in the health field (and no relation to the home run record holder). He noted: "a governance structure of professional baseball clubs that is incapable of enforcing greater revenue sharing is *the* problem. Unless that problem is addressed and solved, labor-management peace will never come to baseball."[22] Lou Hoynes, a legal advisor to baseball, had once said something similar to Bart Giamatti back when he was commissioner. Baseball's top priority, said Hoynes, was to "more evenly distribute its revenues. You don't have to be a genius to figure that out, but you do have to be a genius to figure out how."[23] George Steinbrenner stood on the other side of the argument, but was equally adamant. He made a habit of periodically addressing his fellow owners as "Comrades," then adding, "I want to make it very clear. I'm not going to pay anyone for not working."[24]

With the ownership group split into the big-market and small-market clubs and both working at complete odds with one another, it fell to Ravitch to find a way through the morass. He would have to build consensus around what he termed his "Siamese Twins" – revenue-sharing (the league's wealthiest teams sharing revenues with its less-fortunate partners to ensure a more level economic playing field) and an accompanying salary cap formula (whereby a team was limited in the total amount it could pay its players) – before management could comfortably meet the players' association head on. Then, he and his partners would have to find ways of convincing the union this was the only course of action possible.

As the year 1993 broke, the owners were already considering yet another lockout to support their case – even though they didn't quite know what that case entailed. Their position was weakened, as was the players', by the constant bickering between the two parties, especially in the face of tough economic times and exaggerated salary demands and payouts. The buying public, whose own circumstances were growing more troubled by the day, was becoming tired of the never-ending haggling and back-biting that increasingly defined the tattered icon once proudly called the National Pastime. A marketing specialist who worked with athletes pulled no punches when he told his clients: "if people talk about spoiled, overpaid athletes these days, they're talking about baseball players."[25]

Steve Greenberg, son of the former Detroit Tiger and Hall of Fame inductee (1956) Hank Greenberg, who was baseball's deputy commissioner at the time, was on the mark when he noted: "The economic disparity between the players and the guys who sit in the stands was so much less in my dad's day. The average fan felt much closer to the players. They were working stiffs like them. Now fans say, 'Who can relate to a guy who's making five or six million dollars.'"[26]

Once spring turned to summer and the 1993 schedule ran its course, the situation off the field kept getting worse. The players' association, increasingly concerned that the owners might institute a lockout at season's end, began planning for a pre-emptive Labour Day strike instead. Television contracts, and the rich revenues they generated, hung in the balance and the weaker teams were feeling the pinch more than ever. To counter this uncertainty, Ravitch decided it was time for drastic measures. He convened the owners and their aides to a baseball summit in Kohler, Wisconsin. His intent was to hammer out a revenue-sharing deal they could all accept. Ravitch was clear: "We've got to have a deal...because the consequences of not having one are so much worse than the compromises you will have to make."[27]

It was now up to the owners to sort out the possibilities. This was no easy task. As one member of that select group pointed out, "You can never forget, these guys [owners] don't like each other and they don't trust each other."[28]

Close only counts in horseshoes. And when it comes to negotiations, even negotiations involving partners all sitting on the same side of an issue, coming close to an agreement without sealing the deal means nothing, as the Kohler initiative confirmed. While at various moments it seemed as though consensus were possible, when it came time to leave for home, they all left empty-handed. There was no deal. The owners had dillied and dallied their way around all possible avenues, only to let every option slip through their fingers.

By now, Ravitch was running out of ideas, even as his next challenge was to thwart the union's threatened Labour Day strike. This he managed brilliantly to achieve by guaranteeing that the owners would not entertain the possibility of a lockout during either the 1993 or 1994 seasons. He also promised no off-season decisions would be imposed unilaterally, and made clear that rules on salary arbitration and free agency would remain intact.[29] There was nothing spoken about revenue-sharing.

Ravitch kept the pressure on, insisting the owners reach consensus on their bargaining position – or risk another strike. A difficult proposition at the best of times, it was made more so by the depth of mistrust that owners held toward each other. Controversial A's owner Charlie Finley didn't mince words when he roared: "Stupid. Stupid. Stupid. Stupid. If they'd had a brain they would have been idiots."[30]

The owners' strategic impasse, what Helyar called their "revenue-sharing logjam,"[31] finally broke in January 1994 when the concept's staunchest foe chose to reverse his position. August A. Busch III, owner of both the famed St. Louis Cardinals and the gargantuan Anheuser-Busch brewing company, a worldwide brand famous for both its prancing Clydesdale horses and its Budweiser beer,[32] was a force to be reckoned with inside the owners' group. But when several of his counterparts, businessmen all, convinced him that it was time to bend on the revenue-sharing issue, he deferred to them.

With that barrier out of the way, the vote was called and carried – revenue-sharing was now on the table. The owners were delighted; the union not at all. Its members had not been part of the discussion on the matter. To the MLBPA this omission indicated that direct confrontation was awaiting them just around the corner.

Not all was copacetic in the owners' camp either, for no sooner had one problem been resolved than another bubbled to the surface. What did this sharing of revenues mean, exactly, and how would it be applied? The middle-market clubs moaned about the money they had lost over the past few years, and the precarious position this new plan put them in. Pittsburgh's Doug Danforth pointed out: "We've lost $40 million to $50 million in hard cash over the past six years. The status quo isn't acceptable." Until revenue-sharing was implemented they would have no chance of challenging the top-grossing clubs.

Those clubs, of course, were not about to watch their hard-earned wealth find its way into the hands of paupers without a struggle. The volatile George Steinbrenner spoke for that cohort when late in 1994 he pointed out that money and success on the diamond did not necessarily go hand in hand. "Look at Montreal," he said. "The best record in baseball is the team with the second-lowest payroll. So you can shoot that argument [that without revenue-sharing low-grossing clubs could not compete] right in the butt."[33]

By mid-June, and after hours and days of debate and lobbying, the owners were ready to present their proposal to the union. Revenue sharing was in – taking the form of "a 50 percent share of revenues to players and a guarantee that total pay wouldn't dip below 1994's $1 billion" – on condition that the principle of a salary cap was also adopted. Further, the proposal decreed an end to salary arbitration, offering in exchange a lowering of free-agency eligibility to four years."[34]

Or, to put it another way, as Donald Fehr did, repeatedly, "the owners will do revenue-sharing as long as the players pay for it with a salary cap."[35] He had become cynical. "You go through *The Sporting News* for the last 100 years," he once said, "and you will find two things are always true. You never have enough pitching, and nobody ever made money."[36]

It was clear that among the owners the hard-liners had won out. They were well aware that "the Players Association had been talking for fifteen years about how a salary cap was off the table, that it could never accept such a thing, and [the owners] reacted accordingly."[37]

Fehr was now convinced that the owners had another agenda in the works – to break the union. Should they succeed, he concluded, then "they could go back to setting the salary levels, and over any significant period of time the difference in their revenue would be measured in the billions of dollars."[38]

To Fehr and company the salary cap was anathema. They would never buckle – and so they began to expand development of strike strategies. Such preparation was necessary for under existing labour law it was decreed that if, following a respectable interval, negotiating parties were unable to reach a collective agreement, the employer had the right to declare a bargaining impasse and impose the terms of employment. In other words, if a contract could not soon be reached with the players, "the owners could eventually shove the salary cap down their throats."[39]

In the meantime, not only were there no negotiations in progress, there appeared to be no interest in negotiating. Braves pitching great Tom Glavine had an explanation. "You know, as far as we are concerned, we are ready to play but we're obviously not going to do it under the terms of the salary cap, so as soon as they're ready to come to us with a deal…"[40]

To short-circuit the possibility that the owners could impose their will, which best guesses held would transpire following the end of the season, and to put the pressure back on management, the union began weighing different potential strike dates within the 1994 schedule – when players would still hold the advantage. In their opinion, the union was in a better position than the owners to weather a protracted strike. "The union had a $200 million strike fund to fall back on. The owners had no such war chest. The losses inflicted on them – and the pressure to settle – could be far worse than on the players' side."[41] And thus they chose a date – August 12. If things were not resolved by then, the players would go out on strike.

Almost immediately there ensued a furious flurry of chatter within the groups and across party lines. Any number of suggestions and offers were proposed, but, inevitably, what pleased the owners angered the players, and notions the players thought were fair were coldly rejected by management. The die had been cast: there was little chance the sides might reconcile their differences in time to avoid a calamitous work stoppage.

But wasn't this always the pattern? Ever since the formation of the players' union in 1966, whenever the parties had begun to negotiate a new contract, "tensions with the owners had escalated. A strike or a lockout accompanied every round of negotiations," and over the years court rulings had given the players more and more power. Now, in the middle of the 1994 season, the two adversaries were embroiled in their bitterest contract dispute yet."[42] It could not end well.

Nor did it: the season concluded prematurely, ending with the games of August 11. There would be no World Series. To the average fan this foolhardy battle to the death, pitting billionaires against millionaires, was both incomprehensible and reprehensible. The owners had followed the lead of their chief negotiator Richard Ravitch, who told them, "The question here, ladies and gentlemen, is one very simple one – the players went out on strike, their average compensation is 1.2 million dollars, and all we have been trying to find out is how much more do they want,"[43] and shifted the blame to the other side.

Donald Fehr's response was to point a finger at the ones occupying the VIP loges: "This dispute arises because the clubs could not get their own internal house in order and redefine their revenue-sharing rules."[44] Former pitcher Jim Bouton was even more acerbic. "For a hundred years the owners screwed the players," he declared. "For 25 years the players have screwed the owners – they've got 75 years to go."[45]

By any definition it was a classic standoff, a lose–lose situation, or as Randy Hendricks saw it, "To save the art they burned down the museum."[46] Respected baseball historian John Thorn emphasized that here was a case where two sides were "locked in a battle that neither side thought could be lost. It's like people who go to court thinking the jury's got to see it my way because I'm in the right, but only a fool stops playing baseball in the middle of August."[47]

Expos fans would say he was dead right.

Stan Kasten called the situation a shame. "It made people physically ill, literally sick with what had happened about both sides not coming to an agreement. We knew the repercussions. It could have been avoided and we're proud that we have avoided it since."[48]

Although it would take several more years for the diamond dust to finally settle, Kasten is quite correct. Since 1995, MLB is the only major professional sports organization not to endure a suffocating work stoppage over salaries and working conditions. Hockey and the NHL, to their own and utter shame, have experienced three such lockouts, though the league now has a 10-year CBA, negotiated by Donald Fehr.

Chapter Twenty-Nine

Anatomy of the 1994 Players' Strike:

Conversations with Weiner, Ravitch and Manfred

"It was extraordinarily frustrating dealing with the owners," Richard Ravitch, the owners' chief negotiator, said in conversation not long ago, "even tougher than dealing with the New York state legislature. Absolutely. Convincing owners to adopt a salary cap was a major issue. Big clubs didn't want a salary cap, but smaller clubs wanted the revenue-sharing that came with it."[49]

The owners were bitter, still begrudging the unpalatable compromise that had led to the signing of the 1990 collective agreement. They wanted payback – enough was enough – it was time to put their house back in order. That frustration finally led to a truce in the intramural bickering, and with cooler heads prevailing, in early 1994 the owners accepted a proposal that would impose a salary cap on the game.

Now they were in a position to deal, and with a new kind of muscle behind them, the lions in the owners' den were anxious to challenge the union head on. That hard-line stance led directly to the players' walk-out on August 12 – for if the MLBPA had established anything in its dealings with the owners, it was their absolute determination to never accept a salary cap. Never.

"We knew the owners wanted a salary cap," recalled Michael Weiner, most recently the MLBPA executive director, who was a lower-rung official back in the 1990s. "At spring training in 1993, the owners tried to get their act together on revenue-sharing before they would bargain further. They already had a cap-type proposal in mind."

Once the owners came together with a common purpose in 1994 there was a complete shift in the negotiating landscape. "A lot of owners thought this was their one opportunity to shape the future of baseball," said Ravitch, "even at the risk of a strike. The owners wanted fundamental economic reform."

The result was a complete impasse, even though the parties did try to keep the dialogue open. MLB lawyer Rob Manfred, after checking his files, confirmed that during the 1994 season the two sides conducted 20 full-bargaining sessions and a number of smaller sessions, right up to the eleventh hour. Their twentieth and final meeting took place on August 10, two days before the strike.

But in the end the owners wouldn't budge from their salary-cap commitment, leaving Weiner and union leader Donald Fehr no alternative.

"The 1994 negotiation period was really difficult," recalls Manfred. "The industry economics were bad, very bad. Clubs were losing a lot of money. The state of labor relations was not very good. There was a need for serious economic reform. We aimed at an overall reform of the financial system to promote competitive balance. We wanted payroll compression for all the markets, including the smaller markets to make things as competitive as possible. The combination of wanting to implement reform and the state of labour relations was combustible."

The owners proposed a seven-year contract that would split their total revenue with the players, 50-50, while introducing a salary cap over the next four years. Once an average obligation to the players under that 50-50 split was established, no team could have a payroll greater than 110 percent of that average or lower than 84 percent.

To the players, this kind of limitation ran completely counter to their philosophy. They had made tremendous gains through free agency, and they were not about to give these up. In 1994 alone, they were sitting on guarantees that generated upwards of $1 billion in pay and benefits.

The owners' proposal also eliminated salary arbitration, although it did lower the number of years before which a young player could become a free agent, from the current six to four, with the home club retaining a right of first refusal. For players with fewer than four years of service, a rising scale of minimum salaries was proposed, with the actual minimum amounts to be negotiated later.

Players' licensing revenue (their share from the retail sale of licensed merchandise such as baseball cards, autographed collectables, jerseys, etc.) which was equitably distributed to all 30 teams also came up for debate, with the owners demanding a larger share of the pot. Today the player's share is determined on a pro rata basis depending on length of service. A player's popularity or status are not figured into the calculations.

None of the owners' demands was acceptable to the MLBPA – and true to their word, they walked out on August 12.

In hindsight, Rob Manfred looks back on the strike and cancellation of the season in 1994 as something he deeply regrets. A lot of lessons were learned, however.

"It's called live and learn," Manfred said in an exclusive interview. "Two big lessons: Number one, that the publicity around the strike was all negative. Number two, and this is important to the Collective Bargaining Agreement and efforts to implement reform – it's very hard to fix a problem once and for all. In 1996, for example, we didn't get a salary cap but we did get revenue-sharing. With each negotiation, we improve things, each and every time. Now, there is more balance. I joined the MLB in 1989 as a young man. I was in the room for all of the six contract negotiations, including 1994.

"I'm not surprised the players went on strike. They kept threatening they would. Our positions were completely polarized. Striking in August gave them maximum leverage, that we would be afraid of losing the season. We knew the strike was coming but we thought it would be relatively short."

On the other hand, the owners' negotiator Richard Ravitch was shocked. "I was surprised indeed on August 12 because I thought there might have been some compromise to avoid it," Ravitch said. "You know what I learned afterward, years afterward, that players' agents had significant influence with the owners. You know, it was easier for me to talk to the players' association that it was to the owners. The owners thought I was obstinate. I found Gene Orza of the union to be a terrific guy, same thing with Don Fehr. Don never lied to me. As often happens in a dispute, each side miscalculated a bit. You don't underestimate the resolve of the other side. But the players offered no meaningful exchange, nothing that would help the clubs."[50]

Michael Weiner of the players' association says that "in 1994-95, communications were different. It was quicker to communicate with the players through the media."

As for the salary cap, Weiner agreed with Manfred. "The owners should have taken the incremental approach," Weiner said. "The overriding principle is that to get something you have to give something in return. We never wanted to go on strike. Absolutely not. With Marvin Miller or Donald Fehr, you never enter a bargaining situation planning to go on strike. For any organization that lost out on a championship that year, like the Expos, this was a big thing. And yet, we weren't surprised when Bud Selig cancelled the season.

"It's hard to rewrite history. A cancelled season and the blood that was spilled didn't have to happen.

"Looking at the Expos, they had a great bunch of guys so there was a sense of sadness over what they might have accomplished had the season run its full course. Many of those Expos went on to accomplish a lot after they left the club. On a more personal level, you had guys like Tony Gwynn and Matt Williams who were having great seasons. Losing those opportunities was an unfortunate consequence of the work stoppage."

Continuing in a similar vein, Manfred observed: "Losing the season was a horrible blow. Strikes are kind of like viruses, like wildfire. The players thought we would never cancel the World Series. But the weather was starting to get cold; teams had not played in a month. We would have had to play some games before the start the postseason. The players would not come back to work and that left Bud with literally no choice but to cancel the season."

In hindsight, Weiner does wonder if the players made a tactical error. "Looking back, our strike date was too early," Weiner allowed. "We should have set the strike date late enough in the season so that our players would have received a significant portion of their salary. Placing the strike date later in the season would have put more pressure on the owners."

Weiner does not agree with the assumption that wealthy, large-market clubs like the Blue Jays, Cubs, Phillies, Braves, Dodgers, Yankees, and so on didn't want a salary cap back in 1994.

"There had to be a consensus to go forward with (allowing) the strike," Weiner said. "Pick a fight with the players. The owners wanted radical change. Why, they were even prepared to use replacement players for the 1995 season to try and break the union. The injunction issued against that reminds us all of just how nasty it was."

In 2009 Weiner took over as executive director of the MLBPA when Donald Fehr left his 26-year stewardship to head up the National Hockey League Players Association (NHLPA). Sadly, in August 2012, Weiner, 51, developed an inoperable brain tumor and by the following summer had undergone four rounds and more of chemotherapy and radiation. In May 2013 he wrote in *Sports Illustrated* that he was still able to work full-time most days, trying to live each day to the fullest. Nevertheless, by mid-2013, there was speculation that, faced with difficult choices, MLBPA officials were considering inviting Fehr back into the fold.

In his SI story, Weiner outlined what he most appreciated about the MLBPA in words that in some ways provide a context for the events of 1994. "What I most enjoy about the MLBPA are the people I get to work for, the players," he wrote. "Baseball players understand that the rights and benefits they enjoy did not drop out of the sky but result from sacrifices made by players before them. They also understand that they have a responsibility to the players of tomorrow, to ensure that the rights and interests of players are protected."[51]

Fair enough.

Sadly, Michael Weiner did not live long enough to see his dream fully realized. He passed away at his home in Mansfield Township, New Jersey, on November 21, 2013.

Chapter Thirty

Grit 'N Grin Grissom

It was August 1 and the Expos had just nipped the St. Louis Cardinals, 3–2, thanks mainly to Marquis Grissom. His remarkable tour of the bases in the 10th inning, replicating one of baseball's rarest and most glorious plays, the inside-the-park home run by the home team, had not only brought victory to the home club, it had left fans both speechless and with plenty to talk about.

For a home run scored when the ball doesn't leave the playing field is ultimately a product of raw speed. The race around the diamond nearly always concludes with a bang-bang, hold-your-breath confrontation at home, with the fans on their feet, hollaring. Indeed, the anticipation, the unfolding of the play, makes for some of the greatest drama in baseball. Starting with the throw from the scrambling outfielder at the wall to the relay man positioned just beyond the fringes of the infield grass, then a quick pivot and strong throw to the catcher already steeling himself for a collision. As ball, catcher and runner come together at the last second, all eyes are fixed on the umpire. While a safe call is cause for euphoria and relief for the home team, the opposite makes for a gut-wrenching feeling: for there is almost nothing worse for a ballplayer than to be thrown out at the plate in front of the home crowd, especially when he has covered 360 feet in the frantic attempt to get there.

On August 1, the mad dash around the basepaths ended well for Marquis Grissom.

Batting against Cards left-handed pitcher Rich Rodriguez to lead off the 10th inning, Grissom laced a 1-2 offering deep to centre field. Knowing he had gotten "good wood on it," he quickly tossed his bat aside and charged out of the box, taking that precious extra second or two that all right-handed batters must take to step across in front of the plate and head down the first-base line. As he sped toward first and began the wide turn to cross the bag, he saw the ball bounce off the wall and onto the out-field grass. His eyes remaining fixed on the ball and on the actions of centre fielder Ray Lankford chasing it, Grissom blasted past second base knowing he had a shot at a home run. Pounding toward third with no hesitation in his stride, he got the windmill "go-for-it" sign from excited coach

Marquis Grissom

Jerry Manuel. His back now to the play as Lankford hurriedly threw in to relay man Ozzie Smith, Grissom rounded the bag like a man possessed and made the final charge toward the plate 90 feet away. Speeding along in high gear, he steeled himself for the final act and hit the dirt, barely evading catcher Tom Pagnozzi, a split second ahead of shortstop Smith's desperation relay from just beyond the infield. *The Gazette* columnist Jack Todd claimed that Grissom appeared to leap "a half dozen feet into the air" to drive past Pagnozzi and snare a piece of the rubber. As an exhausted

Grissom rose out of dust pandemonium erupted. The electrifying moment was captured on film and remains one of the most famous highlight-reel moments in franchise history.

"It was the symbolic moment of the season for the Expos," said rapper Annakin Slayd, who included Grissom's achievement on his video tribute to the 1994 Expos. "It showed the Expos' power and talent. Grissom was a superman. Dave Van Horne had the line, 'Marquis Grissom is flying.'" According to baseball-reference.com, Grissom's blast marked the 11th time in baseball history that someone had hit an inside-the-park, walk-off homer. And this one came in extra innings. Grissom admitted later that most players, like himself, would much prefer to hit the long ball over the fence. An inside-the-park jobber just takes the wind out of you. Not only that, it stresses your emotions to the limit. It can also damage you physically in the case of a collision; in this case Grissom was fortunate to avoid hitting the anchored Pagnozzi. The situation would have been quite different had the ball arrived a second earlier.

For the record, meet Grissom's siblings, whose ages in 2013 ranged from 43 to 65:
The Girls: *Barbara, Delores, Dorothy, Elizabeth, Ernestine, Mary, Shirley*
The Boys: *Antonio, Henry, Joe, Marvin, Michael, Phillip, Richard*

In 2012, Grissom, not one to brag about himself, ventured to say he recalled little of that particular home run. "I don't remember. It was before the strike. You'd have to check the video, go to the tape," Grissom said. "It was off the wall, an exciting moment for us but it was just a game we wanted to win. It was a big win for us."

A product of his roots, best described as down-to-earth and genuine, Grissom is one of 15 children born to Marion and Julia Grissom, a hard-working couple in Red Oak, Georgia.

Perhaps it was this self-effacing humility that led teammate Denis Boucher to describe Grissom as "the guy who impressed me most on the 1994 team. He was a great person and I liked the way he went about his business. He led by example and hard work. He talked to everybody at the same level. He made you feel like you were an important part of the team."[52]

A Dave and Dan Tale

"My timing was bad," recalls Expos executive assistant Sina Gabrielli, who has her own Expos memories. "I was away on maternity leave as of mid-April 1994, and then with the strike I just stayed home another six months. So I was not present in 1994, which ended up being one of the most memorable seasons in Expos history! I could not believe that, of all the years, I had to be home on maternity leave during that fantastic year! I missed all the buzz at the office. Even though I kept in touch with everyone, it was not the same as being in the office.

"I had a son in 1994 and I called him Daniel. The running gag was that I named him after Dan Duquette, even though he had Dave Dombrowski's blue eyes! But I just really liked the name. You know some names are harder to pronounce in a different language so I wanted a name that the grandparents were able to say with ease and that was fairly bilingual (English and French)."

Chapter Thirty-One

No Mulligan for Randy

There was no mulligan for the Expos' Randy Milligan after the aborted 1994 season. His luck simply ran out.

Who would have thunk it – that his last game would be August 11, 1994, the Expos' final match prior to the strike. It is odd that he couldn't catch on with any other team. Although the oldest player on the club, he was only 32 when the strike was called, with more good years still left in him. Milligan had enjoyed four decent seasons with the Baltimore Orioles earlier in his career, averaging 15 home runs and 57 RBIs per season. In 1990, he hit three homers in one game against the Yankees and was off to his best season ever when he suffered a dislocated left shoulder in a home-plate collision with Oakland catcher Ron Hassey on August 7. Why is it that baserunners feel the need to be so macho and try to barrel over the catcher, even with serious injury always looming in the background? Milligan – they called him Moose – missed the final 48 games of that season, finishing with 20 homers and 60 RBIs.

Liking what they saw at that time, the Expos acquired the San Diego native in December of 1993 after he played for the two Ohio teams, the Reds and Indians. They picked him up during the 10-day period when Cleveland had designated him for assignment to allow waivers to expire. It was a trade procedure that puzzled Milligan.

"All they had to do was wait half an hour, even less and I would have become a free agent," Milligan told Toronto's *Globe and Mail* newspaper in February, 1994. "Then we could have said what we wanted and they could have told us what they were willing to give. Maybe we could have negotiated something that way (cheaper than arbitration). I would have had no quarrels about signing with the Expos as a free agent. I liked the town."

As it turned out, Milligan went to arbitration, another procedure that puzzled the first baseman. "It's been a strange negotiation," Milligan told the *Globe and Mail*. "The part I don't understand is once you get traded to a new team, that team usually wants you on their squad. In this case, I just didn't feel welcome. That's the part that really hurts me the most. We didn't want it to come down to this but I realize it is part of the business of baseball. It's a bit of a disappointment. I thought we could have had a deal ironed out before Christmas. I don't think we were asking for too much. There was something holding the Expos back."

That 'something' was money. In all fairness to the Expos, they did offer him $600,000, an increase of $125,000 over his 1993 salary. But Milligan and agent Mike Powers wanted more, asking for $1 million. The Expos' chief financial man, Bill Stoneman, was not interested in bumping up their offer to accommodate a career part-timer who figured to be a part-timer in 1994.

"We differ both financially and philosophically as to where Randy fits in with the club," Powers told the newspaper. "We find ourselves hung up on Randy's role, how much they want him. It's a bit of a difficult situation."[53]

As it turned out, Milligan lost his case. There was no way an arbitrator was going to award Milligan a $525,000 raise over his 1993 stipend of $475,000. It is interesting in the context of all this

Randy Milligan

hullaballoo that Milligan earned a healthy $1.2 million with the Orioles in 1992. From there on, his salary only went down.

Milligan got little playing time with the Expos. The club's original plan had been for Milligan to mentor rookie Cliff Floyd at first. However, Larry Walker's injury problems prompted manager Felipe Alou to play the budding superstar at first base much more frequently, putting Floyd in the outfield. This meant Milligan saw even less playing time, leaving him with only 82 at-bats. He managed two homers, 12 RBIs and a .232 batting average.

"Milligan was a very important player," Alou said without any prompting in an interview. "He had some big hits for us. He was really good and helpful with Cliff Floyd at first. He kept everyone loose. It was a perfect situation."

Unfortunately, Milligan never got another major-league job after 1994.

Chapter Thirty-Two

Just How Good
Were These Guys?

The Players

How good were these guys anyway? Well, apart from the fact that they were the best team in baseball and showed no signs of slowing down – what **Butch Henry** called a "built-to-win machine" – they were also very young. Consider this: the only players on the 25-man roster to have reached a thirtieth birthday were Randy Milligan and Jeff Fassero. Promise was the Expos' middle name.

Fassero recalls the first days of the season when, "For some reason, the whole team got off to a poor start. In the middle of May, we were five games under .500 and six games behind Atlanta and John Smoltz of the Braves made the comment that they would walk away with the NL East."[54]

Team members cared for each other. "The best way to put it, we were a family," said Henry. "Sure we had our share of arguments and spats. Some of us were not so close but when it came down to it, we would go to war for each other. Every game."[55]

Rondell White, a rookie in 1994, said: "This was the best team I ever played on. It was electrifying. We couldn't wait to get to the game, to the park. Everything that could go right went right. I thought then we were going to win it all and that's the same way I feel now."

Marquis Grissom didn't have any special moment that he recalled. "Rather what I remember most is the team chemistry, the way we played together. We had a good chance to win every game. Team chemistry was outstanding, the most amazing I ever saw. Even though I won a World Series the next year with Atlanta and went to the World Series with Cleveland in 1997, the chemistry was never the same as in Montreal that year."

Larry Walker draws a comparison between the 1994 Expos and the World Series-bound 2004 Cardinals, his only trip to the Fall Classic. "Both were strong in all departments, but in a seven-game series I would give the edge to the Expos – due to their pitching, especially the relief pitching. Rojas and Wetteland were just lights out."

Walker said the 1994 club made it through without any obvious leaders. "As I recall we all really mingled with each other. Unlike other teams, the pitchers and others all stuck together. There was not any obvious person who stood out ahead of the others. Everyone who wore a uniform was part of the team. We were all a similar age, all fairly young…and of course when you are winning it is a lot easier; everyone is great, even those few who would have been assholes if we were losing. Winning does great things to boost the spirit.

"Following the '94 season we all hoped that we would be able to stay together. We were like the 'we are family' Pirates of 1979; we were very close…and very equal. No one had any say over anybody else."[56]

For pitcher **Gil Heredia**, "The whole starting lineup impressed me, especially Larry Walker and Pedro Martinez. Their physical abilities combined with their unique personalities made them stand out from the rest. John Wetteland was also a special breed. I can go down the whole lineup but those three stood out and impressed me the most."[57]

Backup catcher **Tim Spehr** remembers the whole season "as a big, funny story," although he is reluctant to provide details. "We had fun before the game, fun during the game and lot of fun after the game. Not in a bad way, but when the games were over we weren't about to become straight-laced and be Boy Scouts. We had fun, but it was good, clean wholesome fun."[58]

The Coaching Staff

Expos third base coach **Jerry Manuel** recalled: "We played a whole different brand of baseball. It was tremendous personnel we had. Felipe, as a manager, was fearless, aggressive, a master at putting the team together. Every player was keyed into a proper role. The opposition knew that. What a tremendous opportunity for a manager to grow.

"Baseball had a unique opportunity to witness a style of play that was exciting and executed at a whole different level. Players on the bases knew that unless a decision came from the dugout, they had the freedom to play that certain style. It was a tremendous learning experience for them.

"Whatever Felipe asked you to do, you knew it had a purpose and a way to be done; he explained it to us coaches. He was a machine, he pushed the button and everyone knew the role he had. He did it to the best of his ability without fear, trepidation, or hesitation. He always dug down into the depths of the game of baseball.

"Felipe was the perfect guy for me, oh yeah. All his moves were perfect. We had an understanding of speed. We scored from third base on the contact play; if the ball was hit, we're running home, something that is very rarely seen. One out, runner on third, we'd pull the hit and run, we'd put the ball in play and we get an RBI. We put so much pressure on the other team. Those little things, like squeeze plays. They kept me sharp. That was fun."

Manager **Felipe Alou** always maintained: "No question we were going to the playoffs. The Braves were the only club to compete with us. The biggest memory I have of our team is the incredible unity, the best of any team I managed before or after. They were players developed by the Expos and those who came from other organizations. Just an unbelievable amount of unity, team spirit – and they were a very competent group.

"The club had all the elements of a dynasty: speed, power, hitting for average, defence, incredible bullpen – a young club that could have been good for five or six years. Why, 1995 would have been even better than the 1994 team if we'd been able to keep them together.

"At spring training in 1994 we didn't know how good we might be because of the youth of the team and their lack of experience in winning. We were known for developing players and we knew we had a pretty good team, but what we couldn't know was that we would end up in first place that early in the year. As the season went on, we were really getting better."

The Broadcasters

When **Dave Van Horne** learned that Bud Selig had announced the cancellation of the 1994 season, he decided to pay tribute to the Expos squad in a subtle way. "I wrote the lineup and the stats of the players on a little piece of paper and placed it in my wallet as soon as we realized we weren't going back," the sophisticated, long-time play-by-play man recalled. "I sat down and typed it up on a tiny piece of paper. And I have had it in my back pocket ever since.

"That team obviously had the best chance I thought of ever getting to, even winning, a World Series. The 1981 Expos were undoubtedly an excellent team and there was disappointment when the 1980 team didn't win. But there was something special about the '94 team, because the franchise had survived hard times after Charles Bronfman sold the team, and I thought in 1994 the team really came together.

"They were led by Moises Alou, Larry Walker, Kenny Hill and John Wetteland. They brought dedication and purpose to their play every day. They had terrific talent. Felipe Alou had something to do with it."

Van Horne remembered the Expos winning 94 games in 1993, only to fall short to the Phillies. "The irony of that is the Expos were 20 and one half games ahead of the Phillies in 1994," Van Horne said. "Coming out of the All-Star break, the Expos lost four games against San Francisco but they didn't lose two in a row from then on. It was the way they came together after what happened in San Francisco. I don't think a meeting was formally called. They just said enough of this and everyone elevated their level of play. At the time of the strike, this team was getting better and better day by day. They were pulling away from the Braves at the time of the strike. They were at the head of the class."[59]

Ken Singleton, Van Horne's long-time partner in the broadcast booth, agreed. "I remember how craftily the team was managed by Felipe, like the leader of a finely tuned orchestra. They had everything going for them: speed, defence, some power, their pitching was very good, the bullpen was outstanding," Singleton said. "As the team gained confidence they were like a dynasty in the making; they had that look."

Other Voices

Managing partner **Claude Brochu** could not say enough about the 1994 Expos. "I sensed it from the beginning: I was convinced by Dan Duquette that this team was a winner; that it had a special quality. You could see it in the way the players enjoyed each other. They were very disappointed when the season was cancelled. I learned later that the players had come together and tried to convince their union to accept a special deal whereby the players would keep the same salaries in 1995 as in 1994, just so they could all stay together and have another shot at the championship. Of course, the idea was not approved, but by the very act of asking they were confirming that special bond."

Mark Routtenberg, a member of the ownership group, made a similar observation, adding: "It was a magical team: a team that played together, that believed in its manager and coaches, a team that knew it was on the cusp of greatness."[60]

Expos vice-president **Claude Delorme**, responsible for stadium operations and heavily involved in ticket sales, had his own perspective on just how great the team was in 1994 – and on just how passionate fans became as the season progressed. "After the All-Star Game that year there was so much energy, and in early August we received approval from MLB to start printing postseason tickets. We had about 13,000 strips ordered for the playoffs and the World Series. Those tickets were printed by a company in New York.

"If we had won [the play-offs and the World Series] things would have been substantially different going into 1995. We would have had the impetus for a new ballpark," Delorme said. "It was a turning point in our franchise. We had such a young and talented team, solid enough to win it all. And then it all went down the drain.

"Due to the work stoppage and the cancellation of the season, the tickets were never delivered to us," Delorme said. "Unfortunately, I don't even have samples of those postseason tickets."[61]

Kevin Malone was named the Expos' general manager in 1994. Ten years later he spoke about that club with journalist Stephanie Myles: "A lot of people felt like it was the best team in baseball that year and maybe one of the best to come along in a long time. It's a little frustrating to think back on a team that had that much talent and ability, but didn't get a chance to complete its mission. We felt like we were the best team in baseball, but it wasn't meant to be."[62]

Former Dodgers GM **Fred Claire** thought highly of the 1994 Expos. "As I recall, it was a very well–balanced team, just solid in every way, a solid everyday lineup, with a great, great manager in Felipe. He probably doesn't get the credit he deserves. He was willing to give youngsters a chance and got the most out of all his players. You can't say there was any great superstar player on the team. Larry Walker was a very good player; Marquis Grissom was a great centre-fielder. They had good starting pitching with Ken Hill and Pedro Martinez. They had outstanding relief pitching. Two guys in the bullpen who probably don't get enough attention are Jeff Shaw and Tim Scott."

David Justice, the Braves' outfielder, said much the same thing about the Expos. "They had everything," he said. "You were scared of everything they could do. They could pitch, hit, run, everything.

"What happened to that team was the biggest shame of the whole thing."[63]

Umpire Joe West was positioned behind first base at Olympic Stadium on Blue Monday in 1981 when the Dodgers' Rick Monday hit that famous dinger off Steve Rogers. West also saw the talented Expos team in 1994 and he has little doubt which team was better.

"The 1994 team was the best Expos team ever, better than the team that lost in 1981," said West in 2012, when he was completing his 33rd season umpiring big-league games. "The best, no question about that.

"Position by position, lay them both out on a sheet of paper, the 1994 team was better than the 1981 bunch. Their ace in 1981 was Steve Rogers but I don't remember the supporting cast the way I recall the 1994 cast, which had Ken Hill, Pedro, Jeff Fassero, and others. "That 1981 Expos' team was a bunch of renegades. Put them in a barroom brawl and they came out swinging. Stan Bahnsen, Woodie Fryman, they were rough and tumble like the Oakland Raiders' teams. The 1994 Expos? There were no troublemakers on that team."[64]

A Pirate Bold

In the 1994 Expos media guide, he was listed as "administrative assistant, minor-league operations" in the organization's "baseball management" department. Over time, he served with both the Expos and Cleveland Indians, strengthening his résumé and working his way up the ladder. On September 25, 2007, he was appointed general manager of the Pittsburgh Pirates.

His name? Neal Huntington. His age when appointed? Twenty-eight, and today regarded as one of baseball's top executives.

Chapter Thirty-Three

Heath Haynes

Heath Haynes may not be a familiar name to many who watched the Expos in 1994 but he enjoyed a cup of coffee with the club just the same.

"I was playing for the Ottawa Lynx and we were on the road in Charlotte, North Carolina, when I got the call up to the Expos. It was the very end of May," Haynes remembered. "Jim Tracy was the Ottawa manager and he told me. I was sort of numb. Was it a joke? Was I really going up? I just didn't know what to think. It was like, 'Wow.' It was incredible for me as a non-drafted free agent coming from Wheeling, West Virginia, a small town of 40,000 sandwiched between Pittsburgh and Cleveland.

"I was going up to take the place of Kirk Rueter who had been put on the DL. It was sort of ironic that I was the one to replace him because we were roommates in AA ball. The Expos were in Cincinnati and it was June 1, the last game of a three-game series. I got to the stadium at 6 p.m. pretty excited, and right away put my uniform on. By 8:30 p.m. I was in the game! I was so worked up my depth perception was all wrong. Home plate seemed much closer than 60 feet, six inches away, more like 50 feet."

Haynes entered the game in the fifth inning with two out, two runners on base and the Reds leading 4–0. Tony Fernandez was the batter, but Haynes got him to ground out to second base.

Haynes came back out the next inning and realized then how talented this Expos team was. "There was one play that convinced me I was on a good team," Haynes said. "I gave up a single to the first batter and then the next guy hits this ball that was already through short and third, already in the outfield, when shortstop Wil Cordero hauled it in and turned a double play." Then, with two out, pitcher Johnny Ruffin was safe on an error by Sean Berry, and came home on a Reggie Sanders triple. The run was unearned. Haynes struck out Jerome Walton to end the inning.

In the stands that night, Haynes' parents, his sister and two sets of friends were all looking on. One set sat on the third base side, the other out behind first base. "It sounds incredible now but during the time I was pitching each group of friends managed to nab a foul ball," Haynes said.

"It's a pretty good story. It's hard for anyone to get a foul ball, but this time the balls came into their area and they got them."

Haynes pitched in four games in the week he was up with the big team, but unfortunately, he would never appear in the majors again – even though his ERA was perfect in 3.2 innings of work.

"That year, 1994, was my window of opportunity to at least break in, to prove, in the short time I was up, that I belonged there," Haynes said years later. "I was so happy to get that opportunity. I know a lot of players don't get that close. I wasn't a big thrower. I was 5-foot-10, 180 pounds and my pitches averaged 88-89 miles per hour."

Heath Haynes

Looking back on his week as an Expo, Haynes recalls that "two guys stand out: Pedro Martinez and John Wetteland. Pedro was still young; he always seemed to have a good time. Wetteland was really the same. I got to know him briefly. One of my biggest disappointments was that I never got my picture taken for a major-league card with my photo on it, like from Topps or Upper Deck."[65]

However, Haynes did have the good fortune to marry a young Canadian woman, Eileen King of Cobourg, Ontario. She worked in Ottawa as a paralegal for a firm that had season tickets and occasionally they were given to her. On this one day, she called out to Haynes as he was walking to the bullpen down the left field line, and said hello. Bit by bit, in this same way, they got to know each other – Haynes would show his affection by occasionally grabbing Rice Krispies treats from the clubhouse and giving them to her – and soon enough a beautiful love affair blossomed.

The couple married on New Year's Eve in 1995 in Cobourg in front of minister Lynda King, Eileen's mother. They now live in California, where Haynes works in investment management.

Chapter Thirty-Four

Butch Henry

Butch Henry has no doubt about it. "Of all the teams I played on, that 1994 team was the best; had the most talent.

As Henry looks back on that season, he expresses the utmost respect for Dan Duquette and his role in assembling this group of players, even though he had left for the Red Sox by late January. "Some people may not have good things to say about Dan Duquette as a person," Henry commented in 2012. "I have no opinion on that one way or another – but as a baseball man, he was a genius. He had a contingency plan for every contingency plan. He was thoroughly organized. Look at what he is doing with Baltimore today."

But with regards to an observation made by noted sabermetrician and Red Sox senior advisor Bill James on MLB Network in 2003 that the 1994 Expos were "one of the most overachieving teams in baseball history," and which placed both Henry and pitcher Jeff Fassero in that overachieving category, Henry did have something to say. "Bill James' deductions come strictly from numbers, based on stats and numbers alone. I really didn't pay that close attention to what he said, but when I heard my name I changed the channel.

Butch Henry

"Baseball numbers are a baseline, used to show how players are rated but anyone who played the game knows that stats alone don't always tell the whole story. Maybe we were overachievers, but look at all we accomplished. Why would anybody try to diminish that?"

In 1994 Henry enjoyed his best season in baseball, putting together an 8-3 record and a 2.43 ERA. Behind Ken Hill, Pedro Martinez and Fassero,

Henry did yeoman service in the rotation, with 14 of his 15 appearances coming as a starter.

Henry was placed on waivers and claimed by Boston after the 1995 season. He missed most of 1996 but managed a 7-3 record in the following year. He then bounced around for a couple of seasons as a free agent, but by 1998 was out of the major leagues. He showed up again in 2001 in the International League, although by then his best years were behind him.

Looking back, if there was any one thing that did him in, it would have to be his battle with a host of injuries.[66]

Jim Tracy

On his way to managerial posts in the major leagues with the Los Angeles Dodgers, Pittsburgh Pirates and most recently with the Colorado Rockies, Jim Tracy spent the 1994 season as skipper of the Expos' Triple-A affiliate in Ottawa.

Tracy's Ottawa Lynx enjoyed some success and following the mess of the strike and cancellation of the 1994 major-league season, he was hired as Felipe Alou's bench coach for 1995. Tracy would hold that post through the 1998 season.

Here's a salute to a guy who hung in there and was rewarded with the chance to run his own program in the majors.

Chapter Thirty-Five

Ken – King of the Hill

Marquis Grissom said it best: "Ken Hill was electric." The season had just ended, prematurely, and Hill was tied for the NL lead in wins with a 16-5 record.

Montreal sportscaster Rodger Brulotte says, "The guy I feel sorry for the most as a result of that strike was Ken Hill. You feel sorry for the fans but Hill, heck, he was deprived of a chance to win a Cy Young Award. He would easily have won 20 games. He had a heckuva season, a career year." Indeed, if not for the strike, Hill would likely have become the second 20-game winner in Expos history. Ross Grimsley was 20-11 in 1978.

In the fall of 1991, Hill had been just another treasure sniffed out by GM Dan Duquette. He acquired Hill from St. Louis in return for first baseman Andres Galarraga, a fan favourite who had fallen by the wayside offensively. Just two years earlier, the Expos had given Galarraga a three-year contract worth $6.85 million but he never did produce the way management expected.

Ken Hill

Even though Hill was only 11-10 with the Cards in 1991, Duquette, with his uncanny ability to assess a player, saw something special in Hill. Besides, both Hill and Duquette are natives of Massachussets, Hill from Lynn, Duquette from Dalton.

"I knew Ken Hill a little," Duquette explained in March, 2013. "He attended North Adams State College in Massachussetts and so did my father Denis and my sister Debbie."

Sure enough, Hill blossomed in his first season with the Expos, going 16-9 with a 2.68 ERA. A groin injury suffered on the basepaths in 1993 limited his work, dropping him back to 9-7.

Then came the lofty achievements of 1994. "Kenny Hill was a big pitcher, just a dominant guy," manager Felipe Alou said. Catcher Lenny Webster added: "Ken developed that split-fingered pitch. He was a three-pitch pitcher with that forkball, curveball and fastball."[67]

Hill's banner year in 1994 would be his last with the Expos. He was dispatched in the controversial fire sale of April 1995, along with John Wettleland and Marquis Grissom. Traded first to St. Louis, Hill ended up in Cleveland later in the season and took part in the Tribe's losing effort in the World Series. They were defeated by the Braves, who, ironically, had his old teammate Marquis Grissom in the lead-off spot.

Hill spent a year and more in Texas and then shuffled through Anaheim, Cincinnati and Boston before hanging up the spikes following the 2001 season.

Chapter Thirty-Six

What about the Yankees?

The Expos and Yankees were on a collision course to meet in the 1994 World Series. The two teams were sitting on the best records in baseball on the day the strike was called. Although much more baseball would still have had to be played before either made it to the Fall Classic, most observers believe that, given their respective strengths, New York and Montreal would have been the last ones standing.

Oddly, in an earlier strike-gnarled year, 1981, the same two teams had also seemed destined to meet in the World Series. They didn't – and that year remained the last time either team would even get that close to making a postseason appearance right through 1994. For the Expos, it would never happen again.

In 1981 the Yankees had already qualified for the big meet when the Expos were at home playing the Dodgers in the deciding game of the NLCS. Had Rick Monday's ninth-inning towering fly ball landed in Andre Dawson's glove instead of clearing the wall in right centre, the Expos would have needed only one run in their last at-bat to win the game and advance to the Fall Classic. Even with Monday's home run, the Expos stayed in the fight, getting two runners on base via walks before their two-out rally fizzled.

The Yankees were unable to conquer the Monday-inspired Dodgers, who took the round in six games. As it happened, this was the 11th time those two franchises had met in the postseason, their third in five years. They have not had a postseason meeting since.

After 1981, the Yankees went downhill, not really turning the corner until 1993, similar to the situation experienced by the Expos. As with the Expos, the 1994 season was shaping up to be a turnaround for the Yankees. With manager Buck Showalter at the helm, the Bronx Bombers went 70-43 before the strike.

"It was probably the most fun team I've ever played on," said Paul O'Neill in a 2012 telephone interview. When play was called he was boasting an outstanding .359 batting average, best in the American League. "We had a lot of new players who had come up together. I'd come off a .300 season in 1993 and leaving of spring training, I was getting hit after hit and I kept going.

"I was at the top of my game when it came to mechanics," O'Neill said. "I'd been getting a lot of press about hitting .400 in May but I let the reporters know I didn't really want to talk about it. I told them that if I was hitting .400 on June 1, I would talk to them. That got me off the hook.

"Then June 1 came around – and I was still hitting .400! All the reporters were waiting for me at my locker. Funny thing, for a stretch after that, I went something like 0-for-20."

For O'Neill, an ultra-serious Irishman some called the Warrior, 1994 was all about changing his mental approach to hitting.

"That was a great year for me because I became more comfortable," he said. "I had been a dead-pull hitter but Don Mattingly told me I didn't need to pull the ball. I started hitting line drives all over the place."[68]

The Yankees had acquired O'Neill from his home-state Cincinnati Reds after the 1992 season and O'Neill admits he gained a lot when he left the smallness of Cincinnati for the Big Apple. "I learn a lot more of the mental game," O'Neill said. "In Cincinnati, I tore myself up trying to do too much all the time. In New York, I turned the page."

O'Neill had kind words to say about teammate Jimmy Key, the former Blue Jays pitcher. "He was one of the truest professional pitchers I played with. I felt comfortable out there when he was pitching. He was not going to blow you away with a fastball but when the game was on the line, he would get you an out."

As much as people thought about an Expos–Yankees World Series, O'Neill said he and his mates seldom talked about it. "We were just a team working hard to get into the playoffs." Like everyone else, he was completely gobsmacked when the season and then the postseason were shut down.

Unlike the Expos, though, the Yankees would regroup pretty much unchanged in 1995, and with the addition of closer John Wetteland, would win the 1996 World Series. Since then, they have been in the playoffs more often than not. And O'Neill was a huge part of it until retiring after the 2001 season.

These days O'Neill is a top-rung announcer on the Yankees YES network, working alongside former Expo Ken Singleton, Michael Kay and former Blue Jay Al Leiter.[69]

Chapter Thirty-Seven

Then there were the Jays and the Phillies

Figuring they had the horses after capturing two consecutive World Series championships in 1992 and 1993, the Toronto Blue Jays were looking for a three-peat in 1994. As club president Paul Beeston would say, the team had every belief Toronto would be just as good again. The Jays were baseball royalty in the Queen City, capturing the imagination of fans for several years but especially after they moved into the SkyDome mid-way through the 1991 season. Those were days of wine and roses at the box office, not to mention on the field. Crowds of 40,000-45,000 energetic fans were pretty well the norm back then.

"We believed that we really had a good team in 1994," club president Paul Beeston said. "There was never a thought that we couldn't contend. The core of the team was still young, still aggressive, and full of optimism. Don't forget that from '85 through 1993 we were in the race every one of those seasons, right up to the last week of the season. September meant something for us. It really was an exciting time.

"In 1992 and 1993, there was great depth in the pitching. And in 1994, we still had Paul Molitor, Devon White, Joe Carter, Robbie Alomar, John Olerud, guys like that. But we got off to a slow start and never recovered. It wasn't meant to be."

However, the seeds for a third consecutive World Series title started wilting long before spring training in 1994. Back in the fall of 1993, shortly after the Jays had repeated as Series champs, thanks to Joe Carter's dramatic home run, closer Duane Ward developed lameness in his right arm. The Jays feared at one point that Ward would miss the entire 1994 season with biceps tendonitis, thus dealing their bullpen a big blow.

"It was devastating not to have Ward," recalled Galen Cisco, the Jays pitching coach in that era. "It was almost automatic once he came on in

216

the late innings. He took care of business. We had lost Tom Henke for the 1993 season and then we lost Ward for 1994. We never did recover."

For a number of years, Ward had pitched in Henke's shadow as the setup man, while Henke closed out games. Once Henke left to sign with Texas, Ward stepped in as the closer and saved 45 games in 1993; he was the AL co-leader along with Jeff Montgomery of the Kansas City Royals. And in the AL playoffs and the World Series, Ward was Mr. Dependable like he had been during the regular season.

But he never saved another game after his injury. In fact, his last game was June 26, 1995. Odd but true. "We struggled a long time to find someone to fill that closer role," said former Jays manager Cito Gaston. "When you don't have a closer, you're in trouble. That was the biggest part of our letdown. In 1992 and 1993, once we got to seven innings of ball games, it was all over with Tom Henke and Duane Ward to close the game."

As Ward tells the story, he first started having problems in August of 1993 in New York when his throwing arm suddenly started to feel strange. "I took a cortisone shot and then was great for the rest of the season, the playoffs and the World Series," Ward said from his home in Las Vegas in June 2012.[70]

Then, in the fall of 1993, Ward again felt a sudden problem in his right arm. "One day, I was getting out of bed and my arm was pretty much dead," Ward said. "I don't remember it being painful but I knew something was wrong. I called the Blue Jays and they said to try and build strength. It became a waiting game. But I was getting ready for the next season in December, and the arm still wasn't responding."

By March of 1994, Ward and the team decided he should have surgery done by Dr. James Andrews in Birmingham, Alabama, to repair a torn rotator cuff. "It was not something I looked forward to," Ward said, "but I couldn't throw the ball the way I wanted. The surgery took about 45 minutes. With rehab, it was another six weeks before I could start throwing. To make matters worse, I severed a tendon in my throwing hand throwing a breaking ball. It was disappointing not being able to pitch that season."

So instead of Ward, Cisco and manager Cito Gaston went with a bullpen by committee. It included Danny Cox, Dave Righetti, at the tail end of his career, and a host of others. "Paul Spoljaric (a Canadian) was supposed to step in and that didn't work out," Cisco recalled. "We just didn't get any help out of the bullpen. We replaced Ward with guys with little experience. We gave up more runs than we got."

Cisco admits pushing Ward to the limit and driving his innings total up in 1993, so he wasn't really surprised when the news came down that Ward would sit out the entire season. "Some teams never make it to the

World Series. You don't go back-to-back very often. So you go the limit. You just go for it," Cisco said.

Ward agreed, saying he had no regrets about pitching so much in 1993. "I was with the Jays for six and half years and we won two World Series," Ward said. "Looking back, it was actually a three-peat for us in a roundabout way because since there was no World Series in 1994, technically we were still the World Series champions going into 1995."

Although Ward would pitch some that year, it was his last season.

Other Jays not back in 1994 were Tony Fernandez, Rickey Henderson and Alfredo Griffin. While the club could still call on starting pitchers Pat Hentgen, Dave Stewart, Todd Stottlemyre, Al Leiter and Juan Guzman, somehow things just didn't work out. "We just didn't play quite as well," Cisco said. "As a matter of fact, we were a few games below .500 when the strike came."

Chatting at a cocktail event related to his annual golf tournament in suburban Toronto 18 years later, Joe Carter agreed with Cisco's take on things. "We just got complacent. We should have seized the opportunity. We weren't as good in 1994. We never got it rolling, from the starting pitch in the first game until the strike."

The Blue Jays have never been the same since that strike year, on the field or at the turnstiles.

Blue Jays attendance in their glory years

1989	3,375,884
1990	3,885,284
1991	4,001,527
1992	4,028,318
1993	4,057,947
1994	2,907,933*

*Team was on pace for 4 million in 1994 before the strike

Canadian baseball fans sometimes imagine the "what-would-have-been" had the 1994 season played out to the end – and then brought Canada's two major-league teams to the World Series. "It would have been super had it happened," Cito Gaston said.

"It would have been great for the fans," said Dave Stewart, who pitched for the A's in 1989. "It probably would have been even better than the Oakland-San Francisco series in 1989."

The Philadelphia Phillies, just like the Toronto Blue Jays, could never get on a roll in 1994. The Phillies posted a 97-65 record to win the NL East in 1993, just slightly better than the Expos, and then went on to become NL champions and World Series runners-up. They lost out to the Blue Jays in six games, on Joe Carter's famous home run.

"It's interesting. You get a sort of honeymoon period after the World Series," Phillies president David Montgomery said in 2012. But that honeymoon didn't last very long, as Montgomery and the Phillies discovered the next year. "We had tough news right out of the chute. John Kruk had testicular cancer and wasn't available at spring training," Montgomery said. "Then we parted ways with Mitch Williams. So those two things came out of nowhere. Unfortunately, our success in 1993 was short-lived."

Montgomery pointed out wryly that twice the Phillies had been to the World Series (in 1980 and 1993) only to have a strike occur the following year. "We won the World Series in 1980 and there was a lengthy strike in '81. We were not successful in the 1993 World Series and again a strike took place. "[71] For the record, the Phillies were 54-61 in 1994.

Joe Carter's Spelling Bee

On July 14, 1994, in a game against the Texas Rangers at Arlington, Carter was the victim of a wardrobe malfunction which he considered to be a bad luck omen, and he was steamed. And embarrassed. The clothing factory which produced Blue Jays uniforms had made a mistake on Carter's jersey. They had reversed the "n" and the second "t" in the word Toronto, so that the jersey read Torotno. It took six innings before someone noticed the mistake.

Expos Salaries in 1994

Larry Walker	$4.025-million
Marquis Grissom	$3.575-million
Ken Hill	$2.615-million
John Wetteland	$2.25-million
Moises Alou	$1.415-million
Mel Rojas	$850 000
Darrin Fletcher	$615 000
Randy Milligan	$600 000
Jeff Fassero	$315 000
Sean Berry	$200 000
Wil Cordero	$200 000
Mike Lansing	$200 000
Pedro Martinez	$200 000
Freddie Benavides	$195 000
Lenny Webster	$180 000
Jeff Shaw	$172 000
Tim Scott	$165 000
Lou Frazier	$140 000
Denis Boucher	$135 000
Jeff Gardner	$135 000
Gil Heredia	$135 000
Tim Spehr	$132 000
Butch Henry	$130 000
Kirk Rueter	$130 000
Juan Bell	$130 000
Rondell White	$112 000
Cliff Floyd	$109 500
Joey Eischen	$109 000
Rodney Henderson	$109 000
Gabe White	$109 000
Heath Haynes	$109 000
Brian Looney	$109 000

No Joy In Mudville

1994-1995

Somewhere men are laughing, and somewhere children shout;

But there is no joy in Mudville – mighty Casey has struck out.

Mel Rojas

Mel Rojas, one of the unsung heroes of 1994, was named Expos closer following John Wetteland's trade to the New York Yankees in 1995. Over the next two seasons, he accumulated 66 saves. He left the club as a free agent at the close of the 1996 season.

Chapter Thirty-Eight

Game Over

It gets late early out there.
— Yogi Berra

"**A**ll they told us," Pedro Martinez said later, "was to be ready for the next game and there was no next game."[1]

As the history of the Montreal Expos goes, August 12, 1994, was a very dark day, the day major leaguers from all across the country of baseball went on strike. It would take 232 days – over seven months and more than 940 games cancelled – before cries of "Play Ball!" would ring out again in American and National League ballparks. Not until late April 1995 did the new season open, and then to another truncated schedule.

Baseball, indeed all professional sports, had never experienced anything like it before – for even as both sides waited, wallowing in a state of statis and achieving nothing, the game itself was profoundly altered. To begin with, the 1994 World Series was cancelled, the first time in history that the Fall Classic had been forced to fold its tent and head for the hills. Then, in the spring and with the strike still far from settled, the owners took it upon themselves to unilaterally recruit replacement players to fill in for their striking regulars. They opened spring training camps fully prepared to launch the new season with whatever dross they could find to stick into the lineup, and damn the torpedoes! Amateur Night at the Big Show was coming to a stadium near you!

It was chaos.

Former Los Angeles Dodgers executive Fred Claire called it "a period of division and bitterness between owners and players, and anger and alienation among fans. If ever there was a no-win moment in baseball, this was it."[2]

Stan Kasten, a key management figure with the Atlanta Braves, in a recent telephone interview, went even further. "It made people physically ill, literally sick with what had happened, with both sides failing to come to an agreement," he said. "It was a shame. We knew the repercussions. It could have been avoided and we're proud that we have avoided it since. We weren't trying to be revolutionary. We weren't even asking close to what our competitors already had."[3]

In many quarters, baseball's 1994 players' strike is considered "the worst work stoppage in sports history and it left the fans and the sports world outraged"[4] – and this in a universe that has seen the NHL shut down its operations on three different occasions.

For fans in Montreal, words like 'outrage' don't begin to describe the horror of the moment or their reaction to it. To them, it was more like watching a dear friend tear your heart from your chest, so palpable was the pain.

As every serious follower of the Expos remembers, on August 12 1994, the team, at that moment the best team in baseball, and generally regarded as the best in club history, was sitting in first place atop the National League. With not much more than a month to go before the close of the regular season, the team and its fans were angling toward postseason play and a crack at the World Series.

And then baseball slammed the door. By the time players took the field again the following April, the Expos had been reduced to a scrawny shadow of their former selves. Their dreams, fortunes and, most telling, the very foundation of their existence, had been swept away by the self-serving indifference of both the owners group and the players association.

That story is well known – but worth retelling here, if for no reason other than to provide the context for all that follows. Although no one could have anticipated the debilitating impact of the strike, the fact that the players were restless and preparing for some sort of labour action was not a surprise. For twenty years or so, work relationships between owners and players had steadily deteriorated, with the players almost always coming out of each skirmish better off. Thus, when the most recent collective bargaining agreement expired in December 1993 and negotiations on the new contract began, the owners made clear their intention to retool baseball's broken wage system through a revenue-sharing plan anchored to a salary cap. To the players, the very hint of a salary cap was reason enough to empty out their lockers and walk.

Their stand was important, but their tone perhaps too cavalier. They, or more accurately, their leaders, had lost sight of what was important about the game of baseball – and why it had always occupied a special place in American lore. Even as early as 1990 Donald Fehr was tossing about flippant comments such as: "I don't think American culture would collapse if baseball collapsed."

George Will was having none of it. The acerbic national columnist, whose passion for baseball is well known, replied to Fehr in a March 13, 1990 column.

"That flippancy is trivially true and utterly foolish. Symphony orchestras. Steel mills – American culture could survive without a lot of things. But baseball, unlike, say, the textile industry, depends for its health on the public imagination."[5]

In mid-September, with the strike still ablaze and neither side willing to budge, the chairman of the Executive Council of Major League Baseball, Bud Selig – he would later assume the role of commissioner – cancelled first the balance of the season and then the World Series. The game, which had withstood the travails of World War I, the Spanish flu pandemic of 1918, the stock market crash of 1929 and the Depression that followed, and World War II, had caved with nary a whimper. All because the players went on strike. The players on strike!

Paul O'Neill, whose Yankees were first in the American League and who carried championship hopes similar to those of Expos players, was thrown for a loop. "As a player, you always figure you will get back to work," O'Neill said. "It didn't make sense to me. I watched on television as Bud Selig made the announcement. There was frustration and disappointment. It ended up in a horrible situation."[6]

The folk tale–like epic that unfolded during the winter months tells a sad story of arrogance and stubbornness, a grim saga salted with self-destructive *hubris*. The very fact that the stalemate was permitted to drag on into 1995 with no end in sight is indictment enough. Both sides were so caught up in the minutiae of what they hoped to gain or feared losing, so tied up in the end-game of trying to outsmart the other, they lost sight of their own *raison d'être*: to respect the game of baseball and please the fans.

When this multi-million dollar hissy-fit finally fizzled out, it did so not because the opposing forces experienced some divinely-directed epiphany but rather because a judge of the United States District Court for the Southern District of New York handed down a preliminary injunction that ordered both sides back to work. On March 30, 1995, one day before the new season had been scheduled to open, Judge Sonia Sotomayor ruled that Major League Baseball could not carry through on its plan to unilaterally implement a new collective bargaining agreement and bring in replacement players without the approval of the players union, and found the owners group guilty of negotiating in bad faith.[7] And with that, the 1994 baseball strike came to an end, not with a bang, not even with a whimper, but rather a pathetic 'pop.'

The owners tried appealing but without success. Still, no new leaf was turned over. Bill Gould, chairman of the National Labor Relations Board, whom President Clinton had sent to seek out a solution between the parties, reported back that "there was no lesson learned, no wisdom to be taken from the longest strike in professional sports history. It was, he thought, the perfect waste."[8] Ballparks everywhere unlocked their gates, only to be met by very angry and unforgiving fans. Or no fans at all.

For, of course, nothing had been resolved. The contract in force when the strike began was the one still in effect when the strike ended. All that kerfuffle had been for naught, except, of course, if you counted the collateral damage. That was incalculable, irreparable and irreversible. Baseball, in the eyes of many, through its own stupidity, avarice and thirst for control, had sacrificed its place of privilege on the North American sports scene.

Those many observers were right. Baseball is no longer America's National Pastime: the National Football League has usurped that honour. The summer game remains popular, and is generally successful within it own constituency – except in Florida – but it no longer holds sway. Somewhat like hockey in the United States, its draw is now more regional than national.

Or as Pogo, the philosophical title-opossum in the old Walt Kelly comic strip, might have said, "baseball has met the enemy and he is us."[9]

If there was a lesson to be learned by both sides from this descent into foolishness, it was the one of "never again." Once the legitimate players returned to the playing fields in 1995 and the season began in earnest, MLB and the players reopened negotiations, this time with a fresh sense of direction. They were determined to restore the dignity of the game and find solutions acceptable to both sides – even if that meant adding more water to the wine.

It was a struggle, conducted behind closed doors, beyond the gaze of the media, and took almost two years to sort out. But when all was said and done, it's fair to conclude they got it right. On March 14, 1997, the owners and the players association signed a new contract. It retained the reserve clause, somewhat modified, legitimized revenue-sharing, and substituted the punitive absolutes of the salary cap with what they called a luxury tax.

Peace was restored and, except for a worrisome moment in 2002 when an August strike seemed imminent, both parties to the collective bargaining agreement pulled in their horns and guaranteed that the current period of calm and cooperation would be maintained through 2016. And perhaps beyond.

Chapter Thirty-Nine

Selig's stunning decision

"In order to protect the integrity of the championship season, the Division Series, the League Championship Series and the World Series, the 28 clubs have concluded with enormous regret that the remainder of the 1994 season, the Division Series, the League Championship Series and the World Series will be cancelled and that all clubs will explore all avenues to achieve a meaningful structural reform of baseball's player compensation system in an effort to ensure that the 1995 and future championship seasons can occur as scheduled and uninterrupted."

Text of resolution signed September 14, 1994 by 26 of the 28 clubs, including Expos managing general partner Claude Brochu. Voting against the resolution were Baltimore Orioles majority owner Peter Angelos and Cincinnati Reds principal partner Marge Schott.

"We felt pragmatism dictated this action," Bud Selig told reporters in a conference call from his Milwaukee offices on September 14, 1994. Nevertheless, Selig wants to make clear to Expos fans and all other baseball fans that it was not he who cancelled the remainder of the season and all postseason play in 1994. The owners did: he simply made the announcement.

Speaking to Danny Gallagher in November 2012, Selig said it is incorrect to hang the blame solely on him. "To say I called it off is historical myth," he said. "I didn't call off the World Series. I didn't cancel the season and the postseason. I made the announcement. I didn't want to make any announcement but I felt a moral obligation.

"Managers and general managers were telling me that players would be out of shape. They were concerned about the health of their players. We didn't play for a month so you couldn't just call them back to play. It was a very agonizing decision.

"1994 is one of the low moments in our sport's history because it cost us a World Series, but it was clear the economic system was not working. The industry was in tough shape. It needed a change. This was the eighth work stoppage in my career. There was so much anger building up. It was a seriously outdated system. Small and medium markets were having a terrible struggle. We really had to go through that experience to get at what we have today."

As to how much the cancellation of the season hurt the Expos, Selig had this to say: "It was unfortunate for Montreal. They had a wonderful

baseball team that was playing so great and what happened hurt the club very much. Unfortunately, the Expos' situation was symptomatic of the overall problems facing baseball. There were a lot of wonderful performances that year in baseball but it was the union that went out. It wasn't the owners that caused the problem. I think the union miscalculated the depth of resolve on the management side. As Braves president Stan Kasten said over and over again in committee, we were barely asking for half as much as the other sports already had.

"I know the short-term pain was intense," agreed Selig, "but if this [work stoppage] can be the impetus for a long-range solution, then maybe that will be the good which comes

Bud Selig, Commissioner of Baseball, was still acting commissioner in 1994.

out of this unpleasant moment. The players left us no choice."[10]

That last bit was disingenuous, of course, for the owners always had a choice. One of the reasons the players struck when they did in August was that they feared the owners were preparing to lock them out at season's end and/or impose an agreement of their own. One way or another, they suspected management's long-term goal was to destroy their union.

As a member of the owners' negotiating committee, Philadelphia Phillies president and CEO David Montgomery was an advisor to Selig as he faced the dreadful decision of seeing to the cancellation of the remainder of the season and playoffs.

"One of the aspects I do remember is that I was on the National League schedule committee. John Harrington of the Red Sox and I were a sounding board for Bud," Montgomery said in an interview.[11] "Bud didn't want to pull the plug on the season and wanted to extend the date of making the announcement

"'Can't we go a little longer?' Selig asked. Bud was keen to know just how we felt," said Montgomery. "I told him, 'You can't at this point.'" Montgomery's position was that "the players had been out close to 40 days, they would have to get back into playing shape – probably taking a minimum of 10 days or two weeks. I remember, sadly, we were just running out of days."[12]

Vladimir

Only one player in history has hit at least 30 homers, driven in 100 runs, collected 200 hits, stolen at least 40 bases and hit for an average of .320 or better: Vlad Guerrero, with the Expos in 2002.

Chapter Forty

Presenting Donald Fehr

Donald Fehr, the executive director of the MLBPA during this period, has no qualms about his role in taking his players out on strike and the resulting loss of the 1994 season.

"There has been no second guessing. My job was to protect and represent the players," Fehr said in a recent interview. "It was my job to make the best deal. The owners were the ones who made the decision to force the players to strike. It's an unpleasant memory. That's just the way it is.

"In 1981, the owners tried to gut free agency by imposing crippling compensation for free agents. That is what caused the 50-day strike. In 1985, they tried collusion. In 1990, they locked the players out. In 1994, they tried to impose the salary cap. The owners failed in all of these attempts. And by the way, it was the players who suggested revenue-sharing and the game is in a lot better shape."

Even though acting commissioner Bud Selig was the one to announce the cancellation of the remainder of the 1994 season, Fehr was not about to bad-mouth him almost 20 years later. "Bud's legacy is that the game has been booming under him," Fehr said. Someone has suggested that this comment would make an excellent topic for a debate. "Resolve that during the Selig years baseball has boomed."

Asked if 1994 was the turning point in the Expos' history, Fehr gave this reply: "Other people have told me that. Montreal is a very complicated place with its political and cultural crosscurrents. It was unfortunate. It would have been nice to get a new stadium there like the one in Baltimore."

On the topic of the 1995 Expos fire sale, Fehr called it "unfortunate, so sad." And as for possible use of replacement players in 1995: "It was high-handed pressure."

Fehr was disappointed that the owners agreed to have the Expos play a number of home games in Puerto Rico as a precursor to the team leaving Montreal. "Initially their plan was to contract two teams (one of which would have been the Expos), but what with different ownerships and changes in Montreal, [MLB] was looking for solutions to make the best of a very bad situation," Fehr said.

Regarding the possibility of baseball returning to Montreal, Fehr said: "I hope to see it one day. I hope it happens. Do I envision it? Yes. Do I see it happening? No."[13]

Conspiracy Theory

In a 2009 *Village Voice* overview of the 1994 strike, the editor Allen Barra managed to identify one upside for his readers. "A Canadian team had won the 1992-1993 World Series," he wrote, "and if the Expos had won the Series in 1994, America's pastime might never have recovered from the blow of three straight Canadian world champions."

"That was the cause of the cancellation of the season more than anything else," agrees Michel Spinelli, a former official scorer for the Expos who charted close to 1,000 games from 1980–2004. "The Americans didn't want us Canadians to win the World Series again. It was a real shame."

As conspiracy theorists everywhere have already figured out, the only sure way to guarantee the Expos could not win the World Series was to suspend play and cancel the whole shebang. Why couldn't this be the true reason behind the owners' absolute intransigence – they were willing to forego millions of dollars just to shield themselves from embarrassment?

When Donald Fehr was asked by Danny Gallagher what he thought about the conspiracy theory, he replied, "That can't be a serious question. Until this minute, I have never heard any such suggestion. Complete nonsense as far as I know. It's like the theory that the moon landing didn't happen."

Nevertheless, the ruling powers knew they could stop everything simply by insisting on the salary cap, the players' Achilles heel. The players would have no option but to strike: they would become the bad guys, and for once the owners would have escaped the bullet.

A far-fetched notion? Perhaps, but it sure beats buying into the specious notion that the principle of a salary cap was sacrosanct, especially when one realizes that once talks between the two parties resumed in 1995, the salary cap quickly became a non-starter.

At least this is what some people believe.

Chapter Forty-One

The Fall of Montreal

"I have no reaction because I knew it was coming for a while," Expos closer and player rep John Wetteland told Montreal's *Gazette* the day the strike was called.[14]

"It's a sickening feeling," added Expos catcher Darrin Fletcher. "Some of the guys anticipated this decision better than me. They took everything with them when they left Montreal. I left behind a truck and a lot of clothes belonging to my wife and son (in Kirkland, Quebec). I'll have to fly up there in a couple of weeks and get everything."[15]

Despite the awful news, Expos outfielder Lou Frazier was prepared to say, "I'm going to consider us champions." But it wasn't a feeling shared by Fletcher or pitcher Jeff Fassero.

"Maybe we have the best record in the majors, but there is no champion. We haven't won anything," Fassero said. "To say we are champions has a shallow ring to it," Fletcher said. "You would have to have a serious asterisk attached to anything like that. I don't think anyone would take us seriously."

Expos announcer Dave Van Horne was devastated by the cancellation of the season. "It was just terrible. Heartsick, just heartsick," Van Horne would say in the summer of 2012. "I remember John McHale of the Expos telling me after the Expos had lost to the Dodgers in the 1981 championship series that 10 days after the loss, he still hadn't gotten over it. He was upset. He said you only get these chances once in a while. You have to seize the opportunity.

"I felt like John did. There was the thought of this terrific team in 1994 having a wonderful season, the thought of the franchise perhaps going down over a labour issue, the thought of trying to get a downtown stadium, all of those things were on the table. This was the end of that run for that team, the best team in baseball. It was all torn apart by the great fire sale at spring training in 1995. The big players who drove the 1994 success were now gone. It was like kicking a man when he's down, pounded and then kicked and pummelled. It was a hopeless feeling of despair.

"It was fairly easy to understand the business aspect of what was going on. Nonetheless, even with that understanding, it was still devastating for the franchise. The money wasn't there, corporate support was no longer there, no solid revenue. It was bittersweet – the team saying we're not going to leave town, we are staying in Montreal but, by the way, we can't really keep all of these players."

To Kirk Rueter, news that the season had been wiped out was painful. "To cancel the World Series: it was such a punch in the gut, especially for us," Rueter said on the phone from his home in Nashville, Illinois. "We were an unbelievable team on a mission, such a loaded team. It was a foregone conclusion we were going to the playoffs. We felt we had the best team.

"We definitely had what it takes to go far into the playoffs and generate more revenue to keep all those guys, Walk, Wett, Grip and Ken Hill," said Rueter. "We had a mini-dynasty. We were on some incredible run when the strike came. While the strike was on, we kept hearing from player reps to stay in shape, that there wouldn't be a regular season, just the playoffs."[16]

Said reliever Tim Scott: "I was very disappointed. I was never able to go to the playoffs with anyone. I missed out on a World Series. It's the biggest disappointment I have ever had, to this day."

As it was for Expos fans everywhere, a story of too little and far too late. The world of the Expos, as one knew it, ended in 1994. Even though all of Major League Baseball suffered in the years following, the Expos effectively went into cardiac arrest. Like Humpty Dumpty, their perch on that wall had been precarious at best, and when they fell, it was all over.

As spring training rolled around and with the threat of replacement players taking over was played out, the Expos cut costs by trading three top players and letting free agent Larry Walker go. Fans still refer to this bleak moment as the fire sale. "That was a manifestation of an industry that needed to change systems," Commissioner Bud Selig said in late 2012. "The Expos did what they had to do."

Felipe Alou saw it coming. "I was afraid once the 1994 season was over, I had my fears that they were going to let some of those guys go," Alou said. "We just gave them away. That was awful and the thought of replacement players? It's too bad we were on strike. The Expos would have made a lot of money if we had completed that season."

"If they had kept the team intact, the Expos would still be in Montreal," pitcher Butch Henry said. "I was hoping they would keep the pieces of the puzzle together but I'm not going to second-guess the business side of the game. Around the clubhouse we use to tell what we called the University of Montreal joke – that the front office and ownership group would trade people away and leave the club looking like a University of Montreal roster. We were so close in 1994: for them to not make every effort possible in bringing all of the players back …if they had kept the team intact, we would have kept going the way we left off in 1994."

Keeping the team intact was a topic that received a fair amount of consideration in the fall of 1994. The players made clear among themselves and to management that if it were possible from a technical perspective to keep the team together they were quite prepared to accept a complete freeze of their 1994 wages and waive whatever salary increases or other benefits were due them in 1995, just for the privilege of taking one more crack at the brass ring. As Mark Routtenberg, one of the team's owners and an individual who formed close friendships with the players, has said: "They so hoped that the team would stay together in 1995 that they voted to play for the same wages as '94 if no one was traded."[17]

With the forced termination of the strike occurring at the end of March 1995, the Expos began in earnest to peel away their top talent. Ken Hill was dispatched to his former team, the St. Louis Cardinals, for Kirk Bullinger, Bryan Eversgerd and DaRond Stovall. The Cards in turn sent him on a few months later to the Cleveland Indians. Also in April, reliever John Wetteland was traded to the New York Yankees for the hulking Fernando Seguignol. And still in April, Marquis Grissom was moved to the Atlanta Braves, with the Expos getting back Roberto Kelly, Tony Tarasco and Esteban Yan in exchange. Larry Walker was declared a free agent without ever having received an offer of any sort.

Grissom went on to make three World Series appearances - in 1995, when he earned his victor's ring, and 1996, both with Atlanta, and then with Cleveland in 1997.[18] Hill got to taste the postseason waters in 1995 as well, playing against former teammate Grissom as the Braves won the World Series in six games. It took some time for Walker to make his way into the Fall Classic, but he finally succeeded in 2004 as a member of the St. Louis Cardinals, only to see his team swept by the resurgent Boston Red Sox. Walker, however, excelled in the series, leading the Cards with a .357 batting average, while hitting the club's only two home runs and producing three RBIs. Wetteland saw postseason action on four different occasions, including 1996 when the Yankees conquered the Braves in six to launch their next great run of World Series dominance. He was named Series MVP. At the time, Wetteland's set-up man was a young Mariano Rivera, testing out the bullpen for the first time in his career. When Wetteland left the New York Yankees after his series win, Rivera became the closer and in 1997 saved 43 games, equalling his predecessor's total in 1996.

The Expos' fire sale was awful…so bad, in fact, that the general manager mandated to carry out this carnage, Kevin Malone, himself quit the club at the end of the year. He was "in the building business," he said, "not the dismantling business."[19]

Reaction within the fan base and among the media bordered on the apoplectic. Sportscaster Mitch Melnick of what is today TSN-Montreal, a passionate supporter of all things Expos and one of the most intelligent talk-show hosts in the business, was absolutely unforgiving. He turned his anger toward managing partner Claude Brochu and his colleagues on the board of directors. "The Expos' ownership group had no vision, no balls, no stomach, no understanding," he said in 2012. "It was the year of the franchise. 1994 is on Brochu and the local guys. It's the legacy of Brochu and that gang."

Rodger Brulotte, an equally prominent if less tempered voice on French sports radio, echoed Melnick's comments: "Brochu emptied the house, he abandoned the house, holy God," chomped Brulotte in 2012. "Brochu and Bill Stoneman should have signed the young players to long-term contracts. What he could have done, instead of trading those guys, was to keep them and see what happened in the 1995 season. If at some point there were no ticket sales and no fans, then move those players. The aftermath hurt baseball more than 1994."

Malone took a more philosophical approach. "I think instead of losing Wetteland, Walker, Hill and Grissom, we could have lost only one, maybe two, we could have replaced them, because we had such good players in the system. It's very hard to overcome losing four all-stars at one time."[20]

Chapter Forty-Two

Claude Brochu
Answers Back

Claude Brochu was aware that the 1994 season might well be interrupted by a players' strike, but "I was surprised," he says, "or maybe it was just wishful thinking on my part, that the whole season would be cancelled. We all thought the union would bend somewhat, if only to get players back on the field."[21]

He was half-right. The strike was called on August 12. However, it did not end quickly. Quite the opposite, in fact, as it stretched out across the remaining weeks of summer, then into autumn, then winter, and even through the first days of spring 1995 before a judge's ruling forced players back on the field.

The damage wreaked upon the credibility of the owners, the mystique surrounding the players, and even more so, the passion of fans, was cataclysmic, and still echoes today. Certainly, in Expos land, it cut to the quick – so deeply, some insist, that the unrestrained bleeding led directly to the club's exile 10 years later. Richard Griffin, a long-standing front-office employee of the Expos who left in 1995 to take up a position with the *Toronto Star*, contends: "There is no doubt in my mind that the strike killed baseball in Montreal forever."[22]

Griffin's assessment was, and continues to be, almost a mantra in Quebec. And when blame is assigned and fingers pointed, almost invariably they lead directly to team president Claude Brochu. He was the one at the helm throughout this nightmarish exercise. And he was the one who in early 1995, in a desperate effort to cut costs, elected to dispose of several of the Expos' highest paid (i.e. best) players.

Brochu, as one might expect, rejects this premise. The strike was a major bump in the road, to be sure, but he believes its impact could have been mitigated had not other forces intervened.

But first he had to deal with the facts at hand. The Expos were the epitome of a small-market team. Underfunded ever since Charles

Bronfman sold the club to Brochu and his partners, cash flow concerns were always present. Following the successes of 1993, when the team finished with one of its best records of all time, season ticket sales had declined. Not until the Expos began their great run in July and into August did fans pour back into Olympic Stadium and revenues mount. And that's when everything came to a halt – and the income stream dried up.

"When the 1994 season was cancelled, the impact on the cash flow was devastating," Brochu says today. "It left us with no money coming in." He estimates that with the cancellation of the Expos' final 29 home games right as the team was making its championship run, and allowing for an average attendance pattern in the 30,000-35,000 range over those dates, it is fair to say that the team lost upwards of 900,000 paid admissions due to the strike, a huge hit. Then there was (or in this case wasn't) the portion of revenue shared by those clubs that failed to make it to the postseason, roughly $16 million per team. Of course, had the Expos participated in the playoffs, that sum would have been much greater. But to truly put the icing on the cake, because the strike was so prolonged, season-ticket renewals or purchases declined to almost nothing.

Although little was coming in, recurrent expenses – front-office staff, minor league operations and the like – still had to be met. And since most were paid in American funds, at a time when the Canadian dollar was worth about 75 cents U.S., the cupboard was bare.

The obvious solution was to follow the practice of most other clubs and ask ownership and corporate partners to ante up and help ease the situation. Unfortunately, this option was off the table in Montreal. "I knew very well [my partners] wouldn't want to put another dime into the club. I didn't even have to ask them,"[23] noted Brochu in his autobiography. So he explored the only avenues available to him – secure a line of credit and drastically cut the salary budget. It was brutal.

The moment the strike was declared illegal at the end of March 1995 and the business of baseball started up again, Brochu instructed GM Kevin Malone to dump salaries by trading front-line players for whatever he could get in return. "There was no other way," he said. "We would have lost $20 million, and we had no idea what lay ahead." This was especially true in 1995 as fans everywhere turned their backs on both the players and the owners, and stayed away. Since those on the inside didn't care enough about the game to protect it, they reckoned, why should we?

Tony Gwynn recalls very well the anger and the backlash that accompanied both the strike and its aftermath. "[The fans] just looked at us as millionaires fighting with billionaires. You couldn't talk to them, but you couldn't blame them either. When we walked out, we lost them and it took a good five years to even think we could get them back."[24] In Montreal, the challenge proved to be even more difficult.

For Brochu, recovery started with the fire sale, for it alone removed $20 million in salaries from the budget. He freely admits it was rough. "I knew I was doing the best I could and really didn't let the critics get me down. It was tough on those around me though."

It has been suggested that Brochu (along with most of the owners) had been convinced that the severity of the strike would cripple the union, perhaps even break it, and that salaries would drop as a result. In that scenario, he did not want to be caught with long-term commitments to over-priced players in a period of declining wages. Given the option, his preference was to do the bleeding now, then rebuild anew with new resources.

And he was already busy making plans.

Chapter Forty-Three

Then There Was Larry Walker

While we sometimes confuse the issue, it is helpful to remember that Larry Walker was not part of the fire sale of 1995. He was not traded away in April for a pittance, as were Messrs Grissom, Hill and Wetteland, simply to help the Expos balance the books. His departure from the club to join the Colorado Rockies was even more egregious.

Although Walker didn't sign with the Rockies until April, immediately following the strike's force-fed settlement, he had in fact been in limbo since October 24, the day the Expos granted him free agency without ever presenting him with an offer.

Some years later, Claude Brochu explained that the root of the problem lay with Walker's free-agent eligibility. He had earned $4 million with Montreal in 1994, was primed to expect at least $5 million the following year and, Brochu said, "as a free-agent he would have been looking for a long-term contract. There was no way we could afford that. And even if we made an offer we could have gotten ourselves trapped. We couldn't risk arbitration."[25]

For many of the Expos faithful, the apparently callous way the club rid itself of Walker is still remembered as among the bleakest moments in this darkest period of no baseball and no prospects. Even today it is often considered the tipping point – the moment dreams of a championship team were abandoned to support the bottom line. Arguments to the contrary, and they are often sound, fall on deaf ears. Inevitably, in 1995 and beyond, that expanding number of supporters who had begun to accept the 'new' Expos of 1994 lost faith and once more turned their backs and walked away.

French-language colour commentator Rodger Brulotte spoke for the masses when he said, "Walker was the Expos' Number One player in 1994, without any doubt. He rarely made a bad play. The Expos let Larry Walker go after the 1994 season for nothing. You can't give Walker away for nothing! Larry Walker?' Nothing!"[26]

At the time, even some of Brochu's colleagues closest to him went public with their criticism, suggesting that in difficult times the club president should have turned to the other owners for additional funding – even if it meant buying some of them out.[27] In effect, they were saying there had to be a better way. Why get rid of so many key players, and, especially, why Walker? Even if Brochu was already looking ahead to his next 'generation x,' they thought, how could he not want to keep Walker as the anchor?

Larry Walker was "the best Expo-homegrown player ever," claimed Eddie Haas, the Expos' long-time executive advisor for baseball operations. To third base coach Jerry Manuel, "Walker was the best base runner at the major league level I ever saw. He had the ability to make me look good as a coach. He had tremendous instincts for the game. He was uncanny, the first player as a defensive player to use a decoy to try and hold a runner from scoring. He'd line up in the outfield and pretend he was going to catch it but the ball was going off the wall."

Rodger Brulotte added this perspective: "The Padres had one good right fielder in all of their years and that was Tony Gwynn. But the Expos had Rusty Staub, Ken Singleton, Ellis Valentine, sadly for too brief a period, Andre Dawson, Larry Walker, Vladimir Guerrero. That was our heritage.

"People like to say Guerrero was a fantastic player but they forget Walker, and that Walker was a heckuva player also. He was a five-tool player, you don't find that everywhere. And he did it every day. The pressure never bothered him. He could do everything. He could steal bases when it counted, he had an outstanding arm, could throw out runners."[28]

Walker admits he was not at all keen about leaving Montreal. In fact, he was very anxious to stay. "But it was not going to happen," he said. "I never saw an offer although I understand one was made. Claude Brochu was put in a difficult position; I liked Claude and never had a problem with him. But I understood the strain they were all under."[29]

This is all water under the bridge today. Larry Walker enjoyed great success in Colorado, putting up Hall of Fame numbers and establishing himself as the greatest Canadian-born position player ever. He remained with the Rockies until August 2004, when he was traded to St. Louis, just in time to join his new team members in their jaunt through the postseason where, after defeating both the Dodgers and Astros, they came face to face with the Boston Red Sox in the World Series. This was the only Fall Classic Walker would ever see as a player. Unfortunately, for him and the

Cardinals, it was Boston's year of destiny: they swept the Redbirds in four games.

These days Walker's primary baseball involvement is with Team Canada. Speaking in October 2012, he said, "I am just back from Germany where we qualified for the World Cup. I try to be there whenever they play, although I had to miss last year when they beat the U.S. in the Pan-Am games. That was a great achievement."[30]

When Walker finally ended his active career, he took with him a list of accomplishments as long as his brawny arms. Among the more noteworthy one finds:

Larry Walker's last season in the major leagues was 2005 with the St. Louis Cardinals.

NL Most Valuable Player, 1997; The Sporting News *NL All-Star Team, 1992, 1997 and 1999; NL Gold Glove, outfielder, 1992 to 1993, 1997 to 1999, 2001 to 2002; NL Silver Slugger Team, outfielder, 1992, 1997 and 1999.*

Asked to name the teammate who made the deepest impression on him, he listed two – Albert Pujols and Todd Helton. "I only played with Albert for a year and a half, but would be hard to place anybody above him. I did play with Todd Helton for many years and he was a joy to watch in the field."

For Walker, the personal high points of his career reach back to both Montreal and St. Louis. "I don't tell this to many people," he says, "but often when I can't sleep I find myself thinking back to the '94 and '04 seasons…they are the great 'what if' moments in my career. And even today, so many years later, these two are still the most prominent in my thoughts."[31]

Chapter Forty-Four

La voix des Expos –
Jacques Doucet

Jacques Doucet – *La Voix des Expos*, the voice of the Expos on French-language radio: in recent years he has done play-by-play in French of Blue Jays televised games. A few years back he teamed up with celebrated Quebec author and film-maker Marc Robitaille to produce an exhaustive history of the Expos entitled *Il était une fois les Expos*[32] (*Once upon a time there were the Expos*). It was published in two volumes and totaled 14,000 pages. The work devotes a generous 40 pages to the talented, ill-fated squad from 1994.

When spring training rolled around that year, Doucet already had an inkling the Expos would improve on their excellent 1993 finish. "I thought

The French-language voice of the Expos, Jacques Doucet holds the all-time record for most Expos games attended, home and away, far surpassing whomever else might be runner-up.

they would make a great run for it," Doucet said. "The pitching staff, the outfield, you knew the defence was solid; it was really a team that could contend. Pedro Martinez was an unknown. We gave up a promising second baseman in Delino DeShields.

"At the time of the trade, I said, 'what the heck are they doing?' One thing we didn't know was that he would become a great starter. Everybody was wide eyed. It became a great move. When you get a pitcher of that quality, I mean he was a masterpiece."

Doucet then dug into his notes. "From July 18 – August 11, the Expos were 20-3," he exclaimed. "How great a run is that? It's unbelievable. If they kept up that pace, they were going to win 100 or more games. They were very tough to stop. These guys showed up at the park figuring they could win. If they were down 3-0 in the first inning, they knew they could come back.

"Had it not been for the strike and the fire sale, it could have ensured the future of the franchise for a long time," Doucet said. "To me, the Expos were good in 1981 but 1994 was probably the best team they ever had.

"There was always the possibility the looming work stoppage might happen but you were never expecting the cancellation of the World Series. Prior to the strike, people were buying season tickets, sponsors were flooding in, radio stations were joining the network, it would have snowballed into a bonanza but it turned into a disaster.

"The strike was not the only reason why the Expos left, but it was one of the biggest reasons. It was a nightmare that the World Series was cancelled, and that we had to bear the burden of that decision. It was a very bad climate, baseball-wise."[33]

Chapter Forty-Five

They Also Served – the Forgotten Bench

A nd then there were the different bench and bullpen players in 1994, those who completed the roster of the Expos, even if just for a week in that wonderful but doomed season. Whatever happened to them?

Take, for example, infielder Jeff Gardner, who played his last major-league game ever on May 4, 1994 for Montreal. He was only 30 years old. His case is interesting because just the season before, he enjoyed a respectable campaign with the San Diego Padres. In 404 at-bats, he hit .262 with a homer and 24 RBIs.

Gardner ended up with the Expos in the early part of the '94 season, going 7-for-32 and one run batted in off a triple. That was it. By early May, one year after his decent season in San Diego, he was out of the game.

There were others whose cup-of-tea stopovers with the Expos in '94 were surprisingly brief. Consider pitchers Heath Haynes, who is profiled elsewhere in these pages, and Brian Looney.

Looney was rocked for five runs on four hits in two innings of work in one game in 1994. Even though he had appeared in three games with the club the previous year, that performance ended his days in Montreal. Former Expos GM Dan Duquette gave Looney a chance in 1995 in Boston but the story was much the same there: the former student at The Gunnery in Connecticut surrendered nine runs in 4.2 innings.

Right-handed pitcher Rodney Henderson didn't stay long with the Expos either. Drafted in 1992, he moved so quickly through the minor leagues that by 1993 he spent most of the season with Triple-A Ottawa. He was called up to Montreal on April 19, 1994, but when he surrendered nine hits and nine runs in three games over 6.2 innings, he was sent back to the nation's capital. Henderson remained with the organization until 1998, when he was released. He then signed as a free agent with Milwaukee, but that adventure ended after two games and four runs allowed. He returned to the minors, ending his baseball life in the Pacific Coast League with Sacramento in 2001.

Joey Eischen made his major-league debut with the Expos in June of 1994 but after he was lit up for four runs in two thirds of an inning, he was summarily returned to the minors without much hope of return. However, Eischen persisted, to the point that he resurfaced with Montreal again in 2001 and remained with the organization (including two seasons with the Nationals) through the 2006 season. He was at his best in 2002, when he ran up a splendid 6-1, 1.34 ERA record in 59 appearances out of the bullpen.

Then there are infielder Juan Bell (brother of former Blue Jays star George Bell), and Rondell White. Both played sparingly in 1994, collecting 27 hits in 97 at-bats and delivering two home runs each. The only difference, White out-duelled Bell in RBIs, 13-10. White, of course, went on to stardom with the Expos, remaining with the team into the 2000 season, and spending a total of 15 years in the major leagues before retiring in 2007.

Bell didn't fare quite so well. After his only year in Montreal he moved over to the Red Sox for a brief spell, before eventually winding up playing in

Rondell White

Taiwan. He returned to America after two years or so in Asia, and spent his last three years in professional baseball bouncing around with a number of minor-league clubs, the last being Campeche of the Mexican League in the year 2000.

Tim Spehr was Montreal's third-string catcher behind Darrin Fletcher and Lenny Webster in 1994, going 9-for-36 at the plate. He had been acquired in 1992 along with pitcher Jeff Shaw, in a trade with the Kansas City Royals. He remained on the Expos roster until he became a free agent in 1996. Spehr soldiered on in the major leagues until 1999, providing spot service for Atlanta and the Mets before ending up where it all began, in Kansas City. He eventually wrapped up his career in 2001, with Louisville of the International League.

Tim Spehr

In his notes for the 1994 Expos Media Guide, PR director Rich Griffin wrote the following about a role player who first carved out his place on the club's roster in 1993.

"The Expos began the spring with the knowledge that, barring injuries, the trio of Alou-Grissom-Walker would be in the lineup as outfielders almost every day. As training camp opened, John Vander Wal, Matt Stairs and Archi Cianfrocco were the leading candidates for outfield reserve spots.

"However, a surprise awaited – a seemingly daily member of the Grapefruit League travel squad who was a veteran minor-league outfielder, former UPS driver, recently bespectacled, six-year, minor-league free agent named Lou Frazier. His speed, both on the bases and in the field, earned him the affection of Felipe Alou and a trip north with the Expos."[34]

Frazier (his teammates called him "Sweet Lou") did a yeoman's job for the Expos in 1993, good enough to keep him on the club in 1994. That second year he appeared in 76 games, managed 140 at-bats, drove in 14 runs and collected enough pinch hits to put him near the top of the franchise list with Jose Morales.

"We got Lou through free agency," Felipe Alou said in a 2012 interview for this book. "I saw him in the minor leagues and I said this guy could play for me. I didn't know if he could play for anyone else but he could play for me."

"It was a quite a talented club, with guys like Larry Walker, Marquis Grissom, Pedro Martinez, Moises Alou," Frazier offered in an interview. "The player who really impressed me from 1994 was Larry Walker, the way he conducted himself and went about his business."

When the '94 strike and, ultimately, the cancellation of the season wiped out the Expos' chances, Frazier was a wounded man. "I was very hurt and disappointed," he said.

Lou Frazier

Frazier would go on to play part of the 1995 season with the Expos before being traded to the Texas Rangers. He then played for the Seattle, Baltimore, White Sox and Phillies organizations until 1999, when, following a season at Wilkes-Barre of the International League, he hung up the spikes for good.

Following retirement from the diamond, Frazier remained connected with the baseball world as an outfield/base-running coordinator, hitting coach and first-base coach. His career took on new dimensions in 2010 when he founded the "Louie Sluggers Baseball Club," an Arizona-based non-profit youth organization focused on the development of youngsters' baseball skills.

Perhaps the saddest story of them all concerns Freddie Benavides, an infielder whose last big-league game was the last one played by the Expos in 1994, on August 11. Appearing in a limited role, either filling in at short for Wil Cordero or at second for Mike Lansing, he managed to go 16-for-85 with a triple and six RBIs. But that was it: when it ended, it ended for all time. Never again was he given the opportunity to don a major-league uniform.

Benavides came to Montreal from the Colorado Rockies in odd circumstances. It was while he participated in a fan-promotion tour that former Expos employee and Rockies GM Bob Gebhard quietly informed him he had been traded to the Expos.

"What?" a bewildered Benavides asked Gebhard. "It was a helluva shock." Benavides says today that he never realized "just how good that team was until I got to spring training."

When he arrived in West Palm Beach the following February, Benavides recognized the vast potential that ran up and down the roster; after the team left spring training and began playing regular-season games, he knew this team was special.

"It was a tremendous team. We had a chance to win a World Series with that club. I believed it and we all believed that we were the best team in baseball. We were a very, very good ballclub," Benavides said in an interview July 23, 2011.

"We had camaraderie going into the strike, we won a lot of games, we knew that nobody was going to catch us. The strike came, we said we would be back but it never happened. It really hurt me a lot."

Then came the terrible realization that nobody wanted him for the 1995 season, including the Expos. "It was a big shock," Benavides said. "I played Triple A that season with the Cubs in Iowa."

What didn't help was that Benavides was an arbitration-eligible player: he probably would have earned $500,000 or more for the 1995 season. And in the post-strike era nobody was interested in bringing him on board for that salary. To them, he was just another middle-of-the-road player cast aside by the system, one more speck of dust from the fallout of 1994.[35]

An Expos' Fan Lament

Where were you on the night the Big Owe cried?
When little children wept and parents sobbed;
That night in Montreal when baseball died,
That night of infamy when we wuz robbed?

A rolling, white-hot fever ruled that game
And made a mark that we'll forever bear.
We knew that things could never be the same -
But still we let cold fortune drive us there.

Who cares the hated Marlins finally won?
A bitter prelude to a bitter Fall -
When it was done and over – it was done.
Apocalyptic, times that shaped us all

For we were there that night the Big Owe cried,
That night in Montreal when baseball died.

Bill Young – April 6, 2006

Chapter Forty-Six

Bolting the Organization

In February 1995, long-time Expos PR specialist Rich Griffin made the decision to bolt the organization that had employed him since 1973.

Even before managing general partner Claude Brochu decided to trade away stars Marquis Grissom, John Wetteland and Ken Hill and elected not to offer a contract to Larry Walker, Griffin was preparing to switch jobs himself.

So what did Griffin, the elite media-relations expert, do?

Before spring training started, he accepted a job as baseball columnist for the *Toronto Star*.

"You know Rich, he is so low-key," said his former Expos office mate Claude Delorme, respected director of ticket operations. "He advised Claude Brochu that he had an opportunity to spend more time with the family and improve both quality of life and salary with this new position. After spending so many years with the Expos, I believe the extensive travel and being away from his family finally motivated Rich to look for a new challenge in sports that would provide him more stability. I do not believe that the challenges faced by the organization played any role in his departure."[36]

Griffin's hiring was easily the best choice then *Star* sports editor Dave Perkins would make in his short tenure at that position, even allowing for the fact that Griffin had never written for a newspaper before. All Perkins had to go by were Griffin's annual information guide and the daily Expos game notes for the media, into which he consistently injected his own sense of humour.

Since 1995, Griffin has fashioned a superlative style covering the major-league beat for the *Star*. The Expos replaced him with Montreal native P.J. Loyello, who held the same spot with the Triple-A Ottawa Lynx and who currently has been employed for years by the Florida Marlins, the same organization that hired Delorme.

Griffin's loss to the Expos cannot be compared with the departure of Grissom, Wetteland, Hill and Walker, but it still left a deep impression on the organization. And if there is one word to describe Griffin's reputation and work with the *Star*, it would have to be "esteemed."[37]

Chapter Forty-Seven

They Also Served –
Behind the Scenes

Marcia Schnaar can't remember exactly when it happened. Was it after the strike began on August 12, 1994, or was it after Bud Selig cancelled the season on September 14?

Anyway, it was around that time, shortly after she and her husband Mort had toured Quebec and the Maritimes on vacation, that Expos vice-president of baseball operations Bill Stoneman called her into his Olympic Stadium office to give her some bad news.

"We're going to be laying off a number of people," Stoneman told his long-time executive assistant, "and you are going to be the first one."

"I was sorry that baseball had come to this. It was inconsiderate of Bill because I was a valuable employee," Schnaar said in 2012. "But I was happy too, because it meant I was able to spend more time with my ailing husband. With the strike, there was only one person it was good for and that was my husband. He was on borrowed time."

A few years earlier, Mort had been diagnosed with pancreatic cancer, so shortly after getting the news from her boss, Marcia and her husband decided to travel again.

"We took a trip from Los Angeles to San Francisco on a Parlor Car Tour, then we went on to Hawaii," Schnaar said. "Our motto was 'Have wheelchair, will travel.' Shortly after we returned from Hawaii, we went to the Montreal Neurological Institute, where we spent about seven weeks.

"I probably only went home three times during that time. The Neuro has a cot for each ward. My husband's last week was at the Mount Sinai Hospital in a terminal care ward. I was unable to sleep over there."

Mort died March 8, 1995 and to this day, his widow thinks of him each and every day.

Oddly enough, not long after her husband died, Marcia was hired back by the Expos, this time to hunt out accommodations from various landlords for the replacement players who were expected to arrive shortly because regular major-league players were still on strike.

Schnaar joined the Expos as a Day One employee way back when principal owner Charles Bronfman was hiring people at a suite in the Sheraton Centre.

Out of the blue, Schnaar took a chance and called the hotel, asking if she could speak with Mr. Bronfman. When he answered, she said she wanted to work for the Expos and wondered whom to talk to about a job. "I am as good as anybody," Bronfman replied.

"That tells you the kind of man Charles is, a great human being," Schnaar said. She was hired, although she took about 10 years off at one stage to raise her family. Along the way, she would not only be made an executive assistant in the baseball-operations department but she would also help out in the babysitting department during Expos home games.

Today, she works three days a week at a Montreal medical clinic.

Monique Chibok was employed as an executive assistant with the Expos for 24 years. "I was going 300 mph and I loved it," she remembers fondly. "Now, I am going 60 mph. I miss my job with the Expos even after all of these years. If I had been asked to go with the team to Washington, I would have gone. I wasn't much of a baseball nut, not a baseball freak per se, but I loved what I was doing.

For **Erik Ostling**, the Expos director of team travel, the end of the 1994 season also meant the end of his employment reign. He wanted to move on.

"I saw the writing on the wall, the timing," Ostling said. "And I was about to marry my future wife. The job offered a great life but the travel was tough. There was spring training, the regular season, the winter meetings; it put you on the road 175 days a year. Some days you'd get to the hotel and then suddenly you were trying to remember what city you were in.

"It's the baseball world and some people make it their lives. For me, I realized there was more to life. The strike got me headed in a new direction. I moved to Toronto and it's been fantastic. I joined an organization called the Compass Group back then, now the Hurley Group," said Ostling, who is based in Bedford, Nova Scotia.[38]

How **Michel Spinelli** became an official scorer for the Expos: During the 1980 season Expos PR Director Rich Griffin was looking to get away from the practice of using beat writers like Ian MacDonald of the *Montreal Gazette* and Pierre Ladouceur of *La Presse* as official scorers at Expos home games. On a hunch, he called amateur baseball/occasional major-league umpire Michel Spinelli at home in Montreal and asked him if he would be interested.

"I'm not an official scorer," Spinelli told Griffin.

"But you know the rules because you're an umpire. I'm sure your judgment is good," Griffin replied.

So Spinelli took Griffin up on his offer and went on to serve in that post for close to 1,000 games, from 1980 through the 2004 season, the team's last in Montreal. In later years broadcaster Mitch Melnick and the affable Bob Mann also teamed up with Spinelli in handling most of the scoring duties.

Key people who didn't play for the Expos in 1994 who don't get enough credit including those who helped shape the team before they departed

Claude Brochu, managing general partner

Jacques Menard, chairman of the board

Mark Routtenberg, minority share-holder

Bill Stoneman, vice-president of base-ball operations

Kevin Malone, general manager

Felipe Alou, manager

Tim Johnson, bench coach

Luis Pujols, first-base coach

Tommy Harper, hitting coach

Joe Kerrigan, pitching coach

Jerry Manuel, third-base coach

Pierre Arsenault, bullpen coordinator

Claude Delorme, director of stadium operations

Ron McClain, trainer

Mike Kozak, assistant trainer

John Silverman, equipment manager

Eddie Haas, scout, executive advisor

Ed Creech, scouting director

Marcia Schnaar, executive assistant to Bill Stoneman

Monique Chibok, executive assistant to Claude Brochu

Rich Griffin, media-relations guru

Monique Giroux, media-relations guru 1969-2004

Sina Gabrielli, media-relations assistant

Ron Piché, PR rep, batting-practice pitcher, R.I.P.

Erik Ostling, director of team travel

Suzanne LeMoignan, sales dept. employee 1969-2004

Claudine Cook, director of events

Dan Duquette, former GM

Dave Dombrowski, former GM

Charles Bronfman, former majority owner 1968-1990

John McHale, former president & GM, R.I.P.

Jim Fanning, former do-it-all executive 1968-1993

Buck Rodgers, former manager

Larry Bearnarth, former pitching coach, R.I.P.

Gary Hughes, former scouting director

Frank Wren, former assistant scouting director

John Boles, former farm director

Whitey Lockman, former superscout, R.I.P.

Dave Jauss, former scout

Cheryl Evans, former executive assis-tant, scouting

Denis Brodeur, chief photographer 1968-1996, R.I.P.

Many more too numerous to mention

Compiled by Danny Gallagher

Chapter Forty-Eight

Tony Gwynn – Close and Yet So Far

Tony Gwynn was the definitive leadoff hitter of his generation. During the 1980s and 1990s he hit for high average, drove in runs, and played outstanding defence for the San Diego Padres.

Batting left-handed, his forte was hitting to the opposite field, especially over the shortstop's head. Never mind pulling the ball. He just went with the pitch.

The year 1994 was an almost unbelievable one for him as he became the most recent player in major-league history to toy with the possibility of batting .400. His average when the season ended six weeks short of completion was .394, the closest to that mark since Ted Williams hit an amazing .406 in 1941. Next on that list was George Brett, who over the full season of 1980 hit a pretty neat .390 for the Kansas City Royals.

"I got off to a good start and pretty much maintained it through the All-Star break and August," the classy Gwynn said over the phone some 18 years later. "I was looking forward to finding out how things would be in September to achieve a number like .400. I figured it would be a lot tougher in September than in July or August."[39]

Gwynn thought pitchers would be looking for new ways to make it more difficult for him to get hits. Whatever they tried wasn't working, even at season's end. In his last at-bats, on August 11, Gwynn went 3-for-5 in Houston as the Padres beat the Astros 8-6.

"When we were leaving the park after the last game before the strike, I thought we would be returning to work," Gwynn said. "I didn't think it would be the last game of the season, the end of the road."

A somewhat eerie event occurred post-game on August 11, a harbinger of things to come on the baseball labour front, perhaps. "Our plane had a flat tire," Gwynn said. "We had to sit and wait three hours until they flew in a new tire before we took off." Still, Gwynn figured he would be back playing in two weeks or so. It was not to be. "I was absolutely stunned when the season was cancelled."

As for not getting the chance to reach the magical .400 mark, Gwynn replied, "I don't feel like I lost out on anything. Could I have hit .400? Up until you retire, you don't know if it might ever happen."

Nevertheless, Gwynn remembers 1994 as a great year for baseball. "There were a lot of people having fine years, including the Expos," he said. He then singled out Matt Williams, a member of the San Francisco Giants at the time, who had taken a run at the home run mark, well before Mark McGwire and Sammy Sosa eclipsed Roger Maris' single-season record of 61 set in 1961. Regrettably, Williams saw his run shut down at 43 homers, with six suspended weeks still remaining in the schedule.

"Then there was the All-Star game in Pittsburgh," remembered Gwynn. Held on July 12, the match was tied until the bottom of the 10th inning when Gwynn singled and scored the winning run on a Moises Alou double.

Gwynn was quick to say that while 1994 was a wonderful year for him, it was not his most memorable season. "A better year was 1997, because I drove in 100 runs for the first and only time in my career." Actually it was 119 RBIs combined with a remarkable 220 hits and a .372 average.

Gwynn retired from baseball following the 2001 season, ending his 20-year march through the National League with the astounding totals of 3,141 hits and a .338 lifetime batting average.

He fits nicely as the answer to the question posed in Carole King's best-selling hit *So Far Away: Doesn't Anybody Stay in One Place Anymore?* For Tony Gwynn did. He stayed in San Diego with the Padres for his entire career. In so doing, he joined such notables as George Brett (Kansas City Royals), Cal Ripken Jr. (Baltimore Orioles), Carl Yastrzemski (Boston Red Sox), Al Kaline (Detroit Tigers), Ernie Banks (Chicago Cubs), Craig Biggio (Houston Astros) and, best remembered, Steve Rogers with the Expos. Today Gwynn is a member of the Hall of Fame at Cooperstown. He was inducted in his first year of eligibility, appearing on an astounding 532 of 545 votes cast, a 97.61 percentage. One wonders how 13 writers could opt to keep him off their ballots.

For as a player and as a man Tony Gwynn was a head above most others. For example, when asked what or whom he thought about in the aftermath of the '94 strike, he spoke not of himself or his too-fleeting opportunity to gain baseball immortality. Rather, he said, his thoughts were mostly about Montreal. He had a fondness for the city, in part because it was there at Olympic Stadium that he blasted the single that gave him 3,000 big-league hits and made him the first player to register his 3,000[40] outside of the United States. "They had Grissom and Walker and

Alou...and you know, I think Atlanta's run would have ended that year. And maybe we'd still have baseball in Montreal. Maybe they would have gotten what they wanted."[41]

Tony Gwynn was that kind of ballplayer.

Chapter Forty-Nine

How a Supreme Court
Justice Saved Baseball

In early 1995, U.S. President Bill Clinton spoke publically of his wish that the players' strike end before the hundredth anniversary of Babe Ruth's birth on February 6, a date of some significance. "I identify with Babe Ruth," he told *U.S. News & World Report* at the time. "[Ruth] was a little overweight and he struck out a lot. But he hit a lot of home runs because he went to bat."[42]

In fact, Clinton took the unusual step of actually ordering the two sides to meet and resolve the strike issue by February 6, an order both parties ignored. To the dismay of fans everywhere, the strike not only continued unabated but was about to take a sharp turn for the worse.

On February 16, the owners as a group opened spring training camps and, strike or no strike, made a commitment to start the 1995 season on schedule. They would go with the best players available, they said – and let the union be damned. If it, and its players, refused to take part, they'd find others who would. And thus began the saga of the 'replacement player,' what ESPN's Tim Kurkjian describes as "one of the lowest points in baseball history, a time of anger, confusion and disgrace."[43]

"The important thing is that we keep the game in front of the public and make the best of the situation," said Dodgers vice-president Fred Claire. John Schuerholz, general manager for the Atlanta Braves, was more direct. The strike, he declared, "won't stop me from living up to my responsibility to help provide baseball to the fans or to try and create as normal an environment as I can. All of the surveys indicate the fans are completely behind the replacement concept. They want to see baseball. They don't buy into what the players union says about it."[44] On the other hand, Joe Girardi, catcher with the Rockies at the time, called it a slap in the face for fans. "That's telling the fans: 'You don't know the game. You will pay for any brand of baseball we put out there.'"[45]

The MLBPA's position was clear. It advised "all players on 40-man rosters – generally composed of the top minor leaguers in addition to the major-league regulars – not to report, and all minor leaguers not to play in exhibition games starting in early March."[46]

The replacement players kerfuffle was just the most recent in a series of skirmishes that kept the two sides clawing and scratching at each other's throats – and sending their labour conflict spiraling further away from all sense of reason. When yet another round of negotiations had failed in late December, the owners unilaterally voted to introduce a salary cap. Donald Fehr responded a few days later by declaring that, as a consequence, all 895 unsigned major-league players would become free agents. And shortly afterwards, in an unrelated move, arbitrator Thomas Roberts awarded 11 players a total of almost $10 million as a result of prior collusion charges brought against the owners.[47]

The owners soon rescinded their cap notion – but then replaced it with a new approach: "they abolished salary arbitration, centralized player negotiations with the commissioner's office and ended an agreement not to collude on salaries."[48] It was a strategy that, in effect, would have "essentially let owners fix salaries."[49]

By this time the National Labor Relations Board had seen enough. It launched a challenge before the courts contesting what it called unfair labour practices by baseball owners during the time both sides were still negotiating a new collective bargaining agreement. As noted earlier, the Board's petition was heard by Judge Sonia Sotomayor of the United States District Court for the Southern District of New York. She acted quickly, taking only two hours to hear the case and fifteen minutes to come to her decision. It was decisive.

"[Justice Sotomayor] issued an injunction against the owners that ordered them to restore free agency and arbitration," wrote Sean Gregory in *Time* Magazine some 15 years later. "With the injunction in place, the players agreed to return to work while a new labor agreement was hammered out."[50] The judge was very aware of the fact that Opening Day was only hours away, which explains in part the haste with which she proceeded. She noted in her decision that "issuing the injunction before opening day is important to ensure that the symbolic value of that day is not tainted by an unfair labor practice and the NLRB's inability to take effective steps against its perpetuation," adding that "the harm to the players [would be] the very one the owners' unfair labor practices sought to achieve, i.e., an alteration of free-agency rights and a skewing of their worth."[51]

Although her ruling called for an injunction only, it effectively ended the strike. Major league players returned to work, to an abbreviated three-week spring training session. The season was reduced to 144 games, with Opening Day set back to late April. For the Expos, that day occurred in

Pittsburgh on April 26, where they took two from the Pirates behind the pitching of Jeff Fassero and Pedro Martinez. The following week, over 46,000 greeted the club for Opening Day at Olympic Stadium and once again Fassero guided them to victory, 9–6 over the Mets. From that point on, however, their journey began a slow descent toward last place in the NL East, ultimately ending in the cellar, 25 games behind the league-leading Atlanta Braves. Among the team's few highlights: Carlos Perez represented the club at the All-Star Game; and on June 3, Pedro Martinez pitched nine perfect innings against the San Diego Padres before giving up a hit in the 10th to Bip Roberts. In so doing he became only the second pitcher in history, after Harvey Haddix, to have a perfect game broken up in extra innings. One week later, on June 11, Rondell White had a career day in Candlestick Park against the San Francisco Giants, banging out six hits and hitting for the cycle.[52]

But the story of the year was the Sotomayor decision and its aftermath. For more than simply returning baseball to the parks of America, it afforded the owners and the players union a reprieve within which to resume contract talks. Because her ruling restored the provisions of the previous labour agreement, "it gave both sides an opportunity to take a breath, to take stock of where they were," suggested Randy Levine, later chief negotiator for the owners and, more recently, president of the Yankees. Ultimately "it led to the good-faith bargaining that produced revenue sharing, the luxury tax and interleague play."[53] Although the parties required almost two years to carve out that next agreement, they pretty well got it right: baseball has seen no other work stoppages since, the only major sports league able to make such a claim.

In May 2009, Justice Sotomayor was appointed to the United States Supreme Court. When announcing her nomination, President Barack Obama highlighted her role in 1995: "Some say that Judge Sotomayor saved baseball," he exclaimed.[54] Donald Fehr concurred with the president's assessment, but perhaps in a more round-about way and with less generosity of spirit. "Her ruling did not produce an agreement," he said, "but it gave the parties time to get on with normal business and get back to the bargaining table and produce an agreement. If [the strike] hadn't ended when [Judge Sotomayor] ended it, it would have gone on for some time and it would have gotten uglier and uglier."[55]

As it was, the 1995 season was an ugly affair anyway – what with rebellious fans persisting in hurling abuse at the millionaires and billionaires of the game for their self-centered, selfish and dismissive demeanour. John Thorn, the official historian for Major League Baseball, told film-maker Ken Burns: "I have never encountered such bitterness and such assurances on the parts of my friends that they would never watch another baseball game, that they no longer cared about the game, that they were going to shift their allegiances, not only from one team to another, but from one sport to another."[56]

Opening Day activities were especially nasty. In Pittsburgh, the Expos-Pirates game was delayed for 17 minutes as fans hurled sticks and other objects onto the field to express their displeasure. They desisted only when warned that the game was about to be forfeited. In Cincinnati a plane flew over Riverfront Stadium dragging behind it a banner reading: "Owners and Players: To hell with all of you." Only 5,245 fans showed up for the New York Yankees' first game but those who did turned on Donald Fehr, who was present, calling out such epithets as "Shame on You!" and "You ruined the game."[57]

In fact, had it not been for the record-breaking triumph of Baltimore Orioles star Cal Ripken Jr., who, on September 6, 1995, at Camden Yards, surpassed Lou Gehrig's 56-year consecutive games-played streak of 2130, baseball might well have been brought to its knees.

"You suffer a shocking loss and you think it's never going to be the same again," said controversial journalist and commentator, Mike Barnicle. "And you're thinking, I'm not going to another game, I'm not going to pay the prices that go into the players' pockets, and into managements' wallets, I'm not going to do it, I'm sick of all of them – and then Ripken comes along."[58]

Ripken's feat, along with the joy and humility that cloaked the resolute shortstop's demeanour as accolades rained down upon him, was, without question, baseball's feel-good moment of the year, perhaps even of all time. It certainly played a major role in restoring some measure of the credibility the game had lost over the previous eighteen months.

For the record, the 1995 World Series Champions were the NL's perennial bridesmaids, the Atlanta Braves, who finally had their day in the sun, triumphing over the Cleveland Indians in six games.

Are The Good Times Really Over For Good?

1996-2001

*It is said that every life has its roses and thorns;
there seemed, however, to have been a misad-
venture or mistake in Stephen's case, whereby
somebody else had become possessed of his
roses, and he had become possessed of somebody else's thorns in addition to his own."*

– Charles Dickens, Hard Times

Jose Vidro (second base) and Orlando Cabrera (shortstop) were part of the vanguard of new young players who brought excitement to the Expos even as their universe was collapsing around them.

Chapter Fifty

A snowball headed for hell

Are we headed downhill like a snowball headed for hell?
— Merle Haggard

For 12 years, from the early 1990s until shortly before the club's demise, Mark Routtenberg was a member of the consortium that owned the Montreal Expos. "They were all good years," he says today, "except for the last one, but 11 out of 12 is pretty good. I lost my investment but I made many lasting friendships. I have no regrets – apart from the fact that there is no team here anymore."[1]

A keen follower of baseball and a strong supporter of the Expos, Routtenberg delighted in his association with the organization and its personnel. He was a frequent visitor to the clubhouse where he mingled with players, becoming close to a number of them and a mentor to several. Few objected to this comportment, except perhaps Dan Duquette when he was general manager. As Routtenberg explained a number of years later, "I am an owner. This is what I do; talk to players. If the players say they don't want me in the clubhouse I will stay out. Otherwise I will continue to meet them there."[2]

Given Routtenberg's close association with the Expos, it is not surprising that he has very definite views on those factors which contributed to the club's demise in 2004. In a 2011 interview conducted in his Montreal offices, he quite candidly listed them. Using the players' strike as a jumping-off point, they included: the fire sale; the failed stadium project; problems within the ownership group; the lack of support shown by MLB; the Loria ownership period; and the perception that Montreal was not a baseball town.

The players' strike of 1994

Without question, the players' strike of 1994 and the extraordinary damage it brought down on baseball led the list. Every major league franchise suffered huge losses because of the work stoppage – losses of revenue, credibility, good faith, and respect. Ballparks, once regarded as green cathedrals, sanctuaries of calm, suddenly morphed into unexpected hotbeds of discontent. Sportswriter Selena Roberts believes that "the anger really took baseball officials aback. They really did not think that the anger could sustain itself, and it really did. And I think you saw a fan base saying to baseball, 'you know what, it's not your sport, it's our sport.'"[3]

This anger was very evident in Montreal, beginning right on August 12, the day the strike was called, with much of it directed toward managing partner Claude Brochu. It became especially virulent following the fire sale as fans, media, and even players concluded he was throwing in the towel, protecting his own interests at the expense of the team. The atmosphere around the club grew increasingly toxic and loyal supporters began to pull away.

Inside the organization, however, the long-term goals suggested that no one was giving up. While 1995 became a write-off, the re-energized class of '96 excelled on the field. Brochu was talking about fresh initiatives to breathe new life into the Expos, most specifically via a new stadium, but for many different reasons none of these ever really panned out. In the end, his moral authority suffered such a hit he was left with no choice but to step aside.

The impact of the 1995 fire sale

The 1995 fire sale in Montreal and its impact, both short and long term, are now the stuff of legend in Montreal. When journalist Stephanie Myles asked Claude Brochu in a 2004 interview if, given time and perspective, he might have done things differently, Brochu replied: "I never gave it a thought. I knew what the consequences would be; financially...I never thought for two seconds that we could retain this team, even part of it. For me, we had to get about $20 million of payroll out of there and try to hang on for the 1995 season and see what happened."[4]

Mark Routtenberg believes that the root problem with the fire sale was not so much the loss of four all-star players as it was the club's inability to explain its intent, backed by specific details, to fans in language they could understand. By not doing so, the organization came to be seen as aloof, even callous, and further contributing to a rapidly eroding confidence in the team's management acuity.

Brochu does not accept the premise that the fire sale killed baseball in Montreal. To underscore this opinion, he points out that "the club made a great recovery in 1996."[5] And he is correct. After finishing the '95 season at the bottom of the NL East with a 66-78 record, third worst in the league and 24 games behind Atlanta, Montreal rebounded to finish second in '96, only eight games out and miles ahead of the other clubs in the division.

Leading the charge for Montreal were Moises Alou and the surprising "O Henry" Rodriguez, while Jeff Fassero and Pedro Martinez had solid winning records and Mel Rojas, successor to John Wetteland, notched 36 saves.

The team's performance was so solid it missed out on a wild-card spot only by the slightest of margins – its winning percentage of .543 was just seven points behind Los Angeles. The Dodgers finished with a won-lost record of 90-72, compared to Montreal's 88-74. One victory either way, more or less, and Montreal might have seen the '96 club become the first edition of the Expos to breathe the rarefied air of postseason baseball since 1981. At a time populated with "what ifs," what a world of difference that might have made.

The Expos were back, as Brochu suggested – but not so much the fans. Attendance in 1996 was in the 1.6-million range, third lowest in the National League. Although fan interest generally had declined dramatically throughout baseball following the strike, it had slowly begun to climb back up. Such was not the case in Montreal, where it remained on the decline.

Perhaps this is the reason the Expos were again active in the marketplace at season's end. Some suggest that the impact of personnel decisions in '96 was as damaging as the '95 fire sale. Veterans from the '94 Expos who were cut loose included Sean Berry, Wil Cordero, Jeff Fassero, Kirk Rueter, Tim Scott, and Jeff Shaw, all traded, along with Moises Alou, Mel Rojas, Tim Spehr, and Lenny Webster, who became free agents. Butch Henry was claimed on waivers by the Red Sox.

The general manager who orchestrated most of these transactions was Jim Beattie. He succeeded Kevin Malone, who had left the team, no longer able to stomach the dismantling of his 'championship' club. In conversation, Brochu spoke highly of Beattie, putting him in the same category as the Dombrowskis and Duquettes of earlier days, whom Brochu considered "the best in the business." He concedes that Beattie's job was tougher: "He had less to work with, the [on-field situation] was difficult to handle, and the media were increasingly unforgiving."[6]

All these years later, Montreal's die-hard fan base still holds Brochu accountable for the dream-destroying fire sale and the club's descent into oblivion a decade later. Given the slightest provocation, that anger will still rise to the surface. Even as recently as August 2011, when Brochu was interviewed on sports radio in Montreal and asked about the past, "bitter fans called the station off-air to protest against his presence."[7]

The downtown stadium

"If, for the public, the Expos' misfortunes were summed up by two crucial moments in the history of the club – its elimination on Blue Monday in 1981 and the players' strike in 1994 – I thought we had to add a third date: September 2, 1998. That night…the stadium project died." So wrote Claude Brochu in his autobiography. "The team was on life support. It was the beginning of the end."[8]

For that was the date Quebec's premier, Lucien Bouchard, pulled the plug on the downtown ballpark project. The government's support, which had been assured all up and down the line as development of the stadium project progressed, was shockingly withdrawn, and with no advance warning. Although discussions around the project's revival continued for some time, effectively it had already been consigned to the dead-letter box.

Brochu has written in his autobiography that "I wanted to leave something tangible behind, a facility baseball fans and sports fans in general could enjoy for years to come."[9] It would never happen.

The aging Olympic Stadium, built to receive the 1976 Olympic Games, was growing longer in the tooth with each passing year. Cold and cavernous, it had suffered more than its share of recent mishaps and misfortune – from a retractable roof that refused to retract, to the falling beam in 1991, to the knee-destroying concrete carpet of a playing surface that drove Andre Dawson, for one, from Montreal. Fan confidence in the facility eroded to such a degree that with each succeeding mishap more would conclude it was no longer safe, let alone hospitable, and cease attending ball games.

Charles Bronfman reportedly hated Olympic Stadium. He had always intended to build his own, proper baseball facility, but with the city committed to the Olympics he was never able to secure the municipal support he needed to get such a project off the ground.

Olympic Stadium was one of a host of colossal multi-purpose stadiums built during this period, among them the amphitheatres in Cincinnati, Philadelphia, Atlanta, Pittsburgh and several other cities where major league sports prevailed. Because of the astronomical cost overruns the Montreal facility incurred, it quickly became known, sardonically, as the "Big Owe."

For a time Olympic Stadium was regarded as an architectural marvel, but by 1996 most of these 'donut-hole' facilities had fallen out of vogue and were being replaced. In the country of baseball they were giving way to fresher, more intimate, fan-friendly ballparks designed exclusively for the summer game. The first of these opened at Camden Yards in Baltimore in 1992. When Cleveland followed with Jacobs Field in 1994, a trend was set.

Brochu planned to capitalize on this innovative thrust to build his own new stadium in the centre of town and return baseball to the mainstream of Montreal's sports industry, both geographically and spiritually. The site chosen was an ideally located piece of vacant land that lay in the shadow of the Molson Centre (now the Bell Centre), home of the

Jacob's Field: One example of what a new ballpark in Montreal might have looked like

Montreal Canadiens. Brochu and his planning group were convinced that once it was up and running, and with a new bunch of young players on hand to introduce a revitalized brand of baseball to their sparkling new home field, the nightmare of '94 would fade into history. He was probably correct. As Mark Routtenberg recalls, "At the time everyone was in support of the project and most felt it was a done deal. Kudos to Brochu."[10]

To be called Labatt Park, the new stadium would have been built by the same group responsible for the highly praised Du Maurier Tennis Stadium at Jarry Park, the same Jarry Park where the Expos first hung their hats back in 1969. Labatt Park was to be oval-shaped with a transparent exterior glass wall to enable "spectators to witness activity in the neighbouring streets and public squares. The wall would also reflect the surrounding scenery (sky, trees, etc.) during the day, while at night it would reveal outside activity in the surrounding neighbourhood. It offered many views from the outside to the inside and its design promised a sense of closeness and intimacy."[11]

Brochu and his team had concocted several ingenious schemes to finance construction of the new Labatt Park, some of which involved government participation. One of these was an income tax on salaries of visiting teams and players, revenues the province would not have obtained otherwise. Sadly, it was not enough. Even though the Expos' representatives had prepared thoroughly, when they met government officials on

Labatt Park, artist's representation

that fateful day in September 1998, the last thing they expected was to be turned away. To quote Premier Lucien Bouchard at the time: "We are not about to subsidize the salaries of millionaires (players) when we are closing hospital services." So they didn't. As a result, the millionaires went elsewhere and, unfortunately, there was no let-up in hospital closures.

Brochu, to this day, insists: "if we had built the downtown stadium as we intended to do, the '94 season would have been forgotten."[12]

But it wasn't, and one year later everything fell apart. The team acquired a new owner, Jeffrey Loria, with stepson David Samson riding shotgun. One year after that, the stadium project was officially declared dead, extinguishing the last vestige of the Charles Bronfman legacy. The Expos were now in the hands of strangers from away. Within five years they would be calling Washington home.

One Parti Quebecois politician, not impressed with this turn of events, is reputed to have said: "We were behaving like colonials. Where once we had a Quebec company run by Quebecers, we now had a company controlled by an American."[13]

The contentious consortium

It was ironic. The consortium of 13 investors put together in 1991 by Claude Brochu to purchase the Expos from Charles Bronfman and keep the baseball team in Montreal proved to be remarkably inept when it came to fostering teamwork within its own four walls. It seemed to be every man for himself and the management team be damned, at least so it appeared from the outside looking in.

Established as a limited partnership, the consortium was made up mainly of heads of business and labour groups, all leaders in their respective fields who had agreed to come on board more out of a sense of public duty than anything else. As one member has pointed out, "too many of the limited partners didn't believe in the baseball team. They had no interest in baseball as such."[14] To encourage their participation, Brochu pledged to run things in proper business-like fashion and live within the club's means. Although he didn't say so directly, most understood that this meant they would never be asked to increase their financial stake at a later date. Consequently, the consortium, strapped for cash from the very beginning, was never able to get its head above water.

Brochu held the post of managing general partner and as such was solely responsible for the club's operations, a management model that did not sit well with many of his associates. Given their prominence in the business and social life of Quebec, the partners had expected to play a more active role in club affairs than the one given them. Their dissatisfaction eventually bred conflict, which expanded to such a degree that it ultimately brought down first Brochu, then the consortium, and finally, the Expos themselves.

They were strange bedfellows, these consortium members, a collection of various interests, all with outside alliances and, by nature, often at odds with one another. Most were somewhat beholden to the government, either because they did business with it directly, or represented interests that did. As a simple example, in 1995, when the issue of replacement players and strike-breaking came into the discussion, the union heads in the ownership group went berserk. Then there was the time it seemed Revenue Quebec, collectors of provincial taxes, had singled out the Expos for special attention, and Brochu successfully sued them for harassment. The bankers in the group went bonkers. Much of their institutional revenue was generated through services provided for government and they were loath to upset that apple cart.

Over time, many of the owners appeared to delight in working against Brochu and his interests. Somewhat of a solitary man, not overly gregarious, and inclined to follow his own lead, Brochu never formed a close bond with his colleagues, never gained their confidence. Mark Routtenberg attributed this somewhat to the fact that Brochu "was first a businessman; he had little feeling or passion for the game. For example, he once made a presentation, graphs and all, to show that the Expos led the majors in runs scored per payroll totals. Great. But we were still losing."[15]

Nevertheless, Routtenberg has no doubts about Brochu's integrity. "Whatever he decided to do, he did because he thought it was the right thing, not because he had some nefarious plan in mind." Monique Chibok, formerly Brochu's executive assistant, shared that opinion. "He worked a lot on [the stadium] file and he really wanted it to succeed, despite what people say. A park downtown would have been amazing."[16]

Still, with each passing year, the disconnect between Brochu and the partners grew more pronounced, and in the process it did immeasurable harm to the franchise and its fortunes. Brochu firmly believes that by the time the stadium project arrived on the premier's desk, several of the partners had already intervened with government officials to sabotage the project.[17]

Premier Bouchard's cool response to the plan was discouraging, but as Brochu said at the time, it was only one step in a process of negotiating. The appropriate response by the Expos would have been to up the ante, keeping the pressure on and ultimately threatening to move the franchise if nothing else worked.

The limited partners were having none of this. There would be no hardball tactics, there would be no pushing toward a solution and, most assuredly, there would be no backing of the guy (Brochu) prepared to do the pushing. "The consortium didn't have the heart for it," Brochu said. "They all represented big concerns; there were too many interests in too many other areas that could be affected if things got dirty." And so they turned their backs on Brochu and the stadium. "Fundamentally, the problem was the partnership within the Montreal Expos," Brochu told the *Gazette* in 2011. "They destroyed any chance of (a new stadium) happening. They sabotaged the efforts. We need to take the blame as a partnership group."

Upon reflection he added: "Egos got in the way. People wanted to drive the bus who shouldn't have been driving the bus."[18]

By the end of Brochu's tenure, the tone and timber of comments emanating from a number of the partners and being reported by the media were scandalous. A full-blown mutiny was taking place. It was fuelled in part by escalating tension within the boardroom – but also in part by a widely held perception that once Brochu lost the stadium project he gave up on Montreal. "It seemed to some he was paving the way to move the franchise to Washington and go with it as general partner," recalled Routtenberg. "That was not acceptable, and certainly could not have been done without informing the limited partners."[19]

Commissioner Bud Selig tried several times to get the partners to tone down the invective, but without success. Perhaps he could have tried harder. Brochu noted that "under normal circumstances, Selig would quickly have quashed any form of protest from an ownership group," and cited strong interventions Selig had made previously in Cincinnati and Pittsburgh. "But in Montreal, for obvious reasons, Selig didn't want to…By letting them bark, Selig allowed the situation to deteriorate."[20]

Eventually, Bill Stoneman, Vice President of Baseball Operations, frustrated by the ceaseless off-field bickering, decided to speak his mind. In a scathing letter to Jacques Menard, the club's CEO, he took direct issue with what he called the "emotional Brochu bashing that continues to this day."

Stoneman, who in late 1999 would be appointed general manager of the Los Angeles Angels of Anaheim, was unequivocal in making his point: "My own view is that you and some of your group are more concerned with finding someone to blame for your possible failure than you are with focussing on the issues that will save baseball for Montreal. I am therefore concerned that you are particularly focussed on setting the groundwork for the departure of baseball from Montreal.

"If you fail to keep the club in Montreal will you try to pin it on Claude Brochu? The Expos' marketing department? Bud Selig? Some imagined conspiracy within Major League Baseball? Or rather will it be that you couldn't muster the necessary government, corporate and public interest, assemble sufficient investor capital, build a suitable stadium, or come up with a reasonable business plan to ensure the long-term health of the baseball business in Montreal?"

Stoneman concluded: "Keep in mind that when you take shots at Claude Brochu...or anyone else working for this team, you are shooting my teammates. I hope you will understand when I say I resent it. More importantly, I hope you understand that such emotional nonsense is not productive."[21] Stoneman's strong words were to no avail. It really didn't matter: Brochu was done.

Brochu negotiated his severance package with the limited partnership, reported to be $15 million, and with that he was out the door and gone. At the time, his payout was widely condemned in the media as scandalous. Mark Routtenberg disagreed. "It was well earned," he said. "I bear no grudge on that score. He worked hard, he was honest although he liked to be in control, and he was managing partner. He deserved whatever he could get."[22]

When asked once if he might have wanted to do things differently, Brochu was definite: "I did it the way I thought I should and I was kind of building support on it, doing all kinds of work behind the scenes. A lot of stuff had been done, and we came real close to getting it done. But it all sort of went away. We gave it a good try."[23]

Back to baseball

In the final years of the twentieth century, life on the diamond mirrored the adventures and misadventures taking place in the boardroom. Bit by bit, year by year, the Expos risked becoming irrelevant. After their near-miss in 1996 when they were nosed out of postseason play by a hair's breadth, they settled into a steady decline. Not until 2002 and 2003 did the club again make a race of it, something akin to a deathbed revival, just missing the playoffs both years. It was not for lack of trying: this time they were victimized more by MLB duplicity than by anything they faced on the playing fields.

The 1997 Expos finished in fourth place at 78-84, three wins short of the .500 mark. Attendance dropped to just under 1.5 million, second lowest in the 14-team league behind the Phillies. The story of the year was Pedro Martinez, who rose to extraordinary heights, winning the Cy Young award with a 17-8 record and a stunning ERA of 1.90. It was also the year that 22-year-old phenom Vladimir Guerrero came of age, registering a .302 average, 11 home runs and 40 RBIs in 90 games. What is more, two future stars, Jose Vidro, perhaps the best second-baseman in Expos history, and shortstop Orlando Cabrera, also first made their mark.

The next four years, from 1998 through 2001, sealed the club's fate, both on and off the diamond. In '98 Montreal once again finished fourth, stumbling to a 65-97 record, a whopping 41 games behind the Braves, who had now taken almost permanent ownership of the league crown. Attendance dropped yet again, now below one million, an ominous sign.

The '98 season had been preceded by two trades of note: Mike Lansing was dispatched to the Colorado Rockies and, amid a storm of outrage, Pedro Martinez was air-mailed to the Boston Red Sox. Montreal did receive two legitimate pitching prospects in return, Carl Pavano and Tony Armas Jr., but the story was all Pedro (see below). Other members of the Class of '94 who received their walking papers were Darrin Fletcher, Cliff Floyd and Gil Heredia.

This was the year that the Cardinals' Mark McGwire and the Cubs' Sammy Sosa set out to surpass Roger Maris' record of 61 home runs in a single season. The drama of the close race between the two sluggers established the tone for the year, much as Cal Ripken's heroic perform-ance had done in 1995 when he broke Lou Gehrig's record of 2,130 con-secutive games played. As the season wound down, baseball fans hung onto every game, every home run, watching the two sluggers chase one another into a whole new universe of power hitting. When it was all over, both men had surpassed the Maris standard, Sosa ending up with 66 homers and McGwire with 70.

For that slight margin of four, McGwire can thank the Montreal Expos. The final five home runs he hit were all served up by Expos pitch-ers, five different ones in fact. Number 66 came on a Shayne Bennett pitch in St. Louis on September 27. The next day Dustin Hermanson did the honours for number 67 with Kirk Bullinger following right behind with home run 68. Going into the final game of the season, the burning ques-tion on everyone's lips was: "Is 70 even a possibility?"

The answer came quickly enough. A third-inning blast off Mike Thurman raised McGwire's homer total to 69 and four frames later Carl Pavano wrote himself into the record books as the pitcher who surren-dered number 70.

At year's end Montreal made a number of player moves but the overall effect was much like shuffling chairs on the *Titanic* – not terribly helpful given the circumstances. Vlad Guerrero and Rondell White had strong seasons at the plate, Dustin Hermanson was very impressive on the mound, and Ugueth Urbina led the club with 34 saves.

By 1999, the wheels had pretty well come off the bus. Fewer than 800,000 showed up to watch *Nos Amours* at the Big Owe, roughly half the figure shown for the club with the next lowest attendance figures. Their won-lost numbers, 68-94, had pretty well bottomed out. Few of their efforts made the headlines – apart from the news that Felipe Alou, shortly after he seemed ready to take his services to the Dodgers, was handed a new three-year, $6-million contract. This made him one of the highest paid managers in the big leagues. There was also the unpleasantness of being the victims in a perfect game tossed by the Yankees' David Cone in New York. Overall, Guerrero played the starring role, batting .316, with 42 home runs and 131 RBIs. Rondell White had another .300-plus season, as did Jose Vidro. On the mound, no pitcher managed to reach the 10-win mark, but Urbina was credited with an impressive 41 saves.

All the high drama was left to the boardroom. After a lengthy series of negotiations involving consortium members on the one hand and Jeffrey Loria and stepson David Samson on the other, controlling interest in the Expos changed hands, shifting the club's fortunes from the Claude Brochu era to the days of Loria.

This transfer triggered a bizarre series of events worthy of The Three Stooges, except these happened in real time and affected real people and events. The consortium was so completely horn-swoggled by the new owners that when the deal was finally signed, in Brochu's words, even "the partners would admit that they'd given up control of the organization for peanuts, but that they'd no choice."[24]

Looking back many years later, Dave Van Horne, the iconic voice of the Expos, now with the Marlins and a recent winner of the Baseball Hall of Fame's Ford C. Frick Award for broadcast excellence, mused that much more could have been done to save the team. "From the time Charles Bronfman put the team up for sale to this very day, Montreal, Quebec, the business community, all had an opportunity to step up to the plate and rescue the franchise and they didn't do it. More energy seems to have been spent trying to vilify those who were trying to carry the torch…than going out and trying to come up with a solution."[25]

The (second) controversial Pedro Martinez trade

In 1997 Pedro Martinez was named winner of the Cy Young Award in the National League. He was, says Claude Brochu unequivocally, "without a doubt the best pitcher in Expos history."[26] Already eligible for arbitration, he was only one year away from free agency, and with the club doing poorly at the gate it was evident they would soon be unable to afford him.

Perhaps the smart thing would be to trade him now for young talent that, with good luck, might figure prominently in future plans.

In late September 1997, Brochu called together general manager Jim Beattie, Bill Stoneman, Felipe Alou and the coaches to discuss the team's future. All agreed their goal was to put a competitive team on the field by 2001 when the new stadium was expected to be ready. To achieve this they understood they would have to retool the club. Changes would be necessary, starting with Pedro. As tough as it would be to part with him, there was agreement around the table that rather than lose him to free agency, it would be better to exchange him now for promising future players. Only bench coach Jim Tracy dissented.

On the other hand, when the news got out, fans once again went apoplectic. As soon as this deal – which sent Pedro to the Red Sox in exchange for pitchers Tony Armas Jr. and Carl Pavano – was made public, the multitudes decried it as just another money grab by the bosses, another example of the owners snubbing the fans to add a few more pennies to their coffers. At Montreal's last game of the season, one Pedro supporter marched around the Big Owe's lower concourse holding a sign reading, "Trade Claude Brochu." It was an accurate reflection of the overall mood of the crowd.

Martinez had come to love Montreal and had no desire to be traded. Although he arrived here in 1994 under a cloud of doubt, the fans quickly took to him and he to them, nurturing a mutual warmth that endured well beyond his 1997 departure.

Pedro signed a six-years, $75-million guaranteed contract with the Red Sox following the 1997 season, even though he was really reluctant to go. "I didn't want to leave Montreal," he said in a 2004 interview. "I would have taken $25 million less to stay. And not even like that could they afford me, so I had to actually let go...I feel sad about the whole story, the way Montreal turned out. That's the best city I ever played in and my memories of the fans are incredible."[27]

Pedro collected two more Cy Young Awards in Boston – joining Gaylord Perry, Roger Clemens, Randy Johnson, and, more recently, Roy Halladay as the only pitchers to garner this award in both the National and American Leagues. He also recorded more that 3,000 strikeouts over his career, joining an elite class of just 15 pitchers to have achieved that distinction. And, of course, he was a World Series winner with the Red Sox in 2004.

In the celebrations that immediately followed the last game, a weary and champagne-soaked Martinez faced the television cameras and, speaking from the heart, talked directly to his extended Montreal family. "I would like to share this with the people of Montreal who are not going to have a team any more, but my heart..." The rest of his words were muffled by the celebration going on behind him, but the message was clear. When the gifted rapper/videographer Annakin Slayd put together his brilliant YouTube homage entitled *Remember (A Tribute to the Montreal Expos)* he chose that clip for his opening shot.

Chapter Fifty-One

Pedro goes to Boston

One day during the 1997 season, Expos GM Jim Beattie sidled up to Pedro Martinez for a chat. He wanted the goods right from his star pitcher rather than from his agent, Fernando Cuza. "Pedro, we really like you and we would like to sign you to a long-term deal. Would you be receptive?" Beattie asked Martinez.

"I would sign a deal if you got more guys like me," Martinez replied, "but if you are going to keep trading away players and not trying to improve, then trade me."

The conversation continued along those lines until, at some point, Beattie realized he would have to face the agonizing decision of trading Martinez. The gifted righty had reached his prime that season, with a 17-8 record, good enough to earn him the Cy Young Award. He also became the first pitcher to strike out at least 300 batters and accumulate an ERA of less than 2.00 since Walter Johnson turned the trick in 1912.

"We wanted to trade him so that we wouldn't lose him to free agency," Beattie recalled at spring training in Fort Myers, Florida, in 2013. "We were looking for good, young pitchers not yet arbitration eligible. We tried to get Jared Wright in a package with Cleveland for Pedro but they wouldn't even talk to us.

"We talked to the Yankees and they offered a number of players with big contracts. You wouldn't believe the people they offered. I can't tell you any names. I'll keep them for my book."

In the end, the Red Sox were the winners in the Martinez sweepstakes, and Dan Duquette, Boston general manager from 1994-2002, was the architect of the deal. Four years earlier, when he had been the Expos' GM, Duquette had acquired the promising Pedro from the Dodgers for an established player, Delino DeShields. This time he was taking the opposite approach: acquiring an established player, the now highly prized Pedro, for young talent, Tony Armas Jr. and Carl Pavano. Duquette immediately signed Martinez to a six-year deal worth $75 million.

"The first time we got Pedro, he was a reliever," Duquette said. "Second time, he was an established starting pitcher."

Pedro's won-loss records while with the Expos were 11-5, 14-10, 13-10 and 17-8. His departure marked another symbolic moment in Expos history. When the Expos let him go, it was, if not the beginning of the end, certainly a major step in that direction. It smacked of another fire sale; without him, the team was back to rebuilding again.

Montreal sportscaster Mitch Melnick was infuriated with the Martinez trade, much as he had been with the Martinez-DeShields transaction. "The last thing for me was when they traded Pedro," Melnick said. "I had season's tickets. I was in a group of six people who used four tickets. I threw in the towel. I was not going to reward the Expos anymore.

"I hated the trade for Pedro in 1993. Absolutely. I didn't know anything about Pedro. He was a skinny, middle reliever. And I loved DeShields. He was a throwback. He started to get involved in the community; he seemed the perfect second baseman, like Jackie Robinson. He embraced the history of black stars in baseball. He had star quality.

"However, after we saw Pedro make a few starts early on, though, it was apparent he was good."

Duquette's high regard for Martinez becomes obvious in conversation. When asked who his favourite player from the 1994 Expos was, he answered "Martinez" without hesitation. And then, as soon as Pedro joined the Red Sox, he became Duquette's favourite in Boston.

Pedro also figures in what Dan Duquette considers to be the most memorable moment of his own career, the 1999 All-Star Game at Fenway. "It was pretty special," said Duquette. "Mike Schmidt, Stan Musial and Willie Mays showed up, and all those other great players. It was also Ted Williams' last public appearance – and Pedro was the MVP of the All-Star Game."

With the Red Sox, Martinez maintained the pace he had shown as an Expo, pitching electric, especially in 1999 when he went 23-4. He finished his 18-year career with a 219-100 won-loss record, an ERA of 2.93 and a winning percentage of .687. Then there were those three Cy Young Awards. At some point soon, one can expect to see him welcomed into the Hall of Fame at Cooperstown.

Chapter Fifty-Two

Danse Macabre – the Loria-Samson Horror Show

We wanted people to know that the 'exit' sign is coming down in Montreal and the 'entrance' sign is going up"
 – Jeffrey Loria

Unlike *The Rocky Horror Picture Show*, a celluloid fantasy that is part campy musical, part horror flick and has been a cinema staple for close to forty years, the Jeffrey Loria-David Samson version was all real, all true, and desperately frightening.

These days the dynamic duo makes its home in Miami where, now unmasked but still anchored at the hip à la Batman and Robin, they keep finding new ways to wreak havoc. Although the two managed to slip through the credibility gap when they fled Montreal, they have now been revealed for the rapscallions they are. By their dealings, and mis-dealings, as proprietors of the Miami Marlins, they have managed to turn the baseball community and all of Florida against them.

When Loria made his entry into major league baseball ownership via Montreal in mid-December 1999, the early reviews were favourable. Columnist Jack Todd positively gushed as he described Loria's first days at the helm. In describing Loria's first free-agent signing, pitcher Graeme Lloyd, Todd wrote: "This is the kind of move you make when you're looking to put yourself in a position to win…It's a good indication of the way Loria and Samson will operate, taking a very hands-on approach to personnel moves." He wrapped up his piece by describing these efforts as "good for all the Expos fans who have been thinking, at least since August 1994, that 'someday, maybe' would never come."[28]

Initially, even Mark Routtenberg was open to Loria's entry into Montreal. "I knew he was passionate and he knew baseball. He knew the city and he spoke French. I thought he looked great as an owner. He called me almost every night when he was preparing to take over the team." Speaking ten years after the fact, Routtenberg then added: "He used me. Once he had taken possession, I ceased to be important to him. To his face I would now call him a carpetbagger."[29]

Claude Brochu also had a somewhat sympathetic view of Loria in the beginning, and even today bears little ill-will. "I think they (Loria and Samson) were well intentioned, both of them. I think (Loria) saw, based on that first season, that there wasn't much that could be done here," he told *The Gazette* in 2011.[30]

"Just prior to my departure...I warned the new owner about the unusual group he'd be dealing with. 'Beware and, most of all, never trust them blindly,' I told him.

"Loria smiled. 'I know. I've already realized it,' he said. 'The more I see them go, the more I am convinced that you weren't the enemy. They were.'"[31]

Jeffrey Loria was a successful New York City art dealer who had long harboured a desire to own a baseball team; he had even acquired the Triple-A Oklahoma City 89'ers of the American Association in 1989, only to sell them again in 1993. There were reports he had expressed interest in the Expos back in the early 1990s when the ownership issue was still in a state of flux. When he attempted to buy the Baltimore Orioles in 1994 he was bumped aside by Peter Angelos. Undeterred, in 1999 Loria purchased a minority interest in the Expos for $50 million and was named managing general partner. Unlike Claude Brochu, Loria had no 'cash-call' restrictions built into his agreement with the consortium and during his short tenure never hesitated to take advantage of that right. When a partner refused or was unwilling to ante up, Loria would simply draw against that individual's share of ownership. By the time he left Montreal for good in 2002, Loria owned 92 percent of the team.

Loria's stay in Montreal was defined by bad blood and arrogance. One of his first initiatives was to pick up on Brochu's moribund stadium project, and when the city balked at putting more money into a new ballpark in the face of the millions still owed on Olympic Stadium, he decreed: "We cannot and will not stay there." Later, when new life was poured anew into a somewhat revitalized Labatt Park plan which depended on both public and private financing and would have had the Expos playing there in 2002, Loria balked yet again, insisting that the public share be increased. He even threatened to move the team. These protestations created enough bad blood that the project's other participants chose to step aside and shut the whole effort down.

Rather than rekindle the ardour of that diminishing number of baseball fans in Montreal who still cared, Loria seemed bent on finding new ways of trying their patience. When pressure tactics intended to increase revenues for broadcast rights fell on deaf ears, he chose to play tough – with the result that few games were broadcast on the radio and only a handful were televised, and those only on national networks. In 2000, Dave Van Horne, the voice of the Expos since their inception, and his partner Joe Cannon were reduced to describing games via the Internet, on Expos.com, at a time when the World Wide Web was still regarded as a novelty.

As for the Expos on the field, nothing went right. The team again finished fourth with a 67-95 record, 28 games behind the ever-contending Braves. Attendance remained below one million, still last in the National League. Vladimir Guerrero enjoyed another bumper year, amassing 44 home runs, 123 RBIs and a .345 batting average. He was closely followed by the worthy Rondell White and Jose Vidro. Among pitchers, Javier Vasquez went 11-9, Dustin Hermanson 12-14, and the tandem of Carl Pavano and Tony Armas put together a combined record of 15-13 with a collective ERA that exceeded 5.00. By comparison, in 2000 Pedro Martinez of the Red Sox completed the season with a record of 18-6 and a stingy ERA of 1.71.

If Loria's bull-headedness and disregard for Montreal fans seemed excessive in his first year as owner, it paled in comparison to what he managed to achieve in 2001. On June 1, he fired manager Felipe Alou. The man who had guided the Expos to their great successes from 1992–1994 and kept the flame burning in the face of diminishing returns, was gone. Dismissed. Sacked. He was replaced by Jeff Torborg, a former major league catcher and crony of Loria's.

Declaring that the decision had been a difficult but necessary one, Loria said: "Before the season started and many times since, I have reiterated the fact that we expect to win and the excuses of the past will not be accepted." Loria then added: "Jeff Torborg understands that the pressure for this team to turn around starts now."[32] How well did that turn out? Well, the Expos wrapped up the season still in last place, having improved their record by one full victory to 68-94. Guerrero was still the team's hitting star but even he tailed off somewhat. Vidro kept his numbers pretty constant, but Rondell White was no longer in the picture. He had been traded to the Cubs the previous July for Scott Downs. On the pitching side, apart from Vasquez putting up a solid 16-11 record, there was little of note to report. Tony Armas was 9-14, and Carl Pavano, who missed 119 games with an elbow injury, was only 1-6.

But all that was moot – for by the end of the year Loria and Samson would become the new proprietors of the Florida Marlins – and the Montreal Expos would be owned by Major League Baseball.

Loria and Samson had proven themselves to be an unpleasant crew – a conclusion supported by their more recent history in Florida. They were not well liked, even by their peers. One illustration might be this steamy by-play of invective that occurred between Samson and the Mariners' general manager Bill Bavasi in 2000, when it was widely reported that Bavasi intended to offer Ichiro Suzuki a $100-million contract.

Samson exploded. "I would say it's the end of the world as we know it," he reportedly said. "I am made speechless by that contract...It's unbelievable. Literally, it will take the sport down, that contract. We're right back to the ridiculous contracts. It can't be."

Bavasi, aware of David Samson's congenital discourtesy, was not particularly upset. "My mother always taught me that if the only thing you have to say is, '(expletive) Dave Samson,' then don't say anything at all. So I'm not going to say anything at all. Is my mother the greatest or what?"[33]

Minority Partners

When Jeffrey Loria sold the Expos to Major League Baseball, the club's minority partners were also implicated in the deal. They were:

BCE Inc.; BMO Nesbitt Burns, Inc.; Cascades, Inc.; Stephen Bronfman – Esarbee; Investments Ltd - Fairmont Canadian Resorts and Hotels Ltd.; The Federation des Caisses Populaires Desjardins du Quebec; the Quebec Labour Federations Solidarity Fund; Freemark Holdings, Inc.; Loblaws, Inc.; M & S Sports, Inc.; Provigo, Inc.; Telemedia Communications, Inc.; and two numbered companies: 98362 Canada, Inc., an affiliate of Jean Coutu Pharmacies and 114114 Canada, Inc., an affiliate of a San Francisco chain of clothing boutiques.

This deal, made by MLB to facilitate Loria's purchase of the Marlins, so as to enable John Henry to buy up the Boston Red Sox, bizarre in itself (see below), produced two unlikely anomalies:

A) All of a sudden, the Expos became the property of a limited partnership made up of the other 29 major-league franchises. In other words, every big league team now had a stake in two clubs, its own and the Expos – hardly a healthy situation for Montreal, and an apparent (some would claim real) conflict of interest;

B) Loria acquired, roughly, a 92 per cent share of the Marlins at the time of the sale. This meant that his limited partners – the same limited partners he had with the Expos and who had launched a lawsuit against him – held the rest. In other words, once Loria acquired the Marlins, the plaintiffs now owned approximately 7 per cent of the Florida team.

Indeed, when the Marlins won the World Series in 2003, Loria saw to it that each of the limited partners in the Marlins' ownership group was awarded a championship ring. Now, that was strange.

Chapter Fifty-Three

Boondoggle

With a little sleight-of-hand, a lot of money, and a few winks from Major League Baseball, John Henry bought the Red Sox, Loria bought the Marlins, and the other 29 owners bought the Montreal Expos for $120 million.[34]

– Farid Rushdi, Bleacher Report

Call it scandalous, call it cronyism, call it insider trading, call it farcical – the result was the same. The Yawkey Trust was looking to sell the Boston Red Sox and John Henry was interested. There was just one little hitch. He already owned a baseball club – the Florida Marlins, where he was sole proprietor, and the rules were clear. No one person could own more than one team at the same time. Luckily, Henry had a prospective buyer for his Florida franchise in mind – Jeffrey Loria. Unfortunately, Loria also owned the Expos and was bound by the same ownership regulations as the ones that hobbled Henry.

And that's when Commissioner Bud Selig stepped in and solved the problem. He convinced MLB owners that as the Expos were pretty well moribund and soon to be disbanded anyway, they should collectively pay $129 million to take the club off Loria's hands, thus enabling him to acquire the Marlins. That selling price was a nifty $75 million step-up from the $52 million he originally paid in 1999. It did seem like a risk-free opportunity. After all, the commissioner already had plans to contract the Expos – that is, to erase the franchise from the face of the National League.

When Loria made the move to Miami he took with him everything he could get his hands on – from scouting reports to all the team's computers to a significant number of staff, including broadcaster Dave Van Horne, to even the Expos' new state-of-the-art training facility in Jupiter, Florida.

The door was now open for MLB to eliminate the club entirely. There was one more little glitch to get out of the way before the scheme could work: an apparently ineffectual American League team, i.e. the Minnesota Twins, would have to go as well. Unfortunately for MLB, Minnesota municipal and state authorities were having none of it. The Humphrey Metrodome in Minneapolis sued Major League Baseball for breach of contract – and the whole plan was put in abeyance while MLB appealed. Contraction, while still on the table, was temporarily suspended. The Expos would be returning to Montreal and the Big Owe for at least one more season. That was the good news.

The bad news was that apart from a name and uniforms, and players, the club had been pretty well stripped of everything else. Its ownership was now in the hands of MLB itself, but they were without a field manager and the management staff needed to run the operation. Quick decisions were called for: Tony Tavares, formerly of the Angels, was appointed team president; Omar Minaya, a Mets employee, became general manager; and baseball legend Frank Robinson was coaxed down from his perch as baseball's chief disciplinarian to become field manager. A Hall of Famer, Robinson was one of the greatest players ever to step onto the diamond: he is the only one to be named MVP in both the National and American Leagues. But as a manager, he was not so hot. His lifetime winning percentage is .474, and over his 11-year pre-Expos managerial career he managed to guide his teams to winning seasons on only two occasions. So it was with mixed feelings that this jerrybuilt team of players and staff made its way to Roger Dean Stadium in Jupiter for one last time, to prepare for the season ahead.

The cruelest cut of all

Frank Robinson was hardly the most compassionate manager in Expos history, not that the club's roster was over run with compassionate managers. Case in point: He once asked journeyman outfielder Joe Vitiello, a part-timer who had bounced around from Kansas City to San Diego to Japan before landing in Montreal 2003: "Ever wanted to be a coach, Joe?" He then paused before continuing, "Cause that's the only way you'll ever get to wear a uniform full-time!" Vitiello was cut the next day.

Death by a Thousand Cuts

2002-2004

Baseball in Montreal was over. Oh sure, they played on for another decade, but neither the owners, nor the fans, took it very seriously.

– Bleacherreport.com

Vladimir Guerrero
The last of the Expos superstars, in the last of their days in Montreal

Chapter Fifty-Four

Backing Up the Moving Vans

When the moving van backs up to the door, the sad truth will be this: Baseball abandoned Montreal long before Montreal abandoned the Expos.

— Michael Farber, 2000[1]

Call it the Expos' Violetta moment. Violetta is the tragic figure at the centre of Verdi's brilliant opera, La Traviata. When in the closing minutes of the final act, she is unexpectedly visited at her deathbed by her long-lost lover, Alfredo, she suddenly appears to come alive. Her pain and suffering vanish, and she sings of new beginnings for the two of them. Then, safe in Alfredo's arms, she dies. The curtain comes down and the tearful audience goes home. The end.

So too were the Montreal Expos brilliant in their final act, rising to unexpected heights in 2002 and 2003 before, like Violetta, expiring in 2004. Then, as at the opera house, the curtain fell and the tearful audience went home. The end?

When the 2002 season opened, Bud Selig and his ownership group had already consigned the club to the bone yard. Since the team was to be contracted at season's end once litigation in Minnesota was cleared up, 2002 was seen to be nothing more than a mop-up year. In fact, it was heavily mooted about that the team might even close up shop before the year ended.

Tony Siegle, who was part of the new front-office staff in 2002, remembers it well. Speaking to the *National Post* in 2009 he recalls that when MLB "took control of the Expos they had nothing but some desks… what you have to understand is at the time the team was going to contract, which meant they were going out of business. So we had virtually no money to work with, no staff and, hell, we didn't have computers when we started. I brought mine from home."[2]

And that was the atmosphere under which general manager Omar Minaya approached his job. If, he reckoned, the Expos were about to go the way of the Dodo, why not go out in a blaze of glory? And so, in an effort to give his team a real shot at a winning season, if not the postseason, he dug deep into the player market. With the wisdom of hindsight, some of his deals seem questionable today, but at the time, when there was no tomorrow, Minaya had little choice but to go for the 'now.'

He brought back former fan favourites Andres Galarraga and 'O Henry' Rodriguez, and picked up Troy O'Leary, all now free agents. He traded Graeme Lloyd, Mike Mordecai, Carl Pavano, Justin Wayne and a player to be named later to the Florida Marlins in exchange for Cliff

Floyd, Wilton Guerrero, Claudio Vargas and cash. He traded minor-leaguer Jason Bay to the Mets for Lou Collier. Why, he even gave a March tryout to Jose Canseco.

But Minaya's blockbuster move occurred on June 27, when he sent Lee Stevens, along with minor leaguers Brandon Phillips, Cliff Lee and Grady Sizemore to the Cleveland Indians in exchange for Bartolo Colon and Tim Drew. At the time Colon was one of the premier pitchers in the American League. Minaya thought his pres-

Omar Minaya

ence alone might be enough to make the difference between winning and losing in their final season. Ten years later Colon, Phillips and Lee were still playing starring roles and having an impact on the game.

The Expos opened the 2002 season at home on April 2 against the Florida Marlins – and it wasn't pretty. About 34,000 mostly surly fans turned up, all firmly believing that this would be their last home opener and wanting to say good-bye. "Last night," wrote Sean Gordon in *The Gazette* "was an opportunity for whatever remains of the Expos faithful to gather for one last home opener...for a team that will almost certainly move or cease to exist within six months."[3] David Samson was there as well – his stepfather having wisely decided to remain in New York – and he bore the brunt as pent-up frustration that had been building ever since 1994 came raining down. "An unruly mob of 34,351, thousands of whom were intent on expressing just how angry they were at former owner Jeffrey Loria and his stepson David Samson might have turned the home opener into a riot,"

noted Stephanie Myles.[4] Indeed, when the Marlins took a 6-1 lead in the seventh inning, the restlessness and "Loria Sucks" chants that had prevailed throughout the evening took on a different, menacing tenor.

Co-author Bill Young remembers it well. "Once the Marlins went ahead," he wrote in a letter to his brother the next day, "it was almost as though a football game had broken out, so unruly was the crowd. More like you might expect at a cockfight…you sensed that if things got out of hand they would really get out of hand. There was an air of danger hanging over the Big Owe. At the end of the eighth inning I called home to tell [my wife] to turn on the television: I was afraid something bad was going to happen. I assured her that as soon as the game ended I was outta there, it was that ugly."[5]

But winning can change everything. After the Expos scored three runs in the bottom of the eighth, on Michael Barrett's home run and RBI hits by Vladimir Guerrero and Orlando Cabrera, and then followed with another three in the final frame on key two-out hits by Jose Vidro and Cabrera to nail down a 7–6 Expos win, the mood changed. The hostile atmosphere gave way to something more benign, ranging from rude gestures like 'take that, you jerk David Samson,' to loud paeans of praise for *Nos Amours*. Myles caught the mood when she wrote the next day: "For the Expos players and the manager, it was as though they won the World Series, they were so excited."[6]

One should not be misled, however. The next two games, still against the Marlins, drew 9,000-plus fans total. Montreal lost both.

Nevertheless, the Expos were competitive throughout 2002, finishing second in their division at 83-79, their first winning record since 1996. The starting lineup, with perennial front-liners Guerrero and Vidro leading the way, remained solid all year long. Youngsters like catcher Michael Barrett, shortstop Cabrera and outfielder Brad Wilkerson all performed better than expected, and the pitching was effective throughout. Javier Vasquez, Toma Ohka, Tony Armas and Bartolo Colon accounted for over 50 of the club's 83 wins.

If the Expos seemed to play with a devil-may-care attitude throughout the summer, so what. Everyone connected to the club still believed that contraction was just around the corner, that the new bosses at MLB headquarters were simply waiting for the right moment to pull the plug.

But things were not, in fact, that simple. In mid-July, the 14 former owners of the Expos launched a lawsuit in federal court in Miami "alleging that Bud Selig and former Expos managing partner Jeffrey Loria conspired to eliminate the Expos franchise."[7] They sought millions in punitive and compensatory damages, and an injunction "preventing the contraction, sale or relocation of the Expos franchise, which the owners want to be put in trust." Should steps be taken to generate such moves, the owners were ready to seek preliminary relief.

The minority owners' position was that they had been "fleeced by Loria, a carpetbagger who was aided and abetted by Major League  Baseball in a sinister plot to destroy *Nos Amours*." Loria's camp, on the other hand, summarily dismissed the suit as "revisionist history that smacks of vindictiveness on the part of local owners who are trying to polish their reputations and avoid taking the rap for letting the Expos wither on the vine."[8] It was a nasty, name-calling exercise that carried on for several years, leaving egg on the faces of everyone, but bringing no satisfaction to the minority owners.

And then, in late August, as if there wasn't already enough drama mucking up the heart of a great baseball season for the locals, the Major League Baseball Players Association appeared keen to launch

Michael Barrett

another strike, even setting the walkout date for August 30. The Expos completed their last home stand on August 22, defeating San Diego convincingly 4–0, a week before the anticipated shutdown. At the time it was widely speculated that with a strike in the offing and Bud Selig's declared desire to rid himself of these troublesome Expos, the team had most likely played its last game at home. Ever.

Certainly many in the crowd of 8,000 were convinced the strike and its inevitable aftermath would, in some way or other, stamp *finis* on the club. In his August 22 game report for *The Gazette*, Ian MacDonald wrote: "Should the strike materialize, there is a chance the final month of regular-season play could be wiped out. Major League Baseball insists that while it was unable to contract the Expos last fall, it will either do just that this fall or move the franchise for next season."

MacDonald then suggested that for the fans and for the history books, "If this was the Expos' final game in Montreal, then they served up a classic to remember."[9]

Fortunately, the work stoppage never materialized. Before the month was out, MLB signed a new collective bargaining agreement with the players, clearing the way to the postseason. Among the deal's many provisions was a clause that "prohibited contraction through the end of the agreement in 2006."[10] At least for the moment, the Expos were safe: there would be baseball in Montreal in 2003.

With strike talk out of the way, interest returned to what was happening on the field. Quite unexpectedly, the Expos found themselves in the hunt for the wild card, a possibility the new owners never anticipated, and which created minor panic within their cabal. It was like something right out of the movie *Major League*, the one where the fictional owner of the Cleveland Indians staffs her team with deadbeats and misfits to guarantee a losing season and justify moving the franchise to Florida, only to find that despite her best efforts to see her team finish last she has a winning club on her hands.

In the real world, as the Expos flirted with postseason possibilities *à la Major League*, the team's ownership must had been embarrassed. This was not in their plans: there was no way they were prepared to watch those illegitimate sons of Montreal even come close to knocking their true-blue offspring out of a playoff slot. As so they took action – they sat on their hands.

When September rolled around and clubs were permitted to expand their rosters by bringing up prospects from the minor leagues, or occasionally picking up free agents to help them improve their postseason chances, the lords of the game said no. General Manager Minaya would have to cope with the players he already had on hand. There would be no call-ups, no expanded rosters. The budget couldn't handle it.

As if that were not disappointment enough for the fan-base that still cared, there was more – an outrageous miscarriage of justice that occurred in the second-to-last game of the season, on a Saturday night at the Big Owe. In spite of their short bench, the Expos still managed to get through September with a winning record. In third place at the beginning of the month, by season's end they had climbed into second with that very respectable 83-79 record. This success was largely due to a string of victories in the waning days of September, when they won 12 of their last 15 games.

On Saturday, September 28, the Expos hosted the Cincinnati Reds before another sparse crowd at Olympic Stadium. Most were there hoping to see the great Vladimir Guerrero gain membership in the elite 40-40 club: 40 home runs and 40 stolen bases in the same season. At the time only three ballplayers had managed this feat: Jose Canseco, Barry Bonds and Alex Rodriguez. However, as the 2002 campaign drew to a close, Guerrero was sitting at 40 stolen bases and 39 home runs, just one four-bagger away from joining that exclusive group. And there were still two games to play.

In his second at-bat, Guerrero hammered a line drive toward right-centre and over the wall, his 40th homer, or so it seemed. With a broad smile lighting his face, and as the fans rose to their feet and cheered, Guerrero swung into his home run trot and began circling the bases. He never made it: not all the way around. Second-base umpire Gary Cederstrom stepped in to rule that the ball had never left the field of play, that it had hit the top of the wall and bounded back onto the playing surface. Guerrero was incredulous. "I thought when I hit it that the ball was gone," he said. The game was delayed for some time as the umpires, without the benefit of video review, huddled to discuss the blow. As Myles viewed it, "TV replays, slowed frame by frame, appeared to show the ball hitting the top of the wall, ricocheting off the out-of-town score board and bouncing back into play. If that were the case it would have been a homer." Bill Young was also at that game and he saw it that way also – as did everyone in the ballpark apart from the officiating crew. To them the ball remained in play: Guerrero was credited with a single. And he was running out of chances.[11]

The mercurial Jack Todd this time saved his harsh words for the umpires, accusing them of robbing Vlad of this record-marking home run. "These umpires ought to be ashamed," he wrote. "They saw history and said, 'No thanks.'"

Todd then noted that the indignities didn't stop there, highlighting the umpires' approach to Guerrero on Sunday, the final game, with 25,000 present to bid adieu. "The crew added insult to injury yesterday, first when the home-plate ump called strike three on Guerrero on a pitch that was a foot high, then when the first-base ump completely blew a checked-swing call on Guerrero's last at-bat."[12] Fodder indeed for those suspicious enough to believe the owners would stop at nothing to belittle and besmirch their own Expos.

Nevertheless, Guerrero did have a profitable evening on Saturday. His three hits took him past Al Oliver's franchise record of 204, a mark that still stood 11 years later. And making that achievement ever sweeter, Oliver was present at the ballpark to cheer him on.

The Expos ended the 2002 season with a winning record, something that manager Frank Robinson had achieved only twice before in his career as a skipper. And they did it, not with smoke and mirrors, but with real, legitimate baseball players. Contraction had been avoided, and in spite of the rumours, for the time being the prospect of relocation seemed only a remote possibility. Already the most passionate of Expos faithful were murmuring amongst themselves: "Wait until next year: when we'll have a team just like 1994."

Chapter Fifty-Five

Conflict of Interest

The show is over. The monkey's dead!
    – Tennessee Williams, *Orpheus Descending*

"Wait until next year: when we'll have a team just like 1994." These were words to send shivers up and down the spines of the 29 big-league owners who, much against their better judgment, had unexpectedly become proprietors/owners of not one, but two baseball teams. "A team just like '94" was the last thing they wanted, for, as they well knew, another good showing by Montreal would stretch their own credibility to the breaking point. How could they justify permitting a club as proficient as the Expos to fester on the slag heap rather than offering tangible support? They well understood that the better the Expos performed, the tougher that explanation would become.

Thus, once again, or so many suspect, MLB set out to manipulate the odds to better favour the house. Because the owners had gotten a scare in 2002 when the Expos emerged as surprise contenders for the wild card, this time they wanted to leave no doubt. Their solution was to transfer 22 Expos home games from the Big Owe to San Juan, Puerto Rico and its 19,800-capacity Hiram Bithorn Stadium, named for the first Puerto Rican to play in the major leagues. (Hiram Bithorn had suited up with the Chicago Cubs in 1942-43 and then briefly with the White Sox in the post-war years.) Baseball's intent, or so they claimed, was to assess Puerto Rico's potential as a viable home to a major league franchise in the future. They were also hoping to increase club revenues. They had given up on Montreal.

Club President Tony Tavares justified the move by suggesting that with the Puerto Rican promoters agreeing to a guaranteed revenue base in return for the privilege of hosting major league baseball in their own ballpark, the Expos "will not have to conduct a 'fire sale' of players such as Vladimir Guerrero and Bartolo Colon."[13]

The 22 games were to cover seven series, to be played in April, June and September. The logistics were nightmarish, especially for the players. Following the close of spring training, Montreal opened its 2003 season on March 31 in Atlanta and was scheduled to play eight more away games before returning home. There was nothing unusual in that, except that for most of April, "home" would not be Montreal but rather San Juan. On April 9 they were wrapping up their first road trip, with a 7-1 win over the Cubs in Chicago; on April 10 they were in Puerto Rico, taking part in festivities celebrating their inaugural Puerto Rican home opener.

Instead of enjoying an opportunity to settle into new summer digs in Montreal, the players were far from home, alone, and with little sense of what awaited them. The schedule had them playing 10 games on the island, against the Mets, the Braves and Cincinnati before they would finally reach Olympic Stadium on April 23. Remarkably, after all that, when they arrived in Montreal, they were three games over .500.

Certainly, in the beginning this adventure into Latin America was a successful one for the owners, and the Latin world. "Los Expos" won over the fans, and turned Montreal's Hispanic players into heroes, especially those native to Puerto Rico – Jose Vidro, Javier Vazquez and Wil Cordero. Attendance for the year at Hiram Bithorn averaged 14,000, compared to 12,000 in Montreal, leading to a season total of one million-plus passing through their collective turnstiles. Although this number still left the Expos firmly anchored at the bottom of the National League's attendance lists, the 2003 Expos were the first, and only, edition of the club, to surpass the one million mark since 1997.

If ever a team has shown the capacity to rise to the occasion in the face of adversity it was this band of Expos. They might not have matched the 1994 club in overall superiority, but when it came to grit and team unity, and the ability to put disappointment behind them, the 2003 club was every bit its equal.

Almost nothing went right for the Expos in 2003, starting with spring training. Since the mid-1990s the club had held its pre-season camp in Jupiter, Florida, at Roger Dean Stadium, a state-of-the-art facility built by and for the Expos. A gem in its own right, the Jupiter facility was meant to serve also as the prototype for the proposed Labatt Park in Montreal. However, when Jeffrey Loria sold the Expos to Major League Baseball he put an end to all of that. Literally. He surrendered the Labatt Park project to condominium builders, and, along with the many Expos assets that he deftly squirrelled away on this journey into Florida, he grabbed Roger Dean Stadium as well, all with the tacit approval of the Commissioner's office. This meant that in the late winter of 2003 he moved his Marlins down I-95 to the West Palm Beach area, a major centre for spring baseball, leaving the Expos to fend for themselves further north at the Marlins' former home in Viera, not far from Orlando. The Expos might have been going up the coast, but to them it was a major come-down.

In spite of their chaotic beginnings the Expos got off to a strong start in 2003, wrapping up the month of April tied with the Braves in first place. Their 'real' home opener, the season-launching Big Owe happening, did not occur until April 22 when Montreal hosted the Arizona Diamondbacks. Close to 37,000 watched as the Expos prevailed 4–0 behind the solid pitching of Tomo Ohka and the bats of Jose Vidro and Fernando Tatis. The mood was joyful throughout, much as it had always been for the first game of the season. What was noticeably different this year, however, was the over-riding sense that this home opener was probably a last hurrah of sorts, that the club's 35th year of existence might well be its last.

Nevertheless, the club continued to hold its own in May, slipping somewhat in the standings but still ending the month 11 games over .500. They dropped further back in June, trailing the league-leading Braves and the Phillies, and again in July, barely hanging on to fourth place in their division.

Montreal's second venture into the bizarre universe of home-away-from-home baseball occurred in early June, when the club once again hopped over to the island and Hiram Bithorn Stadium. This time their arrival occurred on the heels of a seven-game road trip to Florida and Philadelphia. Their opponents in Puerto Rico were Anaheim and Texas and the Expos took four of the six games played. That was the good news.

However, following their six days in the Caribbean sun, instead of returning to the comforts of Montreal, they headed out cross-country, right across America to the Pacific Coast and Seattle, where after one day of rest, they opened a three-game series. Then it was three more in Oakland and another three in Pittsburgh before they managed to find their way back home. Incredible! By the time they finally got to sleep in their own beds again they had endured 22 games, almost a month, away from home. Not since the barnstorming days of the Indianapolis Clowns and the House of David had a professional baseball team suffered such discomfort just to play a game. To top it off, for the most part they held their own, not going into a sustained losing spin until the final game in Seattle, when they suffered through a five-game losing streak. For some time afterward they seemed to settle into a pattern of win one game, lose one game. Whatever momentum they generated earlier had apparently dissipated, at least temporarily.

All of this was prelude to what might be seen as the most dramatic month of August in club history, or close to it. Bit by bit the Expos clawed their way back, staying ahead in the win column while other teams faltered, until by the end of the month they were once again back in the race – the wild card race. And when they swept four weekday games from the Phillies before almost 100,000 wildly cheering spectators, a whole new set of believers was born. "Believer Fever" they were calling it, and for a brief moment, before it all came crashing back down, hope had found new hearts to break. "People flock to see playoff contender," read a cutline in *The Gazette*. "Franchise may be down to its last hurrahs, but it's not out of miracles at the Big O."[14] As of the morning of August 29, the Expos found themselves in a five-way tie for the wild card position: beyond question they had demonstrated the moxie to go all the way. It would not be easy, as the other teams in the hunt were the Phillies and Marlins in the East, and the Cardinals and Houston in the Central Division (at that moment the latter two teams were tied for first place). All had the identical winning percentage of .516: only one of them would make it into the postseason.

And then it all went south. Once again, on September 1, when major league clubs could expand their roster to 40 players, the four teams competing against Montreal loaded up. But not Montreal. Commissioner Bud Selig, speaking on behalf of the owners' consortium, refused to grant authorization. In what ESPN's Peter Gammons called "a conflict of interest," the lords of baseball, all owners of other teams, including the Marlins, concluded that there were not sufficient resources to warrant spending an extra $50,000 for the Expos to call up players from the minor leagues. The team would have to do with what it had. This on a salary budget of $35 million and for a team that would only play 59 of its scheduled 82 home games at home and was beat and sore and worn out. That calculated refusal was the final straw. It was "a momentum breaker" according to Omar Minaya. "What killed us," he maintained, "was not getting the call-ups. It was a message to the players."[15]

The Gazette's Stephanie Myles was not impressed. "When it really mattered," she wrote, "the bigwigs turtled. They hid behind disingenuous statements about the team having its highest-ever payroll, about the non-existent interest in Montreal, about how a squad that played 103 of its games on the road had plenty of bodies to finish off without calling up any fresh troops in September." She added: "In other words, they made it look just good enough that no one could lay any blame."[16]

The Expos struggled valiantly in September, but their 12-15 record from August 29 on was just not good enough. They ended out of the wild card race, eight games behind the successful Marlins and in fourth place.

By way of contrast, the Marlins brought back one of their original franchise players, Jeff Conine, to provide moral support, and more. In the playoffs, Florida first took out the Giants before easing their way past the Cubs in a championship series that went the full seven games. They then overwhelmed the Yankees in six games to nail down the club's second World Series triumph in its short history. Former Expo Ugueth Urbina earned two saves in the process.

The Expos ended their home season against Atlanta on a Wednesday night halfway through September, with yet another nine games still awaiting them on the godforsaken road! About 17,000 fans turned out to say good-bye and thank you – and to acknowledge yet again that this last game was quite possibly the LAST GAME, the final time *Nos Amours* would ever play for real in Montreal. Such melancholy obeisance had become an annual ritual of sorts in recent years and for even the most faithful it was beginning to grow old.

Nevertheless, this finale, quite unexpectedly, found itself bubbling over with controversy before it was done. With the Expos having fallen eight games behind the surging Marlins, the team, fatigued, brow-beaten and maligned, was just playing out the string. Baseball's lords had won again.

The game itself was really over in the first inning when Atlanta scored five runs – and by the time the dust settled the Braves had won handily, 14–4. Throughout the match, manager Robinson elected to give as many players as possible a last chance to see action in Montreal, since nothing else was on the line. By the third inning he began making wholesale substitutions, eventually bringing 19 players into the game.

It all went smoothly at first, as the players were gracious and the fans cordial in their response – until Robinson elected to pull Vladimir Guerrero off the field during the seventh inning. With Braves on second and third and one out, the manager thought the opportunity was perfect to call Guerrero in from his post in right field so that his many supporters might sing his praises one final time as he jogged to the dugout. Sadly, however, Robinson's well-meaning gesture was misinterpreted by the paying customers. Guerrero had singled in the sixth inning and was slated to come to up again – and nobody wanted to miss that opportunity to watch their free-swinging colossus wave his bat one last time. Everyone knew he would become a free agent at the end of the season and thus be lost to the club forever. To them, every moment was precious, but none more so than this very last chance to see him standing at the plate wearing an Expos uniform. When the crowd realized that Robinson was about to deprive them of that, they angrily let him know how they felt. Instead of accolades raining down on Guerrero as he left the field, his final moments were accompanied by hoots and hollers directed at his manager. It was not pleasant.

Robinson, proud to a fault some say, never seemed to forgive the fans for what he considered a major insult. When a supporter tried to explain their position, he replied curtly: "If the fans wanted to see him one more time, they should have come out to see him more times during the season."[17]

From then on Robinson appeared to stop caring, about Montreal, about the fans, and about the Expos. His disinterest seemed to grow throughout 2004, from raucous Opening Day to the edgy season finale, and even beyond, into his years with the Washington Nationals. *The Gazette* reported in 2005 that during his time in Montreal Robinson had spent as much time playing golf as he did with the ballclub. When asked why he did not rely more on statistics in drawing up his lineup cards, he allowed that he preferred to go with his gut feeling. It seems that not only in Montreal was Robinson's ability as a manager looked upon with some dismay. Two separate polls of 450 MLB players, conducted in 2005 and 2006 by *Sports Illustrated*, named Robinson as the worst manager in baseball.[18]

But for all that, Robinson greatly admired Guerrero. The youngster from the Dominican Republic was an exceptional ballplayer, an original Expos' find who dominated the game and dazzled the fans. When he did become a free agent following the 2003 season, after eight glorious years in Montreal, he signed with the Angels. There he remained for another six seasons, putting up top-notch numbers every time. In 2004 he was named MVP in the American League. His career wound down with stops in Texas in 2010, where he saw his only World Series action in a losing cause against San Francisco, and then Baltimore in 2011, his last year in the major leagues. Over 16 seasons he failed to bat .300 or better in only three seasons: his first as a novice in Montreal (only 27 at-bats), his final year with the Angels (2009) and his last big-league turn with the Orioles. Even so he still managed to bat .295 with Anaheim and .290 in Baltimore. Not a bad career for one of the greatest free swingers baseball has ever seen.

Not finished with baseball, Guerrero tried out for other big league teams but with no success. He officially retired in 2013. It will be another five years before voters can mark his name on their Hall-of-Fame ballots. Most observers contend that his record is sufficiently consistent across the years to warrant being considered seriously when his turn comes up. Indeed, his all-time career-leading numbers with the Expos – batting average (.323), home runs (234), slugging (.588) and OPS (.978) – will go a long way toward supporting his candidacy. To that one can add his selection as Expos Player of the Year in 1998, 1999, 2000 and 2002. Upon learning of Vlad's retirement, Jack Todd labelled him "the greatest Expo ever to wear the uniform," adding, "it was a dream to watch him play."[19] No one would disagree.

Chapter Fifty-Six

If They Won't Build It, We Won't Come

For more than a year, Bud Selig told the people of Montreal that they had no interest in keeping baseball in their city. The people stopped coming, and they stopped caring.

— Bleacherreport.com

Among the many considerations that pop up when one delves into the reasons behind the Expos' failure, the most insidious has to be the lack of interest, indifference really, demonstrated by Commissioner Selig, the MLB empire and the complete American baseball enterprise, in the well-being and future success of baseball in Montreal.

For, ultimately, the fault pretty well rests with them, the bigwigs who ran the game – from the local bosses, to the carpetbaggers, to the double-jeopardy machinations of the MLB ownership consortium which put the interests of its own members ahead of their impoverished foster club.

That cabal, of course, disagrees, putting the onus of responsibility on the fans – in much the same way that railroads once blamed its ridership for the paucity of passenger rail service today. It worked for the railways, for indeed "the people stopped coming and they stopped caring." Never mind that what they stopped coming to, and why they stopped caring about it, was in direct response to the orchestrated neglect of services provided and the lack of respect shown to customers.

When Cleveland faced difficulties in the recent past, as did Pittsburgh, and even Minnesota, baseball paid attention and lent a hand. Today, all three cities have new ballparks and are seen as stable franchises. But not Montreal. Here, baseball's contribution was to erect roadblocks and barriers, introducing strategies to impede progress and ensure failure. And it worked, but only after those close calls in 2002 and 2003 when the Expos were but a hair's breadth away from postseason play.

In the eyes of most Expos followers, the disappointment of 2003 and the artful micro-management imposed on the club by the owners' consortium – the two-homes-are–better-than-one experiment and the phony reasons given for not authorizing September call-ups – pretty well signalled the end. There was nothing more to give, except to give in. The cloud of despair that enveloped the Big Owe in 2004 defined the season and set the tone. Joy was getting ready to leave the building.   Which was somewhat odd in a way – for, as one correspondent pointed out, "Isn't it ironic that now that baseball is dead in Montreal we have a team that is easy to love and a management crew who actually know and care about the game – and the fans?"[20]

The 2004 campaign began, as it had in 2003, with the Expos opening at home twice, once at the Big O, once on the road at their Puerto Rican home-away-from-home. Again, as in 2003, the Expos were scheduled to play 22 'home' games at the Hiram Bithorn facility, including, as before, the first home game of the season. Before that, however, they were scheduled to stop in Florida, home of the Loria clan and the World Champion Marlins – how MLB delighted in rubbing it in – for three games. They lost two.

Then, it was off to San Juan and their home opener against the Mets. Unlike the previous year, the novelty was wearing thin: only 14,000 showed up for the first game, a far cry from the capacity crowds that had greeted "Los Expos" twelve months earlier. By the time the final game of this home stand rolled around, once again versus Florida, the fan count had dropped to 8,000.

After splitting the first two games with New York, the Expos tumbled into an eight-game losing streak. It was exacerbated, of course, by the fact that upon leaving Puerto Rico they still had six more road games to deal with, in Philadelphia and New York. When they finally struggled into Montreal for their first real home stand and their first real home opener, their record was a bleak 4-12, worst in the National League. As if that were not tough enough, this home stand was only three days long. The club was now off to the west coast and games against the Padres and the Dodgers. It was the fourth of May before the players finally got back to Montreal, long enough to rent lodgings and find a bed.

Brad Wilkerson, a gritty player who wore his heart on his sleeve, commented on the disadvantages that excessive travel placed on the club. "The odds have been against us, both last year and this year," he said. "But this team hasn't made excuses. We have a good group of guys who go out there and play hard for nine innings. We're not going to whine."[21] Maybe they should have. "We wanted to stay in Montreal," he said, "but [MLB[

told us they'd bust up our payroll. Maybe we should have stood up to them."[22]

On a lighter note, Orlando Cabrera developed his own solution to beat the ennui and keep track of the many, many days on the road. In 2003, when the Expos had been dispatched on that 25-day, 23-game odyssey all across America, he bought 25 pairs of underwear at the outset so he could throw away one pair at the end of each day. "A player has never been more excited to look in his suitcase and discover his was out of skivvies."[23] Except perhaps for Cabrera himself: the Expos traded him to Boston in late July, in time for him to play a part

Brad Wilkerson

in the Red Sox curse-busting 2004 World Series victory over the St. Louis Cardinals.

Nevertheless, 30,000 fans did turn out on Opening Night 2004 – quite a reasonable crowd when one considers recent misfortunes and the fact that the Canadiens were still alive in the NHL playoffs. The club that greeted fans bore little resemblance to the hardy Expos crew they had cheered on in 2003. Guerrero and Tatis had been granted free agency, Javier Vasquez had been traded to the Yankees, and Michael Barrett shipped to Oakland. The Opening Night outfield consisted of Endy Chavez, Termel Sledge and Ron Calloway, while around the infield, veterans Orlando Cabrera and Jose Vidro were framed by Tony Batista at third base and Wilkerson on first. Brian Schneider did the catching and John Patterson was the starting pitcher. The evening was, according to *The Gazette's* Dave Stubbs, a "mostly joyful funeral," for, as he pointed out: "Despite the best efforts of Selig and the 29 club owners who have all but unplugged the club' s life support, this town remains at least the mailing address of the baseball team that wouldn't die."[24]

The crowd reflected that mood, noisy and happy, but you could tell expectations were low. The faithful seemed to understand that of all the last Opening-Day games they had attended in recent years, this one really would be the last. So, for them, the time had come to stop worrying about the "what ifs" of tomorrow. They were quite content to settle for the "what is" of today – and "what was" of yesteryear.

The Expos lost both the opener and the game following to the Phillies before taking the get-away match 2-0 behind Zack Day's second win of the season. And that pretty well told the story for the year, one victory for every two games lost.

The Expos returned to the Caribbean twice more before the All-Star break, completing that commitment much earlier than in 2003. This modification to the schedule was a concession built in to ensure that Montreal would not compromise its own home field advantage should, as in the two previous years, the club be caught up in a pennant race late in the season. A thoughtful gesture, to be sure: just a little too late.

The Expos returned to the Island in May, where they lost four of five games. On their final trip to San Juan in July they managed to improve on that performance, winning five of ten games against Toronto, Atlanta and the Pirates. In a truly bizarre illustration of how dysfunctional the Expos' double-home-town circus was, the Toronto-Montreal series had been designed originally to capitalize on traditional Canada Day holiday fare in Montreal. It didn't quite happen that way, of course: the Canadian-ness of the moment sort of got lost in transit.

Throughout the spring, speculation about the Expos' future picked up speed. That the team would be relocated seemed a *fait accompli*: the more pressing question was, where? Although a number of potential locales were tossed about – Las Vegas, Nevada; Monterrey, Mexico; Norfolk, Virginia; Portland, Oregon; and Northern Virginia – the smart money was on Washington, D.C. For one overarching reason: the absence of baseball –The National Pastime - from the nation's capital had been a sore point for the baseball establishment ever since 1971 when the second iteration of the Washington Senators folded its tent and set up camp in Texas. An earlier and more storied version of the club, the one featuring Walter Johnson in the early 20th century, and the Griffith family, had fled for Minnesota a decade earlier. That the city's mayor, Anthony Williams, strongly supported the project made it almost a given. "If baseball makes a commitment to come to Washington, D.C.," he said, "we're prepared to move quickly and move decisively to see that all the approvals are in place, all the financing is in place, all the elements are in place, to see that a team is here in a timely fashion."[25]

And so in this way the season of 2004 unfolded, with the Expos never able to dig out from the bottom of the pack. At the end of July, their record was a dismal 41-63. By August 31 it had climbed to a marginally improved 56-76: by September 29 and their last game at home, they[26] were 64-92, and 38.5 games out of first place. Rocky Rapoport, a long-time season-ticket holder and inveterate Expos fan, described the season as tough, as dismal as any in Expos history. "It's been one disaster after another, almost like they are doing it on purpose so we'll tell them, 'Leave already.'"

Chapter Fifty-Seven

The coup de grâce – September 29, 2004

Things were so bad in that final year in Montreal that I'm surprised they found enough working trucks to haul everything down to Washington in time for the start of the 2005 season.

Fardi Rushdi – Bleacher Report

A s ball games go, the final major league game ever played in Montreal ended early; as memories go, it produced a moment of baseball history in the city that still resonates today.

There was something poetically just about the way the day began. After months and years of speculation, team president Tony Tavares finally made it official on the morning of this last day. "I am here today," he announced from his perch in Olympic Stadium, "to confirm the movement of the franchise from Montreal to Washington." It really was all over – except for the crying.

When 31,395 fans poured into Olympic Stadium that night, the largest crowd of the year, they came to mourn, and to say goodbye – and for some, to vent their anger one last time. The foes were, once again, the Florida Marlins, a nemesis that just added to the melancholy of the moment. Manager Robinson, for whatever reason, either because he wasn't aware of the significance of the occasion, or quite possibly, because he didn't care, sent out a lineup of mostly second-string players the fans barely knew and quickly forgot. By the fifth inning the Marlins had established a 9-1 lead. Leaving little of anything to cheer about.

The winning pitcher was a ghostly reminder of the past in Carl Pavano, part of the trade that sent Pedro Martinez to Boston. Pavano improved his record to 18-8. Sun-Woo Kim took the loss, dropping to 4-6. The only bright light for Montreal was Juan Rivera who managed three hits, one of which drove home Tony Batista with the Expos' lone run, and another, the last hit by an Expo at the Big Owe.

At some point during the middle innings fans became restless and several golf balls were thrown on the field. The umpires called time and issued a warning as Robinson summoned his players back to the dugout. For a few moments tension threatened to spill over onto the field and it seemed the game might be cancelled. But with the help of some timely music over the loudspeakers, including John Lennon's *Give Peace a Chance,* and some heroic cheerleading by Expos mascot Youppi atop the Expos' dugout, order was restored and the game moved ahead. When officially at 10.01 p.m. Terrmel Sledge popped out to former Expo Mike Mordecai behind third base for the final out of the final, final game, it was all over.

Now came the hard part: saying good-bye. This turned out to be a much tougher exercise than the players expected and much tougher than the fans anticipated. No one wanted to leave, at least not until the tears stopped flowing. Livan Hernandez thanked the fans in Spanish, Jamey Carroll who, as Stephanie Myles has written, became a major leaguer in Montreal at the age of 30 and was still in the Show a decade later, spoke in English, and an over-wrought Claude Raymond in French. "I said a few words in French," recalled Raymond in an interview with the *Globe and Mail,* "and Wilkerson grabbed me and said 'I love you and I love these people.' What the hell am I supposed to do? So I started crying. Then he looked at me and he started crying so I grabbed him and both of us were going. I feel like he's my son, this kid."[27]

Photo: Bill Young

Jamey Carroll signs autographs before the last game at Olympic Stadium.

They were not alone in their tears. As one by one the players came out from the clubhouse to signal their appreciation, it became evident there was not a dry eye in the house, literally. Seldom in history have there been more grown men at a sporting event weeping inconsolably on the shoulders of their loved ones than were present at Olympic Stadium on this night. "My father brought me to the Expos when I was a kid," they would sob, in one language or another, "and I will never have the chance to do that with my kids."

"It was kind of overwhelming, really," said Frank Robinson following the game. "The reception makes it tougher to move on. It's like you want to stand still right now and savour the moment because you know when you walk out of this ballpark tonight it'll be for the last time. A lot of the players are in no rush to leave."[28]

But then, in due course, it truly was the last time. As the stadium authorities slowly turned down the lights, one by one we all went home.

Of course, the baseball season was not over; even the Expos had to play out the three matches still remaining, against the Mets at Shea Stadium. Perhaps propelled by the euphoria-induced hangover from the night before, Montreal took the first two games, 4–2 behind pitcher Jon Rauch, and 6–3 on Brad Wilkerson's 32nd home run of the year, a three-run blast in the top of the ninth. It was the last four-bagger struck by a player wearing an Expos jersey. The season ended with the Mets winning convincingly, 8–1, on Sunday, October 3. It seemed only fitting that Montreal should lose to the Mets in the last game they will ever play: back on April 8, 1969, in the Expos' first game

Jon Rauch

that counted for something, *Nos Amours* defeated the Mets in that same Shea stadium 11–10, setting in motion a whole new baseball adventure for Canada.

So who failed whom? The Major League Baseball industry says the fans are to blame. The fans point the finger at club management and too-tight pockets; the players were tired of playing to a sea of empty seats – and Gerry Snyder, the city councillor whose determination brought the team to town in the first place, looked to his old bosses at city hall. "It's disappointing to me that they haven't had the full support of the City of Montreal, and I'm talking from the mayor down." Snyder, who passed away in 2007, was reflecting on the club as it was preparing to leave. "The team brings in tourist dollars, it brings in tax money…and it provides entertainment for the population and gives them something to be proud of."[29]

Benoit Aubin, writing in *Maclean's* magazine, pointed to proponents of the downtown stadium: "I stopped going to the ballpark because the Expos told me to stop going. They've been very stupid, quite often. Claude Brochu wanted a new stadium downtown. In a weird marketing pitch, he convinced everyone the Big Owe was a rotten venue for baseball. I decided to wait for the new digs. They never came, I never went back..."[30] The *Globe and Mail's* Stephen Brunt also turned his eye toward the owners, every one of them from 1991 on. "The truth is that in any sport, in any business, if you don't care about your customers and tell them so, if you peddle a product that requires hope as one ingredient then squeeze out every last drop, the market is bound to die...the fans weren't stupid in Montreal, nor were they masochists. They had limits."[31]

The Gazette's Quebec affairs columnist Don Macpherson plunged into the debate by blaming everyone but the fans; congratulating them for not capitulating to the pressures of Big Business Baseball when tempted to do so. "Those of us without an interest in the Expos – which, to judge from recent attendance figures, is almost all of us – should be relieved that after years of promises, Major League Baseball is finally dragging the stinking, long-dead carcass of local baseball out of town. We should be not only relieved, but grateful and, yes, even proud." Jack Todd applied a similar Gatling gun approach in his analysis of what went wrong, concluding with a comment from Tony Tavares that he (Tavares) could imagine baseball returning to Montreal in 30 years time, as it did in Washington. To this Todd responded, "The question is: Why would anyone want it?"

Manager Frank Robinson, whom many felt had turned his back on the Expos and their fans, was gracious in his parting comments, focusing on the positive. "I think there were a lot more good times than bad times. This is where an expansion ball club grew into one of the best organizations in baseball at one time, and it's sad...the way it is going out now."[32]

A *Gazette* editorial said it best: "There's ample blame to go around; it wasn't so much the failure to build a downtown stadium as it was the failure to find a downtown owner, so to speak, a Bronfman-like owner with deep pockets and a willingness to lose millions. Let's be frank. Making baseball work in Montreal was never easy from Day 1: the new economics just made things all that much more difficult." In this regard the editorial notes that the payroll disparity between the New York Yankees and the Expos in 2004 was $142 million – $183 million for the Yanks against just $41 million in Montreal.[33] Revenue sharing was in the offing, but when it came it was too late to help.

Expos broadcaster Elliott Price called the final out of the final game on October 3. "A throw to first, and the Expos are history – from 1969 to

2004. We'll be back." He then closed his microphone, and we went to commercial.

And with every passing year there are more and more fans who believe that those last words spoken by Price were prophetic, that indeed, someday, as he said, "We'll be back."

I just didn't want it to end

Among the many unusual occurrences that made the final game at The Big Owe so special was one little anomaly that had to do with the scoreboard. When Terrmel Sledge popped out in the bottom of the ninth for the third out to end the game, the scoreboard showed only two outs, and that's how it remained even after the game was over. Somehow, the big board's operator, Eddie Steinman, who had been putting the stats up in lights ever since the team was formed in 1969, had failed to register either Maicer Izturis's earlier flyout or Val Pascucci's groundout. To put it in other terms, if the scoreboard were to be believed, the game never ended: the Expos owed the match at least one more batter.

When this glitch was later pointed out to him, Steinman at first rejected the charge. Shown incontrovertible photographic proof to the contrary, he then conceded the point. And making like a character right out of a W.P. Kinsella novella, he said, smiling, "I guess I just didn't want it to end."

Now that's denial!

The last anthem

It was September 29, 2004 and Olympic Stadium was rocking with the over 30,000 fans who had rolled in to be part of the final game the Expos would ever play.

Tension was running high as fans bristled with melancholic anger and a deep sense of loss. It was apparent that the smallest of missteps could send the crowd into a frenzy, especially as the Expos were facing the Florida Marlins, now owned by Jeffrey Loria and David Samson, former proprietors of the Expos and the miscreants most Montrealers credited with destroying their club.

The first hot spot would be the singing of the national anthems – for both the American and Canadian anthems had the potential to provoke heated reactions from a bitter crowd. The challenge was given to Montreal singer Kim Richardson and she met it head on, softening the tension of the moment through the grace and dignity she brought to the task.

Richardson well appreciated what would face her, standing out on the pitcher's mound very much alone. Many years later she spoke to journalist Richard Burnett about the experience.

"I was prepared for the booing (of the American anthem) because you knew the fans would be pissed the team was moving to the States. So I was able to sing through it." Her example inspired others in the crowd to join her, soon drowning out boos with their cheers.

"I didn't expect fans to start clapping and cheering," she said. "That was a classy thing. Then singing the Canadian anthem I started getting choked up." This time everyone sang along, with English and French-language renditions complementing one another behind Richardson's lead.

By the time the last note was sung, her determination and aplomb had brought calm to what otherwise risked becoming a thoroughly unpleasant situation. It was her moment, and she was heroic.

Take Me Out To the Ball Game

2004-2014

Let me root, root, root for the home team,
If they don't win it's a shame.[1]

Warren Cromartie as a young player with Montreal. More recently he has piloted the drive to bring major-league baseball back to the city.

Chapter Fifty-Eight

A Look Back in Anguish

And silence sounds no worse than cheers; after death has stopped the ears.

To an Athlete Dying Young........A.E. Houseman

Elisabeth Kübler-Ross, the ground-breaking psychiatrist whose study of the terminally ill resulted in a seminal publication entitled, "On Death and Dying," posited that when a person is faced with the impending death of a loved one or some other extreme and awful fate, he or she can expect to experience a sequence of predictable emotional stages. These she identified as: Denial, Anger, Bargaining, Depression, and, ultimately, Acceptance – commonly referred to as the "five stages of grief."[2]

Although it might seem a bit of a stretch to draw on the Kübler-Ross model to explore fan responses, emotional or otherwise, following the Expos' demise, it actually serves well in helping to trace the arc of reactions from the moment all baseball ceased in 2004 up to the present almost 10 years later. David Martin, writing in the *Ottawa Citizen*, even suggested, with tongue in cheek perhaps, that Kübler-Ross had not taken her logic far enough. "Acceptance may be the last stage when it comes to loved ones and pets," he conceded. "But when it comes to a favourite team transferred to another city, there's a sixth, painful, never-ending stage: agony."[3]

Annakin Slayd, the Montreal hip hop artist whose tribute videos to the Expos are powerfully poignant, had a similar take on how the city responded to the Expos' departure: "It's like stages of grief," he told *Canadian Press* in 2012. "I remember being at the last games and not feeling anything – it was just more shock. And then after that it was anger and then (sadness). I think over time the anger turned into reflection, and a little bit of celebration. And that's where we are now."[4]

After the 2004 season ended and reality confirmed that baseball had truly left town, fans poured out their emotional angst in a couple of directions. Anger, disappointment, frustration, even melancholy – all formed a piece of the burning rage that most felt. But, at the same time, they also looked to grab hold of whatever vestiges of the club had survived the debacle. Kübler-Ross undoubtedly would have regarded these behaviours as classic examples of Anger and of Denial.

Anger was most evident in the never-ending post-mortems that inundated newspapers and talk radio as professionals and fans relentlessly directed scathing criticisms at just about everybody associated with the Expos – except the players. In some ways, because the inevitability of the club's departure was so slow and painful in coming, its final death rattle on September 29 was, paradoxically, that much tougher to accept even as it fostered an eerie sense of relief. The second shoe had finally dropped.

Some of this anger was, however, tempered by a more personal sense of loss. "This truly is a sad day," a reader told *The Gazette* in a letter to the sports editor, "a day that only confirms the demise of Montreal as a 'major league' city." Elsewhere, this same correspondent added: "People blamed this on Montreal being a hockey town. Only those from outside Canada would say that. This is about a proud city. We don't care for losers. You don't win here, see ya."

Another reader observed: "It's sad they are leaving. I guess ESPN won't be able to broadcast the team's attendance record anymore and make fun of the Montreal fans." And a third: "The 1994 season is a year I'll never forget. World Champions! The thing is, I felt people did like baseball in Montreal, but when you get the runaround for so long, how much can you put up with."[5]

The print media were supremely critical, as noted elsewhere in this book. As an example, when Jacques Ménard, for many years CEO of the Expos, took a swipe at the different non-local owners who ran the club for its final five years as being out of touch, *Gazette* scribe Pat Hickey refused to let this twisting of the facts pass unchallenged. "The minority owners had their kick at the can," he wrote. "This supposedly sharp group of businessmen were snookered by city slicker Loria. If these guys knew anything about business, they would have invested some money in the product after the team's aborted playoff run in 1994. Instead of trying to make money, they instructed Claude Brochu not to lose money. As a result, Montreal fans not only lost a chance for a winner, they eventually lost the team."[6]

In the beginning, anger bubbled over at every turn, with the media setting the tone. Someone once suggested that had the fourth estate devoted as much ink to the club when they were still in Montreal as they did after it left, it might never gone at all.

A close companion of anger is misery, and in 2004 a blogger with ESPN, Jim Caple, produced the first of what he called his baseball Misery Index – a tongue-in-cheek ranking of the degree to which various major-league baseball teams inflicted misery on their fans. Weighing such factors as Historic despair (i.e. how many seasons have left fans chanting "Wait until next year!" the day after pitchers and catchers report to spring training?); Recent despair; Historic pain; Recent pain; Intangible misery; and Misery outlook, Caple's assessment covered the full span of big league ball. And in a world where the Cubs and the Red Sox had not won the World Series since the jazz age and Seattle was still waiting for the opportunity to even make it there, the team Caple elevated to the top of the Misery Index was (drum roll) the Montreal Expos. They outranked (in order of misery production): Cleveland; both Chicago teams; and Milwaukee (the Red Sox were number 6).

Caple's assessment of *Nos Amours'* misery-inducing features included a list of horrors that haunt us still: from the loss of players like Randy Johnson and Vladimir Guerrero, to Blue Monday, to the 1994 Bud Selig-shortened season, and, of course, the dog's breakfast that was 2003-2004 when the players were the only ones holding up their end of the bargain.

In making his case, Caple wrote: "Threatened with contraction two years ago, 23 of [the Expos'] home games are now played more than 1,000 miles away and the home games in Montreal aren't too pleasant either, due to the exhaust belching from the U-Hauls parked outside Le Stadium Olympique (sic). And baseball wonders why fan support has fallen so far?"[7]

After the Expos packed up and headed south, fans were desperate to get their hands on whatever bits of memorabilia they could find. The team boutique in the bowels of the Big Owe launched its final/going-out-of-business sale a few days after the season ended, and was overwhelmed with customers. Jerseys, used bats, caps – just about anything bearing the Expos logo – went flying off the shelves. The same frenzy found its way into gift shops and sporting goods emporiums until practically every souvenir, every symbol, every reminder of the team, ended up in the hands of folks who absolutely had to have something tangible to help keep alive the wonder that once was *Nos Amours*.

Even today, the interest in Expos memorabilia thrives. Caps, one observer noted, are "seen far more frequently on the streets of Montreal these days than when the star-crossed franchise actually existed." In fact, according to the New Era ball cap manufacturer, Expos hats are the third-biggest seller in Canada, behind only the Toronto Blue Jays and the New York Yankees.[8]

As for the more valuable artifacts and objects or items of historical significance pertaining to the team itself, these were donated to four museums vested in the preservation of Expos history. Montreal's McCord Museum received documentation and photographs chronicling the team's past; the Cinemathèque got film and video amassed by the club over the years; the Quebec Sports Hall of Fame was awarded framed photographs and banners of particular interest, and other similar artifacts; and the Canadian Baseball Hall of Fame in St. Marys, Ontario, obtained an eclectic assortment of items reflecting the Expos' once thriving existence. There was something comforting in the knowledge that thought and care had gone into the preservation of these items, that they were not simply tossed into a dumpster. Every piece protected keeps some part of Expos reality alive.

Denial as a forceful emotional stage didn't really burst forth until the new year. Much as the troublesome dandelion lies dormant in winter only to burst out and cause trouble in early spring, so too did the sense of loss among Expos faithful wait until March to strike, picking a time when spirits were low and stories of spring training activity were finding their way north.

All of a sudden, people recognized that something vital was lacking in their lives: the Expos. Another baseball season was about to begin, except this time there was no Expos team to cheer on.

With each spring training report, the spirit dimmed until April 4, 2005, when total darkness descended. For that was the day the Expos should have opened at home, before the customary 30,000–plus enthusiasts keen to celebrate the end of winter. Except they didn't open at home. They opened in Washington instead. And they weren't our Expos any more – and Washington certainly wasn't our home.

It was then that the penny dropped. Suddenly, for the first time all over again, our hearts were broken once more. For the first time since 1969, we were teamless. And nobody knew how to help us out.

The area's leading sports-radio talk show Mitch Melnick recalled Opening Day 2005 as perhaps his blackest moment in baseball, the day it truly hit home, that our Expos were gone.

Those were the facts, yes. But so unpalatable were they that fans sought to distance themselves from the sad reality, searching instead for other options, anything that could keep the Expos alive a bit longer.

Perhaps another team might fill the void. But which one? Washington was a non-starter. To begin with, they were the bad guys. But, at a more visceral level, we realized, with every sweeping (and unnecessary) change orchestrated by interim general manager Jim Bowden, that the Nationals wanted nothing to do with us. Why, Bowden had even assigned Gary Carter's No. 8 and Vladimir Guerrero's No. 27 to part-time spring-training coaches. ESPN's Tony Kornheiser, based in Washington and familiar to Canadians through his PTI television show on TSN, had this explanation: "We don't know anything about the Montreal Expos, other than they were a vagabond team that played in Canada and Puerto Rico and would have played on barges in the Mississippi River if anybody would have come to see them. Bud Selig tried 5,000 different ways to make the Expos popular in Canada. He did everything but make Shania Twain the second baseman. Nothing worked."[9]

To Stephanie Myles, who was a firsthand witness, such behaviour "tells you all you need to know about how history and tradition are going to be honoured [in Washington]." However, she added, "these sweeping changes have had an unexpected consequence: they make it easier to say good-bye to the team that left Montreal, September 29."[10]

The Washington Nationals saw themselves as the third incarnation of the used-to-be Washington Senators of the American League, a team of honourable but low distinction – two different teams actually – that both ultimately gave up the ghost and moved elsewhere. The first edition went to Minnesota; the second to Texas.

David Martin, the writer whose agony is never-ending, had one soothing balm to offer regarding the Washington Nationals: "I'd like to extend them my heartfelt wish for a season of dropped balls, wild pitches, and doubleheader losses. After all, if there's one thing that baseball has taught me, it's that misery loves company.[11]

The Toronto Blue Jays were an option. A Canadian team. Close to home. But no, they would always be the other guys. Kemp likened a potential courtship with the Jays to a first date "that goes nowhere, no kiss, and a good-bye hug that's as uncomfortable as the day Rick Monday of the Los Angeles Dodgers crushed the fibre of our dreams." Kemp spoke for many when he concluded there was no substitute for *Nos Amours*. "I sit here remembering the day in the early 1970s when I sat along the first-base line at Jarry Park and fell in love with a team that I can't shake from my heart…Maybe I should go for a walk in a cornfield…"[12]

Since Expos faithful were forced to concede there could never be any one team on which they might pin their hopes, most abandoned that notion altogether to follow the fortunes of former Expos players instead.

That was doable, for as long as our favourites were playing, so were the Expos. At least in part. Denial, after all, is more than just a river in Egypt.

For a time, in the years immediately following the Expos' departure, keeping track of former players and lauding their accomplishments became something of a cottage industry. Stephanie Myles and Ian MacDonald wrote periodically on the topic, recording current accomplishments or tracking older alumni still involved in the game at different levels. In 2005, one year after Pedro Martinez and Orlando Cabrera helped their Boston Red Sox to the World Series championship, another group of former Expos played a similar role with the Chicago White Sox in their four-game sweep of the Houston Astros. That club included Dustin Hermanson, Chris Widger, Carl Everett, Tim Raines coaching at first base – and Geoff Blum, the unlikely hero of Game Three. With the score tied 5-5 in the 14th inning, Blum homered to give the White Sox the win, ensuring World Series rewards reached five more former Expos, six if you count manager Ozzie Guillen. He had served as third-base coach for a brief interval at the close of the 2001 season.

Then, courtesy of Stephanie Myles, there is this bizarre factoid that takes a moment or two to sink in. The 1999 Expos bottomed-out with a record of 68-94. And yet, amazingly, by the end of 2005, eight members of that '99 club were wearing World Series rings. Count 'em: Hermanson, Ugueth Urbina (Marlins), Widger, Cabrera, Mike Mordecai (Marlins), Carl Pavano (Marlins), Miguel Batista (Arizona), and Blum.[13] Call it Karma.

When the Nationals traded Livan Hernandez to Arizona in August 2006 and he later had to face Brian Schneider, his battery mate for more than three seasons covering both their Montreal and Washington years, there were few surprises. "He knows everything I throw," said Hernandez later. The wily pitcher, whose choice of offerings included anything from a 56-mph curveball to a fastball in the 90-mph range, on this day was very much in control. The Diamondbacks prevailed 4-2, with Hernandez giving up only six hits over eight innings to nail down the win. Schneider was the only Nats player with more than one hit. He also scored one of his team's two runs. Tony Armas Jr., took the loss. "I got a lot of friends on that team," said Hernandez. "But baseball's baseball."[14]

In 2006, some folks were calling the Anaheim Angels the Exposangels, so numerous and effective were several former Montreal players now with the club. There was no better illustration than what occurred in Boston on Sunday July 30, before a capacity crowd at Fenway Park, with Curt Schilling pitching for the home team. In the third inning, Orlando Cabrera, formerly of the Bosox, led off the inning with a home run over the Green Monster. He was followed by Vladimir Guerrero who slammed a drive so far out of the park, it "landed somewhere in New Hampshire."

After the next batter struck out, DH Juan Rivera – he of the three hits in the tearful last game at the Big Owe in 2004 – banged out yet another home run, his tenth of the month. Three home runs in one inning off Curt Schilling, and all struck by former Expos players. How about that!

Schilling was pulled after five innings and tagged with the loss, only his fourth of the season – but one of his worst performances ever. By the time the game ended, 10-4 in favour of Anaheim, the four Exposangels in the lineup – the other being third baseman Maicer Izturis – had accumulated nine of the club's 16 hits, driven in seven of its 10 runs and scored five. Also in the wings with the Angels that year were Bartolo Colon and Curtis Pride. It might not have been coincidental that the team's general manager was Bill Stoneman, former Expos pitcher and senior administrative officer with the club before moving to Anaheim.[15]

By the time the 2006 postseason rolled around, 10 former Expos were still in the hunt and playing. The Mets had half of them: Endy Chavez, Cliff Floyd, Orlando Hernandez (El Duque), Pedro Martinez, and Guillermo Mota. Also forming part of the team were coaches Manny Acta and Jerry Manuel, and Omar Minaya was the Mets' executive vice president and general manager. Others appearing in the postseason included Randy Johnson (Yankees), Chris Young (Padres), Milton Bradley (Oakland), Rondell White (Twins), and Carl Pavano (Yankees). Russell Martin (Dodgers), while never an Expo, grew up and learned his baseball in Montreal, playing in the shadow of the Big Owe. Oddly, none of these players made it to the Fall Classic, won by the Cardinals over Detroit, four games to one.[16]

Broadcaster Denis Casavant, writing in the Team 990 Sports Radio (now TSN 690) magazine, confirmed there were 45 players associated with the Expos still plying their trade in the major leagues in late 2007. Eleven of them had been on Montreal's roster for the last game *Nos Amours* would ever play, in New York on October 3, 2004. Of the 45, nine wore the Washington Nationals cap. The others were scattered across both leagues.[17]

By the opening of the 2013 season, there were still ten active players who at some point or other had played for Montreal: Luis Ayala, Braves; Jamey Carroll, Twins; Endy Chavez, Mariners; Bruce Chen, Royals; Bartolo Colon, Oakland; Scott Downs, Angels; Brendan Harris, Angels; Maicer Izturis, Blue Jays; Ted Lilly, Dodgers; and Jon Rauch, Marlins. Four of these had taken part in the final game at the Big Owe in 2004 – Carroll, Chavez, Izturis and Harris – while for Montreal's last game against the Mets on October 3 in New York, the trio of Chavez, Izturis and Rauch were in the lineup.[18]

There is one question still to be answered: who will be the last man standing – the man who will be remembered as the last of the former Expos still playing, in the same way Don Drysdale (Brooklyn Dodgers) and Willie Mays (New York Giants) hold that distinction for their New York City-based clubs? The question mattered back in 2004; perhaps it matters still, but either way, we should bear in mind that even in their gloomiest moments of sorrow, the Montreal baseball community has delighted in knowing just how well alumni were doing in their new worlds.

As each year passed and the sharpness of grief lost its edge, Expos fans began expressing a desire, a longing perhaps, to re-establish contact with those who had "gone before." Possibly this imperative was the bargaining phase described by Dr. Kübler-Ross; perhaps it represented the onset of depression, but whatever it suggested, the need was there.

And so began a series of reunion events at which former Expos were given star billing. The first occurred on a softball diamond at Jarry Park in June 2006. Organized by the ALS society (Lou Gehrig's disease) as a fundraiser, the gathering took the form of a celebrity softball game. Present were Andre Dawson, Steve Rogers, Jim Fanning, Warren Cromartie, Derek Aucoin, and Denis Boucher, along with a smattering of local sports celebrities and media personalities. It was a grand occasion: the fans went home happy, weighed down by their autographed memorabilia; the participants were happy; and, best of all, the ALS Society, which raised $240,000, was delighted. Encouraged by their success, they repeated the event the following year, with even more Expos and more celebrities in attendance.

These gatherings helped erase some of the bitterness that had carried over from the Expos' departure and the way it was handled. Describing the first of these as "a reunion, a chance to remember all of the good times that came before the bad times," baseball writer Stephanie Myles noted that although "it could have been bittersweet, in fact, there was much joy."[19]

Later that summer, in July, a similar reunion, but with a different twist, took place in Ottawa, home of the now-defunct Lynx, the former Triple-A farm team of the Expos. Folks were invited to bid on eBay for one of nine slots on the all-fan club that would confront a laid-back team consisting of former Expos Cromartie, Claude Raymond, Rodney Scott, and Dennis (Oil Can) Boyd, and other local celebrities. It was a hoot, even though no one kept score.

Continued interest in the Expos manifested itself in a variety of ways: new associations of baseball fanatics formed, publications, films, and more. To further the knowledge and understanding of baseball in Quebec, including the place of the Expos in Quebec society, local members of the Society for American Baseball Research (SABR) established a Quebec regional chapter. The first post-2004 publication about the Expos was the best-selling *Remembering the Montreal Expos* by Danny Gallagher and Bill Young, authors of this book. David Luchuk came out with *Blue Jays 1, Expos 0: The Urban Rivalry that Killed Major League Baseball in Montreal*, published by McFarland. A film set in 1969 against a background of the Expos' arrival in Montreal, *Un été sans point ni coup sûr*, or, A No-Hit, No-Run Summer (in French with English sub-titles) was released in 2009. It was based on the 2004 novel of the same name by the multi-talented Quebec author, Marc Robitaille. Also in 2009, Alain Usereau produced the well-received *L'époque Glorieuse des Expos*, later translated

Photo: Danny Gallagher

Jim Fanning today, displaying his prized Montreal Expos ring, by the author and published in English by McFarland as *The Expos in Their Prime: The Short-Lived Glory of Montreal's Team, 1977-1984.* Following on its heels was a two-volume encyclopedic history of Expos baseball by the French voice of the Expos, Jacques Doucet, and Marc Robitaille, *Il était une fois les Expos, Tome 1: les années 1969-1984; Tome 2: les années 1985-2004.* The title translates roughly to *Once upon a Time there were Expos.* Unfortunately, this wonderful work is not available in English.

Throughout the period from the year 2000 onward, a number of former Expos were suitably recognized for their excellence. First, Gary Carter, in 2003, and then Andre Dawson, in 2010, were inducted into the National Baseball Hall of Fame in Cooperstown. Joining them as winner of the Ford C. Frick Award for broadcast excellence in 2011 was the voice of the Expos, Dave Van Horne, the man whose "Up, Up and Away" home run call was music to the ear in Montreal for more than 30 years.

At the Canadian Baseball Hall of Fame, the Expos were lauded as well. The list of inductees is long, ranging from Claude Raymond in 1984 to Jim Fanning in 2000, Carter in 2001 and Dawson in 2004. In the years since the Expos took shelter in Washington, that partial listing has expanded. Beginning with Steve Rogers in 2005, the Hall has now made a place for Larry Walker, Rheal Cormier, Rusty Staub and, in 2013, Tim Raines. On the media side, the Jack Graney media award for excellence has gone at various times to Dave Van Horne, Jacques Doucet, and *Montreal Gazette* beat writer Ian MacDonald.

Perhaps the most outstanding tribute to the Expos is the music video prepared by Montreal rapper Annakin Slayd in a salute to the team he knew and followed closely growing up. Called *Remember (A Tribute to the Montreal Expos)*, it is a masterpiece, perhaps the most honest, sensitive and deeply moving salute to a cherished team that one might find anywhere. Quite simply, through his careful selection of words and music, Slayd has managed to draw out the magic that made the Montreal club so beloved.[20]

But for all this effort in keeping the Expos at the forefront, by 2007 interest was waning. "The Expos are dead and all but forgotten," Jack Todd wrote.[21] Fans increasingly found themselves switching allegiance – or switching off. One Expos diehard reported: "We don't have the Expos anymore, so I had to find another team. And everybody hates the Yankees; that's probably why I chose them."[22]

The anonymous curator of the Cardboard Gods (collectibles) website pointed out that even with all the shifting around of franchises since the

Braves moved from Boston to Milwaukee in 1953, there is only one former major league baseball city that does not now host a team – Montreal. In every other situation where baseball had abandoned a city – Kansas City, Seattle, Milwaukee, Washington – the game ultimately managed to find its way back. Even Brooklyn has the Mets just up the road on Long Island at Flushing Meadows.

But, according to Cardboard Gods, the chances of a return to Montreal are slim indeed. "Let's face it," the website declares, "Major league baseball will probably never return to Montreal, so the act of remembering is the only way for the Montreal Expos to endure. In that sense, they are the most important team – in the world of the Cardboard Gods."[23]

Even Stephanie Myles, the last of the Expos beat writers, who once defined herself as "the grownup who lived and breathed every dying moment of the Expos' last eight years," was now ready to say: "But I really don't care about baseball any more. I never thought that would happen, but it has. And it's okay."[24]

Political columnist L. Ian MacDonald shared much the same sentiment in *The Gazette* a few days earlier. "It was time for closure on the Expos," he wrote, "so in Maine the other day I bought a Red Sox cap at the drug store in Ogunquit. This was an intensely personal and exceedingly painful decision." He explained that up until then, "wearing another team cap was out of the question. Certainly not the Yankees...And decidedly not the Toronto Blue Jays, Canada's other team. And if you don't know the why of that, then you're not from Montreal."

In the end, Boston seemed the logical choice for him, even though "since winning the World Series in 2004 and again in 2007 they are no longer beautiful losers...they still have an enduring legacy of heartbreak with which any Expos fan can identify."[25]

"It takes a lot of time to be a baseball fan, to keep up on everything," wrote Myles. "And life goes on, slowly but surely; you just spend that time doing other things; it's a gradual process...I'm just glad it doesn't hurt anymore."

In response to inquiries from American reporters, Myles replied: "No, we don't root for the Jays. Yankees? Maybe. Red Sox? Definitely. Blue Jays? When hell freezes over."

But it's a long, long way from 2008 to 2014. In March of 2014, the Blue Jays will close out spring training with two exhibition games at Olympic Stadium against the Mets. Folks anticipate both will be sold out.

Now wouldn't that be something.

Chapter Fifty-Nine

Au Jeu –
Playing baseball in Quebec

You're too young to start giving up. Too young, and too lovely.
– John Osborne, Look Back in Anger

Just because the Expos vanished from Montreal – and Quebec – in 2004, don't for a moment think that baseball in this province disappeared along with them. Quite the contrary.

The game has a long history in Quebec. It was being played in cities and out in the countryside by the 1860s, if not before. The Montreal Royals won their first Eastern League (later International League) championship in 1898, and were a solid presence in the game right through until 1917 when World War I put an end to all frivolity.

In the hinterland, even before the turn of the century, baseball had usurped lacrosse as the summer game of choice. Its pastoral nature seemed better suited to the times than the increasingly violent and undisciplined "game of the hooked sticks," first introduced by North American natives two hundred years earlier. By 1900, scores of town teams and regional leagues had sprung up all across the province, as the game established itself both as an activity everyone could enjoy – and as the summer alternative to hockey for communities set on establishing bragging rights over their neighbours. To suggest that Quebec does not have a tradition of baseball, or that Quebecers never understood the game, or to make any other of the many uninformed and derogatory comments tossed about in the days of the Expos' fall, was naïve at best, and just dumb otherwise.

Arguably, one of the greatest contributions made to organized baseball in the twentieth century was made in Montreal by Montrealers. And that was to facilitate the entry of African-American ballplayers into the game's mainstream, by establishing a comfortable home base for Jackie Robinson, the first man of colour to cross into the world of whites-only baseball. His immediate success with the Triple-A Montreal Royals in

1946, which he and his wife Rachel readily admit was greatly aided by the warm reception accorded them by the local citizenry, cut through racial hatred so thoroughly that never again have black players been denied the opportunity to play baseball at the highest levels. Had that experiment failed, the cause of integration both in and outside of baseball might have been set back tremendously.

But it didn't fail. Quite the contrary, in fact. Following the last game of the season at Delormier Stadium in Montreal, where Robinson led the Royals to the Little World Series Championship against Kentucky's Louisville Colonels, ecstatic Montreal fans saluted their players by parading them around the outfield. Robinson, unsure of what was happening and in a hurry to fly home to California and his pregnant wife, shied away from the celebration. Nevertheless, the fans ran after him, cheering and calling out his name. Montreal-based sportswriter Sam Maitlin, who witnessed the scene as it unfolded, later expressed the moment in words that have taken on almost iconic significance. "It was probably the only day in history," he wrote, "that a black man ran from a white mob with love instead of lynching on its mind."[26]

But that was just the tip of the colour-line-busting iceberg in 1946. In fact, there were actually six players of colour, including Robinson, who participated in organized ball that year. Four of them played in Quebec. The other two toiled for the Nashua (New Hampshire) Dodgers in the New England League. Both later came to Montreal before heading on, as Robinson did, to the Brooklyn Dodgers. Their names: Don Newcombe and Roy Campanella.

One of the reasons Dodgers general manager Branch Rickey chose Montreal as the location for his challenge of baseball's colour barrier was his awareness that black players had long been a presence at the independent and semi-pro levels in Quebec. Indeed, one year the famous Chappie Johnson Stars barnstorming team actually remained in the Montreal area for a full season, playing in an independent league.

During the late 1940s and 1950s a number of African-American players, veterans of the collapsing Negro Leagues, found a spot in the Quebec Provincial League or other local independent loops. For many, this experience proved to be a stepping-stone to the big leagues; Vic Power, Dave Pope, Connie Johnson, Hector Lopez, and Ed Charles are just some of those major leaguers who found opportunity first knocking for them in Quebec. Even Hall-of-Famer Ray Brown, one of the Negro Leagues' greatest performers, spent the final five years of his baseball life in Quebec, suiting up with teams in Sherbrooke, Thetford Mines and Lachine.

During the pre-Expos days, and apart from the International League Royals, there were a number of other professional circuits scattered across the province. Quebec City and Trois-Rivières were mainstays first of the Can-Am League, and later the Provincial League, as were several other rural centres. Independent leagues flourished across the province, many staffed with a mix of native Quebecers and imports from the United States or Latin America.

Until the Expos came on the scene, the Montreal Royals were the acme of the Quebec baseball world. The top farm club of the Brooklyn Dodgers, the Royals introduced Montrealers to many of the great stars of Flatbush before they became famous. The generous fan support shown to the Royals was proof enough that Quebecers knew baseball, loved baseball, admired baseball – and played baseball.

In the early days of the Big Owe, when it was still considered a phenomenon, the Expos rivalled the Montreal Canadiens in popularity, and drew huge crowds to their games. The sorry ending to their story, as has been demonstrated already, had less to do with the fans and more with the how and what of club management. All this is a roundabout way of repeating yet again that this community possesses a sophisticated appreciation of the game. And that includes knowing when to push the (very real) device called the Bullshit Button, which is available through Amazon for $11.99.

Quebecers have been playing baseball for about as long as the game has existed. And over the years a steady run of them have found their way to the major leagues. Making the leap in the postwar era were: Derek Aucoin, Denis Boucher, Paul Calvert, Eric Cyr, Ray Daviault, Roland Gladu, Tim Harkness, Paul Hodgson, Dick Lines, Georges Maranda, Ron Piché, Claude Raymond, Jean-Pierre Roy, and Pete Ward.

And since 2004, when baseball supposedly died around here, another batch of local players found a home in the big leagues: Philippe Aumont, Eric Gagné, Steve Green, Pierre-Luc Laforest, Chris Leroux, Russell Martin, and Maxime St-Pierre.

Many of those listed were aided along the way by Baseball Quebec, an organization geared to the development of young players, their coaches and to the organization of leagues and officials across Quebec. As players mature, the best are invited to take part in the ABC baseball academy. An elite program that combines academics and baseball, ABC brings a full bag of resources to the table, offering exceptional training opportunities to promising young players.

Each winter Baseball Quebec sends a team of potential all-stars to Florida where they get to play roughly 15 games against U.S. college teams and minor-league professional clubs. The Florida field trip provides a wonderful opportunity for the players to not only play competitive ball during the winter months, but also to be showcased before American scouts, an opportunity that for many of them leads to opportunities with U.S. colleges and universities.

Built in 1938, Stade municipal (Municipal Stadium) in Quebec City is one of the few remaining vintage ballparks in the country. It is currently home to les Capitales de Québec of the Can-Am League.

(Photo: Courtesy Daniel Papillon)

Baseball is played in Quebec at the senior league level across the province and, since 1999, professionally by les Capitales de Québec of the independent Can-Am League. In 2013 the Quebec City club was joined by les Aigles (Eagles) de Trois-Rivières. The circuit, which operates at a level somewhere between A-ball and Double-A, depending, as someone once said, "on who's pitching that day," includes three other teams, two in New Jersey and one in Rockland County, New York. In recent years les Capitales have dominated, winning the league championship for the past five seasons.

Anyone travelling in the Quebec City or Trois-Rivières areas on a warm summer night could do worse than attend a ball game in either city. Both teams play in heritage ballparks of very similar design built within a year of each other during the Great Depression. Both are gems, throwbacks to a time when baseball in Quebec truly was the summer game.

On a lighter note, in 2008 a team from Quebec won the Vintage Baseball World Series played in Westfield, Massachusetts. Quebec's participation was coordinated by John Elias, a graduate of Michigan State and long-time minor-league pitcher who is both a teacher by profession and a Quebec baseball-lifer by avocation. He served for years as the Expos' batting practice pitcher and operated a baseball school in the summer. Russell Martin, catcher for the Pittsburgh Pirates in 2013, was a recent graduate.

Players for the Montreal Vintage Baseball team were recruited from the Quebec Senior Elite Baseball League, one of the loops operating under the aegis of Baseball Quebec. Vintage baseball is an acquired taste: the teams employ the rules, uniforms and equipment of its 19th-century roots.

Montreal Vintage Baseball Club – World Champions 2008
Manager Johnny Elias standing on the right.

Nevertheless, thanks to this modest group, it can honestly be said there was a time when a baseball team from Montreal did indeed win the World Series. No need to qualify the point any further.

Chapter Sixty

The New Beginnings Start Here

The history of other sports seems to begin anew with each generation, but baseball, that wondrous myth....gets passed on like an inheritance.

—Stanley Cohen[27]

Marquis Grissom, Rondell White, Denis Boucher, Mel Rojas and John Wetteland. Manager Felipe Alou was there. So were Pedro Martinez, Cliff Floyd.

Add in mascot Youppi!, head trainer Ron McClain, general manager Kevin Malone, managing general partner Claude Brochu and limited partner Mark Routtenberg. The event? The seventh annual Cummings Jewish Centre for Seniors Sports Celebrity Breakfast held on March 27, 2011, to honour the talent-laden 1994 Expos squad.

Upwards of 700 people packed the room for the hot-ticket affair that raised about $175,000 for the centre's Seniors in Crisis program. It was a sad event – but happy at the same time. All members of the Expos clan present were offered the

Photo by Bill Young

A group of Expos from 1994 prepare to pose for cameras at the 2011 reunion breakfast. Top row, unidentified breakfast guest, Pedro Martinez and outfielder Rondell White. Bottom row, outfielder Marquis Grissom and first baseman Cliff Floyd.

331

chance to say a few words about their run in 1994, cut short by the strike and cancellation of the season.

Just a few days earlier, Martinez had been honoured in Washington when his portrait was added to the permanent collection at the Smithsonian Institution's National Portrait Gallery.

Photo: Dany Gallagher

Pedro Martinez signs one of many autographs at the Cummings Jewish Centre for Seniors Sports Celebrity Breakfast in 2011.

"The Smithsonian recognition was an individual achievement, and this recognition today is a team achievement," said a beaming Martinez, swarmed by autograph seekers as the breakfast concluded. "Any personal recognition I get is related to all the hard work I have put in. But this team was so special. We were so confident we thought we could win every game and beat everybody."

The guest of honour was Routtenberg, a successful businessman who is prominent in Montreal's Jewish community. He was largely responsible for getting Alou, many of the players and non-uniformed personnel to show up.

Routtenberg even induced his former colleague Brochu to come along. Years earlier, Routtenberg had broken off relations with his managing general partner because of disagreements over the way Brochu was running the Expos' ownership group. In a classy move, Routtenberg decided to let bygones be bygones and patch up the rift between them.

A highlight of the event was Annakin Slayd and his heart-warming, touching video of the 1994 squad entitled *Remember (A Tribute to the Montreal Expos)*. Three minutes, 45 seconds of pure joy and melancholy, all rolled into one. Ecstasy to agony. A few months before, Slayd had run into Routtenberg and event organizer Mike Cohen, and all agreed it should be screened.

"I made the video in 2010," Slayd said. "It made sense for them to invite me. I had also done a general video about the Expos, but there was more universal acclaim for *Remembering* . It took me two or three sessions in the studio to complete, about 10 hours for the song and then another 10 hours to edit the video."

Slayd had started with old tapes recorded from TV and highlight reels collected earlier in his life. "These were tapes buried in my mother's basement. They came in handy," said Slayd, who was born in the Montreal suburb of St. Leonard and grew up in Laval. His mother, Effy Louritas, spent close to 10 years from 1980-89 employed by the Seagram Company, whose majority owner was Charles Bronfman.

"John Wetteland was really touched by the tape," Slayd said. "I could see the tears in his eyes when I saw him afterward. He was very emotional. He wanted to take a picture with me. Usually, it's the other way around. His wife took the photo.

"You wouldn't believe how many grown men have come up to me crying. Dozens and dozens. They were all very touched by it. I saw Pedro Martinez a year after the breakfast and he told me he had it on his phone," Slayd said. "I love it so much," Martinez told Slayd. "It was touching and flattering for Pedro to say that," Slayd said.

Perhaps the two most memorable moments in the video are Marquis Grissom's inside-the-park home run off Rich Rodriguez of the Cardinals and Cliff Floyd's golf-shot home run off Greg Maddux.

John Wetteland talks baseball with a reporter at the Cummings Jewish Centre for Seniors Sports Celebrity Breakfast in 2011.

Photo: Bill Young

"The line by Dave Van Horne, 'Marquis Grissom is flying,' was really something," Slayd said. "Absolutely, the Grissom homer was the most rousing moment of 1994, but to me that Floyd home run was my personal, emotional favourite. I was a big Cliff Floyd guy. I saw him as the future of the franchise. Cliff was so good to me. He invited me to stay at his house, the next time I was in Miami."

Chapter Sixty-One

You can go home again
(Part I)

*You can look at it in a number of ways. You can be mad – but you
can also be happy about all the good times you had.*

— Tim Raines

It is hard to know precisely when the groundswell to bring the
Expos back to Montreal gained traction, but that 2011 Celebrity
Breakfast at the Cummings Jewish Centre in honour of the 1994
Expos is probably as good a place as any to begin. Although the
atmosphere that morning was hauntingly nostalgic, the tone was
upbeat: a celebration of what was, measured against the hope of what
might someday be again. And when the Harry Caray–esque Larry
Fredericks, a larger-than-life radio man and sports broadcasting veteran, wrapped things up by leading the audience in a raucous rendi-
tion of *Take Me Out to the Ball Game*, he concluded by calling out:
"Before Quebec City gets the (NHL) Nordiques back, we get the
Expos!" The unqualified optimism he generated had all the patrons
bearing a smile on their lips and a hint of spring in their gait as they
exited the hall.

Some suggest it was at this moment that once-fanciful talk about
major league baseball returning to Montreal took on a more serious
flavour.

In late July of 2011, the Conference Board of Canada released one of
its periodic Briefings entitled, *The Future of Major League Baseball in
Canada*, the sixth in a 14-part series designed to explore "what it takes for
a professional sports team to be successful in Canada." This baseball-ori-
ented Briefing looked at both Toronto and Montreal, but its focus was on
the Expos and their chances of returning to the city.

The study identified four essential market pillars which must be present if a professional team is to be successful. These included: "a large

enough (and growing) population; a relatively wealthy population; a sound corporate presence; and a level playing field." The first three pillars are well represented in Montreal. More problematic is the issue of a level playing field. "It would be tough to find an individual or corporation willing to bring an MLB team back to Montréal knowing that the club would struggle to be competitive," the report said.

Nevertheless, the Conference Board was not prepared to slam shut the door on a return of the game to these parts. The Board said: "If a media conglomerate were to bring a team to Montréal, the synergy could work. With a regular season schedule of 162 games, a team in Montréal would provide great TV and radio content. The number of sports-specialty channels continues to rise, and along with them the demand for content. An MLB team in Montréal would be highly appealing for the right media group."[28]

The debate wasn't long in coming, fueled in part by Rodger Brulotte, a sportscaster/broadcaster for RDS, the French-language version of TSN, and long associated with the Expos. He revealed, on the heels of the Conference Board report, that he had been approached by an anonymous group of local businessmen exploring the possibility of bringing baseball back – and he was taking them seriously. Brulotte suggested that an obvious site for a new ballpark would be the Hippodrome, the once-elegant Blue Bonnets raceway north of downtown where the best of local pacers and trotters once strutted their stuff for the amusement, and profit, of local racetrack habitués and touts. In 2011 the site served to accommodate a concert by U2, and more recently has become the centre point of a proposed housing project.

A *Gazette* article about wealth in Montreal which appeared around this time had its own indirect take on the matter. Author Nicholas van Praet expressed concern that there are "far fewer rich people in this province than in Ontario." He suggested this "lack of affluence is also one of the starkest symptoms of a larger problem. Many Quebecers have a deep distrust of wealth and wealthy people," and he warns that if this doesn't change soon, Montreal risks falling into quiet mediocrity – a kind of non-ambitious lethargy that will hurt not only itself but the rest of the country."[29] If Praet's hypothesis should prove to be true and Montreal tumbles into the kind of mediocrity he suggests, its negative impact would pretty well put an end to any prospects of baseball's return.

Opposition to the Conference Board Briefing and the portrait it presented was swift and cogent, and came mostly via the media. Jack Todd was unequivocal. "Fuhgeddaboudit, folks," he wrote in the *Gazette*. "Sorry but we can't take seriously the reports that say an anonymous group wants to bring the Expos back to Montreal." After listing the reasons why such a venture would not work, Todd concluded by saying, "I don't believe that the kind of people who think the first step is to approach Rodger Brulotte have the foggiest clue about how to bring baseball back to this city. And if these people think they can con the various levels of government to pony up that halfbillion (sic) dollars for a ballpark – they're plain nuts."[30] Stu Cowan, sports editor of the *Gazette*, stated simply that the "Expos' return likely will remain a fantasy."[31] Or a "pipe dream," which is what an August 1, 2011 *Gazette* editorial called it. Pulling out all the negative stops – no salary cap, no indoor stadium, no public money for new stadium construction, too little public support – the paper argued "there are no sound reasons to believe a rebirth of the Montreal Expos is imminent, nor even likely in the longer term." Then in a somewhat indirect rebuttal to the Larry Fredericks boisterous curtain call at the Cummings Celebrity Breakfast a few months earlier, the paper concluded: "Chances are we will be booing the Nordiques before we will be cheering on the Expos."[32]

Academic and poet David McGimpsey, a deeply committed baseball soul, agreed. He was quoted as saying, "Montreal Expos fans are great with patriotic and sentimental remembrance but were not so hot when it came to just going to ball games." He added: "It would have been a pretty blind group who looked into the fan base of Montreal and thought 'Gold.'"[33]

Claude Brochu was of a similar mind as McGimpsey. "As long as Bud Selig is with Major League Baseball," he said in 2011, "Montreal can forget about ever having a team." However, he conceded that "if Pittsburgh can have a team or Oakland or Kansas City or Tampa Bay, there's no reason why Montreal shouldn't have a team."[34]

In early August, the internet site Baseball Digest expressed surprise at the negative tone of the discussion, taking particular exception to the *Gazette*'s reaction. The paper, according to the Digest's unnamed author, makes "the logical mistake of assuming any future MLB team would be run like the Expos under the same circumstances." The writer went on to say the Expos failed because "a crappy owner (Jeffrey Loria) dumped a poorly run franchise into the lap of MLB, whose officials made a bad situation worse before the team moved to Washington. A perfect storm as it were."[35]

Freelance writer Matthew Ross, a baseball junkie and part-time sports radio host on TSN 990 Montreal, in the *Gazette* gave some credence to the data and observations found in the Conference Board report, and to Brulotte's revelations. Ross, who currently heads ExposNation, the grass-roots collection of fans lobbying for baseball's rebirth in Montreal, was, nevertheless, cautious. He likened the notion of baseball return at this juncture to a mid-summer night's dream. However, he did remind readers that a small groundswell of support had been building since the previous July when busloads of Montreal fans trekked to Cooperstown to celebrate former Expo Andre Dawson's induction into the Baseball Hall of Fame. [36]

The debate was on – and, remarkably, whether one supported the prospect of baseball returning home or opposed it, everyone was taking the premise seriously.

Dr. Elisabeth Kübler-Ross would probably have concluded this meant that Expos *aficionados* had finally reached the Acceptance phase of grief's five stages. At peace with what had gone before, no longer mourning its passing, they instead were taking comfort in the joyful memories, and memorials, left in its wake. Their focus was pointed, not toward the anguish of the past, but ahead to something new and better.

A No-Hitter with a Difference

Although the year 2004 represented not much more than a sorry anticlimax to the Expos' sordid story, it did have its moments. Perhaps the most unusual pertained to a couple of strange coincidences involving pitchers Jon Rauch and Tony Armas, Jr. that could have qualified them for entry in the Dictionary of Baseball Oddities, if such a book existed.

On Friday night, August 13, Rauch started against the Houston Astros and Roger Clemens. Relatively speaking, the crowd was larger than usual given that the club was programmed to dematerialize into thin air seven weeks later. Most of the increased attendance could be attributed to the Clemens bump – fans from New England who made the trek across the border to watch Red Sox original Clemens. Rauch was superb: he had a no-hitter going when he injured his arm and was forced to leave after 4.2 innings. And just to make the moment even more memorable for the Expos pitcher, up against the best in the business, Rauch also hit a two-run homer off Clemens, a high and long blast down the right-field line.

Then, to cap this little oddity, the next day's starter for the Expos was Tony Armas, Jr., coming back from injury and working on a pitch count. He made it through five innings before being removed for a pinch-hitter, his day's work done. When he left, the Astros, once again, had yet to score a run or even manage a hit. Thus, over two successive games, two Expos starting pitchers had collectively hurled 9.2 innings of no-hit, no-run baseball at the beginning of each match, before leaving for medical reasons. If this doesn't constitute some sort of a record, it should.

Chapter Sixty-Two

You can go home again (Part II)

And that included Warren Cromartie: he was taking the possibility of baseball returning to Montreal very seriously. A stalwart of the 1980s Expos and a passionate advocate of baseball's return, Cromartie was gearing up for action. He had been struck by the Conference Board report, and well understood that for Montrealers to experience the joys of watching baseball again, even before the long list of impediments could be addressed, there needed to be some lovable and reckless knight in shining armour ready to step right in and get things started.

Even as Cromartie was contemplating a course of action, word came down that on February 16, 2012 Gary Carter had passed away. Carter was, perhaps, the most genial, the greatest, and the most constant of all great Expos players – and probably the one who touched fans the most. All across Expoland the faithful mourned – but a devastated Cromartie deemed this wasn't enough. He and the Kid had been friends during their Expos years and forever afterward – and he wanted to honour that friendship in some tangible way. "Gary was just the best," said Cromartie in a speech given at the Cummings Jewish Centre for Seniors Celebrity Sports Breakfast in 2012, barely a month after his friend's passing. "Everything you saw on camera, that big smile, the things he did with kids, it was all genuine." And then Cromartie closed his remarks "with a passionate call for baseball's return."[38]

He chose his next moment carefully. On April 4, 2012, Opening Day in the major leagues, Cromartie held a press conference to announce the launch of the Montreal Baseball Project. Its mission: to bring baseball back to Montreal. The first step, said Cromartie, is to raise awareness, "getting baseball back on the local radar again. The second is to find a team. And a stadium.".[39] As Cromartie suggested, a new retro ballpark in the downtown area would make the game even more appealing. The gosh-awful Olympic Stadium was still available, but most would agree it has lasted way beyond its best-before date.

Cromartie announced he hoped the Montreal Baseball Project could organize what he envisioned would be an annual fundraising charity event in aid of Carter's West Palm Beach-based foundation and a hospital in Montreal. The first of such events took place two months later, in mid-June. It featured the 1981 Expos team and raised $20,000. Stan Bahnsen, Andre Dawson, Jim Fanning, Wallace Johnson, Bill Lee, Rowland Office, Larry Parrish, Tim Raines, Bryn Smith, Rodney Scott, and Ellis Valentine were there – and, as part of the day's activities, Ballantyne Park, a ball field in the Montreal suburb of Dorval, was dedicated to Gary Carter.

The challenge facing Cromartie after such a glorious happening was to find ways of building on the nostalgia created by the reunion and trans-lating this into corporate support for baseball's eventual rebirth. He announced that plans were already afoot to honour the 1994 Expos at an appropriate opportunity in 2014.

Some months later, in an interview, Cromartie explained his motiva-tion for continuing to spread his vision. "When I went back to Montreal, I did not see anything, anywhere to show the Expos were there," he said. "It was a complete travesty, with the history we have. Roberto Clemente played in Montreal, Jackie Robinson, there is a lot of baseball history there so I decided to take the bull by the horns."

And thus he set his course, first seeking out possible investors inter-ested in his vision. "I'm looking for people with deep pockets," Cromartie said. "Realistically, within five or six years, I'd like to see baseball back in the city."

Cromartie figures the only practical route is to acquire an existing franchise and move it to Montreal. Then there is the issue of a new ball-park that would be needed to attract the interest of the commissioner's office. "A lot of things have changed over eight years since the team left," Cromartie said. "The exchange rate on the U.S. dollar is much better today. Same with corporate rights, revenue-sharing and the playoff sys-tem. But [a transfer of franchise}] won't happen overnight."[40]

While Cromartie was busily drumming up corporate and public sup-port, a small, local group was registering its love affair with baseball in a different way. On Labour Day weekend about 200 Expos fans from Montreal and parts distant gathered in Toronto to take in the Jays-Tampa Bay Rays game at Rogers Centre. And to make a statement, several in fact. When the group purchased their tickets it seemed there was a strong possibility that Vlad Guerrero, attempting a comeback of sorts in the Jays' minor league system, would be a September call-up, and they wanted to greet him in person when he took the field. Sadly for them, he elected to retire from the game a month or so earlier.

Their first aim, however, was to display their fervour for the essence of what baseball once was in Montreal, before a "morass of political and financial machinations...dispatched the franchise to Washington." According to Matthew Ross, one of the group's organizers, "We wanted to come to the closest major-league park to show support, and show that the passion for baseball in Montreal still exists."[41] And thus a grass-roots collection of Montreal baseball fanatics calling itself ExposNation rose to prominence, determined to keep pushing until Montreal can once again boast its own team.

By the end of the year, through the efforts of both the Montreal Baseball Project and ExposNation, the outside world was becoming aware of Montreal's growing interest in the return of baseball to its island shores. The iconoclastic American commentator, Keith Olbermann, once of MSNBC and more recently returned to his ESPN roots, had predicted in late 2011 that what he called the "franchise carousel," which had been "all but quiet since the upheaval of the 1953-1972 era, will begin to spin again." The main problem area he believes lies in Florida, and while he concedes Miami still has a slight chance of survival, Tampa Bay, he insists, has none. Indeed, Olbermann projects that "at the latest, the season of 2020 opens without a Florida team in the majors."

This conclusion prompted Olbermann to consider possible replacement cities, something he pursued by compiling a list of top U.S. metropolitan areas ranked by population *that were not already home to MLB teams*. Heading the list was the San Bernardino area of California, 12th largest of all U.S. metro areas. However, as it lies in the Los Angeles Dodgers' catchment area, San Bernardino is not a plausible candidate for a new ball club. Next largest of the metro areas without major league baseball would have been Montreal, had population centres beyond U.S. borders been included on the list. From that point on, the list is composed of cities just not large enough to merit serious consideration, cities such as Portland (Oregon), Las Vegas and Nashville.

In other words, Olbermann suggests that of all the major centres not served by baseball, Montreal is the one with the greatest potential. Baseball is a major economic generator in its own right, Olbermann maintains, and he believes Montreal is perfectly placed to benefit from all that the modern game has to offer – if it can find a way in.

Speaking in absolute terms, Olbermann regards the Expos as once having been a very successful franchise, even allowing for the fact it played within "the greatest white elephant in the history of North

American sports construction." The Expos were done in, he avowed, not because of fan neglect but by "corrupt government and underfunded ownership and a betrayed fan base. ...then stuff started falling from the roof in a tribute to government graft, and star Expos players started falling off the Expos roster."

With renewed commitment from government, a new stadium and a committed ownership group, "baseball's second try in Montreal could be a triumph." This would be especially true should the city become the new home of the Tampa Bay club, successful on the field and in the management suites.

Something to think about.[42]

Why baseball would succeed in Montreal – Keith Olberman

But wait, didn't things go very badly in Montreal before? They certainly did, but not because of the city nor its love of baseball. Corrupt government and underfunded ownership and a betrayed fan base – all of them saddled with the greatest white elephant in the history of North American sports construction, Olympic Stadium. In every full season between 1979 and 1983 – even in that XXL Airplane Hangar - Les Expos drew at least 2,102,173 fans a year.

The peak total – 2,320,651 in 1983 – edged out the Cardinals for second place in National League attendance, and was just about a million more than the Mets drew in New York. It was about then that stuff started falling from the roof of the tribute to provincial graft, and star players started falling off the Expos' roster. But make no mistake about it: Montreal supported baseball. As late as 1997 the Expos still brought in a million and a half fans (more than the Mets or the Giants).

If all that could not be done in the '90s and '00s could be put together – a downtown stadium with government support, plus a well-run franchise making a long-term commitment – baseball's second try in Montreal could be a triumph. And consider if it were the Rays fleeing north. Not only would Montreal get that well-run franchise, but it would suddenly find itself in a division with rivals from hated cities like Boston and New York...and Toronto.

Chapter Sixty-Three

Hog Tied in Hog Town

Here's a baseball oddity to ponder. In Toronto, baseball has never been the same since the strike fiasco of 1994. The Blue Jays have never made it back to the postseason, and their attendance is way down compared to the glorious box-office figures they amassed from 1991-94.

The Jays were actually headed toward another season of 4 million in attendance when the strike was called. "There have been challenges since 1994," Paul Beeston, team president and CEO admits. "I guess we were a large-market team, by definition, and acted like one. We had won the World Series two years in a row and when we came out of the strike, a lot of fans were angry at pro athletes generally, at professional sports and their teams.

"There were two issues, the hockey issue and the baseball issue. The NHL had the lockout in 1994-95. Fans in Toronto got tired of the bickering between ownership and players. We had enjoyed 10 years of success as a team."

In their heyday, Beeston said, the Jays would routinely halt season-ticket sales at 22,000, keeping another 10,000 names on a waiting list simply to give the average person access to game tickets. That's how hungry Toronto was for baseball.

"We had the good fortune basically to be able to sell out [Rogers Centre]," Beeston said. "After the strike, the number of season-ticket sales evaporated really quickly, and so did the 10,000 people on the waiting list. When we had those great teams, the money was coming in, we were drawing well, we were admired across the country. You don't think the merry-go-round will ever end. We had a state-of-the-art stadium downtown, not in the suburbs, with a roof that opened and closed. And we had a team that was challenging every year. What was constant throughout all that was our excellent play. It was really an exciting time. That's what winning is all about."

Then, half of those 50,000 fans who filled the stands in Toronto from 1991–1994 stopped coming. The lineup for season tickets disappeared abruptly and with no waiting list, revenues plummeted.

"Baseball has always been a secondary sport to hockey in Toronto," pitcher Dave Stewart said. "When the strike came, it was kind of like a slap in the face for fans. They have never forgotten that."

Perhaps it was just coincidence but right after the strike season, Jays GM Pat Gillick left to join the Baltimore Orioles, following which the Jays never made it back to the postseason. When asked to comment, Gillick, in an e-mail, claimed to have "no recollection about 1994. That was many moons ago and I don't have anything of value to offer."

These days, after having earned large revenues for years, the Jays are thankful that revenue-sharing is now part of Major League Baseball. Surprisingly, since 2002, the team has been a regular beneficiary. "It's a significant amount of money," Beeston said, without giving any breakdown and noting that figures aren't released by the commissioner's office. "It's nothing to be proud of. I'd rather be a buyer than a recipient of money. Taking money means you are not covering your costs."

The Jays probably received their largest share of the monies available following the 2010 season when they drew a mere 1.4 million people to the ballpark.

Things appeared to be looking up in the fall of 2012 when GM Alex Anthopoulos overhauled the team by acquiring pitchers Mark Buehrle and Josh Johnson and shortstop Jose Reyes from the Florida Marlins, then took knuckleballer R.A. Dickey from the Mets. And to cap it off, he later signed free-agent outfielder Melky Cabrera to a two-year contract.

Sadly, the bold makeover was a major disappointment. Predicted by many to rule the American League East in 2013, or at the very least return to the postseason after a 20-year absence, the Jays instead dropped to the bottom of their division with a loud splat, mustering no better than a sorry 74-88 record at season's end. Injuries played a part, but the primary source of the problem was that, with few exceptions, the marquee players did not deliver. No one batted over .300, although Jose Reyes was close at .297. Only Edwin Encarnacion managed more than 100 RBIs and 30 home runs, though four other players did hit 20 or better. In fact, the team as a whole amassed 185 homers, ninth best in baseball.

Among the pitchers, the sole regulars to put together winning records were Buehrle and Dickey, but with ERAs above 4.00. Closer Casey Jansen saved 34 games, nearly 50 percent of the club's wins. Collectively, the Jays' pitching corps ranked no better than 25th out of 30 teams.

There was one area where Toronto made a big comeback. Home attendance climbed above 2.5 million, sixth best in the 15-team American League. Fans remained optimistic to the end – and hopes are still high for 2014.[43]

Chapter Sixty-Four

A Revenue-Sharing Primer

 One truism that applies to almost all discussions involving strikes and salary caps and revenue-sharing is that most people have at best very little understanding of what they claim to be talking about. To help improve understanding, co-author Danny Gallagher invited Pat Courtney, publicist for the Commissioner's Office, to give us his explanation.

Mr. Courtney very kindly replied. He provided three interpretations, what he called the Short, Slightly Longer and Long versions. Here is what he wrote:

The Short Version:
Each Club pays 48% of its locally generated revenue into a pool, which is then distributed equally among the 30 Clubs.

The Slightly Longer Version:
The Plan runs on Net Defined Local Revenue ("NDLR"), which is all locally generated revenue related to baseball operations less actual stadium expenses. The plan runs in two parts – the Base Plan and the Supplemental Plan. In the Base Plan, each Club contributes 34% of its NDLR into a pot which is then split equally among the 30 Clubs. In the Supplemental Plan, the total amount transferred is set such that the total Plan transfer is equivalent to a 48% straight pool plan. Each Club either pays or receives a fixed percentage of that transfer amount based on its Performance Factor, a collectively bargained number. The sum of a Club's payment or receipt in the Base Plan and the Supplemental Plan is its Plan obligation for that year.

The Long Version:

Clubs share their Net Defined Local Revenue ("NDLR"), which is aggregate operating revenues collected from baseball operations less stadium operations expenses. NDLR excludes revenue generated from the postseason and is lagged one year (i.e., in 2012, Clubs share based on 2011 NDLR). The plan operates in two parts, the Base Plan and the Supplemental Plan.

In the Base Plan, each Club contributes 34% of its NDLR into a pot and receives 1/30th of the pot back. In the Supplemental Plan, the total amount transferred is set such that the total Plan transfer is equivalent to a 48% straight pool plan. Each Club either pays or receives a fixed percentage of that transfer amount based on its Performance Factor. Performance Factors are fixed for each Club through the 2014 Revenue Sharing Year, at which point any Club who has signed a new or renegotiated broadcast agreement that materially increases its TV revenue is adjusted and the Performance Factors for each Club are recalculated beginning in the 2015 Revenue Sharing Year.

In the new Basic Agreement, the Clubs in the fifteen largest markets (as defined in Attachment 26 to the Basic Agreement) will be incrementally disqualified from receiving Revenue Sharing Proceeds. Any Revenue Sharing proceeds that those Clubs would have received is redistributed to the Payor Clubs in proportion to their payment.

The sum of each Club's payment/receipt in the Base Plan and in the Supplemental Plan is its Net Payment/Receipt under the Revenue Sharing Plan.

Chapter Sixty-Five

Oh! Oh! – Let's talk about Olympic Stadium

The great mistake was to have considered Jean Drapeau as a spendthrift politician, whereas he will remain forever a visionary for his city and his country.

– Roger Taillibert website

Steve Rogers loved Olympic Stadium. And he has little good to say about Jarry Park, that idyllic field of dreams which still symbolizes the heart of what it meant to be an Expo. However, by the time Rogers made it to Montreal, quaint Parc Jarry had grown old, and tired. Her charm had worn thin – and so when the chance came to play in Olympic Stadium, it was smiles all around. "I loved to play baseball there," said Rogers in 2013. "It was pitcher friendly. Huge foul territory, very forgiving in the power alleys in centre field. It was a big ball park. So, from a pitcher's standpoint, it was pretty good...so much better to play baseball in than Jarry Park. It was definitely a huge step up."[44]

Not any more. Today the Big O is seen in the same light as the aging Jarry Park, old and tired, but without the magic. The complaints are many and discussed elsewhere, but what sealed its doom, as far as fans were concerned, was the stark, untempered, negative terminology used by advocates of a new downtown ballpark to describe its deficiencies, and hence boost the desirability of their own project.

So negative was the criticism of Olympic Stadium that when the project to build a new downtown ballpark (tentatively called Labatt Park) failed, there was no going back. Not to the Big Owe at any rate. As Claude Brochu put it: "I wouldn't go there. There's no way. It's the memories and everything."

In a footnote to this story, in November of 2006, Olympic Stadium rid itself of its Big Owe sobriquet. Anyone still of a mind call it by that familiar term should know that from now on, it will have to be written as

Big O, an entirely different euphemism which also originated at the time of the 1976 Olympics. Big Owe is no longer justified because, finally, 20 years after the stadium's $1.5-billion debt was incurred, it has now been paid in full. Most of this revenue was generated through a tax on cigarettes.

According to a law adopted in 1976, the Quebec government was to return Olympic Stadium to the City of Montreal once the debt was repaid. That was then. By the time the loan was actually squared away, Montreal wanted nothing to do with the cash-hungry stadium. "The stadium was paid for by all Quebecers," said city representative Francine Senécal, "so it should belong to all Quebecers."[45]

If baseball is ever to come back to Montreal, one can be fairly certain that, for a few years anyway, the new team will be quite content to call the Big O home. The two exhibition games scheduled for March 2014 at Olympic Stadium might well go a long way toward exorcising the demons that perhaps for too long were allowed to roam its concrete corridors. Loud cheers and happy faces, little boys and girls holding mom and dad's hand and young lovers, still on page one of their memory books, will all bring a new kind of energy to the place.

Perhaps in the spirit of Opening Days of yore, the old ballpark will come alive yet again, nurturing new dreams and lofty aspirations.

Chapter Sixty-Six

You can go home again (Part III)

Larry Anderson's brief pitching career with the White Sox and Brewers in the mid-1970s was over almost before it began. However, his take on the relevance of the classic ballpark anthem "Take Me Out to the Ball Game" is a folly that will live forever.

"In the seventh inning fans all get up and sing 'Take Me Out to the Ball Game,' and they're already there," he once said, apparently with a straight face. "It's really a stupid thing to say and I don't know who made 'em sing it. Why would somebody that's there get up and sing "take me out to the ball game? The first person to do it must have been a moron."[46]

Well, the one thousand or so ExposNation folks who crowded into the Rogers Centre in the summer of 2013, draped in their Expos regalia, might disagree. For to them, the idea of being taken to a ball game, especially a

y

major league game, especially one played in Montreal, in a brand new major league stadium, is precisely what they have wanted for a long time – and they're not ready to settle for anything less. Theirs is a burning desire that never completely left, not even after MLB managed to squirrel the real thing out of town one dark night in late 2004. So that day in Toronto, cheering as the Blue Jays

Photo by Bill Young

Fern Lapierre – the organist at Parc Jarry

faced the Tampa Bay Rays, they were on a mission, to let the baseball world know exactly how they felt. And singing "Take Me Out to the Ball Game" was part of it

Former Expos pitcher Derek Aucoin is associated with the ExposNation group, and he is impressed with the organization's energy and commitment, along with its basic street smarts. Although he too mourns his old club's demise, he concedes that "maybe this had to happen. Maybe the club had to go, so that we could get a second chance, the opportunity to do things better."[47] Certainly he is among those who believe strongly that baseball will rise again in Montreal.

Almost from the start of 2013, efforts to drive the future of baseball in Montreal kept gaining momentum. The sad first anniversary of Gary Carter's February 2012 passing was occasion enough to stir Expos memories. Carter was important to Montreal – but, in turn, Montreal was almost as important to him and the Carter family. Daughter Kimmie was born in the city, and she recalled just how much her father loved "being up there…he knew the national anthem in French. He was part of the Expos and he wanted to be part of that world as much as possible."[48] Later that same year Gary would be remembered by the city in a more formal way.

In late March, Warren Cromartie returned with an update on the progress of the Montreal Baseball Project. At that time he announced that his group had linked up with the Montreal Board of Trade on a feasibility study "to see if conditions are right and the interest is there" to support baseball's return. Convinced that they are, Cromartie pointed to several positive factors – revival of the Canadian dollar, more television money, immediacy of social media, and revenue sharing in baseball. He stated his goal is "to change the attitude. I know people were angry eight years ago…this is a new era, new times."

According to Michel Leblanc, CEO of the Board of Trade, "the signal we're getting is there's an appetite for a baseball team. We're going to test that over the coming months." He then added: "our belief is that Montreal is strong, our economy is strong, and we might have a viable product that will be good for Montreal and good for our brand abroad."[49]

As might be expected, not everyone agreed. Henry Aubin, the *Gazette's* expert on city affairs, declared that the Board of Trade's announcement left him dumbfounded. "You don't need a $400,000 study…to know there isn't the fan base here to support a team," he huffed. More significantly, he questioned the board's priorities. "This scandal-ridden city is suffering a lot less from a lack of a baseball team than it is from a lack of integrity in business," he wrote in a *Gazette* opinion piece. Aubin hammered away at the board, urging it to shift focus and face head on the rot at the core of city operations. Harm to the city's reputation will not go away on its own, he noted. When a board official told Aubin "a sign of a major-league city is a major-league team," the journalist retorted, "Yes, but an even more desirable sign is major-league integrity."

Other commentators, while conceding that Board of Trade involvement now gave the Montreal Baseball Project more credibility, were still calling it just a dream. Nevertheless, calling it a dream was one very big step up from what they had called it before – a fantasy.

Cromartie's project was given a further shot in the arm in April when Stephen Bronfman, son of the Expos' first owner Charles Bronfman and a limited partner with the team in its consortium days, included words of encouragement in remarks he made to the Junior Chamber of Commerce of Montreal. He suggested that given revenue sharing, TV deals and luxury taxes, "a reincarnation of the Expos may be possible." Calling it a "long shot," he added: "but if it could happen, it would be great for the city. A lot of people are supportive of the idea. It's a major undertaking and it can't be done 100 per cent privately."

As the year progressed, one sensed a fairly steady flow of baseball talk and baseball activity taking place within the city. There was even the night that pro ball came back to Montreal, if only for one match. In a Can-Am (Independent) League exhibition game at cozy Ahuntsic Park on a cool evening in May, the Quebec Capitales, perennial league leaders in both championship rings and attendance figures, met up with Aigles de Trois-Rivières. Over 1,000 came to watch.

To the organizers the match was a test of sorts – to help determine if there was sufficient interest to warrant entering a Montreal-based team in the Can-Am League, and, in a modest way, to gain some sense of the extent to which locals would welcome a more permanent return of the game to Montreal.

Michel Laplante is a former Triple-A player from the Abitibi region of Quebec who, in recent years, incrementally, has served as the Capitales' premier starting pitcher, field manager, and now club president. He also owns and operates the growing B-45 Yellow Birch Bat business outside Quebec City, and he happens to possess one of the more astute baseball minds in the province. When asked about the chances of baseball returning to Montreal he offered this comment:

"Montreal's baseball roots are stronger than most people think. People in this city were negative about the game of baseball in the early 2000s…To even think about getting a major league team back, you have to go back to baseball's roots and build it back up. Tonight's game means a lot."[50]

Less than one month later, Ahuntsic Park was in the spotlight again. This time the honoured guests were not a couple of ball clubs, but two members of the Carter family. Mrs. Gary Carter (Sandy), accompanied by her daughter Christy were there to take part in the renaming of the old ballpark as Gary Carter Stadium, in honour of the man many consider the greatest Expo of them all.

To Warren Cromartie, who claims that the "enthusiasm behind the Montreal Baseball Project is fuelled in part by the spirit of Gary Carter," said of his friend: "He was a Montrealer. He loved it here."[51]

In addition to Ahuntsic Park acquiring a new appellation, a few days later the section of Faillon Street closest to the Expos' original home at Jarry Park was also renamed in honour of "the Kid." In a brief elegy, the effusive baseball broadcaster Rodger Brulotte captured the essence of the man with flawless accuracy. "When we signed him," said Brulotte, "he became the image of the Expos, our gladiator; and our gladiator left us for another world. Gladiators aren't supposed to die."[52]

Photo: Gary Carter Foundation

Gary with wife Sandy Carter, son D.J. and daughters Kimmie and Christy

Nor, apparently, are baseball franchises. At least that's what one might infer from a Q&A session Tampa Bay owner Stuart Sternberg had with Jon Paul Morosi of FoxSports.com in mid-2013. Asked if major league baseball could work again in Montreal, Sternberg answered, "Yes, I know it can." When asked how he knew, Sternberg replied, "My gut. I was at Olympic Stadium the day after they got Bartolo Colon. I've been convinced – this is before I bought the (Rays) – that it would be an incredible place for baseball. That doesn't mean *my* baseball team, but *a* baseball team."

Sternberg was very precise on this topic. He is aware of the speculative chatter that has the Rays possibly moving to Montreal, even though his lease at Tropicana Field (capacity 34,078; average attendance 17,909, lowest in the American League for the past six years) has the team locked in until 2027. City officials, understandably, have shown little interest in letting the team off the hook. The situation is dire enough to have even caught the attention of Commissioner Selig. "We have a stadium problem there," he concedes. "There's no question about it."[53]

Sternberg said it is unlikely for a Montreal baseball revival to occur within the next five years or so. "In the next 20 years, yes," he said. He added: "You need a decent-to-good corporate base to have a successful baseball franchise."[54]

In late October 2013 the *Boston Globe* weighed in on the issue, noting that "now there's some real talk about the possibility that the Rays, for instance, could see Montreal as a real alternative if plans for a new stadium don't work out in the Tampa area." According to one American League official, just as cities like Washington and Seattle "have received second chances for franchises…Montreal would be a viable second-chance city given the financial opportunity there now. There have always been great baseball fans there. They never had a venue that was desirable for baseball and the economics never allowed them to keep the great talent they developed over the years."[55]

Thus, it was not at all by accident that when the ExposNation folks chose the date for their invasion of the Rogers Centre they zeroed in on July 20, a day when the Tampa Bay Rays, perhaps baseball's most vulnerable team – and one of its best – were in town.

About 1,000 Expos loyalists took part, all sharing a common purpose: to demonstrate to the larger baseball community that people in Montreal are still passionate about the game. "They want to continue to show that they miss the Expos, " said ExposNation founder Matthew Ross[56] "Our hope is that this event will lead to sponsorship in order for us to put on related events, to further the cause of bringing an MLB team back here," said Ross. "We want to start a season-ticket drive to present to prospective investors and the government."[57]

Less than a month later, out on the grounds of Jarry Park, there was another gathering of the expanding ExposNation clan, this time for what was billed a Pitch and Catch Rally with four former Expos – Derek Aucoin, Denis Boucher, Claude Raymond, and Steve Rogers. When asked about the prospects of the game making a comeback in Montreal, Rogers said: "I believe there is always a possibility…you have to start somewhere and the grassroots efforts of the ExposNation and the grassroots efforts of Warren Cromartie and his group to try for a franchise to return here…that's where you start."[58]

Then, in late September Cromartie, speaking for the Montreal Baseball Project, had more positive news to deliver – and this of a decidedly quantifiable nature. According to a Léger Marketing poll taken as part of the Montreal Board of Trade study into baseball's potential viability in the city, 69 per cent of the 1,589 respondents were "in favour of baseball's return to the city," with only 11 per cent being opposed. Forty per cent even said they were ready to purchase tickets at $40 each. Major League

Baseball is keeping an eye on the Cromartie project but to date has not reacted to any of its initiatives. This is not surprising because the Cromartie group is still at the stage of raising awareness and seeking some individual or company with deep pockets to help sustain the effort.

John McHale Jr., MLB's chief information officer and executive vice-president of administration and son of the late Expos executive John McHale Sr., has talked with Cromartie a few times. "I have known Cro for many, many years, decades, I guess, and he calls me from time to time simply to keep someone in our office aware of what he and his group are doing," McHale said in a recent email to Danny Gallagher. "We have no role in his activities, do not make suggestions, nor do we give advice other than to explain MLB rules."[59]

The first of these rules, McHale said, requires that "an owner wishing to explore relocation must, before discussing the possibility with anyone, secure permission from the Commissioner's office."

Cromartie's report on Léger Marketing's preliminary findings came on the heels of another major step in the pilgrimage toward baseball nirvana in Montreal, the return of a major league team to the city. Two teams actually.

Felipe Alou

On March 28 and 29, 2014, the Toronto Blue Jays will play two late pre-season games at Olympic Stadium against the New York Mets, in preparation for the opening of their regular schedules a few days later. There are also plans to hold a gala at the Queen Elizabeth Hotel with Felipe Alou and Claude Raymond as guests of honour.

Claude Raymond

Efforts are underway to bring most members of the 1994 team back to Montreal, to give fans a chance to say thank you – and perhaps even pay homage to the World Series they never won.

As Cromartie has underscored, however, this weekend event will be about much more than simple nostalgia. "I can't emphasize enough how critical it is for fans to show up for these two games...The whole world is going to be watching...I want all Expos fans. I want

ExposNation fans...to let the whole world know we want our baseball back here in the city."

Jack Todd is all for it. In fact, he has even suggested the 1994 players be honoured with a parade, one that "would allow the entire city to come out to thank the 1994 team." He calls it *The World Series Parade That Never Was – for the official unofficial champions of '94.* "Let's make it happen," he urges.

Todd's proposal not only makes sense, it also creates an appropriate opportunity for us, the authors, to conclude this modest attempt at chronicling the slow descent of the 1994 Expos from ecstasy to agony over a 10-year span. And happily for us, Todd has provided absolutely the most fitting words upon which to exit:

So you could say this parade has been a long time coming.
Not only does the 1994 team deserve a parade,
it would be a reaffirmation
of a truth
that becomes clearer with every passing month:
Major league baseball belongs in Montreal.

Danny Gallagher's 36 Expos Memories

1   First game in New York in 1969.

2   Rusty Staub running off the field to change his uniform because he had soiled his pants.

3   Bill Stoneman's first no-hitter, April 17, 1969.

4   Bill Stoneman's second no-no, Oct. 2, 1972.

5   Ross Grimsley's 20-win season in 1978, the only player to win that many games in franchise history.

6   Rusty Staub's electrifying, pinch-hit/at-bat moment before 59,260 fans in Montreal July 27, 1979 shortly after he returned to the team in a trade with Detroit.

7   Finishing two games shy of the Pirates after the last day in 1979 on Sept. 30, finishing with a 95-win season.

8   Mike Schmidt's home run off Stan Bahnsen Oct. 4, 1980, leaving the team just missing a playoff berth.

9   Tim Raines steals 71 bases in the strike-shortened 1981 season.

10   Rick Monday's home run off Steve Rogers Oct. 19, 1981, sealing the NL championship for the Dodgers.

11   Pitcher Bill Lee, the late Expos scout Terry Steeves and Montreal Gazette cartoonist Terry (Aislin) Mosher retreat to a bar on May 8, 1982 near Olympic Stadium after Lee took the day off to protest the release of his friend and teammate Rodney Scott.

12   Lee got released the day after Scott, never to play another game in the majors. He was only 37. Was he blackballed?

13   Pete Rose gets 4,000th hit off Jerry Koosman of the Phillies April 13, 1984.

14   Gary Carter traded to the Mets in December, 1984.

15   Workhorse/warhorse Steve Rogers spends entire career with the franchise.

16   Andre Dawson gallantly playing for so long on gimpy knees.

17   Buck Rodgers' managerial reign 1985-1991.

18   Randy Johnson started his fabulous career with the Expos before being traded to Seattle.

19   22-inning game Aug. 23, 1989 at Big O, Expos lose 1-0 to the Dodgers.

20   Talented 1989 team chokes, prompting majority owner Charles Bronfman to sell the team and resulting in Claude Brochu doing excellent work in cobbling together a consortium of owners.

21 Spotting Halle Berry sitting across from the visitors' clubhouse at the Big O in 1990, waiting for then boyfriend/husband David Justice of the Braves, not long after she was living in a homeless shelter waiting for her fabulous acting career to take off.

22 Part of Olympic Stadium collapses in 1991.

23 Dennis Martinez's perfect game July 28, 1991.

24 Felipe Alou's managerial reign 1992-2002.

25 The strong, quiet leadership of classy, genuine Tim Wallach, the only captain in Expos' history.

26 Having a few brews at the popular Crazy Horse bar in West Palm Beach across the road from the spring-training park.

27 Jeffrey Loria's awful attempt at being a team owner, resulting in the dream of a new downtown ballpark fading to dust.

28 Gary Carter inducted into Cooperstown in 2003, wearing an Expos' cap.

29 Jose Vidro's dream 2000 season: 200 hits, 101 runs, 51 doubles, .330 average, 97 RBI, the best campaign of any second baseman in franchise history.

30 Vladimir Guerrero falling short of a 40/40 season in 2002 with 39 homers and 40 steals.

31 The awful experiment of playing home games in Puerto Rico in 2003 and 2004.

32 Hopping on Montreal's subway train and getting off at the Pie 1X station at the ballpark.

33 Calling the Expos' Big O office at 514-253-3434 so many times.

34 Dave Van Horne's "Up, Up and Away" home-run call.

35 Jim Fanning. All class.

36 Last game in New York in 2004.

Afterword

Acknowledgments

It's been a three-year journey for Bill Young and me in putting this book together, and without the help of many people, it would not have been possible.

Close to 100 uniformed and non-uniformed people in baseball were interviewed for the book. I would like to thank the many people from the Expos' organization for agreeing to interviews. A special appreciation goes out to Marquis Grissom for consenting to a number of chats and helping me get through to other people. As it turns out, we caught up to 26 of the 32 players who donned an Expos' uniform in 1994.

It was a particular pleasure to talk with Commissioner Bud Selig, former MLBPA executive director Donald Fehr, Blue Jays president Paul Beeston, 1994 NL batting champ Tony Gwynn and 1994 AL batting champ Paul O'Neill. The same holds true for Derek Jeter, who was passed over by the Expos in the 1992 draft. Ditto for NL executives John Schuerholz, Stan Kasten and David Montgomery.

Thanks to Norm King of Ottawa for the time he took to look over portions of the manuscript and in search of typos and grammatical errors. Nephew Greg Gallagher and niece Lauren Gallagher were also key figures in the editing process.

We are also profoundly grateful to Carl Lemyre who put this book together for us. He is a man of great patience and understanding, both of which he drew on many times throughout the production of this book.

Most of all I wish to thank my brother Jim Gallagher of Ottawa for the hours he put in, poring over the book, making corrections and offering wise suggestions and perceptive comments. This book would have been the lesser without his keen participation. Nevertheless, for whatever errors remain, please note that the fault lies entirely with the authors.

My girlfriend Sherry Bacchus needs to be lauded for her love and understanding as I slipped away to the computer so many times to work on the manuscript.

Bill and I first produced the best-selling *Remembering the Montreal Expos*, which came out just before Christmas in 2005. It has been a pleasure working with Bill because of his eloquence, stellar prose and organizational skills. He put all the time and effort into laying out all of the chapters.

Danny Gallagher
Toronto
dannogallagher@rogers.com

I echo Danny's words. He and I are a team, proud to work together. This project is a labour of love, borne in part from our refusal to accept that the Expos are gone, and partly in the blind faith that baseball will return to Montreal once again – preferably in our lifetimes. We are deeply grateful for the many friends and colleagues who over the years offered their encouragement and suggestions - and we thank all of you who have read and enjoyed our earlier work, *Remembering the Montreal Expos*. We hope you find this book equally enjoyable.

I would be remiss if I did not say thank-you to my wife Sandra who so graciously stood by my side as this book was taking shape, no matter what the mood of the day...

Bill Young
Hudson, Quebec
williamyoung@videotron.ca

Who we are

Bill Young (left) and Danny Gallagher with Stephanie Myles, The Gazette's last baseball writer. Stephanie, who told it with compassion and a wry wit, kept the faith long after others had turned to other things – for that she is to be admired.

Danny Gallagher has been writing for media outlets since 1972, either full-time or as a freelancer. He has written extensively about the Montreal Expos since 1988 when he joined the staff of the *Montreal Daily News*. This is his third book on the franchise. *You Don't Forget Homers Like That* was published in 1997 and *Remembering the Montreal Expos* co-authored with Bill Young hit stores in late 2005. Gallagher has worked in retail for the Liquor Control Board of Ontario since 2000. He lives in Toronto with girlfriend Sherry Bacchus.

Bill Young of Hudson, Quebec, a retired CEPGP (community college) administrator and founding director of the historic Greenwood Centre for Living History in Hudson is currently a free-lance writer and baseball historian. In addition to a column on topics of community interest that appears monthly in *The Gazette's West Island Edition*, he also writes periodically for the Quebec Heritage News, SABR-International, local publications and the SABR-Quebec website. *Remembering the Montreal Expos*, co-authored with Danny Gallagher, was his first book. In 2012 he was awarded the Queen's Diamond Jubilee medal for community service.

End-notes

Prologue

1 *WARREN GILES*, president of the National League, spoke these words on August 14, 1968 at Montreal's Windsor Hotel upon officially receiving Montreal's first franchise payment from owner Charles Bronfman and his six-man group of sponsors. (*Montreal Gazette*, August 15, 1968 and reprinted in that same paper August 20, 2011)

2 The off-day had provided Dodgers pitching sensation Fernando Valenzuela with sufficient rest to enable him to step in as L.A.'s starting pitcher. His opponent on the mound for the Expos was Ray Burris. Both men pitched masterfully in the penetrating chill of an unforgiving open ballpark, and after eight innings the game was all tied, 1–1.

   Unexpectedly, Montreal manager Jim Fanning, who had recently replaced a summarily fired Dick Williams as Expos field boss, and who was new to the role, decided to pull Burris and send in Steve Rogers to open the ninth. Rogers, the ace of the pitching staff, had been lights out during the postseason but had never before appeared in relief. Nevertheless, in the fading glow of a gloomy Monday afternoon he quickly retired the first two batters he faced, Steve Garvey and Ron Cey. His final hurdle, Rick Monday, managed to drive the ball toward right-centre and beyond the reach of centre fielder Andre Dawson. It hung, for what seemed like forever in the heavy dampness, before it soared above the twelve-foot wall and then plummeted out beyond the black and for-bidding night deep into the bleachers, and deeper into the most fearful night-mare of our times. The Dodgers had won. They then went on to win the World Series as well. Blue Monday? Yes, Expos fans know all about Blue Monday.

3 JOE BTFSPIK was a character created by legendary cartoonist Al Capp for his Li'l Abner comic strip. A sad-eyed little man who walked through life with a rain cloud hanging just above his head, he was "the world's worst jinx, bringing disastrous misfortune to everyone around him." His caricature, not to mention his impossible-to-pronounce name, came to represent the symbol of jinxes and misfortune for generations of Li'l Abner followers into the 1970s. (http://en.wikipedia.org/wiki/Li'l_Abner#Main_characters)

4 Richard Sandomir, "Sotomayor's baseball ruling lingers 14 years later," *New York Times*, May 26, 2009.

5 Ibid.

Beginnings

1   Claude Brochu, with Daniel Poulin and Mario Bolduc, *MY TURN AT BAT: The Sad Saga of the Expos* (Translated from, "La saga des Expos" by Stephanie Myles) (Toronto: ECW Press, 2002), p. 26.

2   Biographical Information, "Charles Bronfman," Baseball reference.com.

3   Jerome Holtzman, "Expos owner Bronfman would be sorely missed," *Chicago Tribune*, February 4, 1990.

4   Ibid.

5   Ibid.

6   Steve Marcus, "Gary Carter and the trade that won the Mets a World Series," *Long Island Newsday*, February 16, 2012.

7   Danny Gallagher, "From Jamestown to Montreal to HOF, Carter recalled by Fanning," Canadian Baseball Network: Sportsnet, February 19, 2012. http://www.canadianbaseballnetwork.com/articles/from-jamestown-to-montreal-to-cooerstown-carter-recalled-by-fanning/

8   Jerome Holtzman, Ibid.

9   Ibid.

10 Claude Brochu, Ibid.

11 Biographical Information, "Charles Bronfman," Baseball reference.com

12 Ibid.

13 John Helyar, <u>Lords of the Realm: The Real History of Baseball</u>. (New York: Random House; Ballantine Books, 1995.), p. 488.

14 Gary Hughes: Telephone conversation with Danny Gallagher, October 15, 2012.

15 Mike Kozak: Interview with Danny Gallagher, 2012.

16 Danny Gallagher recalls working with Monique Giroux when he covered the Expos. He considered her cooperative, helpful and friendly, the perfect person in the perfect position.

Deep Despair

1   http://en.wikipedia.org/wiki/Montreal_Expos#1990s).

2   Conversation with Bill Young, Bradenton, FL, April 12, 2011.

3   Gallagher, Danny, with Bill Young, *Remembering the Montreal Expos* (Toronto: Scoop Press, 2005), p. 161.

4   http://www.baseballlibrary.com/ballplayers/player.php?name=Buck_Rodgers_1938&page=chronology.

5   "Roland Hemond Named Recipient of Buck O'Neil Award," February 11, 2011. http://cooperstownchamber.wordpress.com/2011/02/22/roland-hemond-named-recipient-of-buck-oneil-award/

6   Bill Young, "Canadian Hall of Fame Inductions: Cormier and Melvin, Part I," July 11, 2012. http://seamheads.com/2012/07/11/canadian-hall-of-fame-inductions-cormier-and-melville/.

7   Olympic Stadium (Montreal) http://en.wikipedia.org/wiki/Olympic_Stadium_(Montreal).

8   Gary Hughes: Telephone conversation with Danny Gallagher, July 12, 2012.

Felipe Returns

1   Ecclesiastes 3:1.

2   http://en.wikipedia.org/wiki/1992_Los_Angeles_riots.

3   Scott Miller, "Expos forced to wait as L.A. violence grows," *Los Angeles Times*, May 1, 1992.

4   Curt Smith, Pull Up a Chair: The Vin Scully Story (Washington, DC: Potomac Books, Inc. 2010), p. 183.

5   Miller, Ibid.

6   Claire Smith, "Baseball: Dodgers are trying to put turmoil behind them," *New York Times*, May 6, 1992.

7   Etienne Bouchard, "Alou relives Expos days," QMI Agency, May 23, 2012.

8   Matthew Ross, "Alou's Expos legacy..." *Montreal Gazette*, April 1, 2012.

9   Ross Newhan, "Felipe Alou to Guide the Expos: Baseball: He replaces Runnells and becomes the first major league manager from Dominican Republic," *Los Angeles Times*, May 23, 1992.

10 Mark Armour, "Felipe Alou," *The Baseball Research Journal*, Vol. 42, Spring 2013, Number 1, from Michael Farber, "Diamond Heirs," *Sports Illustrated*, June 19, 1985.

11 Newhan, Ibid.

12 Claude Brochu: Conversation with Bill Young, October 12, 2011.

13 These and all statistical information courtesy of retrosheet.com/.

14 Stu Cowan, "Memories of Tim Wallach and the Expos," Stu on Sports (*Montreal Gazette* Blogs), September 14, 2012... http://blogs.montrealgazette.com/2012/09/14/memories-of-tim-wallach-and-the-expos/.

15 Ibid.

16 Kevin Malone: Telephone interview with Danny Gallagher.

17 All comments from Kevin Malone based on telephone interview with Danny Gallagher.

18 Paul Morgan, *Kalamazoo Gazette*, in conversation with Danny Gallagher, summer 2012.

19 Derek Jeter: Conversation with Danny Gallagher, May 2012.

20 Bill Young, "The search for joy on Opening Day," *Montreal Gazette West Island Supplement*, April 4, 2012.

21 Danny Gallagher, "From Jamestown to Montreal to HOF: Carter Recalled by Fanning," Ibid.

22 Gary Carter: Interview with Danny Gallagher, summer 1992.

23 Danny Gallagher, Ibid.

24 Ibid.

25 Kirk Rueter: Telephone interview with Danny Gallagher, 2012.

26 Felipe Alou: Interview with Danny Gallagher, 2012.

27 Dan Duquette: Interview with Danny Gallagher, March 7, 2013.

28 John Wetteland: Telephone interview with Danny Gallagher, 2012.

29 Montreal Expos Media Guide '93, Montreal Baseball Club, Inc., Montreal, 1992.

30 Dan Duquette, Ibid.

31 Mel Rojas: Telephone interview with Danny Gallagher, 2012.

32 Tim Spehr: Telephone interview with Danny Gallagher, 2012.

33 Ibid.

34 Gil Heredia: Telephone interview with Danny Gallagher, 2012.

35 Danny Gallagher, Article on John Wetteland, *the Globe and Mail*, Toronto, June 1996.

36 John Wetteland: Conversation with Danny Gallagher, March, 2012.

37 Mitch Melnick: Telephone interview with Danny Gallagher, 2012.

Fly Me to the Moon

1 Leonard Cohen, <u>Beautiful Losers,</u> (McClelland and Stewart Ltd., Toronto, 1966).

2 Bill Marks, "The American passion," *The Sporting News*, April 12, 1993, pp. 12-13.

3 Michael Bowker, "The Loudest Cheer," http://lafargue.tripod.com/pride.htm.

4 Jonah Keri, "Gary Carter and the Meaning of Memories," Friday, February 17, 2012, 2:10:24 PM I http://jonahkeri.com/tag/montreal-expos/feed/.

5 vhttp://en.wikipedia.org/wiki/Curtis_Pride.

6 Jeff Blair, *The Sporting News*, January 11, 1993, p. 30.

7 Jeff Blair, *The Sporting News*, February 8, 1993, p. 30.

8 Jeff Blair, *The Sporting News*, February 22, 1993, p. 18.

9 Jeff Blair, *The Sporting News*, July 26, 1993, p. 18.

10 Jeff Blair, *The Sporting News*, August 2, 1993, p. 18.

11 Jeff Blair, *The Sporting News*, August 30, 1993, p. 17.

12 Jeff Blair, *The Sporting News*, September 13, 1993, p. 15.

13 Ibid.

14 Ibid.

15 March 20, 1994 I FROM INQUIRER WIRE SERVICES, Philly.com/.

16 September 19, 1993 , Ibid.

17 Jeff Blair, *The Sporting News*, October 8, 1993, p. 33.

18 Ibid.

19 Peter Pascarelli, "Baseball Report," *The Sporting News*, p. 12.

20 Jeff Blair, *The Sporting News*, October 25, 1993, p. 22.

21 Ibid.

22 Jeff Blair, *The Sporting News*, November 1, 1993, p. 23.

23 Ibid.

24 Peter Pascarelli, "DeShields Derailed," *The Sporting News*, November 29, 1993, p. 34.

25 Ibid.

26 Claude Brochu, with Daniel Poplin and Mario Bolduc, *My Turn at Bat: The Sad Saga of the Expos*, pp. 78-80.

27 Jeff Blair, *The Sporting News*, December 6, 1993, p. 40.

28 Claude Brochu, in "Triumph and Tragedy: The 1994 Expos," a film produced by Major League Baseball Productions, 2010.

29 George Verrell, *The Sporting News*, December 27, 1993, p. 30.

30 Jeff Blair, *The Sporting News*, December 6, 1993, p. 40.

31 Felipe Alou: Telephone interview with Danny Gallagher.

32 David Jauss: Telephone interview with Danny Gallagher.

33 Dan Duquette: Interview with Danny Gallagher, March 2013.

34 Marquis Grissom: Telephone interview with Danny Gallagher.

35 Darrin Fletcher: Conversation with Danny Gallagher, spring 2011.

36 Tom Treblehorn: Telephone interview with Danny Gallagher.

37 Kirk Rueter: Telephone interview with Danny Gallagher, May 2012.

38 Rich Griffin, *Expos Guide 1994*, (Montreal: Montreal Expos Baseball Club, Monique Giroux, editor).

39 Butch Henry: Telephone interview with Danny Gallagher, May 2012.

40 Bill Young, "Letters from Quebec: The Kirk Rueter revelation," November 18, 2010, seamheads.com.

41 Danny Gallagher, "Expos' prize prospect swings a powerful bat," Toronto *Globe and Mail*, March 30, 1993.

42 Ibid.

43 Danny Gallagher: Unless otherwise noted in the footnotes, all quotes in the Cliff Floyd story are drawn from interviews conducted by Danny Gallagher (2010-2012).

44 Rich Griffin, Ibid.

45 Tim Scott: Telephone interview with Danny Gallagher, May 2011.

46 See: http://www.youtube.com/watch?v=bFX92ALqxlk.

47 On March 8, 2012, Cliff Floyd and Danny Gallagher enjoyed breakfast together at the Turnberry Isle resort near Miami.

48 Ibid.

49 Denis Boucher: Telephone interviews with Danny Gallagher, November and December 2012.

50 Jeff Blair, *The Sporting News*, September 13, 1993, p. 15.

51 Note: all statistical information courtesy of Baseball-reference.com; Retrosheet.org and baseball-almanac.org.

52 Dennis Martinez: Conversation with Danny Gallagher, Spring, 2012.

53 Jeff Blair, "Martinez remembers El Perfecto 'like it was today,'" Toronto *Globe and Mail*, July 26, 2011.

54 Delino DeShields: Conference Call, November 17, 1993.

55 *Montreal Gazette*, November 14, 1993.

56 Dan Duquette: Interview with Danny Gallagher, March 2013.

57 Claude Brochu, *My Turn at Bat: The Sad Saga of the Expos*, pp. 78-80.

58 Dan Duquette: Ibid.

59 Fred Claire and Steve Springer, My 30 Years in Baseball (Internet Publishing Company), www.sportspublishinb LLC 2004), p. 131.

60 Mitch Melnick, in "Triumph and Tragedy: The 1994 Expos," a film produced by Major League Baseball Productions, 2010.

61 Ibid.

62 Fred Claire: Telephone interview with Danny Gallagher, 2011.

63 Pedro Martinez: Interview with Danny Gallagher, Montreal, March 2011.

The Gathering Storm

1   Stephen Omes, "Whatever happened to Chaos Theory?" *Discover Magazine*, April 4, 2007 (internet: http://discovermagazine.com/2007/apr/whatever-happened-to-chaos-theory).

2   Tobias J. Moskowitz and L. Jon Wertheim, <u>Scorecasting: The Hidden Influences Behind How Sports are Played and Games are Won</u> (New York: Crown Archetype, 2011), p. 99.

3   Richard Goldstein, "Marvin Miller, union leader who changed baseball dies at 95," *New York Times*, September 12, 2007.

4   Malcolm Gladwell, in *The New Yorker*, Quoted in "Marvin Miller, union leader who changed baseball dies at 95," Richard Goldstein, *New York Times*, September 12, 2007.

5   Ben Reiter, "Marvin Miller, 1917-2012," *Sports Illustrated*, December 10, 2012, p. 42.

6   Allen Barra, "Running Scared: Once again, one of baseball's greatest is kept from Cooperstown," *The Village Voice*, as quoted in the Wikipedia entry on Marvin Miller.

7   William Shakespeare, *Julius Caesar*, Act I, Scene ii.

8   Ben Reiter, Ibid.

9   *Steve O's Baseball Umpire Resources*, "Steve O's Menu: Baseball Work Stoppages," http://www.stevetheump.com/baseball_stoppages.htm.

10 John Helyar, Ibid., p. 23.

11 Ibid., p. 24.

12 Buzzie Bavasi and Jack Olsen, "The Great Hold-out," *Sports Illustrated* SI Vault, May 15, 1967.
(http://sportsillustrated.cnn.com/vault/article/magazine/MAG1079835/index.htm)

13 Ibid.

14 Helyar, Ibid., p. 119.

15 Ibid., p. 122.

16 *Steve O's Baseball Umpire Resources*, Ibid.

17 Helyar, Ibid., p. 129.

18 *Steve O's Baseball Umpire Resource*, Ibid.

19 Helyar, Ibid., p. 122.

20 http://en.wikipedia.org/wiki/Major_League_Baseball_Players_Association.

21 Helyar. Ibid., p. 167.

22 John Gaherin, "Cot's Baseball Contracts ; http://mlbcontracts.blogspot.com/.

23 Helyar, Ibid., p. 179.

24 Ibid., p. 180.

25 *Steve O's Baseball Umpire Resources*, Ibid.

26 Gussie Busch, 1976 "Cot's Baseball Contracts, Ibid.

27 Helyar, Ibid., p. 210.

28 Ibid., p. 212.

29 Ibid., p. 224.

30 Ibid.

31 Ibid., p. 228.

32 Ibid., p. 234.

33 Ibid., p. 236.

34 *Steve O's Baseball Umpire Resources*, Ibid.

35 Helyar, Ibid., p. 294.

36 Ibid., p. 284.

37 http://www.baseball-reference.com/bullpen/1981_strike.

38 http://keepingscore.blogs.time.com/2011/03/04/top-10-u-s-sports-strikes-and-lockouts/slide/the-1981-baseball-strike/#the-1981-baseball-strike.

39 Helyar, Ibid., p. 307.

40 A. Bartlett Giamatti, "Men of Baseball, Lend an Ear," *New York Times*, June 16, 1981, p. 19.

41 Helyar, Ibid., p. 307.

42 Ibid., p. 308.

43 Ibid.

44 Murray A. Clemens, Q.C., "Final Offer Arbitration: Baseball, Boxcars and Beyond," Materials prepared for the Continuing Legal Education Society of British Columbia, 2011.P. 2.2.3 http://www.cle.bc.ca/PracticePoints/REAL/11-FinalOfferArbitration.pdf.

45 Mike Norris: pitcher for the A's, "Cot's Baseball Contracts, Ibid.

46 Helyar, Ibid., p. 325.

47 Ball Park Figures? Better Believe It: Thanks to Arbitration, Tim Raines of the Expos is the 36th million-dollar-a-year man in baseball," *Sports Illustrated*, March 4. 1985, in SI Vault. (http://sportsillustrated.cnn.com/vault/article/magazine/MAG1119191/2/index.htm)

48 Helyar, Ibid., p. 325.

49 Ball Park Figures? Better Believe It: Ibid.

51 Helyar, Ibid., pp. 327-328.

52 Ibid.

53 Ibid., p. 329.

54 *Time* magazine, January 7, 1985.

55 Helyar Ibid., p. 351.

56 *Steve O's Baseball Umpire Resources*, Ibid.

57 Helyar, Ibid., p. 355.

58 Ibid., p. 354.

59 Ibid., p. 356.

60 Ibid., p. 362.

61 Ibid., p. 365.

62 Murray Chase, "Baseball owners lose arbitration on free agents…ruling backs players on collusion charges against teams in '85," *New York Times*, September 22, 1987.

63 Ibid.

64 Mitch Melnick, "Melnick in the Afternoon," on TSN Radio 990, Montreal, June 19, 2012.

65 Helyar, Ibid., p. 364.

66 Ibid., p. 365.

67 Murray Chase, Ibid.

68 Helyar, Ibid., pp. 373-4.

69 Ibid., p. 375.

70 Retrosheet: http://www.retrosheet.org/.

71 Helyar, Ibid., p. 376.

72 Mitch Melnick, "Carter was the face of the Expos," *New York Times News Service*, February 16, 2012.

73 Helyar, Ibid., p. 377.

74 Ibid., p. 380.

75 Helyar, Ibid., pp. 381-82.

76 Ibid., pp. 375-76.

77 Retrosheet: http://www.baseball-reference.com/players/s/smithbr01.shtml.

78 Paul Dickson, Baseball's Greatest Quotations: An Illustrated Treasury of Baseball Quotations and Historical Lore. (New York: Collins Publishers, 2008), p. 200.

79 Helyar, Ibid., p. 421.

80 Charles Siebert, "Baseball's Renaissance Man: Bart Giamatti," *New York Times*, September 4, 1989.

81 Ibid.

82 Helyar, Ibid., p. 421.

83 *The News and Courier*, Charleston, South Carolina, November 29, 1989, p. 13d.

84 Bob Verdi, "Sign Langston this time Cubs," *Chicago Tribune*, September 12, 1989.

85 Ibid.

86 Retrosheet: http://www.baseball-reference.com/players/s/smithbr01.shtml

87 Mark Landsbaum, "Langston finds seller's market," *Los Angeles Times*, December 2, 1989.

88 Random Retro Baseball Player: Pascual Perez, posted by Matt Clapp, 1/28/1009 at http://www.sharapovasthigh.com/2009/01/random-retro-baseball-player-pascual.html.

89 *The News and Courier*, Ibid.

90 Helyar, Ibid., p. 441.

91 Ibid.

92 Ibid., p. 442.

93 Ibid., p. 452.

94 *Steve O's Baseball Umpire Resources*, Ibid.

95 Helyar, Ibid., p. 452.

Camelot

1 **Camelot** is a musical by Alan Jay Lerner (book and lyrics) and Frederick Loewe (music). It is based on the King Arthur legend as adapted from the T. H. White tetralogy novel, *The Once and Future King*. Original production 1960.

2 *THE TENTH INNING*, a documentary film, directed by Ken Burns and Lynn Novick and presented in the Fall 2010 as a new chapter in their nine-part documentary film series, *BASEBALL* (1994). *THE TENTH INNING* is a production of Florentine Films and WETA, Washington, DC.

3 Jeff Blair, *The Sporting News*, January 17, 1994, p. 31.

4 Jeff Blair, *The Sporting News*, December 20, 1993, p. 35.

5 John Schuerholz: Telephone interview with Danny Gallagher, Spring 2012.

6 Jeff Blair, *The Sporting News*, January 24, 1994, p. 35.

7 Jeff Blair, Ibid.

8 Claude Brochu, e-mail exchange with Bill Young, October 12, 2012.

9 Jeff Blair, *The Sporting News*, March 14, 1994, p. 22.

10 Peter Pascarelli, "A central location is just what the Indians needed," *The Sporting News*, January 31, 1994, p. 31.

11 Peter Pascarelli, "Duquette will change Boston's approach," *The Sporting News*, February 14, 1994, p. 22.

12 Danny Gallagher, "Poor season could put Montreal Expos on life-support," *The Globe and Mail*, April 4, 1994.

13 Jeff Blair, *The Sporting News*, March 14, 1994, p. 22.

14 Jeff Blair, *The Sporting News*, April 4, 1994, p. 66.

15 The information used here was obtained free of charge from and is copyrighted by Retrosheet. Interested parties may contact Retrosheet at "www.retrosheet.org."

16 Baseball Almanac: 1994 All-Star Game: http://www.baseball-almanac.com/asg-box/yr1994as.shtml.

17 *Montreal Gazette*, August 1, 1994.

18 "Six days on the road," by Earl Green and Carl Montgomery, made famous by country singer Dave Dudley (1963).

19 John Schuerholz: Telephone interview with Danny Gallagher, spring 2012.

20 Marquis Grissom: Telephone interview with Danny Gallagher, spring 2012.

21 Mitch Melnick: Telephone interview with Danny Gallagher, October 7, 2012.

22 Roland Hemond: Telephone interview with Danny Gallagher, October 1, 2012.

23 Lindsay Applebaum, "Davey Johnson on why the Nats can't date porn stars," DC Blog, August 21, 2013.

24 Darrin Fletcher: Conversation with Danny Gallagher, 2012.

25 Jacques Doucet: Conversation with Danny Gallagher, 2013.

26 Dave Van Horne: Conversation with Danny Gallagher, 2012.

27 Felipe Alou: Conversation with Danny Gallagher, 2012.

28 Mike Kozak: Conversation with Danny Gallagher, 2012.

29 Expos Media Guide, 1994.

30 Erik Ostling: Conversation with Danny Gallagher, 2011.

31 Tony Gwynn: Conversation with Danny Gallagher, 2012.

32 Andre Dawson: Conversation with Danny Gallagher, 2012.

33 Sean Berry: Conversation with Danny Gallagher, 2012.

34 Freddie Benavides: Conversation with Danny Gallagher, July 2011.

35 Tim Scott: Telephone interview with Danny Gallagher, 2012.

36 Ibid.

37 Gil Heredia: Interview with Danny Gallagher, 2013.

38 Marquis Grissom: Telephone interview with Danny Gallagher, 2012.

39 Darrin Fletcher: Interview with Danny Gallagher, 2012.

40 Unless otherwise noted, all quotes drawn from conversations between Danny Gallagher and the individuals cited.

The Good, the Bad and the Ugly

1   "The Good, the Bad and the Ugly," Film by Sergio Leone in which Clint Eastwood plays the character Blondie.
2   Barbara W. Tuchman ,The Guns of August. (New York: The Macmillan Company, 1962).
3   Baseball Reference.com/ BR Bullpen – 1994 Philadelphia Phillies.
4   Larry Walker: Conversation with Bill Young, October 25, 2012.
5   Bill Young, "LETTERS FROM QUEBEC: The Day the 1994 Expos Came Back to Town," Seamheads.com, March 30, 2011.
6   Fred Claire with Steve Springer, Fred Claire: My 30 Years in Baseball. Ibid. p. 112.
7   Ibid.
8   Ibid., p. 113.
9   George Will, "*Millionaires and billionaires*," from the 10th Inning, a film by Ken Burns first televised September 28, 2010. The latest chapter of the seminal Burns work, entitled "Baseball."
10 John Helyar, Lords of the Realm: The Real History of Baseball, p. 452.
11 Ibid., p. 488.
12 Ibid.
13 Ibid., p. 492.
14 Ibid., p. 506 .
15 *King James Version of the Bible*,The Revelation of St. John the Divine, Chapter 6, verses 1-8.
16 Bud Selig, "*Millionaires and billionaires*," from the 10th Inning, a film by Ken Burns first televised Sept ember 28, 2010. The latest chapter of the seminal Burns work, entitled "Baseball."
17 John Helyar, Ibid., p. 553.
18 Ibid., p. 533.
19 Ibid., p. 555.
20 Ibid., p. 569.
21 Stan Kasten: Exclusive telephone interview with Danny Gallagher, July 7, 2012.
22 Helyar, Ibid., pp. 555-556.
23 Ibid., p. 557.
24 Ibid. p. 557.
25 Ibid., p. 564.
26 Ibid., p. 566.
27 Ibid., p. 577.
28 Ibid.
29 Ibid., p. 581.
30 Ibid., p. 585.
31 Ibid., p. 590.
32 Wikipedia, http://www.google.ca/search?q=budweiser horses.
33 Helyar, Ibid., p. 592.
34 Ibid., p. 594.
35 Ibid., p. 595.
36 Donald Fehr, "Cot's Baseball Contacts, Ibid.

37 Andrew Zimbalist, *Millionaires and billionaires*," Ibid.
38 Donald Fehr, *Millionaires and billionaires*," Ibid.
39 Helyar, Ibid., p. 595.
40 Tom Glavine, *"Millionaires and billionaires*," Ibid.
41 Helyar, Ibid., p. 596.
42 Narrator, *"Millionaires and billionaires*, Ibid.
43 Richard Ravitch, *"Millionaires and billionaires*," Ibid.
44 Donald Fehr, *"Millionaires and billionaires*," Ibid.
45 Jim Bouton, "Cot's Baseball Contacts," Ibid.
46 Helyar, Ibid., p. 603.
47 John Thorn, *"Millionaires and billionaires*," Ibid.
48 Stan Kasten: Telephone interview with Danny Gallagher, July 7, 2012.
49 Ibid.
50 Unless otherwise noted, all quotes in this section are drawn from telephone conversations that Danny Gallagher had with Messrs. Ravitch, Manfred and Weiner, in April 2012.
52 Michael Weiner, "Making this the right place and the right time," *Sports Illustrated*, May 6, 2012.
53 Denis Boucher: Conversation with Danny Gallagher, 2012.
54 Tim Spehr: Conversation with Danny Gallagher.
55 Jeff Fassero: Conversation with Danny Gallagher, 2011.
56 Danny Gallagher: Conversation with Dave Van Horne, 2012.
57 Mark Routtenberg: Conversation with Bill Young, September 7, 2011.
58 Claude Delorme: Conversation with Danny Gallagher, September 2012.
59 Stephanie Myles, "'The best city I ever played in' – Red Sox ace," Ibid.
60 Howard Bryant, Ibid., p. 26.
61 Paul O'Neill: Conversation with Danny Gallagher, December 2012.
62 Duane Ward: Conversation with Danny Gallagher, June 2012.

No Joy in Mudville

1 Howard Bryant, Ibid., p. 26.
2 Claire, Fred with Steve Springer. Fred Claire, Ibid.
3 All quotations in this section, unless otherwise noted, are drawn from conversation between the individual cited and Danny Gallagher in 2011, 2012 or 2013.
4 Mark Maske, "After the strike, baseball's disgusted fans decide to strike back," *The Washington Post*, April 30, 1995.
5 Paul Dickson, Baseball's Greatest Quotations: An Illustrated Treasury of Baseball Quotations and Historical Lore (New York: Collins Publishers, 2008), p. 170.
6 Paul O'Neill: Conversation with Danny Gallagher.
7 Howard Bryant, Ibid., p. 44.
8 Ibid., p. 45.
9 Pogo (a possum who inhabited the Okefenokee Swamp) was the name of a popular comic strip created by Walt Kelly and distributed by the Post-Hall Syndicate. It ran regularly in newspapers from 1949 to 1975. A distinguishing

characteristic was its willingness to engage in political and social satire at a time when such things were often frowned upon, or even censored.

10 Bud Selig: Conversation with Danny Gallagher, November 2012.
11 David Montgomery: Conversation with Danny Gallagher, April 2012.
12 Ibid.
13 Donald Fehr: Conversation with Danny Gallagher, spring 2013.
14 *Montreal Gazette*, September 15, 1994.
15 Unless otherwise noted, all quotations in this chapter are drawn from conversations Danny Gallagher had with the individuals cited.
16 Kirk Rueter: Conversation with Danny Gallagher, April 2012.
17 Mark Routtenberg: Conversation with Bill Young.
18 All statistical information courtesy of Baseball-Reference.com and Retrosheet.org.
19 "Expos' G.M. Decides to Go," *New York Times*, October 10, 1995.
20 Stephanie Myles, "'The best city I ever played in – Red Sox ace,'" Ibid.
21 Claude Brochu: All quotations in this section, unless otherwise noted, are drawn from conversations between Claude Brochu and Bill Young in 2011-2012.
22 Bryant, Ibid., p. 29.
23 Claude Brochu, with Daniel Poulin and Mario Bolduc, p. 86
24 Howard Bryant, Ibid., p. 46.
25 Claude Brochu: Conversation with Bill Young, October 12, 2011.
26 Rodger Brulotte: Conversation with Danny Gallagher, 2011.
27 Rodger Brulotte and others: Conversation with Danny Gallagher, 2011.
28 Larry Walker: Conversation with Bill Young, October 25, 2012.
29 Ibid.
30 Ibid.
31 Jacques Doucet et Marc Robitaille, *Il était une fois les Expos*[28](*Montréal, Québec: Hurtubise, 2011*).
32 Jacques Doucet: Telephone interview with Danny Gallagher, June 8, 2012.
33 [1] Expos Media Guide, 1994.
34 All Freddie Benavides comments in this chapter from conversations with Danny Gallagher, July 2011.
35 Claude Delorme: Telephone interview with Danny Gallagher, August 9, 2011.
36 Neither Griffin nor Perkins would comment for this book.
37 Erik Ostling: Conversation with Danny Gallagher, spring 2012.
38 Tony Gwynn: Unless otherwise noted, all comments in this chapter drawn from a telephone conversation with Danny Gallagher, June 28, 2012.
39 "Tony Gwynn recorded his 3,000th hit in Montreal," by Cooperstowners in Canada.
40 Bryant, Ibid., p. 65.
41 Bill Clinton in *US News & World Report* (February 6, 1995), as quoted in Paul Dickson, Baseball's Greatest Quotations: An Illustrated Treasury of Baseball Quotations and Historical Lore (New York: Collins Publishers, 2008), p. 108.
42 Tim Kurkjian, in ESPN *The Magazine* (August 2002) in Baseball Almanac.
43 Ross Newman, "*Strike throws curve into start of spring training: Baseball:* Both sides express mixed emotions. Teams of replacement players are ready to take to the field," *Los Angeles Times*, February 16, 1995.

44 Ibid.

45 Ibid.

46 1994–95 Major League Baseball strike, from Wikipedia, the free encyclopedia.

47 Richard Sandomir, "Sotomayor's baseball ruling lingers, 14 years later," *New York Times*, May 26, 2009.

48 Ibid.

49 Sean Gregory, "How Sotomayor 'Saved' Baseball", *Time* magazine, May 26, 2009.

51 Sandomir, Ibid.

52 Wikipedia.

53 Sandomir, Ibid.

54 Ibid.

55 Ibid.

56 John Thorn, speaking on the documentary, *Millionaires vs. Billionaires*, from "The Tenth Inning."

57 1994-1995 Major League Baseball strike , from Wikipedia, the free encyclopedia.

58 Mike Barnicle, speaking on the documentary, *Millionaires vs. Billionaires*, from "The Tenth Inning."

Are the Good Times Really Over for Good?

1   Mark Routtenberg: Conversation with Bill Young, September 7, 2011.

2   Ibid.

3   Selena Roberts, *Millionaires vs. Billionaires*, Ibid.

4   Stephanie Myles, "Darkest day in Montreal," *Montreal Gazette*, August 12, 2004.

5   Claude Brochu: Conversation with Bill Young, October 11, 2011.

6   Ibid.

7   Matthew Ross, "Brochu sticks to his guns," *Montreal Gazette*, August 4, 2011.

8   Claude Brochu, MY TURN AT BAT: The Sad Saga of the Expos, p. 159.

9   Ibid.

10 Mark Routtenberg: Ibid.

11 http://www.ballparks.com/baseball/national/monbpk.htm.

12 Matthew Ross, Ibid.

13 Claude Brochu, Ibid., p. 211.

14 Mark Routtenberg, Ibid.

15 Ibid.

16 Monique Chibok: Conversation with Danny Gallagher, spring 2011.

17 Ibid.

18 Matthew Ross, Ibid.

19 Mark Routtenberg, Ibid.

20 Claude Brochu, Ibid., pp. 169-170.

21 Ibid., pp. 259-260.

22 Mark Routtenberg, Ibid.

23 Stephanie Myles, Ibid.

24 Brochu, Claude, Ibid., p. 211.

25 Stephanie Myles, "Van Horne back for 'final final,'" *Montreal Gazette*, September 28, 2004.

26 Claude Brochu, Ibid., p. 135.

27 Stephanie Myles, "'The best city I ever played in:' Red Sox ace," Ibid., August 12, 2004.

28 Jack Todd, "Expos flashing the entrance sign," *Montreal Gazette*, December 21, 1999.

29 Mark Routtenberg, Ibid.

30 Matthew Ross, Ibid.

31 Claude Brochu, Ibid., pp. 214-215.

32 "Alou is fired by Montreal," *Reading Times and Reading News*, June 1, 2001.

33 Bill Bavasi, "Cot's Baseball Contacts," Ibid.

34 Farid Rushdi, "How Jeffrey Loria destroyed the Montreal Expos/Washington Nationals," *Bleacher Report*, October 20, 2009.

Death by a Thousand Cuts

1 Michael Farber, whose comments were first made in 2000 and resurrected years later by Wayne Scanlan in a *Montreal Gazette* article (April 1, 2011). Scanlan then added the following observation: "As usual, Michael Farber of *Sports Illustrated* put it best, long before the team was gone, when he wrote that the pending Expos obit was bound to get it wrong, blaming the fans in Montreal."

2 Dave Gross, "League ownership has spotty pedigree," *National Post*, August 28, 2009.

3 Sean Gordon, "Fans to Team: Love Ya," *Montreal Gazette*, April 3, 2004.

4 Stephanie Myles, "Fans go home happy," *Montreal Gazette*, April 3, 2002.

5 Bill Young, letter to his brother, April 3, 2002.

6 Stephanie Myles, *Montreal Gazette*, September 30, 2004.

7 Jeff Blair, "Ex-owners of Expos go to court over sale," *The Globe and Mail*, July 8, 2002.

8 Sean Gordon, "Suit unlikely to keep Expos here," *Montreal Gazette*, July 18, 2002.

9 Ian MacDonald, "One for the scrapbook," *Montreal Gazette*, August 20, 2002.

10 Wikipedia.

11 Stephanie Myles, "40-40 quest is futile," *Montreal Gazette*, September 30, 2002.

12 Jack Todd, "Umpires rob Vlad of 40th," *Montreal Gazette*, September 30, 2002.

13 SI.com, "'Los Expos' to play 22 games in San Juan next season," Spanning the globe, November 20, 2002.

14 Bill Brownstein, "Neglected team suddenly hot," *Montreal Gazette*, August 29, 2003.

15 Wikipedia.

16 Stephanie Myles, "Baseball brass bailed on Expos," *Montreal Gazette*, September 29, 2003.

17 Wikipedia.

18 Ibid.

19 Jack Todd, "Guerrero's tool box overflowed with talent," *Montreal Gazette*, September 16, 2013.

20 Bill Young, Letter to the editor, *Montreal Gazette*, February 2, 2004.

21 Tom Haudricourt, "Last stand for the Expos," *Ottawa Citizen*, reprinted from the *Milwaukee Journal Sentinel*, May 18, 2004.

22 Ibid.

23 Ibid.

24 Dave Stubbs, "The world's longest wake continues," *Montreal Gazette*, April 24, 2004.

25 "Washington makes new pitch for Expos," *Associated Press, Montreal Gazette*, May 8, 2004.

26 Dave Stubbs, "Super fans stick it out to the end," *Montreal Gazette*, June 29, 2004.

27 Larry Millson, "Expos make their final out," *The Globe and Mail*, October 4, 2004.

28 Stephanie Myles, "31,395 say goodbye Montreal," *Montreal Gazette*, September 30, 2004.

29 "Snyder has idea why team failed," *The Canadian Press* in, *The Globe and Mail*, September 29, 2004.

30 Benoit Aubin, "Bye-bye to the Big Owe," *Maclean's*, October 11, 2004.

31 Stephen Brunt, "Washington exposed as not such a great home for Senators," *The Globe and Mail*, October 1, 2004.

32 Jack Todd, "A dream is laid to rest in our Field of Condos," *Montreal Gazette*, September 29, 2004.

33 "Montreal Expos: 1969-2004," Editorial in the *Montreal Gazette*, September 30, 2004.

Take Me Out to the Ball Game

1 "Take Me Out to the Ball Game," written by vaudevillian Jack Norworth and Albert Von Tilzer, in 1908 Baseball Almanac, http://www.baseball-almanac.com/poetry/po_stmo.shtml/.

2 Wikipedia.

3 David Martin, "A cruel curveball," *Ottawa Citizen*, February 25, 2005.

4 Benjamin Shingler, "Making a fashion statement," *The Canadian Press* in, *Montreal Gazette*, August 16, 2012.

5 *Montreal Gazette*, "Expos gone, but not forgotten," Letters to the sports editor, October 4, 2004.

6 Pat Hickey, "Expos owners blew it in '94," *Montreal Gazette*, November 16, 2004.

7 Jim Caple, "The MLB Misery Index," ESPN.com, page 2, April 5, 2004. (http://sports.espn.go.com/espn/page2/story?page=caple/040407).

8 Benjamin Shingler, Ibid.

9 Tony Kornheiser, *Washington Post*, as seen in the *National Post*, February 5, 2005.

10 Stephanie Myles, "Expos tradition fades," *Montreal Gazette*, February 23, 2005.

11 David Martin, Ibid.

12 Brian Kemp, Ibid.

13 Stephanie Myles, "Some former Expos leave their marks on White Sox historic Series victory," *Montreal Gazette*, October 28, 2005.

14 Barry Svrluga, "In Nats' loss, former mates use old tricks on each other," *Washington Post*, September 13, 2006.

15 "Batting cleanup," compiled by Stephanie Myles, *Montreal Gazette*, August 1, Montreal 2006.

16 Stephanie Myles, "Nos Amours live on in playoffs," *Montreal Gazette*, October 2, 2006.

17 Denis Casavant, "Last of the fallen," The Team 990, Montreal Sports Radio, undated.

18 Art Yellon, "The Last Expos," www.bleedcubsblue.com/, April 25, 2013.

19 Stephanie Myles, "Expos aid ALS battle," *Montreal Gazette*, June 2007.

20 This Anakin Slayd video can be found on YouTube at http://www.youtube.com/watch?v=bFX92ALqxlk/.

21 Jack Todd, "Nos Amours were born out of optimism from Expo 67," *Montreal Gazette*.

22 Stephanie Myles, "Diehard Expos fans were nostalgic," *Montreal Gazette*, July 21, 2007.

23 Cardboard Gods, cardboadkgids.baseballtoaster.com/ %, May 2008.

24 Stephanie Myles, "Baseball buzz left town with Expos," *Montreal Gazette*, July 18, 2008.

25 L. Ian MacDonald, "My painful decision to don a Red Sox ball cap," *Montreal Gazette*, July 6, 2008.

26 Bill Young, "Quebec and the integration of baseball, Part I: Jackie Robinson in Montreal, Quebec Heritage News, summer 2011.

27 Stanley Cohen, quoted in, John Sexton, <u>Baseball as a Road to God: Seeing Beyond the Game</u> (New York: Gotham Books, 2013), p. 200.

28 Glen Hodgson and Mario Lefebvre, "The Future of Major League Baseball in Canada," Briefing 6 in the series PLAYING IN THE BIG LEAGUES, The Conference Board of Canada, July 2011.

29 Nicolas Van Praet, "Where are all the Quebec millionaires? *Montreal Gazette*, from the *Financial Post*, July 19, 2011.

30 Jack Todd, "Don't bet on a return of the Expos," *The Montreal Gazette*, August 1, 2011.

31 Stu Cowan, "Expos return likely will remain a fantasy," *Montreal Gazette*, August 6, 2011.

32 *Montreal Gazette*, editorial, "Return of the Expos is a pipe dream, for now." August 1, 2011.

33 David McGimpsey, in Mike Boone, "Whatever the stats, baseball isn't coming back to Montreal," *Montreal Gazette*, July 13, 2011.

34 Matthew Ross, "Brochu sticks to his guns," *Montreal Gazette*, August 4, 2011.

35 "Return of MLB to Montreal draws debate – mostly negative," *Ballpark Digest*, ballparkdigest.com, August 1, 2011.

36 Matthew Ross, "Will we get another chance with Nos Amours?" *Montreal Gazette*, July 28, 2011.

37 The Story of the Phoenix, http://www.phoenixarises.com/phoenix/legends/story.htm.

38 Daniel Sailofsky, "Gary Carter remembered for his friendship, generous smile," *The Senior Times*, April 2012.

39 Stephanie Myles, "Cromartie has a dream: to return baseball to Montreal," *Montreal Gazette*, April 4, 2012.

40 Warren Cromartie: Conversation with Danny Gallagher, October 2012.

41 John Lott, "Delegation of Expos fans fails to ignite the Blue Jays, *National Post*, September 3, 2012.

42 Keith Olbermann, "The Marlins: A modest proposal," 2012/11/13, (http://keithol-bermann.mlblogs.com/2012/11/13/the-marlins-a-modest-proposal/.

43 Danny Gallagher: Conversations with Paul Beeston and Dave Stewart, summer 2012.

44 Stu Cowan, "Former Expo Steve Rogers wasn't a fan of Jarry Park," *Montreal Gazette*, August 17, 2013.

45 Alana Coates, "Finally! Olympic debt is a Big 0," *Montreal Gazette*, December 20, 2006.

46 Larry Anderson, frequently quoted in various sources: Baseball Almanac, *USA Today*, etc. This version is the complete comment.

47 Derek Aucoin, Speaking with Mitch Melnick on TSN Radio in Montreal, August 13, 2013.

48 Dave Kaufman, "The Kid remembered one year later," *Montreal Gazette*, February 16, 2013.

49 Canadian Press, "Cromartie group touts baseball's return to city," in, *Montreal Gazette*, March 21, 2013.

50 Matthew Ross, "Pro baseball returns to Montreal for one night," *Montreal Gazette*, May 13, 2013.

51 Christopher Curtis, "Montreal is home, Sandy Carter says as Ahuntsic Park is renamed for Expos' Gary Carter, *Montreal Gazette*, June 18, 2013.

52 CTV (Montreal), "Fans celebrate Gary Carter Street renaming," May 21, 2013.

53 Ronald Blum, "Baseball 'cleaner than ever': Selig," *Associated Press*, in, *Montreal Gazette*, July 16, 2013.

54 Jon Paul Morosi, "Rays owner talks future, possible move," Fox Sports, June 24, 2013 (http://msn.foxsports.com/mlb/story/tampa-bay-rays-owner-stuart-stern-berg-talks-future-of-franchise-possible-move-evan-longoria-david-price-062213).

55 Nick Cafardo, "Montreal now seen as a viable alternative," *Boston Globe*, October 20, 2013.

56 Stu Cowan, "Memories of 'Nos Amours' live on," *Montreal Gazette*, July 22, 2013.

57 Jack Todd, "Bring baseball back to Montreal," *The Gazette*, July 22, 2013.

58 "ExposNation shows its colours at rally," *Montreal Gazette*, August 19, 2013.

59 John McHale Jr., e-mail exchange with Danny Gallagher, October 14, 2013.

Autographs

Autographs

Autographs